Archaeology
A Brief Introduction
Seventh Edition

Brian M. Fagan

University of California, Santa Barbara

CARL A. RUDISILL LIBRARY
LENOIR-RHYNE COLLEGE

Prentice Hall
Upper Saddle River, New Jersey 07458

CC
165
.F28
1999
Dec 2005

Library of Congress Cataloging-in-Publication Data
Fagan, Brian M.
   Archaeology : a brief introduction / Brian M. Fagan.—7th ed.
    p.   cm.
   Includes bibliographical references (p.   ) and index.
   ISBN 0-321-04705-2
   1. Archaeology.   I. Title.
  CC165.F28   1999
   930.1—dc21   99-25580
                                           CIP

Editorial Director: *Charlyce Jones-Owen*
Editor in Chief: *Nancy Roberts*
Director of Production and Manufacturing: *Barbara Kittle*
Full Service Production Manager: *Joseph Vella*
Buyer: *Benjamin D. Smith*
Manufacturing Manager: *Nick Sklitsis*
Project Coordination and Text Design: *York Production Services*
Electronic Page Makeup: *York Production Services*
Cover Design: *Jayne Conte*
Marketing Manager: *Christopher DeJohn*
Photo Researcher: *Mira Schachne*
Printer and Binder: *The Press of Ohio*
Cover Printer: *The Press of Ohio*

©1999 by Prentice-Hall, Inc.
Upper Saddle River, New Jersey 07458

All rights reserved. No part of this book may be reproduced, in any form or by any means, without permission in writing from the publisher.

Printed in the United States of America

10 9 8 7 6 5 4 3 2 1

ISBN 0-321-04705-2
Prentice-Hall International (UK) Limited, *London*
Prentice-Hall of Australia Pty. Limited, *Sydney*
Prentice-Hall Canada Inc., *Toronto*
Prentice-Hall Hispanoamericana, S.A., *Mexico*
Prentice-Hall of India Private Limited, *New Delhi*
Prentice-Hall of Japan, Inc., *Tokyo*
Simon & Schuster Asia Pte. Ltd., *Singapore*
Editora Prentice-Hall do Brasil, Ltda, *Rio de Janeiro*

TO

Lucia, Karen, and other friends at Whittier College who first gave me the idea for this book.
And, as usual, to our cats, who were as subversive as ever. They did everything they could to prevent me from revising the manuscript by stepping on it with muddy paws and by dancing intricate *pas-de-deux* on the computer keyboard. As you can see, they failed!

CARL A. RUDISILL
LIBRARY

LENOIR-RHYNE COLLEGE
ἡ ἀλήθεια ἐλευθερώσει ὑμᾶς
1891
HICKORY, N.C.

Gift of

In Memory of Professor

John P. Fogarty

Contents

Chapter 3   Culture   37

Chapter 4   The Present and the Past   55

Chapter 5   Time and Space   76

Chapter 6   Ancient Climate and Environment   98

Preface

Archaeology—a romantic subject, redolent of lost civilizations and grinning skeletons dripping with gold, the realm of pith-helmeted men and women who are adventurers and scholars at the same time, of movie hero Indiana Jones. But is this reality? Most archaeologists have never worn a pith helmet, have never discovered gold, and will never unearth a long-forgotten civilization. Nor do most archaeological sites yield rich treasure, or even human remains. The romance is not always there, but the world of modern archaeology is deeply fascinating all the same. This book is a journey through this world in all its intriguing diversity and is designed to give you some idea of how archaeologists go about studying human behavior of the past.

Archaeology: A Brief Introduction, Seventh Edition, is a brief introduction to the fundamental principles of method and theory in archaeology, beginning with the goals of archaeology, going on to consider the basic concepts of culture, time, and space, and discussing the finding and excavation of archaeological sites. The last four chapters summarize some of the ways in which archaeologists order and study their finds. Throughout the book, I emphasize the ethics behind archaeology and end with a discussion of how we should act as stewards of the finite records of the human past.

Most readers will encounter this book as a supplement to an introductory anthropology course, or as part of a broader archaeology offering. It is designed for complete beginners, so every attempt has been made to keep technical jargon to a minimum. Inevitably, a book of this length and scope glosses over many complex problems or smoldering controversies. I have proceeded on the assumption that at this stage, a positive overstatement is better than a complex piece of inconclusive reasoning. Errors of overstatement can always be corrected in class or at a more advanced stage.

If there is a theme to this volume, it is that the patterning of archaeological artifacts we find in the ground can provide valuable insights into human behavior in the past. In pursuing this theme, I have attempted to focus on the basic concepts of archaeology and leave the instructor to impose his or her own theoretical viewpoints on the various chapters that follow. In the interests of simplicity, too, I have drawn again and again on a few relatively well-known sites from New World and Old World archaeology, such as Olduvai Gorge and Teotihuacán, rather than distracting you with a multitude of site names. I have added brief descriptions of these major sites in a special "Sites and Cultures" information section at the back of the book, where a glossary of technical terms will also be found.

The seventh edition of *Archaeology* has been revised throughout to reflect the latest advances in the field, and includes suggestions by dozens of instructors and students who have used the book in its earlier editions, as well as my own updatings.

Highlights of the Seventh Edition

This is an exciting time to be writing about archaeology, for the major scientific advances in many fields are transforming our ability to reconstruct the remote past. Increasingly, archaeology is becoming a multidisciplinary field, and the seventh edition of this book reflects this. In general, however, the book remains much the same, because the basic principles of archaeology remain unchanged through the years, whatever new and sophisticated theoretical approaches or high-tech scientific methods are brought to bear on the past. These basic principles provide the foundation for all the many research projects that archaeologists carry out, whether close to home or far afield, whether academic research or cultural resource management.

Updating and Rewriting

- *New perceptions of archaeology.* Chapter 1 includes new discussion of archaeology and alternative perspectives on the past, reflecting new thinking on this important topic.
- *Chronological methods.* An update of chronological methods appears in Chapter 5.
- *Expanded coverage of environment and climate.* A new Chapter 6 summarizes ways in which scientists study long- and short-term climatic change. The study of ancient climate and its impact on ancient societies has been revolutionized in recent years and reflects a major advance in archaeology sufficient to justify an entire chapter.
- *New discussion of survey and excavation methods* reflecting the increasing impact of nonintrusive fieldwork appears in Chapters 7 and 8.
- *People in the past and the study of beliefs* receive expanded coverage in Chapter 12, including the spectacular Ice Man discovery from the European Alps.
- *Expanded coverage of ethics and gender,* both important topics in archaeology today, both throughout the book and in Chapters 12 and 14.
- *Update of theory* appears in Chapter 13.
- *Revision and updating throughout.* The entire text and Guide to Further Reading have been revised and updated on a page-by-page basis. Over a third of the book has been completely rewritten for this expanded edition.

New and Revised Art Program

The seventh edition's art program has been expanded with new photographs and fresh or revised line art. The new illustrations provide additional background on recent discoveries, amplify the narrative, or replace older art with new pictures. Some expanded captions serve to integrate the illustrations more closely into the text.

Acknowledgments

The seventh edition has benefited from the expertise of many colleagues, too numerous to list here. I am deeply grateful for their encouragement and assistance. I would like to thank the following reviewers for their help in revising the seventh edition. I appreciate their frank comments:

René Péron, Santa Rosa Junior College
Philip Duke, Fort Lewis College
Robert H. Tykot, University of South Florida
Lynn Gamble, San Diego State University
Ellis E. McDowell-Loudan, State University of New York, College at Cortland
Gary M. Shaffer, Scottsdale Community College

Lastly, my thanks to my editor of many years, Alan McClare, also to photographic researcher Mira Schachne, and the editorial and production staff at Addison Wesley Longman and York Production Services. They have turned a complex manuscript into an attractive book and done all they can to minimize unexpected difficulties.

As always, I would be most grateful for criticisms, comments, or details of new work, sent to me c/o Department of Anthropology, University of California, Santa Barbara, CA 93108 (E-Mail: brian@brianfagan.com).

Brian M. Fagan

Author's Note

Dates

The following conventions are used:

- Dates before 10,000 years ago are expressed in years Before Present (B.P.)
- Dates after 10,000 years ago are expressed in years Before Christ (B.C.) or Anno Domini (A.D.).

Another common convention is B.C.E./C.E. (Before Common Era/ Common Era), which is not employed in this book. By scientific convention, "present" is A.D. 1950.

Please note that all radiocarbon dates and potassium-argon dates should be understood to have a plus and minus factor that is omitted from this book in the interests of clarity. They are statistical estimates. Where possible, radiocarbon dates have been calibrated with tree-ring chronologies, which adds a substantial element of accuracy (see Chapter 5). For tree-ring calibration of radiocarbon dates, see *Radiocarbon,* 1998.

Measurements

All measurements are given in miles, yards, feet and inches, with metric equivalents.

1

The Birth of a Science

Chinese terra-cotta soldier from the Royal Sepulcher of the Emperor
Shihuangdi of China, c. 221 B.C.

In the absence of history, the spade becomes no mean historian.

William A. Miles, *The Deverill Barrow* (1826)

"**I** contrived to sit, but when my weight bore on the body of an Egyptian, it crushed like a bandbox. . . . I sank altogether among the broken mummies, with a crash of bones, rags, and wooden cases, which raised such a dust as kept me motionless for a quarter of an hour, waiting until it subsided again." Giovanni Battista Belzoni (1820:183), circus strongman turned tomb robber, explored and ravaged ancient Egyptian sepulchers in 1817. Belzoni was adept with levers, ropes, and gunpowder, but by no stretch of the imagination could he be called an archaeologist. He was an adventurer of restless ambition, who thought the ancient Egyptians would be a way to fame and fortune.

Unsolved mysteries, lost civilizations, and swashbuckling adventure: the mythic Hollywood archaeologist Indiana Jones cuts a broad swath across the movie screen. Many people think of archaeologists as larger-than-life adventurers, or consider them eccentric pith-helmeted professors perpetually deciphering ancient inscriptions. Although Indiana Jones is said to be a fictional composite of several early twentieth-century excavators, I have never met a professional archaeologist who even vaguely resembled him, and only a handful who ever wore pith helmets. The heroic days when one could discover an ancient civilization in a month and several royal palaces in a week are long gone. Today's archaeology is a sophisticated multidisciplinary science, with roots in anthropology and history.

Archaeology is the scientific study of ancient human societies, from the earliest times right up to the present.[1] As such, archaeology is part of a much wider discipline, **anthropology**, which studies all aspects of humanity, ancient and modern. But archaeologists are unique among scientists in that they study changes in human cultures over long periods of time.

For all its apparent glamour, archaeology is often an unspectacular discipline. Most archaeologists spend their entire careers working on obscure sites far from the popular limelight. They have never dug a buried city or unearthed a gold-laden burial. But our journey through the world of archaeology must begin in the adventurous days of Victorian archaeology. The specialized academic discipline of today is a product not only of modern scientific innovation, but of the work of flamboyant pioneers who did indeed find lost civilizations in remote lands. This chapter tells the story of how archaeology began.

Early Speculations and Excavations

People have speculated about human origins and the remote past for centuries. As early as the eighth century B.C., the Greek writer Hesiod wrote that humanity had passed through five great ages of history. The earliest was an Age of Gold, when

---

[1]Key terms defined in the Glossary at the end of the book are highlighted in bold type. Archaeological sites, cultures, and civilizations whose names are italicized are described in the section on sites and cultures at the back of the book.

"people dwelt in ease," the last an Age of War, when everyone worked terribly hard and experienced great sorrow. In the sixth century B.C., the Babylonian monarch Nabonidus dug deep into ancient city mounds near the Tigris and Euphrates rivers. His workmen uncovered the foundations of the temple of the goddess Ishtar at Agade near Babylon. The find, says an ancient tablet, "made the king's heart glad and caused his countenance to brighten." In later centuries, the Greeks and Romans were intensely curious about their primitive ancestors, about Scythian "barbarians" living on the northern plains who drank from cups made from human skulls, and the Britons far to the northwest who painted themselves blue. Classical writers wrote of the long-term continuity of human life. "Thus the sum of things is ever being renewed," wrote the Roman poet Lucretius in the first century B.C. "Some races increase, others diminish, and in a short space the generations of living creatures are changed and like runners hand on the torch of life" (*De Rerum Natura* II: 75).

The history of archaeology really begins in the European Renaissance, which saw quickened intellectual curiosity, not only about the world beyond the narrow confines of Europe, but about the Classical civilizations as well. People of leisure and wealth began to follow the path of Renaissance scholars, traveling widely in Greece and Italy, studying antiquities, and collecting examples of Roman art. The same travelers were not above some illicit excavation to recover statuary from ancient temples and Roman villas. Soon the cabinets of wealthy collectors bulged with fine art objects, and the study of Classical lands became a major scholarly preoccupation. In 1738, Italy's King Charles III commissioned Spanish engineer Rocque Joaquin de Alcubierre to excavate the famed Roman city of *Herculaneum*, buried under deep layers of volcanic ash by an eruption of Vesuvius in A.D. 79. Alcubierre blasted and tunneled his way through rock-hard ash, tunneling sideways into underground galleries where he found jewelry, statues of well-known Herculaneans, and fragments of bronze horses. Visitors climbed down narrow shafts to walk through the buried theater, marble-columned houses, and frescoed rooms. Hundreds of men, including prisoners, labored below ground, recovering bronze busts, hundreds of texts written on papyrus scrolls, and copies of now-lost Greek masterpieces. Toxic gases, slime, and collapsing tunnels brought an end to this glorified treasure hunt.

Many **antiquarians** were not wealthy enough to travel to Classical lands, so they stayed at home and searched for antiquities in their own backyards. *Stonehenge* on the uplands of southern England was the most famous curiosity, a place where "stones of wonderful size have been erected after the manner of doorways." The antiquarians indulged their insatiable curiosity by digging into burial mounds and river gravels, recovering all manner of prehistoric finds—clay vessels, stone axes and adzes, bronze implements, even occasional gold ornaments. Their digging methods were brutally crude, usually little more than a hasty pit sunk into the center of a mound to recover a skeleton and its grave goods as quickly as possible (Figure 1.1). Some expert diggers would open two or three mounds a day. The accounts of their excavations frequently include complaints that a delicate find "crumbled to dust before their eyes," hardly surprising considering the crude digging methods they employed. Until well into the nineteenth century, archaeology was little more than a glorified treasure hunt, even a sport. Not only that, but the archaeological record of prehistoric times was a complete jumble. "All that has come down to us . . . is wrapped in a thick fog," complained one Danish scholar in 1806.

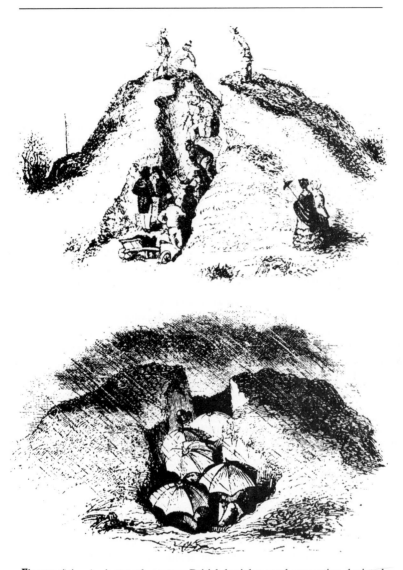

Figure 1.1 A nineteenth-century British burial mound excavation depicted in *Gentleman's Magazine*, 1840. The excursion was little more than a picnic. "Eight barrows were examined. . . . Most of them contained skeletons, more or less entire, with the remains of weapons in iron, bosses of shields, urns, beads, brooches . . . and occasionally more vessels."

The Three Ages and
the Antiquity of Humankind

Although some eighteenth-century collectors were content to display their finds in cabinets, others puzzled over the people who had made their artifacts. Were they hunter-gatherers and farmers like the American Indians, or little more than animals? Had they developed more complex societies as time passed? What was needed was some way of classifying and dating the past.

The first breakthrough came in 1807, when Danish archaeologist Christian Jurgensen Thomsen opened the National Museum of Antiquities in Copenhagen to the public. For years, scholars had talked of three ages—a Stone Age when people had no metals, a Bronze Age, and an Iron Age. A man with a passion for order, Thomsen took the confusing jumble of artifacts in his museum and laid them out in different rooms. In one gallery he displayed implements of the Stone Age, "when little or nothing at all was known of metals." In another he showed those with stone and bronze but no iron, and in a third, grave finds belonging to the Iron Age. His new scheme soon became known as the **three age system**, a system still used to this day for classifying the prehistoric past. Thomsen knew his scheme was mere theory, but one of his assistants, Jens Jacob Worsaae, went out and excavated more burial mounds and other sites. Worsaae proved that Stone Age occupations did, in fact, underlie Bronze Age levels, and that Iron Age sites were the latest of all. The validity of the three age system was now soundly established and it was in widespread use by the 1860s.

But how long had human beings lived on earth? Between medieval times and the late eighteenth century, everyone believed in the literal historical truth of the Scriptures. Genesis 1:1 stated that God had created the world and its inhabitants in six days. The story of Adam and Eve provided an entirely consistent explanation for the creation of humankind and the world's population. In the seventeenth century, Archbishop James Ussher used the genealogies in the Old Testament to calculate that the world was created on the night preceding October 23, 4004 B.C. These bizarre calculations soon became theological dogma and were defended with great fanaticism by theologians in the early nineteenth century, when another group of experts showed that humans had lived on earth much longer than a mere 6,000 years.

The Industrial Revolution of the late eighteenth century with its massive canal and railroad building schemes created a demand for a new breed of scientist—the field geologist. Men like Englishman William "Strata" Smith made their living surveying the earth's layers. Smith realized that the earth had been formed not by divine creation but by natural processes such as erosion, weathering, and sedimentation. These processes had been operating for a very long period of time, far longer than 6,000 years. This theory of the earth's formation became known as **uniformitarianism**. Many of Smith's geological strata contained the fossils of long extinct animals, fossils that French scientist Georges Cuvier pieced together. Cuvier reconstructed pterodactyls and mammoths, and he used his fossils to place geological layers in order, each with its distinctive fossil animals. But how old were these strata? Cuvier believed that God had created each successive layer of the earth, after great floods had wiped out earlier life. Humans belonged to the time of the last flood. In other words, the world was but 6,000 years old.

Cuvier was wrong, for the proof that human beings had lived in far earlier times was in front of his very nose. As early as 1600, the bones of an elephant and a stone ax were found in the heart of London, but no established scientist took these, or many subsequent finds of the same type, seriously. Uniformitarian theories were well established in geology by the 1830s, notably by the writings of British geologist Sir Charles Lyell, whose *Principles of Geology* strongly influenced Charles Darwin. In 1836, an eccentric French customs officer named Boucher de Perthes began digging for fossils in the gravels of the Somme River near Abbeville in northern France. He was surprised to find dozens of stone axes alongside the bones of extinct animals like the hippopotamus. De Perthes claimed that these tools were the work of people who had lived long before the biblical flood, but scientists just laughed at him. It was not until stone artifacts and the bones of rhinoceroses, mammoths, and cave bears were found in the sealed layers of a cave near Brixham in southwestern England in 1858 that the scientific establishment finally sat up and took notice. There could be no doubt of the association, and a steady stream of British geologists and archaeologists crossed the Channel in 1859 to examine de Perthes's finds.

The same year—1859—saw the publication of Charles Darwin's book *Origin of Species*, the pivotal scientific essay of the nineteenth century. It described the theory and mechanisms of evolution and provided a theoretical framework for a human history not a mere 6,000 years long, but one that extended back far into the remote past. Darwin himself said little about human ancestry, but this assumption that human beings were descended from apelike ancestors horrified many devout Victorians. "My dear, let us hope it is not so," exclaimed one distraught mother (Figure 1.2). As the controversy over evolution raged, scientists began the long search for human ancestors, which continues to this day.

In 1857, quarrymen working in the *Neanderthal* cave near Dusseldorf in Germany unearthed an odd-looking skull with beetling brows quite unlike anything anatomists had seen before. Many experts dismissed the find as that of a modern hermit, or even as one of Napoleon's soldiers, but the great Victorian biologist Thomas Huxley thought otherwise. He examined the skull and compared it to those of modern humans and chimpanzees, pointing out that it had some apelike characteristics. Here, then, was the first scientific evidence that humans had some evolutionary links to the apes. In the decades that followed, the search for what was soon called the "missing link" between apes and humans took hold of the popular imagination. Even today, discoveries of early human fossils cause considerable excitement and often turn their finders into media figures. Raymond Dart caused an international furor when he announced the discovery of a primitive ape-human, *Australopithecus* ("southern ape-man"), in South Africa in 1924. The celebrated Leakey family, Louis, Mary, and son Richard and his wife Meave, have added more chapters to early human evolution than all other scientists put together, through a combination of expert fieldwork, intuition, and sheer patience. For example, Louis and Mary Leakey searched at *Olduvai Gorge* in Tanzania for human fossils for more than a quarter century before they unearthed a magnificent 1.75-million-year-old *Australopithecus* skull in 1959. Not that the numerous fossil finds of the last half century have dampened controversy. The ferocious debates over human evolution and early human behavior rage just as stormily today as they did in Darwin's time.

Figure 1.2   A Thomas Nast cartoon from the British humor magazine *Punch* lampooning Charles Darwin's linking apes with humans.

Early Civilizations: Ancient Egypt and Mesopotamia

The Ancient Egyptians

The Greeks and Romans considered the ancient Egyptians the fountain of wisdom and medical knowledge, the source of all the institutions of civilization. But ancient Egyptian civilization remained a mystery until French general Napoleon Bonaparte invaded Egypt in 1798. Napoleon professed an interest in science, so he took 40 scientists along with him to record all that was known of Egypt, ancient and modern. The scholars, "Napoleon's donkeys," as the soldiers called them, were electrified by what they found. For six years they sketched and explored, collected antiquities, and compiled a magnificent record of an exotic civilization that had built temples and pyramids quite unlike anything in Greece or Italy. Among their finds was the famous Rosetta Stone, a trilingual inscription that allowed the young French linguistic genius Jean François Champollion to decipher ancient Egyptian hieroglyphs in 1822. This was the scientific breakthrough that unlocked the secrets of civilization on the Nile, but by that time the scientists' remarkable discoveries had brought another breed of visitor to Egypt—the tomb robber.

Egyptian antiquities were so exotic and valuable that they commanded enormous prices in Europe, where the newly founded British Museum and the Louvre in Paris were competing for sensational exhibits. Well-organized, ruthless tomb robbers like Giovanni Belzoni descended on the Nile. For three eventful years, Belzoni blasted and tunneled his way from one end of Egypt to the other. He searched for papyrus inscriptions in mummy caves, found the (empty) royal tomb of Pharaoh Seti I in the *Valley of Kings* near Thebes, and was the first in centuries to penetrate the spectacular temple of *Abu Simbel*. A tall man of immense strength and considerable charm, Belzoni, as mentioned previously, was an expert with levers, weights, and gunpowder, essential qualifications for an early nineteenth-century tomb robber. He left Egypt precipitously in 1819 (after a fracas with his enemies in which shots were fired), exhibited some of his finds in London, and perished while searching for the source of the Niger River in West Africa.

Tomb robbing and looting continued unchecked in Egypt until the late nineteenth century; indeed, it persists to this day. But Jean François Champollion's decipherment of hieroglyphs brought another new kind of visitor to the Nile—the dedicated scientist. For example, Englishman John Gardiner Wilkinson spent ten years recording inscriptions in Egyptian tombs. He wrote a detailed account of the daily life of the ancient Egyptians, which revealed a colorful, cheerful civilization, but one that was intensely conservative, deeply religious, and preoccupied with the afterlife.

All modern Egyptology has built on the work of Champollion and his contemporaries, and on the more scientific excavation methods introduced to the Nile in the late nineteenth century by the British archaeologist Flinders Petrie and others.

The Assyrians and Sumerians

"He will stretch out his hand and destroy Assyria," thundered the Old Testament prophet Zephaniah, "and will make Nineveh a desolation, and dry like a wilderness." To the occasional adventurous European visitor, the lands by the Tigris and Euphrates in what is now Iraq seemed like a confirmation of the prophet's fulminations. All that remained of *Nineveh* were some desolate earthen mounds covered with crumbling bricks. And all that survived of the Assyrians were some vague references in the Scriptures.

In 1840, the French government sent Paul-Emile Botta as consul to the small town of Mosul on the Tigris River opposite the ruins of Nineveh. His real assignment was to dig into Nineveh to make spectacular archaeological finds. Botta had no archaeological experience, and he did not excavate Nineveh deep enough to find anything worthwhile. He listened with interest when one of his men described the riches that lay under his home on another mound at *Khorsabad*, 14 miles (22.5 km) away. The consul sent him away with a few men to see what he could find. A week later he returned with tales of walls covered with carvings of strange animals. Botta gasped at the bas-reliefs: winged, human-headed animals and processions of men with long beards. He put more than 300 men to work on what turned out to be the Assyrian king Sargon's palace, a vast multiroomed structure adorned with grandiloquent reliefs that boasted of the monarch's triumphs.

Five years later, a restless young Englishman named Austen Henry Layard started digging at the city of *Nimrud* downstream of Nineveh. He found two Assyrian buildings the first day and was soon tunneling deep into magnificent palaces (Figure 1.3). This was the stuff of which archaeological legends were made. The visitor to

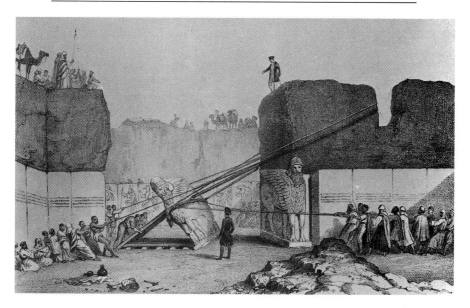

Figure 1.3 Mesopotamian archaeology, nineteenth-century style; Austen Henry Layard recovers a human-headed lion from an Assyrian palace at Nimrud, Iraq.

Nimrud, and later Nineveh, where Layard worked with much greater success than Botta, wandered through deep earthen tunnels that followed the rooms of the palaces. Here one gazed at "the portly forms of kings . . . so lifelike that they might almost be imagined to be stepping from the walls to question the rash intruder on their privacy" (Layard, 1849: 226). Layard excavated with a small army of workmen and acted like a tribal chieftain. He arranged marriages, settled quarrels, supervised the dig all day, and recorded inscriptions until late at night. The young archaeologist was a brilliant writer; his books on Nineveh are still in print. His discoveries caused a sensation in Europe. Among other things, he uncovered a bas-relief of a royal lion hunt and a frieze that commemorates the siege of Lachish, a city of Judah mentioned in the Old Testament. His diggers even uncovered the limestone slabs at the entrance to King Sennacherib's palace that bore the ruts made by his army's chariot wheels.

Layard's greatest discovery came at Nineveh, where he unearthed a complete royal library, piles of clay tablets lying a foot deep on the floor of a special chamber. He shoveled them into baskets and shipped them down the river, like all of his finds, on a wooden raft supported by inflated goatskins. A quarter century was to pass before even a small number of the tablets were deciphered, and when they were they yielded further sensations. In 1872, a young cuneiform expert named George Smith, who had never been to Mesopotamia, discovered a tablet that told of a prophet named Hasisadra, who survived a great flood sent by the gods to punish humankind by building a large boat. Hasisadra's boat went aground on a mountain, and he sent out birds to find a resting place. The entire story bore a remarkable resemblance to the biblical story of the Great Flood. Seventeen lines of the story were missing, so Smith was sent out to Iraq to find them. Incredible though it may seem, he discovered the tablet fragments in Layard's excavation dumps in a mere five days!

Those who believed in the historical truth of the Bible were, of course, electrified by the Flood tablets. But scholars were more interested in the evidence they gave for far earlier civilizations, for the Assyrians had merely copied the legend from earlier accounts. In 1877, another French diplomat, Ernest de Sarzec, excavated the ancient city of *Telloh* in southern Mesopotamia, where he discovered clay tablets and the remains of a great temple far older than those of the Assyrians. What Sarzec had found was the Sumerian civilization, the earliest literate society in the world and a civilization as old as, if not older than, that of the ancient Egyptians. A whole series of long-term excavations at other Sumerian cities like *Nippur* and *Ur* between the 1890s and 1930s chronicled many more details of this flamboyant, warlike civilization, a patchwork of small city-states that flourished 5,000 years ago between the Tigris and Euphrates rivers.

Troy and Mycenae

Many of the best known nineteenth-century archaeologists were either professional travelers or adventurers. A few, like German businessman Heinrich Schliemann, were obsessed with the past. Schliemann became fascinated with the Greek poet Homer at an early age. He retired from business at the age of 46, determined to prove that Homer's *Iliad* and *Odyssey* were true stories. In 1871, he started excavations at *Hissarlik* in northwestern Turkey, which he soon proclaimed was the site of Homeric Troy. Schliemann thought and acted on a large scale. He employed engineers who had worked on the building of the Suez Canal in Egypt to supervise his excavations and discovered seven ancient cities superimposed one on top of the other. His excavations culminated in the discovery of what Schliemann claimed to be a treasure of more than 8,000 gold ornaments and artifacts. He insisted that this was the Treasure of Priam, the Homeric king of Troy. Schliemann was no scientific saint—almost certainly his treasure was assembled from isolated gold pieces found over many months. Interestingly, the Treasure disappeared in the final days of World War II, and was considered lost until it surfaced in Russia after the breakup of the Soviet Union (Figure 1.4).

Schliemann's Troy discoveries caused a popular sensation, which reached a height when he moved to *Mycenae* in Greece in 1876. This was, he thought, the legendary burial place of King Agamemnon, leader of the Greek armies at Troy. More than 125 men tore into Mycenae and uncovered a circle of stone slabs. Schliemann found more than 15 burials at Mycenae, many of them covered in jewels, golden death masks, and adorned with fine inlaid weapons. "I have gazed on the face of Agamemnon," cried Schliemann. He believed he had found the Homeric king, but archaeologists now date these finds to at least three or four centuries before the Trojan War, which raged in about 1190 B.C.

Heinrich Schliemann was the last of the great adventurer-archaeologists to work in Mediterranean lands, for his methods were too unscientific even for his day. By the 1870s, Austrian and German archaeologists were working on Classical sites like *Olympia* with a new precision that was a far cry from the methods of Belzoni, Layard,

Figure 1.4   Heinrich and Sophia Schliemann. She wears the treasure allegedly found in a single hoard at Troy.

or Schliemann. A team of architects worked with the archaeologists. The Germans renounced all claims to the finds, and they built a special museum for them at Olympia itself. A new era in archaeological research was beginning that put scientific recording before spectacular discovery, precise excavation before rapid shoveling.

Early American Archaeology

From the moment Christopher Columbus landed in the Bahamas in 1492, people speculated about the origins of the American Indians. In 1589, a Jesuit missionary named José de Acosta first proposed the general theory of their origins that provides the basis for modern thinking on the subject. He believed it was entirely possible that "small groups of savage hunters driven from their homelands by starvation or some other hardship" had taken an overland route through Asia to their present homelands with only "short stretches of navigation." He wrote this a century and a half before Vitus Bering sailed through the Bering Strait in 1728. Today, all scientists agree that this was one route taken by the first Americans, but the date of their arrival remains a controversial subject. While some scholars speculated about Indian origins, others marveled at the great diversity of Native American populations. Some, like the Eskimo of the far north, were hunter-gatherers; others lived in large villages or, like the Aztec of Mexico and the Inka of Peru, in sophisticated civilizations. How could one account for this diversity, and why were some societies more complex than others? These questions still preoccupy archaeologists today.

The "Moundbuilders"

When land-hungry colonists moved west of the Allegheny Mountains in the late eighteenth century, they were surprised to find large earthworks and burial mounds doting the landscape. Those who dug into them found no gold, only human skeletons, copper and mica ornaments, and stone pipe bowls. Who had built these earthworks? Many colonists and intellectuals refused to believe that the "savage" Indians could have done so. They argued they were the work of long-vanished civilizations from foreign lands. Only a few scholars disagreed, among them Thomas Jefferson. Fascinated by what were already known as the Moundbuilders, he dug into a burial mound on his Virginia estate and uncovered several layers of human skeletons. Unlike many of his treasure-hunting contemporaries, Jefferson made careful note of the strata in the mound, the first stratigraphic excavation in the Americas.

The Moundbuilder controversy continued to smolder through the nineteenth century, pitting those who believed in an exotic explanation for the earthworks against more sober scholars like Samuel Haven of the American Antiquarian Society, who argued that the artifacts in the mounds often bore a resemblance to those used by living Native American groups. Writers churned out dozens of literary fantasies about the Moundbuilders, writing about "white people of great intelligence and skill" who had waged wars of conquest over the Midwest thousands of years ago. These racist theories had no founding in scientific fact, but it was not until the 1890s that Cyrus Thomas of the Bureau of American Ethnology proved beyond all reasonable doubt that the mounds were in fact of Native American manufacture.

Maya Civilization

Further south, the Spanish conquistadors had marveled at the Aztec capital *Tenochtitlán*. "We were amazed on account of the great towers and buildings rising from the water. And some of our soldiers even asked whether the things we saw were not a dream," wrote one soldier after the Spanish Conquest. However, the Aztec and earlier native American civilizations sank into almost complete historical oblivion. Dense forest covered the great Maya centers in the lowlands of Mexico and Guatemala. Only a few Catholic priests recorded details of Maya civilization before it vanished, among them Spanish bishop Diego da Landa. He visited Maya temples and recorded some of their script in 1566 while torturing and imprisoning Indians for refusing to accept the Christian faith, and burning their unique hieroglyphic documents as well.

Only a few reports of temples and pyramids deep in the forest kept interest in the ancient Maya alive. It was these that excited the imaginations of two men who are among the immortals of early archaeology—lawyer-turned-traveler John Lloyd Stephens and artist Frederick Catherwood. Both were experienced archaeological travelers who had visited Egypt and the Holy Land; Stephens and Catherwood sailed for Central America in 1839, a journey that took them on foot and by mule into the depths of the tropical lowlands. They struggled through dense rain forest to the Maya city of Copán, where they found monuments "some in workmanship equal to those of the finest monuments of the Egyptians." The jungle-covered ruins covered miles. While Catherwood settled down to draw the intricate carvings, Stephens tried to buy the site from the local people for $50 so he could exhibit his finds in New York. When the deal foundered, he contented himself with writing a famous description of Copán. "The only sounds that disturbed the quiet of this buried city were the noise of monkeys moving among the tops of the trees, and the cracking of dry branches broken by their weight. They moved over our heads in long and swift processions, forty or fifty at a time" (Stephens, 1841: 112).

Stephens and Catherwood recorded as much as they could of Copán, then visited Palenque, where they searched for parallels to ancient Egypt among the human figures at the site. Back in New York, Stephens penned one of the first assessments of Maya civilization. "The works of these peoples, as revealed by the ruins, are different from the works of any known people," he wrote. "We have a conclusion far more interesting and wonderful than that of connecting the builders with the Egyptians or any other people. It is the spectacle of a people . . . originating and growing up here, having a distinct, separate, indigenous existence; like the plants and fruits of the soil, indigenous" (Stephens, 1841: 332). All subsequent scientific work on Maya civilization has been based on these famous words. Stephens and Catherwood were to journey to the Yucatán a second time, to study *Uxmal*, *Chichén Itzá*, and other famous locations (Figure 1.5). These studies convinced Stephens that "these cities . . . are not the works of people who have passed away . . . but of the same great race which . . . still clings around their ruins" (p. 332).

Like Austen Henry Layard, John Lloyd Stephens was a superb popular writer, whose books about the Maya became instant bestsellers. And Frederick Catherwood's

Figure 1.5   John Lloyd Stephens and Frederick Catherwood examining a Maya temple deep in the Yucatán rain forest.

pictures of the ruins are among the finest of all archaeological illustrations. In writing his books, Stephens corresponded with the Boston historian William Prescott, whose *History of the Conquest of Mexico* set the Spanish Conquest against a background of the Aztecs' rapid rise to power. The books by these two men, more than any others, helped readers realize there was more to America's past than merely Moundbuilders and mythical, exotic civilizations.

Southwestern Archaeology and the Direct Historical Approach

By the late 1800s, archaeologists and anthropologists were convinced that living American Indian societies were the descendants of the first Americans. So they began to work back from the present into the past. In 1879, Frank Hamilton Cushing of the Smithsonian Institution traveled to Zuñi Pueblo in New Mexico, intending to stay only three months. He ended up staying for nearly five years, observing Zuñi life in remarkable detail, even being initiated into membership of a secret society, the Priesthood of the Bow. His widely read book *My Adventures in Zuñi* (1882) described the life and customs of a Pueblo society whose roots stretched far back into the past. His contemporary, anthropologist Adolph Bandelier, spent years wandering around the Southwest on a mule, tracking down oral histories at *Pecos* Pueblo and other locations (Figure 1.6). These oral traditions were to become a foundation of the archaeological research conducted by Alfred Kidder of Harvard University at Pecos from 1915 to 1929. Bandelier and Cushing were two of the pioneers who showed the close relationship between anthropology, the study of living peoples, and archaeology, the study of past societies (Chapter 2). Thus it was logical for Kidder to excavate the intricate strata of Pecos using a direct historical approach, working backward from well-documented historic levels far into prehistory. All American archaeology is based on the general principles developed by these and other pioneers, who showed the close links between ancient and modern Native American societies.

Explaining the Past

As archaeologists began to study the early prehistory of humankind and the great civilizations, anthropologists were looking at the many diverse societies that explorers and missionaries were revealing every year. These societies ranged from the simple hunter-gatherers of the Tierra del Fuego Indians and Australian Aborigines to the complex and well-organized Japanese and the Pueblo Indians of the American Southwest. Then there were the ancient Egyptians and the Sumerians of Mesopotamia, early civilizations that could be linked to the early development of Western civilization. How could one explain all of this diversity, and the change of human societies from hunting and gathering to city dwelling?

"From Them to Us": Unilinear Evolution

The nineteenth century was a period of remarkable industrial and technological change, to the point that notions of human progress and achievement dominated popular thinking. Darwin's theories of biological evolution seemed a natural extension of the doctrines of social progress. Archaeologists and anthropologists alike soon wrote

Figure 1.6   Pueblo Bonito, New Mexico, a large southwestern pueblo built and occupied between about A.D. 850 and 1130. The pueblo had five stories of rooms in a semicircle. The round structures are kivas, subterranean ceremonial rooms. Pueblo Bonito was part of the Chaco Phenomenon, an Anasazi trade and ritual network centered on Chaco Canyon, New Mexico.

of millennia of gradual human cultural evolution throughout early prehistory into modern times (for definitions of culture, see Chapter 3).

British anthropologist Edward Tylor (1832–1917) surveyed human development in all of its forms, from the crude stone axes of very early humans to Maya temples in Mexico, to Victorian civilization. He developed a three-level sequence of human development, from simple hunting savagery, as he called it, through a stage of simple farming and pastoral nomadism, which he called barbarism, to civilization, the most complex of all human conditions. American anthropologist Lewis Henry Morgan (1818–1881) went even further and outlined no less than seven periods of human progress, starting with savagery and culminating in a "state of civilization."

Such notions of **unilinear cultural evolution**, of linear human progress from the simple to the complex, were easy to defend in a world whose frontiers were still being explored. Archaeology was still in its infancy, the remote past known mainly from Europe and the spectacular discoveries of ancient civilizations in southwestern Asia. It was easy for late nineteenth-century scholars, living as they did in societies where doctrines of racial superiority were unchallenged, to speculate that human societies had evolved in a linear way, from simple unsophisticated hunter-gatherer bands to complex literate civilizations.

Such simplistic hypotheses are long discredited.

Diffusionism: How Did Civilization Spread?

As more and more data accumulated from archaeological excavations all over the world, it became clear that a universal scheme of unilinear evolution was far too simplistic an explanation for the past. Could cultures have changed as a result of external influences? Did, for example, the ancient Egyptians spread the institutions of civilization to other parts of southwestern Asia, perhaps even further afield? Could one account for the differences between human societies as the result of the **diffusion** of ideas and the migrations of peoples? In its more extreme forms, diffusionism is an assumption that many major human inventions originated in one place, then diffused to other parts of the world as a result of trade, migration, cultural contact, even exploration.

Diffusionist theories of prehistory were popular in the early twentieth century, when scholars like the Egyptologist Elliot Grafton Smith argued that the "Children of the Sun," ancient Egyptians, had voyaged all over the world, taking sun worship and their civilization with them. Like unilinear cultural evolution, extreme diffusionism like Grafton Smith's did not stand up to detailed scientific scrutiny, especially when twentieth-century archaeologists realized they were dealing with very complex problems of culture change over very long periods of prehistoric time. It is very tempting to write of bold Egyptians in great ships voyaging to America, or of sword-wielding Bronze Age chieftains fighting their way from Hungary to Belgium 3,500 years ago, but, unfortunately, the human past is much more complicated than that. Not that this deters the lunatic fringe, who still write of epic voyages and lost civilizations buried under Antarctic ice, to say nothing of ancient astronauts landing on earth and creating ancient Maya civilization.

By the 1920s, both unilinear evolution and diffusionism were discredited explanations for the past as archaeology became a fully fledged scientific discipline.

The Development of Modern Scientific Archaeology

The development of scientific archaeology and the discovery of the prehistoric past ranks as one of the outstanding achievements of nineteenth- and twentieth-century science. The process of development began with the establishment of the antiquity of humankind and the development of the three age system for subdividing prehistory. The crude excavations of Layard and Schliemann are part of the story, as are the pioneer efforts of Cushing and Bandelier to work from the present back into the past. But the technologically sophisticated archaeology of today can be said to stem from four major developments: the invention of modern scientific excavation techniques, the use of multidisciplinary approaches to study relationships between people and their environments, the increasing impact of science on archaeology, and the refinement of archaeological theory since the 1960s.

Scientific Excavation

The science of excavation as a systematic way of recording ancient human behavior began with the work of the Germans at Olympia in Greece during the 1870s. These meticulous excavators placed recording before spectacular discoveries. However, an eccentric retired British Army general, Augustus Lane Fox Pitt-Rivers, refined their methods even further during the 1880s. Pitt-Rivers was a firearms expert who developed a passion for artifacts and the evolution of weapons. In later life, he inherited a vast fortune and huge land holdings in southern England and devoted much of his time to excavating the ancient burial mounds and earthworks on his estates. Pitt-Rivers was no ordinary excavator. He ran his digs like a military operation, employing expert supervisors who were trained surveyors. Unlike his contemporaries, who dug to find spectacular artifacts, Pitt-Rivers believed that every find, however small, was important. He insisted on accurate recording, built model reconstructions of his sites, and observed even the most minute details of the various layers (Figure 1.7). The military discipline of his work was apparent everywhere, even in his photographs. "The figure standing at attention in the foreground gives the scale," reads one of his captions.

Pitt-Rivers's remarkable excavations fell on deaf ears until the 1920s, when a new generation of fieldworkers refined his methods even further. The most famous was another British archaeologist, Mortimer Wheeler, who, between the 1920s and 1950s, carried out a series of beautifully executed excavations on Roman and Iron Age sites in Britain and on cities of the *Harappan civilization* in Pakistan's Indus Valley. Wheeler also had a distinguished record as a military man. Like Pitt-Rivers, he insisted on precise recording, employed photographers and other experts, and pioneered the use of trained amateur diggers on his sites. Wheeler was a strict teacher who realized that all excavation was destruction. He also realized that scientific archaeology could be dull and did everything he could to enliven his writings about the past. "Dry archaeology is the driest dust that blows," he once remarked. How true!

Late twentieth-century excavation still draws on the basic principles laid down by Wheeler and his contemporaries, but has added many refinements (Chapter 8). These include specialized methods for excavating waterlogged sites, minute recording methods using electronic instruments, and sophisticated ways of excavating minute discolorations, some of which even record the positions of long-vanished burials in sandy soil. Most important of all, today's archaeologists have moved away from the study of single sites to large numbers of sites within regions. They also realize that all excavation is destruction, that any digging should be kept to a minimum to preserve the finite record of the past for future generations.

Archaeology and Ecology

Few archaeologists thought of archaeological sites in their wider environmental context until the 1950s, although many of the tools for environmental reconstruction were developed early in the twentieth century. In 1916, Swedish scientist Lennart van Post invented the science of palynology, the study of minute fossil pollen grains as a means of studying ancient environments (Chapter 5). Archaeologists eventually realized that this new technique offered a chance to study ancient societies in the context of their environments, but the study of cultural ecology, as it is called, did not reach a full level of sophistication until the 1950s and 1960s.

Cultural ecology is the study of the ecological relationships between human cultures and their environments, a study pioneered by anthropologist Julian Steward. Archaeologically, a concern with environmental relationships began in the late 1940s

Figure 1.7   A Pitt-Rivers excavation of a prehistoric burial mound at Wor Barrow, Cranborne Chase, in southern England during the early 1880s. His sites were remarkable for their careful excavation, precision, and attention to minute details.

with British archaeologist Grahame Clark's excavations at the Star Carr hunter-gatherer site in northeast England. Using pollen analysis, plant remains, and animal bones, he was able to show that this 10,000-year-old hunting site once lay in a bed of reeds backed by birch forests. He even demonstrated that the site was occupied in late winter by studying the red deer antler in the deposits (Clark's Star Carr interpretations have now been revised by later work; see Chapter 6). Clark relied heavily on botanists and zoologists in his research. Today, teams of scientists from many disciplines routinely work together in the field, reconstructing the environments of late Ice Age societies in France, examining the landscape exploited by 100,000-year-old hunters in southern Africa, monitoring the modifications made by farmers to midwestern landscapes 1,200 years ago.

Scientific Methods

Archaeology is an integral part of history and anthropology, the study of living peoples, but the high-tech methods of the sciences have had an ever-increasing impact on the field. Pollen analysis was one early contributor, as was aerial photography, which gave archaeologists an overhead view of the past (Chapter 4). Perhaps the great revolution came in the 1950s, when radiocarbon dating revolutionized prehistoric chronologies, providing the first secure time scale for the last 40,000 years (Chapter 5). Since then, the impact of science on archaeology has been universal, in everything from computers to sophisticated ways of searching for archaeological sites through rain forest canopies, to methods for studying prehistoric diets through the carbon isotope content of human bones. The marriage between archaeology and other sciences is now so close that both the methods and theoretical approaches of many disciplines have affected the ways archaeologists go about their work.

A New Generation of Theory

The impact of science and more scientific approaches has revolutionized explanations of the past, too. The simplistic unilinear and diffusionist theories of yesteryear are long gone, for archaeological theory has become far more sophisticated in recent years (Chapter 13).

A major theoretical furor in archaeology began during the 1960s with archaeologist Lewis Binford and others arguing for more explicitly scientific approaches to the study of culture change (cultural process) in the past. Recent years has seen a strong reaction against the somewhat impersonal study of culture change epitomized by science. Post-processualists (Chapter 13) argue that archaeologists should be concerned about the people of the past and the effects of individual and group actions on culture change, not just about impersonal processes of culture change.

At the same time, there has been an explosion of new perspectives on the past. There are those who argue passionately for a feminist approach to prehistory, others who believe the very term *prehistory* is racist and demeaning, that archaeology does not present a true picture of the remote past. Archaeologists have always considered themselves scientists, scholars with a dispassionate and objective view of what happened in ancient times. Now many scholars argue that archaeologists bring their own cultural biases and perspectives to their interpretations of ancient society, that they should consider themselves "mediators" of the past rather than objective scientists. These issues are causing a considerable theoretical ferment in archaeological circles as American archaeologists, and researchers working elsewhere in the world, grapple with tricky issues like the treatment of burials and alternative views of the past based on oral traditions. We explore some of these issues in later chapters.

This chapter has described some of the early developments in archaeology and provided some insights into the exciting history of our discipline. The romantic days of archaeology, the days of Layard, Schliemann, and Stephens, are long gone. Today, archaeology is a serious, meticulous scientific discipline, which seems, at times, somewhat dull to pursue, even if the issues and sites it explores are of great importance. But the thrill of archaeological discovery is always there, even after a long day of digging in the hot sun or fog and cold wind. Perhaps the greatest moment of archaeological discovery ever came in 1922, when Egyptologist Howard Carter pried a small hole through the sealed doorway leading to the tomb of the pharaoh Tutankhamun. He shone a candle through the aperture and was struck dumb with amazement. "What do you see?" his companion Lord Carnarvon asked impatiently at his side. "Wonderful things," whispered Carter, as he stepped back from the hole. Few of us will ever be fortunate enough to experience such a unique thrill as Carter's, but the excitement of archaeology is just as great with smaller, less important finds. And it is well in these days of science that we never forget these thrilling moments. In the pages that follow, we describe the basic principles of archaeological research that make such moments possible.

Summary

Archaeology began in the European Renaissance as travelers collected Classical antiquities. Collecting led to excavation at the Roman city of Herculaneum in 1738, followed by widespread digging throughout Europe, especially into burial mounds. The chaotic finds from these investigations were first classified by Danish Museum curator Christian Jurgensen Thomsen, who developed the three age system for subdividing prehistory in 1807. The antiquity of humankind was established by stratigraphic excavation of stone tools associated with the bones of extinct animals in 1859; other excavators in Egypt and Mesopotamia unearthed the early civilizations of southwestern Asia. In the Americas, John Lloyd Stephens and Frederick Catherwood investigated ancient Maya civilization in the 1840s, and other investigators worked back from the present into the past investigating ancient Pueblo and Moundbuilder cultures in North America. Early archaeological theories invoked unilinear cultural evolution and diffusion as explanations for such developments as the origins of civilization. Modern scientific archaeology developed out of meticulous excavation techniques, a concern with environmental change, and explicitly scientific methods that allowed the study of cultural change in the past.

2

The World of Scientific Archaeology

Classical Greek vase from Athens, c. 400 B.C.

Archaeology is the special concern of a certain type of anthropologist.

James Deetz, *Invitation to Archaeology* (1967)

This volume takes you on a journey through the world of scientific archaeology, an adventure as engaging as it is many sided. Any thinking person who visits an archaeological site faces the reality of the past, a vista of human experience that stretches far back in time. How, visitors may wonder, do archaeologists know how old a site is, and what do their finds mean? What do archaeologists really do? How do they unravel the complexities of early human societies? It all seems very complicated to dig for the past. And the unchanging, incredibly ancient structures that surround one add to the sense of romance and awe.

Our complex world is full of so-called unexplained mysteries and hidden surprises, phenomena that sometimes defy obvious explanation. Many people believe the archaeologist lives in the mysterious regions of our world, with "missing links" and long-lost civilizations. Enterprising authors and movie producers take us on fantasy rides into the strange territories of their specially selected archaeologists. From the comfort of our armchairs, via television, we can search for lost continents, reconstruct Noah's Ark, and trace the landing patterns of extraterrestrials' spaceships. Such searches are not only fantasy fun, they are big business as well. Millions of dollars have been made from this type of archaeology, which, unfortunately, bears little resemblance to reality.

The romance of archaeology has taken people all over the world in search of the past. Every year thousands of tourists visit the pyramids of *Giza* in Egypt (Figure 2.1). To promote tourism, the Mexican government spent millions of pesos restoring the ancient city of *Teotihuacán* in the Valley of Mexico. Most popular package tours abroad now include visits to an archaeological site or two (Figure 2.2). Many sites— for example, Stonehenge in England and the Stone Age painted cave at *Lascaux* in France—are in danger of permanent damage from the sheer volume of visiting tourists. As a result, you can no longer wander among the uprights at Stonehenge. The French government has built a magnificent replica of the Lascaux cave paintings for tourists to enjoy, but the original cave is closed to all but scientists.

Most such archaeological sites now boast a museum. Eagerly, the tourist peers into the display cases and admires the glittering gold of a fine necklace or the crude stone tools made by a human hand more than a million years ago. Perhaps, at the door, the visitor pauses to buy a replica of the archaeological find in the case. It is a pleasing reminder of a fleeting visit to the past, a memento to be displayed to admiring friends at home. But, unfortunately, many people are greedier—they covet the past and want to own a piece of the real thing.

Collectors and treasure hunters, many of whom regard themselves as legitimate archaeologists, are the curse of archaeology. The vanity of the ancients decreed that they be buried with riches to accompany them in the afterlife. The greed of their descendants decrees that people today covet these riches. The antiquities dealer and the private collector pay enormous prices for painted pots and other fine antiquities looted from otherwise undisturbed sites. Major museums compete to acquire the finest specimens of prehistoric art. In perhaps the most blatant case of all, the

Figure 2.1   The pyramids of Giza in Egypt. "The romance of archaeology has taken people all over the world in search of the past." These pyramids were the culmination of more than a century of aggressive royal pyramid building by ancient Egyptian kings of the Old Kingdom, c. 2600 to 2100 B.C. Each served as the burial place for a king and was connected by a causeway to a mortuary temple where offerings were made to the deceased. The pyramid shape is thought to represent a symbolic sun ray descending to earth through the clouds, a symbolic ladder for the divine king to ascend and join the sun god in the heavens.

Metropolitan Museum of Art in New York paid a cool million dollars for one Greek vase, which was probably looted from an Italian tomb.

There seems to be some fundamental human desire to collect things and display them in the privacy of one's home. Collecting is a passion once described as "so violent that it is inferior to love or ambition only in the pettiness of its aims." People collect everything from barbed wire to beer cans, and many think of archaeology as the acquisition of objects. But when people collect archaeological finds, they are collecting a part of an endangered, finite resource that is rapidly vanishing, a unique archive that can never be replaced. Every object they buy or dig from a site is the product of ancient human behavior. This behavior can be partly reconstructed from objects found in the earth, but much of our insight depends on the contexts (positions) in time and space in which the objects occur in the ground. Removing an artifact from its context is an irreversible act that cheats us all of knowledge. Perhaps it should be mentioned that professional archaeologists also destroy sites as they excavate them, but they record the context of their finds as they go along, a critical ingredient in scientific archaeology.

Modern archaeology is not treasure hunting, nor is it a fantasy search for lost worlds; it is the systematic study of humanity in the past. This general definition includes not only ancient technology and human behavior, but social organization, religious beliefs, and every aspect of human culture.

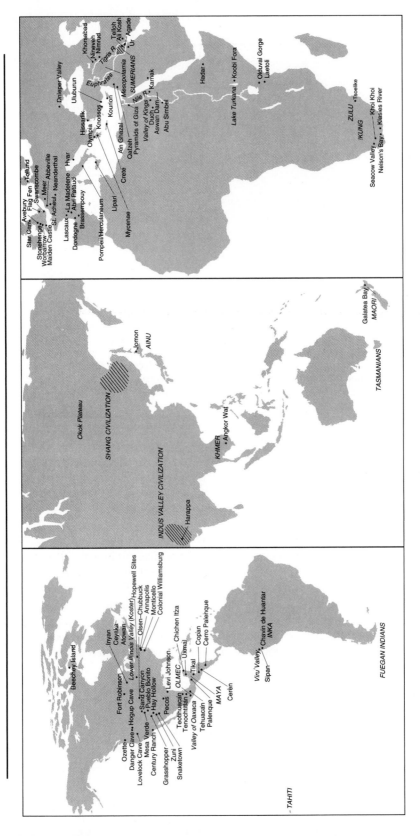

Figure 2.2 The archaeological sites mentioned in this text. Obvious geographic place names are omitted.

Who Needs the Past?

There is not yet one person, one animal, bird, fish, crab, tree, rock, hollow, canyon, meadow, forest. Only the sky alone is there; the face of the earth is not clear. Only the sea alone is pooled under all the sky; there is nothing whatsoever gathered together. . . . Whatever is that might be is simply not there: only the pooled water, only the calm sea, kept at rest under the sky. (Tedlock, 1996: 64)

The Maya *Popol Vuh*, a book of counsel, tells the story of the creation and recounts the deeds of gods and kings in a brilliant celebration of the Quiché Maya past. Sometimes called the Maya Bible, the impact of its creation myth is as powerful as that in the Book of Genesis.

All societies have an interest in the past. It is always around them, haunting, mystifying, tantalizing, sometimes offering potential lessons for the present and future. The past is important because social life unfolds through time, embedded within a framework of cultural expectations and values. In the high Arctic, Inuit preserve their traditional attitudes, skills, and coping mechanisms in some of the harshest environments on earth. They do this by incorporating the lessons of the past into the present. In many societies, the ancestors are the guardians of the land, which symbolizes present, past, and future. Westerners have an intense scientific interest in the past, partly born of curiosity, but also out of a need for historical identity. There are many reasons to attempt to preserve an accurate record of the past, and no one, least of all an archaeologist, should assume they are uniquely privileged in their interest in the remains of that past.

We have no monopoly on history. Many non-Western societies do not perceive themselves as living in a changeless world. They make a fundamental distinction between the recent past, which lies within living memory, and the more remote past that came before it. For instance, the Australian Aborigine groups living in northeast Queensland distinguish between *kuma*, the span of events witnessed by living people, *anthantnama*, a long time ago, and *yilamu*, the period of the creation. Furthermore, many societies also accept that there was cultural change in the past, among them Hindu traditions of history, which mention early people who lived without domesticated animals and plants, and the Hazda hunter-gatherers of East Africa who speak of their homeland's first inhabitants as being giants without fire or tools.[1]

---

[1] Some simple definitions will be helpful.

Hunter-gatherers (foragers): human societies that lived by hunting wild game, large and small, by fishing, and by gathering wild vegetable foods. Hunting and gathering was the only human lifeway from the earliest prehistoric times up to the development of agriculture and animal domestication in southwestern Asia in about 8800 B.C. Only a handful of hunter-gatherer societies, such as the San of the Kalahari Desert, survive.

Urban: city-dwelling. Archaeologists have argued for years about how to define a city. In general, cities have more than 5,000 inhabitants and are far more complex entities than villages or towns, especially i their social organization and nonagricultural activities.

City-states: cities with large, very complex social organizations that controlled specific territories. Satellite settlements throughout this territory provided food and other resources to the controlling city. City-states contrast with villages, which farmed much smaller areas of land owned by individual kin groups. Early Sumerian civilization flourished over a huge area between the rivers Tigris and Euphrates that is now Iraq. It was made up of dozens of competing city-states that controlled much smaller areas of land

These paradigms of the past take many forms, with mythic creators of culture, usually primordial ancestors, deities, or animals establishing contemporary social customs and the familiar landscape, or a more remote, discontinuous heroic era like that of the Greeks, which allowed writers like the playwright Aeschylus to evaluate contemporary behavior.

Most human societies of the past were nonliterate, which meant they transmitted knowledge and history orally, by word of mouth. The Aztec oral histories, partially set down after the Spanish Conquest of the fifteenth century A.D., are an excellent example of history transmitted by word of mouth. They were recited according to a well-defined narrative plot, which focused on great men, key events, like the dedication of the sun god Huitzilopochtli's temple in the Aztec capital in 1487, and the histories of favored groups. In these, as in other oral histories, there were formulas and themes, which formed the central ingredients of a story that varied considerably from one speaker to the next, even if the essential content was the same. Many oral histories are mixtures of factual data and parables that communicate moral and political values. But to those who hear them, they are publicly sanctioned history, performed before a critical group, and subject to the critical evaluation of an audience who may have heard the same stories.

Oral traditions are hard to use because their antiquity is very difficult to establish. In some cases, in Australia for example, oral histories and archaeology coincide in general terms. For example, the traditions speak of the arrival of the first people from overseas, of flooding of coastal areas after the Ice Age, and of the hunting of giant marsupials (pouched animals like the kangaroo). So Australia's past can be said to come from two sources: archaeological data and oral traditions. In some instances, the archaeologists and indigenous people have shared interests and come together in identifying sacred places and historic places, often to ensure they are preserved, even if the two groups differ on the "significance" of a particular location, where the archaeology finds no buildings or artifacts, yet the local people consider it a "sacred place."

But, all too often, the archaeologist and a local community have different interests in the past. To the archaeologist, the past is scientific data to be studied with all the rigor of modern science. To local people, the past is often highly personalized and the property of the ancestors. Such histories are valid alternative versions of history, which deserve respect and understanding, for they play a vital role in the creation and reaffirmation of cultural identity. And they raise a fundamental question, which lies behind many Native American objections to archaeological research. What do archaeologists, usually outsiders, have to offer to a cultural group that already has a valid version of its history? Why should they be permitted to dig up the burials of the ancestors or other settlements and sacred places under the guise of studying what is, to the people, a known history? It is a question that archaeologists have barely begun to address.

We should never forget that alternative, often compelling, accounts of ancient times exist, which play an important role in helping minority groups and others maintain their traditional heritage as it existed before the arrival of the Westerner. However, all of us, whether scientist or layperson, native American, Australian Aborigine, or Asian America, whatever our cultural and ethnic background, holds the past, however we think of it, in stewardship for future generations. An awareness of the past and of its lessons is one of the most precious legacies we can pass on to those who come after us.

"Village at the Rapids"

Inyan Ceyaka Atonwan (Dakota: "Village at the Rapids") (the Little Rapids site) lies on the Minnesota River about 45 miles (72 km) southwest of Minneapolis. The settlement was occupied by Eastern Dakota people between the early and middle 1800s and lay close to a trading post at Fort Snelling, where artist Captain Seth Eastman sketched and painted an invaluable record of the local Native Americans. Archaeologist Janet Spector excavated the site in 1980–82 and used artifacts from the excavation to identify different men's and women's activities in the village. As she wrote her report, she worried whether she as a non-Indian could do Indian-centered work. In 1985, she made contact with the local Dakota, one of whom was related through his mother to a man named Mazomani, who was a prominent member of the Little Rapids community in the early 1800s. They visited the site and then began a collaborative project between Dakota and archaeologists, combining oral history with archaeology, written records with modern-day experiences with the local people.

In 1980, Spector had found a small antler handle for an iron awl used for perforating leather. Red ocher-filled dots adorned the handle, which she learned from historical sources recorded important accomplishments by the owner. She felt certain it had belonged to a woman because they are responsible for hide work among the Dakota. Mazomani had a daughter named Mazaokiyewin ("Woman Who Talks to Iron"), who was a skillful leather worker. In her book *What This Awl Means*, Spector tells Mazaokiyewin's life story and constructs a scenario for the awl's loss just as it was worn out. She later presented her narrative to Mazaokiyewin's descendants, a story of a once vibrant place reconstructed by a skillful mediation between past and present, archaeology, oral tradition, and Native Americans' relationships with their history. The Inyan Ceyaka Atonwan project is a model of sensitive research that mediates conflicting perspectives on the past.

Spector writes (1993: 129), "I still find myself wishing for a time machine. I dream of spending time just one day at Little Rapids with some members of our project . . . and some of the nineteenth century figures linked to Inyan Ceyaka Atonwan. . . . I can visualize the day, but it is difficult to picture how we would communicate, given the distances between us."

What archaeologist, at one time or another, has not wished for a similar time machine? Therein lies the frustration and fascination of archaeology.

Archaeology and Anthropology

Archaeology has close links to the much wider science of anthropology. Indeed, archaeologist James Deetz has called the archaeologist a special kind of anthropologist concerned with ancient rather than modern societies.

Anthropology is the scientific study of humanity in the widest possible sense. Anthropologists study human beings as biological organisms and as people with a distinctive and unique characteristic—culture. They carry out research on contemporary human societies and on human development from the very earliest times.

This enormous field is divided into subdisciplines. **Physical anthropology** involves the study of human biological evolution and the variations between different living populations. Physical anthropologists also study the behavior of living nonhuman primates, such as the chimpanzee and gorilla, research that can suggest explanations for behavior among very early humans. **Cultural anthropology** deals with the analysis of human social life, both past and present. It is primarily the study of human culture and how culture adapts to the environment. Among cultural anthropologists, **ethnographers** describe the culture, technology, and economics of living and extinct societies, and **ethnologists** engage in comparative studies of societies, a process that involves attempts to reconstruct general principles of human behavior. **Social anthropologists** analyze social organization, ways in which people organize themselves. Finally, **linguistic anthropologists** study human languages, a field of research that is sometimes important to the study of the past.

Archaeology and cultural anthropology are part of the same discipline. However, archaeologists study past societies, ancient and relatively modern, which means they cannot speak to their informants. Their excavations and site surveys yield the material remains of human behavior in the past—stone tools, pot fragments, broken animal bones, and so on—all manufactured or modified by deliberate actions possibly centuries, even millennia ago. The archaeologist links these material remains to actual human behavior by developing theoretical models to explain such behavior and cultural change over long periods of time. As we have said, archaeology is a unique way of study human culture change from the time of the earliest human beings 2.5 million years ago up to the present.

The Diversity of Archaeologists

The stereotype of the pith-helmeted professor dies hard, for many people assume that every archaeologist studies ancient Egyptian pyramids or royal tombs. Like all scientific disciplines, archaeology has become a highly specialized field, to the point that an archaeologist working in the Ohio Valley or China may know as little about ancient Egypt as a well-informed layperson. There are probably about 10,000 archaeologists in the world, making for a relatively small community of practitioners, many of whom know one another well. The scientific interests of this community is astonishingly diverse. Archaeology is now a discipline and profession of specialists, often in dauntingly obscure topics. During the course of my career, I have worked with prehistorians and Egyptologists, historical and underwater archaeologists, to mention only a few relatively broad specialties. I have also collaborated with experts on ancient Egyptian wine, Ice Age earthworms, southern African mice, reindeer teeth growth rings, and eighteenth-century Colonial American gardens! All this without mentioning the many resource managers and private sector specialists who have crossed my path. We can only mention a few major archaeological specialties here.

Classical archaeologists study the ancient civilizations of Greece and Rome. They rely heavily on written sources. Many of them concentrate on architecture and the objects they excavate as fine examples of Classical art. Until recently, they have had relatively little interest in the minute economic, environmental, and social problems that absorb archaeologists working in earlier periods. But this inclination is changing as the prehistoric scholars' theories and methods influence archaeologists working on later periods. Much recent research has concentrated on such topics as rural landscapes in Roman Italy and on Mediterranean trade routes.

Historical archaeologists practice what is sometimes called "document-aided archaeology," where written records are available to amplify archaeological discoveries. Some excavate cities like Saxon London and medieval Winchester, which flourished in the dim yet documented past. Much historical archaeology covers an enormous range of sites and historical problems associated with the spread of Western civilization around the world during the European Age of Discovery after A.D. 1430, everything from remote trading forts to pioneer burial grounds and convict settlements in Australia. American historic-sites archaeology focuses on pioneer settlements, such as Colonial Williamsburg, slave communities in the South, Spanish missions in the Southwest, or nineteenth-century frontier forts. Scholars at these sites frequently specialize in such objects as pottery imported from England, Italy, and China, Spanish-style architecture, and uniform buttons. Some archaeologists study factories or slum housing dating from the Industrial Revolution or even later. Much of historical archaeology leads to reconstruction of ruined buildings as part of our national heritage. *Colonial Williamsburg*, Virginia, is the most famous of early American towns. It has been reconstructed with active help from archaeologists (Figure 2.3). One of the most famous discoveries of recent years was an African American burial ground in the heart of Manhattan, unearthed during ground clearance for a new federal building. The burials are providing a mine of information about a largely invisible segment of New York's population two centuries ago and will eventually be reinterred.

Figure 2.3   Excavations at Colonial Williamsburg. Historical archaeology was applied here to discover details of a colonial mental hospital. Colonial Williamsburg has been meticulously restored to its eighteenth-century form, including both private residences and public buildings. Archaeology has played an important role in reconstruction research.

For each of these projects, the archaeologist supplies details lacking in historical records. Contemporary historical records are usually filled with political and religious matters, with the deeds of civic leaders and statesmen. Archaeologists uncover the anonymous players of history, the humble folk who labored in the shadow of the palace wall, lived out their lives in mines or remote frontier towns, or in slave plantations. Their long-forgotten artifacts tell their story, reveal their complex interactions both with one another and with society at large. For example, more than a decade of excavations in the cellars and foundations of eighteenth-century Annapolis, Maryland, have revealed an ethnically far more diverse urban population than one might suspect from reading historical records alone.

Archaeology has been used to study modern households, too. Using methods developed for studying prehistoric rubbish heaps, archaeologist William Rathje delved into thousands of Tucson, Arizona, garbage bags, studying the waste disposal of lower-, middle-, and upper-income households. He found that most people discard rubbish indiscriminately, low-income families consume the most vitamin pills, and the average Tucson family wastes about $100 worth of beef a year. The implications of this research for consumers and manufacturers are fascinating. The Tucson project, and similar research in Milwaukee and other cities, also provides useful theoretical information for studying ancient middens (garbage heaps), even if Tucson itself happens to be several sizes larger than ancient Nineveh or the ancient Aztec capital, Tenochtitlán.

Increasingly, historical archaeologists are studying the archaeology of the European expansion and colonization of the world since A.D. 1400, focusing on such issues as ethnic diversity and the survival of indigenous cultures after the arrival of foreign settlers. For example, many archaeologists are excavating African American free and slave communities in North America, discovering many details of subtle resistance to the dominant culture.

Underwater archaeologists study ancient wrecks and submerged sites like ancient ports in the Mediterranean, around Florida, and elsewhere. Special recording techniques have been devised to recover the smallest details of shipwrecks and the cargoes in their holds. Unfortunately, many people believe that wrecks hold rich treasure and gold doubloons. Thus many wrecks are robbed or destroyed by inquisitive divers long before archaeologists can get to them. Although many people think of underwater archaeology as different from excavation ashore, it is not. Archaeologists working underwater have exactly the same intellectual goals as their dry land colleagues—to recover, reconstruct, and interpret the past. Their scuba gear and recording and recovery technology for recovering finds are specialized, but they are still studying ancient cultures. The famous *Uluburun* Bronze Age ship, wrecked off southern Turkey in 1305 B.C., yielded raw metals and precious objects from all over the eastern Mediterranean world, a startling testimony to the sophistication of maritime trade over 3,000 years ago (see Chapter 11). Many important ports and waterside cities now lie under shallow water and can be investigated with scuba gear. The most famous of them is *Port Royal* in Jamaica, famous for its pirates, submerged by an earthquake on June 7, 1692. Two thirds of the settlement vanished underwater. Underwater archaeologists have mapped the submerged buildings and recovered many artifacts from houses and storage areas. In recent years, archaeologists have also investigated underwater military sites in the western Pacific and historic shipwrecks in North America.

Prehistory is that portion of human history which extends back from before the time of written documents and archives. In contrast to Classical and historical archaeologists, prehistoric archaeologists deal with an enormous time scale of human cultural evolution, which extends back at least 2.5 million years. Prehistoric archaeology is the primary source of information on 99 percent of human history, for it encompasses the unwritten past, which can extend right into modern times in areas like Africa and the Amazon Basin. Prehistoric archaeologists investigate how early human societies all over the world came into being, how they differed from one another, and, in particular, how they changed through time.

No one could possibly become an expert in every aspect of prehistoric archaeology. Some specialists deal with the earliest human beings, working closely with geologists and physical anthropologists who are interested in human biological evolution. Others are experts in stone toolmaking, in the early peopling of the New and Old Worlds, or in the lifestyles of hunter-gatherers. Specialists in the origins of agriculture or urban civilization work closely with experts on topics ranging from architecture to cattle. All of this specialist expertise and knowledge means that most larger-scale prehistoric excavations involve teams of scientists cooperating to study early human settlements in the context of their natural environments. We give many examples of this type of research in later chapters.

In recent years, some groups, among them Native Americans, have argued that the term *prehistory* is racist and demeaning, on the grounds it implies that "prehistoric peoples" were inferior, and had no history, when, in fact, they had flourishing oral traditions and often sophisticated perspectives on human existence and the cyclical nature of time. However, the term is well established in science, and has never been used as an explicitly pejorative or racist term by any reputable archaeologist.

Cultural resource management (CRM) is a major and highly important part of archaeology today, so much so that most archaeological research conducted in North America is conducted under such activities. CRM is exactly that, the management of the finite sites and other records of the past within a framework of federal, state, tribal, and local records designed to minimize destruction of the material remains of the past. The key phrase is "resource management," where investigation of an area to be impacted by, say, strip mining, highway or home construction, or logging results in an archaeological investigation, usually under contract, to determine what archaeological remains are present and how to minimize their destruction. This is achieved by avoiding them, leaving parts of sites to be destroyed intact, or by rescue excavation before construction begins. CRM archaeology is extremely demanding, often carried out under very tight deadlines, and involves scientists from many disciplines. This is probably one of the hardest kinds of archaeology to do well and offers unique challenges. **Public archaeology** is a growing part of archaeology and covers the general activity of public education about the past. It is an integral part of CRM and sometimes academic archaeology, too.

World Prehistory

Africa was the cradle of humankind and of modern humanity as well. Geneticists believe anatomically modern humans, the ancestors of ourselves, first developed in Africa between 100,000 and 200,000 years ago. Their descendants radiated across the Sahara Desert and throughout the world during the late Ice Age, after 100,000 years ago. Thus the only way we can understand the origins of human biological and cultural diversity is on a truly global canvas. The study of world prehistory, the early history of humankind throughout the globe, requires a truly international perspective on the past, not one based only on part of the world like Europe or North America.

Prehistory covers an enormous span of time, starting more than 2.5 million years ago with the emergence of the first toolmaking hominids (humanlike beings) in East Africa and extending right into modern times. A common, and conventional, distinction between prehistory and **history** is the existence of historical documentation for historic times. In these periods, archaeological finds can be amplified with documentary evidence. For example, there are inscribed clay tablets that constitute the archives of the Sumerian peoples of Mesopotamia some 5,000 years ago, so we are technically in historic times.

Unlike our Victorian and early twentieth-century predecessors, we are able to examine human prehistory on a truly global scale. Unfortunately, in many areas of the world, such as Southeast Asia and Siberia, little or no excavation has been carried out, so our knowledge of the peopling of the globe remains very incomplete. Prehistoric archaeologists are trying to document and understand the ways in which humanity adapted itself to the many and diverse environments of the globe. By studying these adaptations, we can begin to understand the astonishing diversity of human cultures that make up our world.

The study of prehistory is, of course, far more than just the reconstruction of an engrossing epic of human biological and cultural evolution. It is the study of a series of intricate and still little-understood developments in our long history and of our ever-changing relationships with the world's myriad natural environments. In 1863, the great British biologist Thomas Huxley stated, "The question of questions for mankind, the problem which underlies all others, and is more deeply interesting than any other—is the ascertainment of the place which man occupies in nature and of his relations to the universe of things" (Huxley, 1863:1). To a considerable degree, this remains one of the fundamental questions of archaeological research.

For the sake of convenience, we can divide prehistory into a series of broad chapters, each spanning long periods of time and increasingly complex cultural developments. In fact, it is more appropriate to refer to these chapters as "developments," for archaeologists are concerned, in the final analysis, with the study of evolving human cultures over very long periods of time.

Early Prehistory

The immensely long span of prehistoric time, from the emergence of toolmaking, upright-walking hominids in tropical Africa more than 2.5 million years ago, up to between 200,000 and 100,000 years ago when modern human beings first appeared, is known as early prehistory (Figure 2.4). This was the archaic world of early prehistoric times, when the hominids evolved slowly into more advanced *Homo erectus* some 1.9 million years ago. Cultural evolution was even more glacially slow, with little fundamental change in human lifeways or technology for more than a million years. Then, about 1.8 million years ago, human beings spread north out of the tropics into more temperate latitudes, into Europe and Asia, adapting to far greater climatic extremes.

That they were able to do so was in part the result of the control of fire—for heat, perhaps cooking, and certainly for protection against predators living in deep caves, natural shelters for human beings.

For at least 800,000 years, these widely scattered *Homo erectus* populations evolved in the general direction of anatomically modern humans, showing great genetic and anatomical variation subsumed under the general term early *Homo sapiens*. Among these populations were the squat, heavily built Neanderthals of Eurasia who flourished from before 100,000 until about 33,000 years ago. They lived in Eurasia during the intensely cold climate of the last Ice Age glaciation.

The Origins and Spread of Homo sapiens sapiens

Sometime between 200,000 and 100,000 years ago, anatomically modern humans evolved in the savanna woodlands of eastern and southern Africa. A minority of scientists believe, however, that *Homo sapiens sapiens* emerged in many parts of the Old World at roughly the same time. These modern people, known to us more from genetic studies than fossils, were still hunter-gatherers, but apparently they were more efficient in their adaptations than their predecessors. By 100,000 years ago, *Homo sapiens sapiens* had spread out of Africa into southwestern Asia, coming into contact with other, earlier *Homo sapiens* hunter-gatherer populations.

The Peopling of the Globe by Modern Humans

In perhaps the most dramatic chapter of the human past, *Homo sapiens sapiens* spread widely over the Old World and into the New World (the Americas) during the closing millennia of the Ice Age. Human beings had crossed into Australia by 40,000 years ago. Less than 20,000 years later, people had developed the intricate technology needed to survive months of subzero winter cold. They flourished in a deep-frozen Ice Age Europe and on the open plains that stretched far northeast into Siberia. By 15,000 years ago, perhaps earlier, some tiny human bands had probably crossed into Alaska and the Americas. Only the far offshore islands of the Pacific remained uninhabited by humans, awaiting the development of deep-water canoes and offshore navigational techniques.

The Origins of Food Production

The worldwide thawing at the end of the Ice Age some 15,000 years ago led to dramatic changes in global climate and geography. Human populations in the Old World and the Americas had to adapt to radically new circumstances, to highly diverse postglacial environments. It was about 8800 B.C. that some largely sedentary hunter-gatherer communities in southwestern Asia started cultivating wild cereal grasses such as wheat and barley, perhaps in response to a severe drought triggered by a sudden cold snap that signaled a partial return to glacial conditions in the north. The new adaptation was highly successful. Within a few centuries, village farmers were flourishing in many parts of the region, and soon further afield. The herding of goats, and then cattle and pigs soon replaced hunting as a primary means of subsistence. The new economies

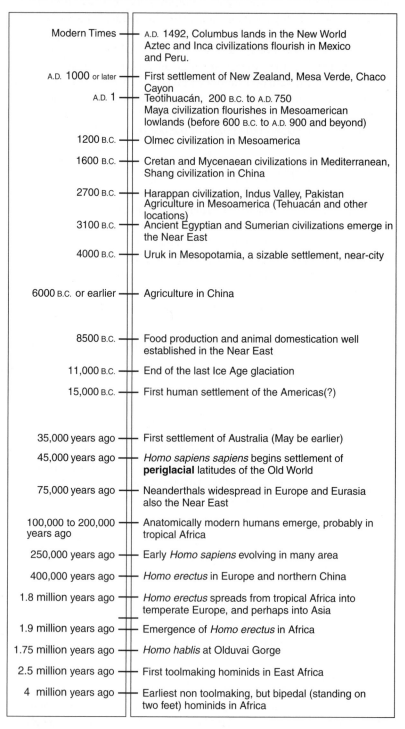

Modern Times — A.D. 1492, Columbus lands in the New World
Aztec and Inca civilizations flourish in Mexico
and Peru.

A.D. 1000 or later — First settlement of New Zealand, Mesa Verde, Chaco
Cayon

A.D. 1 — Teotihuacán, 200 B.C. to A.D. 750
Maya civilization flourishes in Mesoamerican
lowlands (before 600 B.C. to A.D. 900 and beyond)

1200 B.C. — Olmec civilization in Mesoamerica

1600 B.C. — Cretan and Mycenaean civilizations in Mediterranean,
Shang civilization in China

2700 B.C. — Harappan civilization, Indus Valley, Pakistan
Agriculture in Mesoamerica (Tehuacán and other
locations)

3100 B.C. — Ancient Egyptian and Sumerian civilizations emerge in
the Near East

4000 B.C. — Uruk in Mesopotamia, a sizable settlement, near-city

6000 B.C. or earlier — Agriculture in China

8500 B.C. — Food production and animal domestication well
established in the Near East

11,000 B.C. — End of the last Ice Age glaciation

15,000 B.C. — First human settlement of the Americas(?)

35,000 years ago — First settlement of Australia (May be earlier)

45,000 years ago — *Homo sapiens sapiens* begins settlement of
periglacial latitudes of the Old World

75,000 years ago — Neanderthals widespread in Europe and Eurasia
also the Near East

100,000 to 200,000 years ago — Anatomically modern humans emerge, probably in
tropical Africa

250,000 years ago — Early *Homo sapiens* evolving in many area

400,000 years ago — *Homo erectus* in Europe and northern China

1.8 million years ago — *Homo erectus* spreads from tropical Africa into
temperate Europe, and perhaps into Asia

1.9 million years ago — Emergence of *Homo erectus* in Africa

1.75 million years ago — *Homo hablis* at Olduvai Gorge

2.5 million years ago — First toolmaking hominids in East Africa

4 million years ago — Earliest non toolmaking, but bipedal (standing on
two feet) hominids in Africa

Figure 2.4 Major developments in human prehistory referred to in the text.

spread like wildfire south through the Nile Valley and north, deep into Europe. Independent centers of plant and animal domestication may have developed in India, Southeast Asia, and China within a few millennia. The cultivation of indigenous plants and cereals began in the Americas by at least 4000 B.C., probably earlier.

Some of the major controversies in archaeology surround the origins of food production. Why do humans turn from hunting and gathering to agriculture and animal herding, a development that led to immediate, long-term changes in global environments because of overgrazing, forest clearance, and plowing? The first scholars to speculate about early agriculture searched for the village occupied by the genius who had first planted wheat grains and watched them germinate into a new and predictable food supply. No one has ever found this mythical genius. We now realize that farming and the domestication of animals were complex changes in human culture that took place over thousands of years, not only in southwestern Asia but in other areas of the world as well. Was climate change responsible for food production, or a multiplicity of environmental, cultural, or social factors? The debate continues.

Throughout prehistory, human societies experimented with new ideas and technologies. Only a few caught on, and only a handful—among them agriculture, metalworking, writing, and wheeled transport—have polically affected the development of human societies on a global scale.

The Origins Of States (Civilizations)

Before 3000 B.C., new, highly centralized urban societies appeared in Egypt and Mesopotamia (now southern Iraq). These were state-organized societies, civilizations headed by supreme rulers and governed by a bureaucracy of officials and priests (for more discussion of a state, see Chapter 12). People lived in much larger communities, in cities of more than 5,000 people, in societies with ranked social classes, under a social order where conformity was assured by the threat of force, and under an official religion that sanctified the deeds of the tiny minority who ruled the state.

The Sumerians of Mesopotamia, the ancient Egyptians, the Harappans of the Indus Valley in Pakistan, the **Shang** of northern China, and other early peoples were followed by much larger empires and imperial civilizations, for example, those of the Persians, Greeks, and Romans. The process of early state formation—still only partially understood—also took hold in the Americas, where European explorers like Hernán Cortés came into contact with amazingly sophisticated native American civilizations, such as the Aztecs of Mexico and the Inkas of Peru in the fifteenth century A.D.

A continuous historical record takes us from the Sumerians of Mesopotamia through biblical times right up to the conflicts and astonishing economic and technical achievements of Western civilization.

European Expansion

The final chapter of prehistory coincides with the expansion of Western civilization outward from its European homeland during the Age of Discovery after A.D. 1430. The five centuries that followed found Westerners coming into contact with all manner of human societies, covering the entire spectrum from Tasmanian hunting bands to the civilizations of the Khmer of Cambodia and the Inka of the Andes. These were the centuries when the world's diverse societies were first drawn into what historians and anthropologists often refer to as a world system—the system of economic and political interconnectedness that is pervasive in the late twentieth-century world.

Prehistory, then, is the compelling story of unfolding human existence, one that began at a few locations in tropical Africa and now takes us to the frontiers of outer space. The recorded archives of history take us back to but a tiny fraction of our long past, which means the study of prehistory has much to tell us about why we are so similar and why we are so different.

Summary

Archaeology is the systematic study of humanity in the past, not only human behavior and technology, but of every aspect of human culture. The discipline is an integral part of anthropology, the study of humanity in the broadest sense, with archaeologists studying past societies from all time periods. There are many types of archaeologists, among them Classical archaeologists, who study ancient Greece and Rome. Historical archaeologists study sites and societies that are also recorded in written documents. Underwater archaeologists are specialists in shipwrecks and other underwater features, which are excavated like those on land, to acquire information about ancient societies. Cultural resource management (CRM) is a major area of archaeology that involves managing the finite remains of the past. However, archaeologists have no monopoly on the past, for each society has its own worldview and perceptions of history. World prehistory is a global study concerned with the following developments: early prehistory and human origins, the emergence and spread of modern humans, the origins of food productions and early civilization.

3

Culture

Painting from the base of Mimbres bowl, from the Mimbres Valley, New Mexico, c. A.D. 1000 to 1130.

An archaeologist of 6666 A.D. may find himself obliged to rely on the divergences between assemblages of kitchen utensils to help him recognize that by 1950, the United Kingdom and United States of America were not occupied by the same society.

V. Gordon Childe, *Piecing Together the Past*
(1956)

Many times, while excavating in Africa, I have woken on a cool winter's morning deep in the bush and watched a modern-day farming village close to our site come alive as the sun rises. The air is still, a slight chill hugging the ground, where dew glistens in the soft light of dawn. You smell wooden smoke and cattle dung, see figures wrapped in blankets moving out to cattle enclosures or huddling around fires. The thatched huts are still quiet as the timeless rhythm of another day begins. You sense the timelessness of it all, the annual cycles of planting and harvest, birth, life, and death. Again and again, I think of the continuity between ancient and modern, for, like it or not, we live with the past as well as the present. In places like Africa, where many people still live much as their predecessors did centuries ago, the links between past and present seem particularly strong and you remember the close links between archaeology and anthropology.

"Archaeology is anthropology" is a fundamental principle of our discipline, for the archaeologist is a special type of anthropologist, who studies past rather than living societies. Archaeology and anthropology have developed together for more than a century, ever since sociologist Herbert Spencer espoused doctrines of human progress in the mid-nineteenth century. Spencer's theories were the cultural equivalent of Charles Darwin's biological evolution and natural selection. They strongly influenced early anthropologists like Edward Tylor and Lewis Morgan, who developed the first universal schemes of human cultural evolution in the 1870s and 1880s. Edward Tylor wrote the first global essays on anthropology. He was well aware of the close links between ancient and modern non-Western societies, for he had visited Maya ruins and excavated in Stone Age caves in France. Tylor and his contemporaries made comparisons between the simple nonmetal-using culture of the Tasmanian aborigines and Stone Age hunter-gatherers, between living Eskimo groups and late Ice Age Cro-Magnons, who lived in western Europe 18,000 years ago.

The Victorians worked at a time when little was known of the prehistoric past, and even less about the remarkable diversity of human societies in the non-Western world. Today's archaeologists would not dream of comparing Eskimo culture to that of the Cro-Magnons, but they still make extensive use of fundamental concepts developed by anthropologists working among hunter-gatherer and subsistence farming societies around the world. The great strength of anthropology is its insistence on participant observation—field research carried out by living among one's subjects. Anthropology indeed has a long and distinguished record of such studies conducted by remarkable people: Franz Boas, who worked among the native Americans; Bronislaw Malinowski, who observed the Trobriand islanders of the western Pacific; Margaret Mead, who worked in Samoa; and many others.[1]

Archaeology shares with anthropology a concern with culture and culture change. In particular, the concept of culture provides a framework that archaeologists can use both to describe and explain the past. In this chapter, we examine culture and culture change, the goals of archaeology, and the nature of archaeological evidence. This provides a framework that archaeology can use to both describe and explain the prehistoric past. The term **culture** has both general and specific connotations in anthropology, which we must now define.

Human Culture

Everyone lives within a cultural context, one that is qualified by a label like "middle-class American," "Roman," or "Sioux." These labels conjure up characteristic objects or behavior patterns typical of the particular culture. We associate hamburgers with middle-class American culture and kayaks with maritime Eskimos. Romans are thought to have spent their time conquering the world, Sioux wandering over the Great Plains. But such stereotypes are often crude, inaccurate generalizations. In fact, the label "American Indian" is really a biological term that includes incredibly cultur- ally diverse peoples, ranging from family-size hunter-gatherer bands to large, com- plex civilizations.

Each human society has its own recognizable cultural style, which shapes the behavior of its members, their political and judicial institutions, and their morals. Every traveler is familiar with the distinctive flavor of various cultures that one expe- riences when dining in a foreign restaurant or arriving in a new country. This distinc- tiveness results from a people's complex adaptation to greatly varied ecological, societal, and cultural factors.

Human culture is unique because much of its content is transmitted from genera- tion to generation by sophisticated communication systems. Formal education, reli- gious beliefs, and day-to-day social intercourse all transmit culture and allow societies to develop complex and continuing adaptations to aid their survival. Such communication systems also help rapid cultural change to take place, as when less

---

[1]There are, of course, many types of anthropologists, who study all manner of specialized topics:

Social anthropologists work primarily with social organization and the more intangible aspects of human society. Some are specialists, although they may combine their specialty with theoretical insights from social anthropology in the field.

Ethnographers study technology and economic life, and collect data on social organization and other aspects of human culture.

Ethnologists generalize from the information collected by the ethnographer, and linguistic anthropologists study the great diversity of human languages and their development.

Physical anthropologists study human biological evolution and the biology of human beings and their clos- est relatives, apes and monkeys.

Then there are medical, psychological, urban, and other anthropologists who study aspects of modern industrial and nonindustrial society. A large number of anthropologists now work in the private sector on problems of human diversity in the workplace.

technologically sophisticated societies come into contact with those with more effective technology. Culture is a potential guide for behavior created through generations of human experience. It provides a design for living that helps mold responses to different situations.

Human beings are the only animals to use culture as the primary means of adapting to the environment. Although biological evolution has protected the polar bear from arctic winters, only human beings make thick clothes and igloos in the Arctic and live in light thatched shelters in the tropics. Culture is an adaptive system; it is an interface between ourselves, the environment, and other human societies. Through the long millennia of prehistory, human culture became more elaborate. If this cultural buffer were now removed we would be helpless and most probably doomed to extinction. As our primary means of adaptation, human culture is always adjusting to environmental, technological, and societal change.

Language, economics, technology, religion, and political and social organization are but a few of the interacting subdivisions of human culture. These elements shape one another and blend to form a whole. For instance, the distribution of water and food supplies as well as flexible social organization helps determine the distribution of home bases among the San hunter-gatherers of the Kalahari Desert in southern Africa.

Culture is the dominant factor in determining social behavior; human society is the vehicle that carries our culture. Societies are groups of interacting organizers. Insects and other animals have societies but only humans have culture as well.

What is culture? Anthropologists have tried to define this most elusive of theoretical formulations for generations. All such definitions are concepts that are a means of explaining cultures and human behavior in terms of the learned, shared ideas held by a group of people. One of the best definitions was that put forth by the great Victorian anthropologist Sir Edward Tylor more than a century ago. He wrote (1871: 4) that culture is "that complex whole which includes knowledge, belief, art, morals, law, custom, and any other capabilities and habits acquired by man as a member of society." Most archaeologists prefer to define culture as the primary nonbiological means by which human societies adapt to and accommodate their environment. An archaeologist's view of culture is that it represents the cumulative intellectual resources of human societies. These resources are passed from generation to generation by the spoken word and by example. Culture is the primary means of nonbiological adaptation to the environment and regulates relationships with the environment through technology and social and belief systems.

The concept of culture provides anthropological archaeologists with a means for explaining the products of human activity. When archaeologists study **patterns of discard,** or the tangible remains of the past, they see a patterned reflection of the culture that produced them, of the shared behavior of a group of prehistoric people. This patterning of archaeological finds is critical, for it reflects patterned behavior in the past.

Cultural Systems

Archaeology can be very frustrating. I remember sitting in the middle of an ancient African farming village that I had excavated over many months. My laboratory was stacked high with boxes of animal bones, pot fragments, and other artifacts. Despite weeks of excavation under the hot sun, I felt a deep sense of frustration, for there was so much about the inhabitants that was hidden from me. As the afternoon shadows lengthened, I found myself conjuring up a living village on the now-silent mound. As images of huts and cattle enclosures passed through my mind, I felt an overwhelming desire for a few minutes conversation with the ancient inhabitants. So much was lost, so much was intangible and beyond reconstruction with the archaeologist's spade.

Herein lies the great challenge of archaeology—reconstructing not only the material, but trying to comprehend highly perishable aspects of human cultures: long-vanished religious beliefs and social interactions, the day-to-day transactions between individuals, within families, and with a wider world that make up our lives.

So far, no one has been able to dig up a religious philosophy or an unwritten language. Archaeologists have to work with the tangible remains of human activity that still survive in the ground. But these surviving remains of human activity are radically affected by intangible aspects of human culture. All cultures reflect their owner's worldview, their idea of the universe in which they live. In many ancient societies, the living and spiritual worlds were thought of as one, so that religious beliefs and symbolism affected architecture, art, and the design of ceremonial artifacts. Great Maya cities like Copán and Tikal were reproductions in stone and stucco of the supernatural world of trees (carved uprights), sacred mountains (pyramids), and openings to the Otherworld (caves and temple entrances). The same kinds of symbolism affected artifact design in many cultures. Eighteen hundred years ago, the *Hopewell* people of the American Midwest traded, over enormous distances, finely made ornaments fashioned of hammered copper sheet (Figure 3.1). These ornaments turn up in Hopewell burial mounds. The copper technology that made them was simple, but the symbolism behind the artifacts was not. They were probably exchanged between important individuals as symbolic gifts, denoting kin ties, economic obligations, and other social meanings that are beyond the archaeologist's ability to recover. Thus the artifacts found in an excavation reflect not only ancient technology, but also the values and uses that a society placed on such objects. Ancient tools are not culture in themselves, but a patterned reflection of the culture that produced them. Such patternings provide a link between archaeological remains and the behavior of their makers.

I have always found it helpful to think of cultures as systems of different, interacting parts, which interact, in turn, with their ever-changing environments. In thinking this way, I, and many archaeologists, have been strongly influenced by the work of anthropologist Leslie White. In the 1950s, he studied peoples' means of adapting to their environment. He argued that human culture is made up of many structurally different parts which articulate with one another within a total cultural system (Figure 3.2). This **cultural system** is the means whereby a human society adapts to its physical and social environment and is a useful conceptual tool for studying the past, even if theoretical approaches to cultural systems vary widely from one archaeologist to another.

All cultural systems articulate with other systems, which also are made up of interacting sets of variables. One such system is the natural environment. The links between cultural and environmental systems are such that a change in one system is

Figure 3.1   Hopewell bird claw in mica. The Hopewell people traded such prestigious objects over large distances in eastern North America during the first millennium B.C.

linked to changes in the other. Thus a major objective of archaeology is to understand the linkage between the various parts of cultural and environmental systems as they are reflected in **archaeological data.** It follows that archaeologists studying cultural systems are more interested in the *relationships* between activities and tools within a cultural system than in the activities or tools themselves. They are profoundly interested in cultural systems within their environmental context, and in the intangible beliefs and values that helped create them.

To be workable, any human cultural system depends on its ability to adapt to the natural environment. A cultural system can be broken down into all manner of subsystems: religious and ritual subsystems, economic subsystems, and so on. Each of these is linked to the others. Changes in one subsystem, such as a shift from cattle herding to wheat growing, cause reactions in many others. Such relationships give the archaeologist a measure of the constant changes and variations in human culture that can accumulate over long periods as cultural systems respond to external and internal stimuli.

By examining the systematic patternings of archaeological finds, we can discover more about the intangible aspects of human behavior. By dropping their

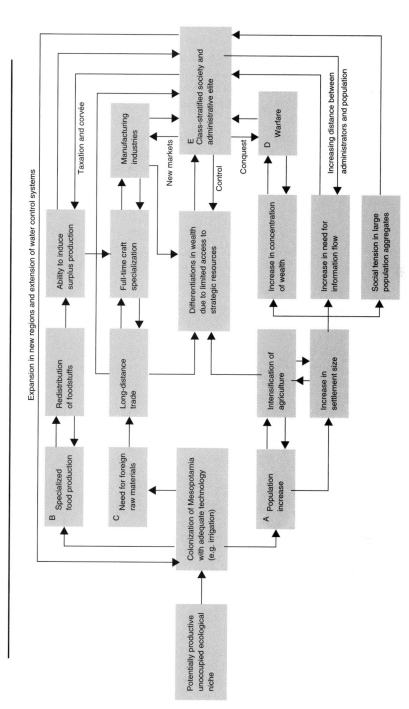

Figure 3.2 Cultural systems are, of course, theoretical formulations used by archaeologists to interpret the past. This systems model illustrates a systems approach to understanding human culture. It is an attempt to document the relationship between cultural and environmental variables that led to state-organized societies in Mesopotamia between 5000 and 2000 B.C. (*From The Rise of Civilization* by Charles L. Redman. Copyright © 1978 W. H. Freeman and Company. Reprinted with permission.)

possessions on the ground or burying their dead in certain ways, people have left vital information about many more elements in their cultural system than merely their tools or skeletal remains (Figure 3.3). One can examine the relationship between individual households by comparing the artifacts left by each; one can study trading practices by analyzing the products of metalsmiths; one can discover religious beliefs by mapping temple architecture. Also, the carefully arranged grave offerings in a royal cemetery tell much about the ranked members of a royal court buried in a communal grave.

British archaeologist Sir Leonard Woolley excavated a Royal Cemetery of 2800 B.C. in the city of *Ur* in southern Iraq, which is a classic example of how archaeology reveals social ranking. An important prince died. The priests supervised the hasty digging of a vast pit. Dozens of workers carried basketloads of earth up a lengthening ramp and dumped their loads to one side. Next, a few masons built a stone burial chamber with a vaulted brick roof. A small procession of high officials carried the royal corpse into the empty mausoleum and laid the dead man out in all his finery. They arranged food offerings alongside the bier in gold and silver bowls. Then the dead man's closest personal attendants knelt silently by their master. They took poi-

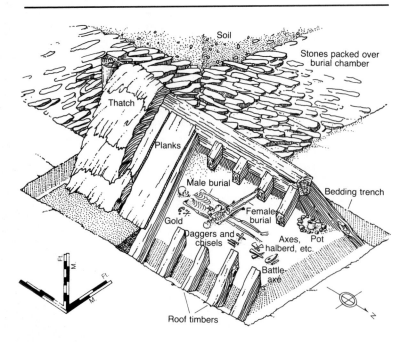

Figure 3.3 A wooden burial house from Leubingen, Germany. The two burials were deposited in a wooden house under a mound. The archaeologist recovers not only the burials and the objects with which they were buried, but also reconstructs the burial layout and sequence of construction of the burial house. Further, the archaeologist tries to infer the funerary rituals from the artifact patterning and the structures under the mound.

son and accompanied the prince into eternity. The walled-up chamber stood at the back of the empty pit, where the priests presided over a lavish funeral feast (see Figure 12.3).

A long line of soldiers, courtiers, and male and female servants filed into the mat-filled burial pit. Everyone wore their finest robes, their most brilliant uniforms, and badges of rank. Each courtier, soldier, or servant carried a small clay cup brimming with poison. The musicians bore their lyres. The royal charioteers drove the ox-drawn wagons down the ramp to their right place in the bottom of the great hole. Grooms calmed the restless animals as the drivers held the reins. Everyone lined up in their proper places in correct order of precedence. Music played. A small detachment of soldiers guarded the top of the ramp with watchful eyes. At a quiet signal, everyone in the pit raised their clay cup to their lips and swallowed poison. Then they lay down to die, each in his or her correct place. As the bodies twitched, then lay still, a few men slipped into the pit and killed the oxen with quick blows. The royal court had embarked on its long journey to the afterlife.

The priests covered the grave pit with earth and a mudbrick structure before filling the hole and access ramp with layers of clay. A sacrificial victim marked each stratum until the royal sepulcher reached ground level. When he uncovered the royal grave, Woolley was struck by the order and strict protocol of death. He wrote, "A blaze of colour with the crimson coats, the silver, and the gold; clearly these people were not wretched slaves killed as oxen might be killed, but persons held in honour, wearing their robes of office" (Woolley, 1982: 122).

The precise and sophisticated recovery of such patterned data as that in the Ur burial is crucial for **analysis** and **interpretation** in archaeology.

Cultural Process

Every cultural system is in a constant state of change. Its various political, social, and technological subsystems adjust to changing circumstances. We ourselves live in a time of rapid cultural change, in which measurable differences set apart different ten-year periods. We would find it hard to identify the thousands of minor daily cultural changes that occur, but we can easily recognize the cumulative effects of these minor changes over a longer period.

Consider the many minor changes in automobile design over the past decades. In themselves the changes are not very striking, but if one looks at the cumulative effect of several years' steady change toward safer cars—energy-absorbing bumpers, padded steering wheels and dashboards, air bags, seat belts, more aerodynamic shapes—the change is striking. The automobile of today is different from that of the 1960s, and many of the changes are due to stricter governmental safety regulations, which in turn are due to greater public safety consciousness. Here we see a major cumulative change in part of our enormous technological subsystem. By examining the relationship between technological and political subsystems, we can understand the processes by which culture changes.

The word *process* implies a patterned sequence of events, one event leading to another. A contractor builds a three-bedroom house in an ordered sequence of events, from foundation footings up to final painting. (Archaeological research itself has a process—research design and formulating objectives in the form of hypotheses, collecting and interpreting data to test those hypotheses, publishing the results.) To analyze **cultural process,** we attempt to consider all of the factors that cause changes in human culture and how they affect one another.

How did human cultures change in the past? What cultural processes came into play when people began to cultivate the soil, or when complex and elaborate urban states developed 5,000 years ago? As we saw in Chapter 1, new discoveries like agriculture or ironworking were once thought to have spread throughout the world by mass migrations or by long-distance trading over continents and oceans. But as more and more archaeological data have accumulated in all corners of the world, people have realized that such straightforward explanations of cultural process as universal evolution, or the spread of all ideas from one place of invention, are simplistic and do not reflect reality.

Most changes in human culture have been cumulative, occurring slowly over a long period of time. Ancient Egyptian civilization began with the unification of Upper and Lower Egypt into a single state by the pharaoh Menes in about 3100 B.C. Intensively conservative and seemingly unchanging, Egyptian civilization endured for 3,000 years, until the Nile Valley became part of the Roman Empire. This impression of unchanging civilization is misleading, for, in fact, the institutions of Egyptian kingship developed long before the unification of the state and evolved constantly as circumstances changed along the Nile. The basic institutions remained much the same, but the pharaohs trimmed their rule to accommodate new technologies, new political and social circumstances. One of the reasons Egyptian civilization endured so long was that it was flexible enough to adjust to widely fluctuating Nile flood levels and changing outside political conditions. Studying these often subtle processes of cultural change requires highly sophisticated research work.

Processes of culture change in prehistory were the result of constantly changing adaptations to a myriad of external environments. Cultural systems were constantly adjusting and evolving in response to internal and external **feedback.** Clearly, no one element in a cultural system is a primary cause of culture change because a complex range of factors—vegetation, technology, social restrictions, and population density, to mention only a few—interact with one another and react to a change in any element in the system. From the ecologist's point of view, therefore, human culture is merely one element of the **ecosystem,** a mechanism whereby people adapt to this environment. This viewpoint provides a useful framework for much modern archaeological research and for studying cultural process, although, of course, cultural systems encompass much more than merely environmental adaptation.

We look more closely at ways in which people have sought to interpret ancient cultural process in Chapter 13.

The Goals of Archaeology

Modern archaeology is a complex discipline that covers the entire compass of human history. However, whatever their specialty, archaeologists everywhere agree that their research has these three broad goals:

- Studying culture history
- Reconstructing past lifeways
- Explaining why cultural change has taken place.

In practice each objective usually complements the other, especially when archaeologists design their research to answer specific questions rather than merely digging a site as a preliminary to describing rows of excavated objects.

These three goals are fundamental to all archaeological research, but are concerned with the actual process of field and laboratory research. Archaeology has three additional, wider goals, which relate to both cultural heritage and the role of the discipline in modern society:

- Preserving the world's cultural heritage, as found in archaeological sites, for future generations. This is the notion of stewardship, central to archaeology.
- Making society aware of the origins of, and importance of, human biological and cultural diversity.
- Using the lessons of the past to serve the present, especially in the context of economic development and environmental adaptation (see Chapters 6 and 10).

Culture History

Culture history (technically, *culture prehistory,* but the term *history* is usually employed) means, quite simply, the description of prehistoric human cultures as they extend back thousands of years into the past. **Culture history** is derived from the study of sites—and the artifacts and structures in them—in a temporal and spatial context. By investigating groups of prehistoric sites and their many artifacts, it is possible to erect local and regional sequences of human cultures that extend over centuries, even millennia (see Chapters 9, 13). Most of this activity is descriptive, and an essential preliminary to any work on lifeways or cultural process.

Past Lifeways

The study of past lifeways, the ways in which people have made their living in the past, involves the study of prehistoric cultures within their environmental context. Environmental data come from many sources, including ancient plant remains, fossil pollen grains, and animal bones. Ancient subsistence patterns, and even diet, can be reconstructed from food residues such as animal bones, carbonized seeds, and fish remains recovered during the course of meticulous excavations. Over the past half century, archaeologists have achieved miracles of lifeway reconstruction. In one notable example, southwestern archaeologists have used tree rings to reconstruct a great drought that affected the western United States between A.D. 1275 to 1299. As the drought settled over the Four Corners region, the Anasazi groups who lived in the area dispersed from their large pueblo towns like the Cliff Palace at *Mesa Verde* and *Sand Canyon* and settled elsewhere (see Chapter 6).

Reconstructing ancient lifeways is another form of descriptive archaeology, but one that relates archaeological contexts in time and space to the complex interplay of changing patterns of human settlement, subsistence strategies, and ancient environments (Chapter 10). The theoretical framework for this kind of research is the systems approach, which sees human cultures as complicated, ever-changing systems that interact with one another as well as with the natural environment.

Serving the Present

Archaeology gives us a long perspective on history, especially of ways that different societies have adapted to changing environments and developed solutions to such problems as the use and abuse of water sources, overgrazing of pasturelands, and growing crops in frost-prone regions. In a remarkably successful experiment, archaeologists like Clark Erickson of the University of Pennsylvania have reconstructed ancient irrigated field systems on Bolivia's high grasslands (*altiplano*), grown potatoes successfully in them even in severe frosts, and reintroduced the ancient methods to modern-day local villages. Some archaeologists spend their careers studying traditional botany and medical practices that use wild plants of all kinds, work that often involves working with native informants. Much of this research serves to reinforce a pride in cultural heritage among people whose traditional cultures have been decimated over many centuries of European contact. William Rathje's pioneering studies of modern urban garbage have provided valuable information on waste disposal for recyclers and others interested in resource management, as well as basic theoretical data for archaeologists digging ancient cities.

Explaining Cultural Process

How can one explain why human cultures in all parts of the world reached their various—and diverse—stages of cultural development? Why did cities and civilization first appear in southwestern Asia, then much later in India and China? Why did agriculture never take hold in Australia and spread so rapidly in the Americas? What were the processes of cultural change that caused the great diversity in human societies, that triggered widely differing rates of culture change in different places, even in very similar environments?

Many early archaeologists were content to talk generally of migrations, the diffusion of ideas, and revolutionary inventions. In fact, cultural processes were much more complicated than this, for they were responses not only to environmental change but to a myriad of social, political, and even religious factors that affected the way people made decisions about their lives. Today, a commonly used approach called **processual archaeology** involves the application of rigorous scientific methodology to the archaeological record, developing propositions that can be tested using meticulously collected archaeological data. Processual archaeology is based on the notion that archaeology is far more than merely a descriptive activity, and that it is possible to explain cultural change in the past. Many archaeologists believe this processual approach is too impersonal, that it takes little account of the way *people* make decisions about their lives. Much recent research (commonly called **postprocessual archaeology**) factors in both a scientific approach and information from other sources such as oral history to counteract the relative impersonality of the processualists (see Chapter 13).

Theory in Archaeology

The debate between processual and postprocessual archaeologists reflects the constant debate over theory in archaeology. Theory is the overall framework within which the archaeological scholar operates. Over the past century and a half, archaeologists have devised many theoretical approaches to the past, approaches that relate a body of theory to a battery of ever more sophisticated methods and techniques for describing the past. Archaeologists are constantly at work devising new theoretical approaches to expand the scope of their research. These evolving theoretical frameworks are a means for archaeologists to look beyond the facts and material objects for explanations of cultural developments and changes that took place during our long history. Ideally, research in archaeology would be a constant, interactive dialogue between theory and observation, a more or less self-critical procedure based on inference about the past built on phenomena in the contemporary world.

These three broad goals of archaeological research provide the basis for all archaeology, for our ultimate objective is very simple—to describe, understand, and explain human behavior of the past.

Archaeological Evidence

Archaeologists construct ancient cultures from archaeological data, the material remains of the past. This material data comes in many forms, as an entire city, a humble farmer's dwelling, the golden mask of the Egyptian pharaoh Tutankhamun, or a scatter of broken bones or stone tools. As we see in Chapter 4, such data makes up the archaeological record. The realities of long-term preservation in the ground enter into the equation because only the most durable artifacts survive under normal circumstances, objects like stone tools and baked clay potsherds. Thus some aspects of ancient cultural systems such as technology and hunting activity tend to be better preserved than, say, art styles or perishable ornaments. And some subsystems like religious beliefs and philosophies often defy interpretation altogether.

Archaeology is based on the scientific recovery of data from the ground, on the systematic excavation and recording of the archaeological record as it survives in sites, as artifacts, food remains, and other finds.

Archaeological Sites

The archaeological **site** is a place where traces of ancient human activity are to be found. It is the archaeologist's archive, in much the same way as government files can yield a day-by-day record of historical events. Sites are normally identified through the manufactured tools, or artifacts, found in them. They can range in size from a huge prehistoric city, such as Teotihuacán, in the Valley of Mexico, to a small meat cache used by hunter-gatherers at Olduvai Gorge, Tanzania. An archaeological site can consist of a human burial, a huge rockshelter occupied over millennia, or a simple scatter of stone tools found on the floor of Death Valley, California. Sites are limited in number and variety by preservation conditions and the activities of the people who occupied them. Some were used for a few short hours, others for a generation or two. Some, like Mesopotamian city mounds, were major settlements for hundreds, even thousands, of years and contain numerous separate occupation layers. The great mounds of the city of Ur in Mesopotamia contain many occupation levels, which tell the story of a long-established ancient city that was abandoned when the river Euphrates changed its course away from the settlement.

Archaeological sites are most commonly classified according to the activities that occurred there. Thus cemeteries and other sepulchers, like Tutankhamun's tomb, are referred to as *burial sites*. A 20,000-year-old Stone Age site in the Dnieper Valley of the Ukraine, with mammoth-bone houses, hearths, and other signs of domestic activity, is a *habitation site*. So are many other sites, such as caves and rockshelters, early Mesoamerican farming villages, and Mesopotamian cities—in all, people lived and carried out greatly diverse activities. *Kill sites* consist of bones of slaughtered game animals and the weapons that killed them. They are found in East Africa and on the North American Great Plains. *Quarry sites*—where people mined stone or metals to make specific tools—are another type of specialized site. Prized raw materials, such as **obsidian,** a volcanic glass used for fine knives, were widely traded in prehistoric times and are of profound interest to the archaeologist. Then there are such spectacular ceremonial and religious sites like the stone circles of Stonehenge in southern England; the Temple of Amun at *Karnak*, Egypt; and the great ceremonial precincts of lowland Maya centers in Central America at Tikal, Copán, and *Palenque* (Figure 3.4). *Art sites* are common in southwestern France, southern Africa (see Figure 12.8), and parts of North America, where prehistoric people painted or engraved magnificent displays with deep, and still little-understood symbolic meaning. Some French art sites are more than 30,000 years old. Each of these site types reflects a form of human activity, which is represented in the archaeological record by specific artifact patterns and surface indications found and recorded by the archaeologist.

Figure 3.4 The Acropolis complex at Copán, Honduras, as drawn by Tatiana Proskouriakoff. The ceremonial precincts of Copán are surrounded by several square miles of residential quarters and outlying settlements, making it one of the largest pre-Columbian cities in the Americas. The pyramids and plazas of central Copán were laid out as a symbolic representation of the Maya sacred world, complete with sacred mountains (pyramids), with the temple entrance at the top of the pyramid serving as the symbolic entrance to the underworld.

Artifacts, Features, and Ecofacts

Artifacts are objects found in archaeological sites that exhibit features resulting from human activity. The term covers every form of portable archaeological find, from stone axes to gold ornaments, as well as food residues such as broken bones. **Features** are structures such as houses, hearths, storage pits, and so on. They can also include buried fields, workshop areas, and drainage systems. Artifacts are distinguished from nonartifacts simply because artifacts display patterns of humanly caused features, or attributes. These objects can be classified according to their distinctive attributes. Artifacts are the product of human ideas, ideas that people had about the way objects should look or be used. Every culture has its own rules, which limit and dictate the form of artifacts. Our own society has definite ideas of what a fork should look like, or an automobile, or a pair of shoes. We are so familiar with the artifacts of other cultures that seeing, say, a skin kayak, we at once identify it as "Eskimo."

Most craft skills, such as stone toolmaking, pottery manufacture, basketry, and metallurgy, are learned by each new generation. Each generation passes the skills on to the next, usually resulting in relatively slow, sometimes very slow, changes in artifacts and artifact technology. This inborn conservatism, which we might call tradition, strongly influences perpetuation of artifact forms.

The variation in a group of similar artifacts, such as stone projectile points, may reflect varied ideas behind them. Archaeologists study and classify artifacts, as we discuss in Chapter 9. These **classifications** are really research devices by which we study the products of human behavior and, indirectly, human behavior itself. For the archaeologist, every artifact has a number of **attributes,** identifiable properties that combine to give the object its distinctive form. The vessel illustrated in Figure 3.5 has several obvious attributes: painted motif, rounded base, and so on. Each of these attributes contributes to the form of the pot and was part of the mental template that produced it. Each attribute has a different reason for being there. The band of decoration is purely ornamental, part of the decorative tradition among the people who made it. The shape of the pot is determined by its function—it was designed for carrying liquids and for cooking, for which a bag-shaped, round-bottomed body is essential. Attributes can be present because of traditional, functional, technological, or other reasons. Just occasionally a new attribute appears, a new decorative motif perhaps, which may vanish just as fast as it appeared. Why? Because it did not catch on with other potmakers. Occasionally, too, a new attribute may achieve wide popularity and be adopted by everyone. Then the innovation becomes part of the pottery tradition.

The dictates of fashion and style play an important role in the changes that occur in attributes over short and long periods of time. These fashions and the styles associated with them are a major factor in studying culture change. To take a relatively modern **analogy**, Victorian explorers who penetrated deep into the East African interior traveled in caravans laden with cheap imported goods such as glass beads, cotton cloth, and iron hoes. Sometimes they would find that the trade goods they brought with them to barter for food, goods once thought to be prime commodities, were no longer of interest to peoples in the interior. Fashions had changed, and different bead colors had assumed greater desirability. If one were to investigate sites where such trade was taking place over several centuries, one would find changes in proportions of different bead types, shapes, and colors. In this case, they are the result of changing fashions.

Figure 3.5 Painted vessel from the American Southwest. Attributes include rim shape, height, paint colors, design motif, clay composition, and so on.

The archaeologist is deeply concerned with how artifacts vary and with the changing forms of the many manufactured objects found in archaeological sites. Variation in the form of artifacts is a complex subject, but one of critical importance to archaeologists. It is the cumulative result of thousands of minor changes in the mental templates of dozens of different artifacts that provides the tangible evidence for culture change in the prehistoric past. And that, as we have seen, is a major concern to anyone studying prehistory.

Ecofacts are archaeological finds of cultural significance that were not manufactured by humans. These include bones and plant remains.

Context

The thin line of the 1,000-year-old cattle dung–covered hut floor appeared in the bottom of the trench, a hard semicircular patch of fire-baked clay lined on its outer side with the charred bases of wall posts. We removed the overlying ashy soil with slow care, using trowels, then paint brushes to ease the matrix off the long-abandoned floor surface. Three large boulders appeared in the soil. We brushed them off, exposing a patch of charcoal between them, also a broken ox jaw and the broken fragments of a small clay pot. The exposed floor was about 10 feet (3 m) across, with the hearth set near the center of the house. Before we lifted the hearth, artifacts, and hut floor, we measured the exact position of every find and feature three-dimensionally, tying our measurements into a site grid linked in turn to the map of the area. I remember thinking as we took up the boulders that in themselves they were just three large stones. Taken together, plotted in relationship to the charcoal and artifacts, they became something quite different. They told a story of long-forgotten household behavior. The finds had a context.

Artifacts are found in archaeological sites. Archaeological sites are far more than just a concentration of artifacts, however. They can hold the remains of dwellings, burials, storage pits, craft activities, and sometimes several occupation levels. Each artifact, each broken bone or tiny seed, every dwelling, has a relationship in space and time to all of the other finds made in the site. An artifact can be earlier than, contemporary with, or later than its neighbors in the soil. A thousand obsidian flakes and half-completed projectile heads scattered over an area several square feet in diameter are, in themselves, merely stone fragments. But the spatial patterning of all the fragments is significant, for it tells us something of the various manufacturing activities carried out by the person who flaked the thousand fragments from chunks of obsidian. In this instance, and many others, the context of the artifacts in time and space is vital (see the section on site-formation processes in Chapter 4).

To every archaeologist, an artifact is of limited value without this context. The museums and art galleries of the world are filled with magnificent artifacts which have been collected under circumstances that can only be described as highly unscientific. Generations of treasure hunters have ravaged ancient Egyptian cemeteries and dug up thousands of pre-Columbian pots for museums and private collectors. Few of these objects have any **archaeological context.** Any expert can look at a pre-Columbian pot and say at once, "Classic Maya." But, tragically, rarely will our expert be able to consult excavation records and say, "Classic Maya, Level VIB from Temple of the Inscriptions, Palenque, excavation C, 1976, associated with burial of an adult male, 35 years old, date about A.D. 680." An artifact removed from its context in space and time in an archaeological site is merely an object that yields only limited cultural information. An artifact carefully excavated from a recorded archaeological context is an integral part of history, and as such has far more significance. This context of space and time lies at the very foundations of modern archaeology.

But before we examine archaeological context more closely, we must explore the complex relationship between the remote past and the archaeological record of the present.

Summary

Archaeologists are a special type of anthropologist, concerned with the study of ancient cultures and societies. Human culture is unique, its content transmitted from one generation to the next, allowing societies to develop and continue adapting to aid their survival. Humans are the only animals to use culture as the primary means of adapting to the environment. Human culture is constantly adjusting to environmental, technological, and societal change. The patterning of archaeological finds reflects patterned behavior in the past, the shared behavior of ancient peoples, and the material remains of their culture. Human cultures are made up of interacting components, often called cultural systems. Cultural process is the process of cultural change. Archaeology has three research goals: studying culture history, reconstructing past lifeways, and explaining why cultural change takes place. The study of archaeology proceeds within an overall theoretical framework, theoretical models that are part of the constant dialogue between theory and observation of archaeological evidence. Archaeological evidence comes in many forms, but is limited by the realities of long-term preservation in the ground. Both sites and artifacts have contexts in time and space, which are the vital dimensions that allow the study of ancient societies in spatial and chronological frameworks.

4

The Present and the Past

Artist's impression of a European Bronze Age warrior of about
1000 B.C. in ceremonial dress based on excavations from England,
Denmark, and the Netherlands. (Picture by Jo Richards)

The archaeological record is contemporary. It exists with me
today and any observation I make about it is a contemporary
observation.

Lewis R. Binford, 1983

A tiny silk thread on an ancient Egyptian mummy of 1000 B.C., a perfectly preserved basket from a 500-year-old Indian village in the Pacific Northwest, and a deep-frozen Siberian horsewoman's grave from Siberia, where even horse trappings survive: these exceptional finds and many others show us just how much of the past has vanished in the soil. The archaeological record is tantalizing complete, for what survives is but a fragment of what was once fabricated, built, and used. I once discovered a series of stone tool scatters on the banks of the Victoria Nile River in northern Uganda. Thousands of tiny quartz chips and hundreds of discarded stone arrow barbs marked a site visited again and again by Stone Age hunter-gatherers over many millennia. Everything organic and perishable had vanished soon after the visitors departed, leaving only stone tools and the by-products of their manufacture for the archaeologist to study. There were no traces of the brush shelters where the people had slept, of their wooden spears, arrow shafts, and digging sticks, of the skin cloaks they had used to collect ripe nuts. Sun, rain, and wind, even trampling hippopotamuses feeding at night, had leached out the organic remains of human activity or trampled them into dust.

Sometimes the archaeologist can achieve miracles with just stone artifacts and reconstruct amazingly complete portraits of moments in ancient life. For example, in 7000 B.C., a small group of Stone Age foragers camped in a sandy clearing near Meer in northern Belgium. One day, someone walked away from camp, sat down on a convenient boulder, and made some stone tools, using some carefully prepared flakes and lumps of flint he or she had brought along. A short time later, a second artisan sat down on the same boulder. He or she had also brought along a prepared flint cobble, struck off some blanks, and made some borers. Later the two same stone workers used their finished tools to bore and groove some bone. When they finished, they left the debris from their work lying around the boulder.

When Belgian archaeologist David Cahen excavated the site 9,000 years later, all he found were some scatters of stone debris. He plotted the clusters and painstakingly refitted the stone flakes onto their original cores. After months of work, he reconstructed the stone workers' day and showed the second one was left handed. No spectacular excavation this, just months of meticulous field and laboratory work studying a seemingly unpromising scatter of stone artifacts. A greater contrast in research with Austen Henry Layard's large-scale diggings at Nineveh is hard to imagine.

Most archaeological sites are far from spectacular, yet they can yield priceless information while the well-preserved finds grab the headlines. How, then, is the archaeological record formed? What humanly caused and natural factors affect the preservation of artifacts, food remains, and sites? This chapter looks at these issues and at some of the ways archaeologists used the dynamic, living present to gain access to the remote past.

The Archaeological Record

The discards of the past—food remains, structures, and artifacts—are of priceless value as a means of studying ancient human behavior. These material remains form the **archaeological record,** the archives used by archaeologists to study the past. The archaeological record comprises all kinds of archaeological finds, from the pyramids of Giza to an early human butchery site at Olduvai Gorge, Tanzania, occupied nearly two million years ago. California shell mounds, Ohio earthworks, Inca cemeteries—all are part of the archaeological record. So are isolated artifacts—the throne of Tutankhamun ("King Tut"), a wooden religious mask from a midwestern burial mound, and a Polynesian stone adze.

We seek to find out about prehistoric people from the traces of their activities. The carcass of a mammoth butchered 20,000 years ago is a mine of information on ancient hunting practices. Analysis of dried-out seeds or ancient human body **feces** found in archaeological sites tells us much about prehistoric diet. What we can find out about the past is severely limited, however, by the state of preservation of archaeological finds. Some substances, such as baked clay or stone, will survive indefinitely. But wood, bone, leather, and other organic materials soon vanish except under waterlogged, frozen, or exceptionally dry conditions. Everyone has heard of the remarkable tomb of Egyptian pharaoh Tutankhamun, whose astonishing treasure survived almost intact in the dry climate of the Nile Valley for more than 3,000 years (Figure 4.1). This archaeological record is exceptionally complete and informative. We even know, from the bouquet of wildflowers laid on his inner coffin, that Tutankhamun's funeral took place in the spring.

But most archaeological sites are found where only a few durable materials survive. Constructing the past from these finds is a challenge, the sort of problem faced by the detective piecing together the circumstances of a crime from a few fragmentary clues. The analogy is close: take two spark plugs, a fragment of a china cup, a needle, a grindstone, and a candlestick. Imagine someone from Patagonia digging them up in 1,000 years' time and trying to tell you how the makers used the objects. This analysis is precisely what the archaeologist does in going about the work of being a special type of anthropologist. The data we amass from **surface survey** (looking for sites) and **excavation** (digging) make up the archaeological record (Chapters 7, 8). The two basic units studied by archaeologists are sites and artifacts. These come down to us much modified by the ravages of centuries and millennia: the site-formation processes.

Site-Formation Processes

The time machine, which has enchanted generations of readers and moviegoers, is a fictional artifact for transporting people through time. Although archaeologists would welcome a time machine, we are satisfied by the remarkable fact that objects made, used, and deposited in the past survive into the present. We need not go to the past, for it comes to us.

Archaeologist Michael Schiffer's point (1987:3) is well taken, for the objects from the past that survive come down to us in two forms, either as historically documented

Figure 4.1   The throne of Egyptian pharaoh Tutankhamun, one of the many wood artifacts recovered from the richest royal sepulcher ever found. Tutankhamun died in his late teens in about 1323 B.C., having come to the throne in infancy. During his reign, the worship of the sun god Amun was restored at Thebes after a period of religious confusion.

artifacts, such as, for example, Orville and Wilbur Wright's first airplane, or in the archaeological record as abandoned artifacts like a clay vessel or a stone ax that are no longer part of a living society. The past in the form of artifacts does not come down to us unchanged, for complex processes have acted upon these objects, be they tools, dwellings, burials, food remains, or other manufactured or humanly modified items. Archaeologists not only have to study these artifacts but to untangle the many events and processes that contribute to the great variability in the archaeological record.

The factors that create the historic and archaeological records are known as **site-formation processes.** Site-formation processes are those agencies, natural or cultural, that have transformed the archaeological (or historical) record since a site was abandoned. There are two basic forms of site-formation processes: cultural processes and noncultural processes.

Cultural factors are those where human behavior has transformed the archaeological record. They can vary widely in their impact and intensity. For example, later occupants of a surface that was a hunter-gatherer camp in the Nile Valley may have been farmers and goat herders rather than hunters. The foundations of their houses cut deeply into underlying soil, and the hooves of their penned goats trampled on, and scattered, small stone artifacts lying on the surface.

People also reuse artifacts. To conserve prized tools and valuable raw materials, one may change the use of an artifact from a knife to a scraper or recycle a projectile point to another use. Sometimes prestigious or valuable objects become prized heirlooms passed down from generation to generation, or are buried with the dead—as soapstone pipes and other artifacts were with Hopewell kin leaders in the Midwest more than 2,000 years ago. Reuse, especially of such commodities as building materials, can become a potent factor in settlements that are occupied for longer periods of time, where people recycle old bricks and other materials for new dwellings. The wooden beams used in southwestern pueblos were recycled again and again, often generations, even centuries, after they were first cut. Then there is the dumping of trash. Whether underfoot or in secondary locations, trash heaps may form. These heaps often tend to cluster in specific locations that can be used for many generations, perhaps in a convenient, abandoned storage pit or an old dwelling. Disposal of the dead can also be viewed as another form of discard behavior.

It is a great mistake to think of any form of human discard behavior as random. The archaeologist must decipher the complicated behavioral processes—perhaps the logic, if you will—behind the accumulation of trash heaps, the disposal of the dead, and many other activities. In short, the archaeological record is not a safe place for artifacts, for myriad human activities can disturb them after deposition—plowing, mining, digging of foundations, land clearance, and even artillery bombardment, to say nothing of pothunting and site looting.

Noncultural processes are the events and processes of the natural environment that affect the archaeological record. The chemical properties of the soil or bacteria may accelerate the decay of organic remains such as wooden spears or dwellings or even increase the chances of superb preservation. Rivers may overflow and inundate a settlement, mantling the abandoned remains with fine silt. Windblown sands, ice, and even earthworms can disturb the archaeological record. A great earthquake can topple a settlement in a few minutes, as happened to the Roman port at *Kourion* in Cyprus in A.D. 365. David Soren's excavations revealed poignant scenes of sudden tragedy. The quake struck just before dawn. Moments before, a young girl had stepped out into a house courtyard to calm a restless mule. The surrounding walls collapsed, killing her and the mule, who were found sprawled under the debris removed during the excavation. A man and his family perished in bed, the husband frantically sheltering his wife and young child with his body. The moment of death and terror was frozen in time for archaeologists to uncover. It is easy to picture the crashing sounds, the rumbling earth, and the frantic cries of buried victims that soon give way to the silence of death.

Whether site-formation processes are cultural or noncultural, the important point is that one can never take the archaeological record at face value. What the archaeologist sees in the ground is not necessarily a direct reflection of human behavior. It is not enough to observe conditions of unusually good preservation or to describe the complex layers of a prehistoric rockshelter. One must also analyze and interpret the ways in which the archaeological record was formed. As Michael Schiffer put it (1987: 4),

> The real time machine, then, is the archaeological process: the principles and procedures that we as scientists apply to material traces in the historical and archaeological records. If we desire to obtain views of the past that are closer to reality . . . then we must build into our time machine a thorough understanding of formation processes.

A large component in this hypothetical time machine is that of preservation.

Preservation

The environment is a hostile place for human artifacts. The process of interacting with it causes deterioration and drastic modification to many properties of artifacts, affecting everything from color and texture to weight, shape, and chemical composition.

The environmental agents of deterioration can be grouped into chemical, physical, and biological categories. Chemical agents are universal, for the atmosphere contains water and oxygen, which create many chemical reactions—for example, corrosion of some metals. Different water temperatures, irradiation of materials by sunlight, and atmospheric pollutants all cause chemical reactions. Buried objects are often subject to rapid chemical change, especially as a result of dampness. Soils also contain reactive compounds such as acids and bases, which contribute to deterioration—acid soils dissolve bones, for example. Many archaeological deposits are somewhat salty, a condition caused by salts derived from wood ash, urine, and the neutralization of acids and bases. Such saline conditions can retard some decay, but react severely with copper, iron, and silver.

Physical agents of deterioration such as water, wind, sunlight, and earth movement are also universal. Water is especially potent, for it can tumble artifacts on the shoreline, sometimes even fracturing them in ways that suggest human intervention. Rainwater can cascade off roofs and tunnel deep grooves into walls. Cycles of wetness followed by dryness can crack wood and cause rot, and melting and freezing ice cracks rocks and concrete. Physical agents operate on small and large scales alike. For example, the effects of the Kourion earthquake in Cyprus not only flattened the small port, but affected the landscape for miles around.

Living organisms are the main agents of biological decay. Bacteria occur almost everywhere, and are usually the first to colonize dead organic matter and to begin the processes of decay. Fungi also occur widely and are especially destructive to wood and other plant matter, particularly in warm, damp climates. Beetles, ants, flies, and termites infest archaeological sites, especially middens and abandoned foods. Dogs, hyenas, and other such animals gnaw, chew, and scavenge bones and other organic materials from the surface of abandoned sites and game kills. The fragmentary animal bones scavenged by early hominids at Olduvai Gorge, Tanzania, bore clear signs of hyena teeth, for the predators had moved in on the abandoned hominid sites as soon as they departed.

Processes within the natural environment affect not only artifacts, but the actual physical sites that form their context in time and space. Archaeologists who spend most of their time in the field are often known as "dirt archaeologists" because they are always working with one of the primary constituents of an archaeological site—the soil. The first human activity at any site takes place on a natural surface, on sediments sitting on underlying bedrock. Sometimes this sediment was weathered over a long time, and may contain pollen grains, plant remains, or other sources of environmental information. Some Stone Age and Bronze Age burial mounds in Europe were erected on undisturbed soils that contained forest pollen grains, giving a picture of the local environment at the time of construction. For example, these pollens tell us a large burial mound near the famous stone circles at Avebury was located on recently cleared forestland, close to cultivated fields. The original land surface under another nearby mound still bore the plow marks from recent cultivation (Figure 4.2)

After a site is abandoned, additional sediments usually accumulate on top of the archaeological remains, sediments accumulated by wind or water action, such as the windblown sands that accumulate in the rooms of southwestern pueblos. The footsteps of humans and animals as well as burrowing animals, earthworms, wall

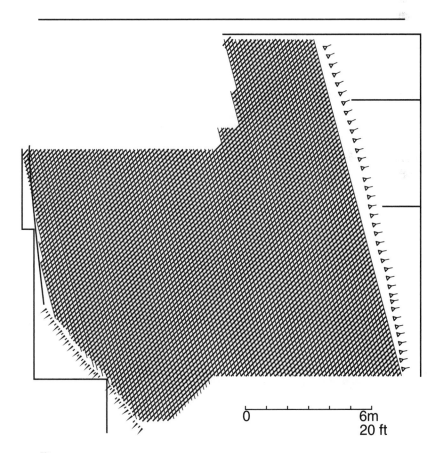

Figure 4.2 Plow marks on a cultivated field buried under a burial mound at South Street, Avebury, England.

flakings from overhanging cliffs, and the deteriorating elements of artifacts and structures contribute to the alteration of archaeological deposits. Stone Age rock-shelters in southwestern France, for example, were occupied intermittently by hunter-gatherer groups between 50,000 and 15,000 years ago. Some of the larger ones contain densely packed layers of hearths, ash accumulations, boulders, and decaying structures. Untangling how these levels were formed is a complex process. Some of the larger rockshelters, like the famous La Madeleine shelter on the banks of the Vezère River, were occupied for months on end, especially when salmon were running or during spring and fall reindeer migrations. How does one distinguish longer-term occupation from repeated short visits on the basis of what remains in the deposits? A myriad of different environmental processes contribute to site formation and can transform the archaeological record in ways that can be mistaken for traces of human behavior.

The preservation of such fragile organic archaeological remains as bone, leather, skin, textiles, and wood depends on their physical environment. Soil and climatic conditions very strongly influence archaeological materials. The inorganic artifacts—stone, baked clay pots, mud bricks, gold, copper, and bronze—are preserved best. Much of the surviving archaeological record consists of such durable **inorganic materials** in the form of human tools (Figure 4.3).

Prehistoric peoples used many organic substances, materials that survive at relatively few locations. Bone and antler were commonly used by early hunter-gatherers, especially in Europe some 16,000 years ago. The desert peoples of western North America relied heavily on plant fibers and baskets for their material culture. Both hard and soft woods were used for digging sticks, bows and arrows, and other tools and

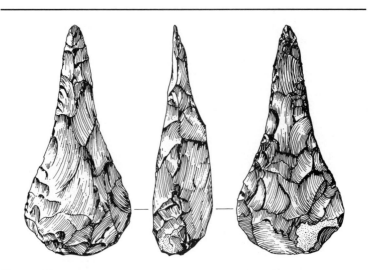

Figure 4.3   Three views of an Acheulian stone ax from Swanscombe on the River Thames, England. One-third full size. Acheulian hand axes were general-purpose artifacts used widely by archaic humans in Africa, Europe, and southern Asia from before a million years ago up to after 200,000 years ago.

weapons. Cotton textiles were much prized in coastal Peru 2,000 years ago. Nearly every human society collected wild vegetable foods for part of their livelihood. These and traces of broken animal bones and other food remains are sometimes found when preservation conditions are favorable.

Favorable Preservation Conditions

What are the most favorable conditions for preservation of archaeological finds? The fantastically rich tomb of the Egyptian pharaoh Tutankhamun, who died in 1323 B.C., yielded incredible finds, including his personal wooden furniture, much of his clothing, and the perishable ritual objects that accompanied the dead king to the next world (see Figure 4.1). Tutankhamun's tomb is the only pharaoh's burial ever to be discovered intact, undisturbed by tomb robbers. The richness of the grave furniture came as a complete surprise and included not only his personal possessions, but his chariots, broken down in easily assembled parts. (In a recent study, French archaeologists have reconstructed the chariots and concluded they were drawn by small horses, even ponies.)

The Moche Lords of Sipán in northern coastal Peru were buried under an adobe clay platform in about A.D. 400. The dry conditions of the Peruvian desert preserved their lavishly adorned sepulchers, where three lords lay in graves stratified one above the other, each wearing their complete ceremonial regalia, including golden masks and elaborate gold and silver jewelry. We know from scenes painted on Moche pots that these were warrior-priests, who presided over warfare and ceremonies that involved the sacrifice of prisoners of war. In life, the lords would have glittered brightly in the sun, when they appeared in public, in a dazzling display of political and spiritual power. They would have seemed like gods on earth (Figure 4.4).

Dry conditions like those of the Nile Valley have led to remarkable discoveries in the desert of the western United States as well, where caves in Utah and Nevada have yielded not only sandals, bows and arrows, and other wood and fiber objects, but thousands of seeds, and even human excrement (coprolites or feces), which can be analyzed to give information on prehistoric diet (Figure 4.5) (Chapter 10).

Waterlogged, flooded sites also aid preservation. They can seal off organic finds in an oxygen-free atmosphere. Danish archaeologists have found prehistoric dugout canoes deep in ancient peat bogs, along with leather clothing, traps, and wood spears. Their most famous finds are the corpses of sacrificial victims buried in the bogs more than 2,000 years ago. We can gaze on the serene countenance of *Tollund Man*. His corpse is in such excellent condition that we know he did not eat for at least 24 hours before his death, and his last meal was a porridge of barley and wild grasses (Figure 4.6).

Richard Daugherty gained unusual insights into prehistoric whale hunting on the Northwest Coast of North America by digging a Makah Indian village at *Ozette,* Washington, long buried by sudden mud slides. The wet mud crushed cedar plank houses by the ocean, sealing their contents from the destructive effects of the atmosphere. The Ozette village was occupied for more than 2,000 years, right into the twentieth century. The buried houses provided a wealth of information about Makah life and artistic traditions of centuries ago. The thick mud preserved walls and beams, sleeping benches, and fine mats. Wood fishhooks, seal-oil bowls, cedar storage boxes,

Figure 4.4   A mannequin wears the complete regalia of a Moche Lord of Sipán, Peru, c. A.D. 400.

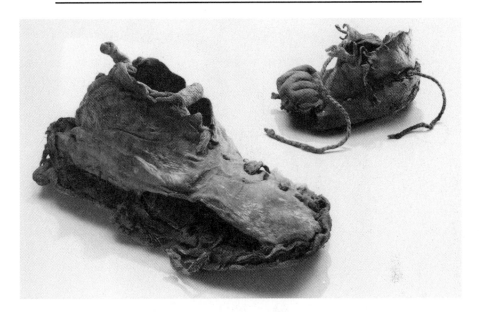

Figure 4.5   Dry preservation: sandals from Hogup Cave, Utah.

and whaling harpoons were uncovered by using fine pressurized water jets to wash mud from the soft wood. The most remarkable find of all was a whale fin carved out of red cedar and inlaid with sea otter teeth, a unique ritual object without parallel in North America (Figure 4.7).

Fortunate is the archaeologist who finds a site with conditions as good as those at Ozette. They are very much the exception rather than the rule.

Arctic cold can literally refrigerate the past and preserve the minutest details of clothing, even skin tattoos. In 1993, Russian archaeologist Natalya Polosmak excavated an undisturbed burial chamber on the Ukok Plateau of southern Siberia, once home to ancient herders from the sixth to second centuries B.C. The chamber contained an ice-filled log coffin, which Polosmak thawed by pouring hot water onto it for days. The casket contained the body of a 25-year-old woman wearing an elaborate headdress. Five feet six inches tall, she had been laid to rest on her side, her strong hands crossed in front of her. The still-soft skin of one shoulder bore an intricate tattoo of a mythical creature. Her burial robe included a woolen skirt of horizontal white and maroon stripes and a yellow silk top, perhaps from China, which mantled her shoulders. A wood-handled mirror lay by the body. Nearby were the remains of horses that had been led to the graveside, dispatched with swift axe blows, then laid in the pit next to their mistress.

Everyone has heard of Roman Herculaneum and Pompeii, entire towns overwhelmed in A.D. 79 by an eruption of nearby Vesuvius. The volcanic ash and lava buried both communities, even preserving the body casts of fleeing victims. Such sites are rare, but when they are discovered they yield remarkable finds. In the sixth century A.D., a volcanic eruption in a nearby river suddenly buried a small Maya village

Figure 4.6   The head of Tollund Man, whose remarkably well-preserved corpse was discovered in the peat bogs of Denmark. He probably was a ritual sacrifice.

at Cerén in San Salvador. The people had eaten their evening meal, but had not yet gone to bed. They abandoned their houses and possessions and fled for their lives. Not only did the ash bury the village, it also smothered the nearby crops, burying corn and agave plants as they stood in the fields. Payson Sheets and his research team have recovered entire dwellings and outhouses, and the artifacts within them, just as they were when abandoned. Each Cerén household had one building for eating, sleeping, and other activities, and a storehouse, a kitchen, and sometimes other structures (Figure 4.8). Substantial thatched roofs projected far beyond the walls, providing not only covered walkways, but places for processing grain and for storage. Each household stored grain in clay vessels with tight lids, suspended some corn and chilis from the roof, and kept sharp knives in the rafters. The excavations have uncovered outlying maize fields where the plants were doubled over, with the ears still attached to the

Figure 4.7   Richard Daugherty examining a whale fin carved of cedar wood, found at the Ozette site, and inlaid with 700 sea otter teeth. The teeth at the base are set in the design of a mythical bird with a whale in its talons.

stalk, a "storage" technique still used in parts of Central America today. Judging from the mature maize plants, the eruption occurred at the end of the growing season, in August. Cerén provides an unusually complete look at life in a humble Maya settlement far removed from the great ceremonial centers where the elite lived.

However, as we have said, most archaeological sites yield only a fraction of the organic materials buried in them. The fortunate archaeologist may recover not only

Figure 4.8   Artist's reconstruction of the dwelling, workshop (right), and storehouse (left), Household 1, Cerén, San Salvador.

manufactured tools but some food remains as well—animal bones or a handful of shells, seeds, or other vegetable remnants—but only rarely does anything more survive. Obviously the picture one obtains of the inhabitants at such a site is incomplete compared with that from Cerén or Ozette.

Middle-Range Theory and the Archaeological Record

The archaeological record is static, whereas the present is ever changing and dynamic. How, then, does one study the relationship between the static and dynamic, between the past and the present? This issue is of critical importance to archaeology, for most of our research is based on the assumption that because an artifact is used in a specific way it was used in that way millennia before. This assumed relationship has two parts:

- The past is dead and knowable only through the present—by archaeologists studying it.
- Accurate knowledge of the past is essential to understanding the present.

Middle-range theory comprises methods, theories, and ideas that can be applied to any period and anywhere in the world to explain what we have discovered, excavated, or analyzed from the past. The general concept comes from sociology and describes a body of theory that is being formed as archaeologists try to bridge the gap between what actually happened in the past and the archaeological record of today. Lewis Binford and other archaeologists have searched for "Rosetta stones" that permit one to use observations of the static past to make statements about its long-vanished dynamics. They believe middle-range theory provides the conceptual tools for explaining artifact patternings and other material phenomena from the archaeological record.

Middle-range research is important to archaeology, whether one believes that this research is meant to specify the relationships between behavior and material remains or to understand the determinants of patterning and structural properties of the archaeological record. It is conducted by **ethnographic analogy,** by studying living societies (**ethnoarchaeology**), and/or by using historical documents or controlled experiments (**experimental archaeology**).

By no means do all archaeologists agree that the archaeological record holds no direct information on human behavior. Many argue that the relationship between human behavior and material culture in all times and places is what archaeology is all about. The controversy continues, but it is safe to say that ethnoarchaeology and experimental research as well as analogy have leading roles in today's research into the past.

The Living Past

We live in a world inhabited by an astonishing diversity of human societies. A century ago, many of them were still living in much the same way as their prehistoric ancestors. But the unchanging routine of planting and harvest, of life and death, of the seasons of game and vegetable foods, has withered in the face of Western exploration and industrial civilization. Today, few of these societies still enjoy their traditional lifeways. Many are extinct. The Tasmanians effectively vanished within 70 years of white settlement; the Indians of Terra del Fuego disappeared in the 1950s (Figure 4.9). Ishi, the last California hunter-gatherer, managed to live in his home territory in the northern California foothills until 1911. He saw all of his companions wiped out by white settlers. The surviving Indian peoples of the Amazon region are rapidly fading away in the face of large-scale mining operations that are decimating their rain forest environment.

Anthropology has traditionally worked with non-Western societies and with peoples who have had to make far-reaching adjustments to encroaching industrial civilization. Anthropologists have followed the fates of these people as they have adjusted, often becoming impoverished minorities in large industrial cities. Since the nineteenth century, many of the societies once studied by anthropologists have, by their death or transformation, become part of the archaeological record. No longer living groups, they have left behind them surface scatters of artifacts and sites that are now the only chronicle of their societies other than early historical records, oral traditions, or anthropological studies of some generations ago. In short, they have become human cultures of the past.

For years, archaeologists talked about an "ethnographic present," a moment in time when a non-Western society first came in contact with Europeans, such as when Captain James Cook landed on Tahiti in the South Pacific in 1769. They tended to think of Tahitian, and other cultures for that matter, as frozen like time capsules, when, in fact, these cultures had changed continually for centuries, and still changed after European contact. There has never been an ethnographic present, but archaeologists have long recognized the value of records of such societies as a way of interpreting much older cultures. They approach the problem by using ethnographic analogy and ethnoarchaeology.

Figure 4.9 A group of Fuegan Indians walking along the shore; these and many other hunter-gatherer peoples are now virtually extinct.

Ethnographic Analogy

Early anthropologists collected vast quantities of information on traditional material culture of diverse societies all over the world. This material gave archaeologists a chance to compare still-living peoples and prehistoric peoples who had a basically similar technology. Thus, it was argued, the African San, Australian Aborigines, and other living hunter-gatherers who had no metals could be considered living representatives of prehistoric, stone-using hunter-gatherers. Under this approach, an archaeologist who dug a 20,000-year-old campsite in an arctic environment could turn to the Eskimo of today for comparative modern material. They believed that Eskimo and arctic Stone Age cultures bore remarkable similarities, on the grounds they adapted to the same environment.

This type of reasoning was obviously simplistic because each human society, ancient or modern, has, or has had, its own distinctive adaptation to its environment, which helps shape all aspects of its culture in many ways. For example, some 18,000 years ago, the late Ice Age Magdalenian hunter-gatherers of southwestern France were expert reindeer hunters whose sustenance relied heavily on the seasonal migrations of these animals. Similarly, modern subarctic hunter-gatherer groups in northern Canada live off migrating herds of caribou, a close relative of the reindeer. The late Ice Age environment of southwestern France and that of the Canadian subarctic are radically different, as are the technologies each group uses or used. It would be naive indeed to claim that the Magdalenians of 18,000 years ago were prehistoric examples of modern subarctic caribou hunters.

Archaeologists then began to make analogies with recent societies in new ways. They worked back from known, living peoples into earlier times. They began by digging sites of historically documented Indians and studying their contents, making full use of historical records to interpret their finds. Thus photographs of Northwest Coast Indian homes taken in 1890 would be compared with excavated home foundations from comparatively recent times, say, A.D. 1500. If the features of both were the same, then it was reasonable to interpret the design of prehistoric houses from this model. The house would then be traced backward into prehistoric times in sites many centuries earlier than the historic settlements.

This method, very simply stated, is the basis on which archaeologists use ethnographic records to interpret prehistoric artifacts and sites. Considerable controversy surrounds such interpretations, for sophisticated research methods are needed if comparisons are to be made between modern artifact patternings and those found in prehistoric sites. For this reason many archaeologists believe "living archaeology" (or ethnoarchaeology) is a more effective approach.

Living Archaeology (Ethnoarchaeology)

Much of the ethnographic material available to archaeologists was collected when anthropology was much less sophisticated than it is today. Very often ethnographers collected object after object or information on customs without recording detailed information on settlement layout or artifact patternings, the types of information that archaeologists now need so badly. One can hardly blame the pioneers, for they were out to record as much information about vanishing cultures as they could before it was too late. And subtle settlement details hardly seemed a high priority. Today, many of the settlements the anthropologists studied have themselves become archaeological sites. They are now virtually indistinguishable from prehistoric sites with their middens and crumbled hut foundations. They offer a unique opportunity to study the processes by which abandoned settlements turn into archaeological sites. Understanding these processes makes archaeological interpretation in general much easier, and so some archaeologists have gone out in the field to study "living archaeology" for themselves.

The !Kung San. (The ! symbol denotes a click sound made with tongue against the roof of the mouth.) Anthropologist Richard Lee, who has spent many years studying the !Kung San of southern Africa, took archaeologist John Yellen with him on one of his expeditions. Yellen spent many months studying the ways in which the San butchered animals and the fragmentary bones that resulted from butchery, cooking, and eating (Figure 4.10). He drew plans of recently abandoned sites of known age, recorded the positions of houses, hearths, and occupation debris, and talked to people who had lived there as a way of establishing precise population estimates and the social relationships of the inhabitants.

Yellen found that the San camps developed their layouts through conscious acts, such as building a shelter or a hearth, as well as through such casual deeds as discarding animal bones and debris from toolmaking. There were communal areas that everyone used and private family areas gathered around hearths. Some activity areas, such as places where women cracked nuts in the heat of the day, were simply located under a convenient shady tree. Yellen recorded that most food preparation took place

Figure 4.10   Living archaeology: a !Kung San brush shelter and windbreak in the Kalahari Desert, southern Africa, recorded by archaeologist Francis Van Noten shortly after it was abandoned.

in family areas. Most activities in San camps were related to individual families. Theoretically, therefore, one should be able to study the development of the family through time by studying changing artifact patternings. To do so in practice, of course, requires very comprehensive data and carefully formulated research designs.

Tucson, Arizona: Modern Garbage.   Although ethnoarchaeological investigations have tended to focus on hunter-gatherers, there are numerous instances of fascinating research on more complex societies, even our own. A major long-term study of modern urban garbage in Tucson, Arizona, for example, is based on the latest archaeological methods and research designs. The project is designed to investigate the relationships between resource management, urban demography, and social and economic stratification in a modern context, where control data from interviews and other perspectives are available to amplify an archaeological study of a type that might be conducted at an ancient urban center. The Tucson garbage study has produced remarkable results, showing widely different patterns of resource management from one segment of the city's population to another, with the middle class being the most wasteful.

Maya Metates.   When archaeologist Brian Hayden was examining Maya stone tools of the post-Conquest colonial period near the Mexico-Guatemala border, he discovered that some present-day Mayan-speaking communities still made and used stone metates (grinders) and pounders, metates and manos, in the traditional way. Hayden designed a broad-based research project to examine the properties of the stone collected for tool manufacture, the efficiency of stone technology, and the evolution of the forms of stone tools as they were used and reused. He worked closely with a 50-year-old metate maker named Ramon Ramos Rosario. Hayden followed Rosario through the entire manufacturing process, from the selection of the material to the final surface smoothing of the artifact (Figure 4.11). Time and motion studies showed that it took this expert 2.5 days to rough out and smooth a metate blank using only stone tools and 4.5 to 5.5 days to finish both a metate and a mano. Finally, Hayden examined the characteristics of the picks used to chip and peck the rock as if they were archaeological finds, combining these studies with use-wear analysis. Hayden seriated the picks on the basis of the intensity of edge-wear development and as a way of estimating the relative length of use of comparable tools. He compared his results to prehistoric artifacts and was able to show that many blunt-edged Maya woodworking tools in archaeological sites were probably used by women to roughen used manos and metates.

The Hayden study demonstrates the power and potential of a many-sided approach to ethnoarchaeology, using data from the dynamic present to evaluate archaeological evidence from the static archaeological record.

Nunamiut Eskimos.   In another instance, Lewis Binford's study of the Nunamiut caribou hunters of Alaska was designed to learn as much as possible about an Eskimo group's hunting practices. The Nunamiut depended heavily on meat, supplementing their flesh diet with the partially digested contents of caribou stomachs and about a cupful of vegetable foods a year. They relied extensively on stored food for eight and a half months a year, fresh meat being freely available for only about two. Binford soon found that the Nunamiut food-procurement strategy was based on complicated decisions that involved not only the distribution of food at different seasons, but the

Figure 4.11   Ramon Rosario making a stone metate.

storage potential of different animals and their parts, as well as the logistics of procurement, carrying, and storing meat. Was it easier to move people to the herds or to
carry meat back to base? His research convinced him that the linkages between the
facts of animal anatomy and the realities of lifeway strategies held the key to meaningful analysis of animal bones.

Binford studied the annual round of the Nunamiut, and also their butchery and
storage strategies, developing indexes to measure utilization of different body parts.
He also compared observations from modern kill sites to 42 archaeologically known
locations that dated to earlier times. The Nunamiut research is valuable not only for
the large body of empirical data it generated, but also because it showed just how
locally confined any cultural adaptation is.

The Nunamiut research and other ethnoarchaeological projects serve as a cau-
tionary tale, for they show that differences in artifacts and human behavior at different
locations can result from entirely local considerations and not necessarily from cultural differences.

Experimental Archaeology

Archaeologists love experimenting with the past. One ardent early experimenter, Robert Ball of Dublin, Ireland, blew a prehistoric horn so hard that he produced a sound like a bellowing bull. Unfortunately, his heroic effort caused him to burst a blood vessel and die. Not all experimental archaeology is so risky, however. Archaeologists have been making stone implements, floating over oceans on rafts, and trying to recreate the past ever since the eighteenth century. Some of their achievements are remarkable.

Louis Leakey, the famous Stone Age archaeologist, not only dug early hominid sites, but also spent many years perfecting his skills as a stone toolmaker. He could shape a perfect prehistoric hand ax and skin an antelope with it in a few minutes—a favorite demonstration at conferences. One of the most remarkable experiments of all was Norwegian Thor Heyerdahl's *Kon-Tiki* expedition in 1947, on which he attempted to prove that Polynesia had been settled by adventurous Peruvians who had sailed balsa rafts across thousands of miles of ocean. Heyerdahl did succeed in reaching Polynesia. His expedition merely proved, however, that long ocean voyages in *Kon-Tiki* rafts were possible. He did not prove that the Peruvians settled Polynesia.

People have cleared thick Danish woodland with stone axes and grown prehistoric crops in the American Southwest under conditions identical to those of centuries ago. The latter experiments lasted 17 years. Good crop yields were obtained in all but two years, when drought killed the young crops. Experiments in living the prehistoric lifestyle have proved popular, especially in Britain and Denmark, where television networks have financed long-term experiments with volunteer "prehistoric peoples." One British experiment centered on several families who were provided with crops and livestock and isolated in a reconstruction of an Iron Age village of about 200 B.C. They were left alone to survive for a year, the only concession being modern antibiotics and birth control pills. Such experiments are of questionable scientific value, but they do provide superficial insights into the realities of prehistoric life. Controlled burnings of some faithful reconstructions of ancient houses have been undertaken, too, to show what structures would look like when reduced to ashes—as structures are in many actual sites. British archaeologists have even built an entire experimental earthwork that they are digging up at regular intervals over 128 years. The resulting information on soil decay and artifact preservation will be invaluable for interpreting equivalent prehistoric sites.

Many recent experimenters have concentrated on replicating such phenomena as wear on the working edges of prehistoric stone tools. Lawrence Keeley and other researchers have examined stone artifacts such as Paleo-Indian points under high- and low-power microscopes. They are now able to distinguish between wear polishes associated with materials, including wood, bone, and hide. This approach is now reliable enough to discern whether a tool was used to slice wood, cut up vegetables, or strip meat from bones.

Sometimes, edge-wear studies can yield remarkable results, especially when combined with **refitting,** reassembling flakes with the parent **core** from which they were struck. These techniques enabled David Cahen and Lawrence Keeley to identify the left-handed stoneworker at Meer, Belgium, mentioned earlier in this chapter. By reassembling some of the stone flakes and cores, studying the wear patterns on tool working edges, and examining distribution of stone fragments throughout the site, they were able to show that two people, one of them left handed, had made some tools used to bore and shape fragments of bone.

In this, and many other innovative projects, archaeologists are using the present to better understand the past, attempting to overcome the limitations imposed on us by the archaeological record and the formation processes that have affected it.

We must now examine archaeological context, another basic principle of archaeology, which is also fundamental to understanding and interpreting the archaeological record. The notion of context in time and space is the subject matter of the next two chapters.

Summary

The archaeological record comprises all kinds of archaeological finds, from vast cities to small scatters of stone artifacts. But preservation conditions severely limit the amount of information that can be learned about ancient societies. Dry, frozen, or waterlogged conditions offer exceptional preservation environments, which allow the survival of leather, skin, wood, and other organic substances. Complex site formation processes affect the archaeological record, natural and humanly originated processes that change the artifacts and other finds, also their contexts in the ground. Such processes can be cultural (of human origin) or noncultural. The archaeological record is static, whereas the present is ever changing and dynamic. Archaeologists assume the past is dead and knowable only through the present, by archaeologists studying it. They use middle-range theory, methods, theories, and ideas that can be applied to any period and anywhere in the world to explain what they have discovered about the past. This body of theory, derived from ethnographic analogy, ethnoarchaeology, the study of living cultural systems, and controlled experiments, is used to bridge the gap between what actually happened in the past and the archaeological record today.

5

Time and Space

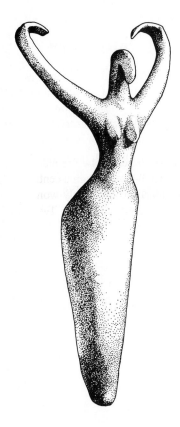

Birdlike goddess from Predynastic Egypt, c. 4000 B.C.

What seest thou else in the dark backward and abysm of time?

William Shakespeare, *The Tempest*

Time—our hectic lives depend on it. Only this morning, a harried student made an appointment with me after sifting through the crowded pages of her day-planner. I could see that every half hour of the day was crammed with lectures, meetings, and sports practice. We both commented on the tyranny of schedules, which never seem to get easier, only more hectic. The hours of the day are the framework of our daily lives, of our jobs and leisure time. Not for us the broad sweep of changing seasons or days measured by sunrise and sunset. We depend on the clock to guide us through the day, to regulate our lives. I write these words at precisely 5.10 P.M. in the late afternoon, and could, if I wished, obtain a reading for the exact second that I write the number 5. We Westerners are obsessed with the passage and measurement of time. Chapter 5 describes the critical dimensions of time and space in archaeology.

Our sense of linear history spans our own lives, those of our parents and grand-parents. I have a dim memory of balloons on my second birthday, and continuous rec-ollection from about age 8. My parents saw the elderly Queen Victoria driving in a carriage in a London park in 1898—more than a century ago. An Irish archaeological colleague's father talked regularly to an elderly woman in his village, who remem-bered French soldiers landing in Ireland in 1798. Two centuries is a long span of liv-ing memory, but the history books give us a linear past that extends back to the beginnings of writing in southwestern Asia more than 5,000 years ago. They tell us Washington, D.C., was founded in A.D. 1790, that Rome was established in 753 B.C., and that the famous Egyptian pharaoh Ramses II reigned from 1304 to 1237 B.C.

Looking earlier than 3000 B.C., however, we enter a chronological vacuum, a blank that archaeologists have labored to fill with carefully assembled sequences of sites and artifacts. Except in a very few areas, such as the American Southwest and parts of Europe, where tree rings can be used to date prehistoric sites very accurately, prehistoric time must be measured in centuries and millennia, rather than individual years. We know that Washington, D.C., was founded in A.D. 1790. We will be lucky if we can ever date the beginnings of the city of Teotihuacán to closer than 200 ± 100 years B.C. Some idea of the scale of the problem can be gained by piling up 100 quar-ters to represent the time that humankind has been on earth. The length of time cov-ered by historical records is considerably less than the thickness of one quarter because 99.9 percent of human experience lies in prehistoric times. Small wonder time is important in archaeology.

The prehistoric past is like a vast, empty landscape, which archaeologists have peopled with thousands of archaeological sites large and small, each with their own characteristic artifacts and other traces of long-forgotten human behavior. Each of these sites and their contents has a precise context in time and space. Some sites, like Teotihuacán in Mexico, were occupied for hundreds of years. Other localities, such as Olduvai Gorge, were inhabited for hundreds of thousands of years. Without dates, prehistory would be a jumble of confusing sites and cultures devoid of order. How, then, do archaeologists date the past?

Linear and Cyclical Time

Westerners think of the passage of the human past along a straight, if branching, high-way of time. The great nineteenth-century German statesman Otto von Bismarck called this the "stream of time," on which all human societies ride for a time. The analogy is apt if you think of time in a linear fashion, as archaeologists do.

An unfolding, linear past is not the only way of conceptualizing ancient times. Many non-Western societies, ancient and modern, think of time as a cyclical phenom-enon, or sometimes as a combination of the linear and the cyclical. The cyclical per-spective stems from the passage of seasons and of heavenly bodies, from the close relationships between foragers and village farmers and their natural environments. It is also based on the eternal verities of human life: fertility and birth, life, growth, and death. The endlessly repeating seasons of planting and harvest, of game movements or salmon runs, and of ripening wild foods governed human existence in deeply sig-nificant ways. The ancient Maya developed an elaborate cyclical calendar of inter-locking secular and religious calendars to measure the passage of the seasons and to regulate religious ceremonies.

But we should not assume that societies with a cyclical view of time did not have linear chronologies as well. The celebrated Maya "Long Count" was a linear chronol-ogy, which formed an integral part of the close relationship between Maya rulers and the cosmos. The ancient Egyptians developed a linear chronology for administrative purposes. But, in general, societies develop linear chronologies only when they need them. For example, Western societies use linear time to regulate times of prayer, to control the working day, and for airline schedules. It is hard to generalize, but soci-eties with centralized political systems tend to use the reigns of chiefs or kings as signposts along a linear time scale. For instance, the history of the rulers of the state of *Benin* in West Africa shows a significant shift in the interpretation of time. Before the fourteenth century A.D., Benin history is essentially mythological, with inaccurate chronology and a variable number of kings. But with the founding of the Yoruba dynasty, the deeds and reigns of every *oba* (king) are remembered in detail with chronological accuracy right down to modern times.

Archaeologists refer to two types of chronology:

- *Relative chronology*, which establishes chronological relationships between sites and cultures, and
- **Absolute chronology** (sometimes called **chronometric chronology**), which refers to dates in calendar years.

Relative Chronology

My aged tortoiseshell cat has just come into my study. Bulging with breakfast, she gives me a plaintive meow and looks for a patch of sunlight on the carpet. She spots one, just where I have laid down a pile of important papers. Thump! With a sigh, she settles down on top of the documents and dozes blissfully as I write. Time passes. I realize that I need one of the articles in the pile under my faithful beast. I debate whether to have a cup of coffee and procrastinate or to disturb her, knowing there will be angry claws. In the end, writing deadlines prevail and I gently elevate the cat and slip the papers out from under her. She protests half-heartedly and settles down again as I congratulate myself on escaping grievous injury . . .

The case of the cat and the papers is a classic example of relative chronology in action. Consider the sequence of four events. I am sitting at my computer, consult some documents, then lay them on one side on the floor. This is the first event in the sequence. Some time later, the second event takes place. The cat settles on the publications and goes to sleep. More time passes. I need an article in the pile, lift the cat, and remove the papers. This third event is followed by the final act of this stirring drama as the cat goes back to sleep. We have observed a sequence of events. However, beyond establishing that they took place "after breakfast," we have no idea exactly how much time passed between each event in the sequence. In other words, we have a relative chronology of human (and feline) behavior.

The Law of Superposition

Our relative chronology of the cat and the papers is based on a fundamental principle of archaeology and relative chronology: the law of superposition. **Superposition,** the notion that underlying levels are earlier than those that cover them, came to archaeology from geology. The geological layers of the earth are superimposed one upon another almost like layers of a cake. Easily viewed examples are cliffs by the seashore or road cuts along the highway, which show a series of geological levels. Obviously, any object deposited in the lower horizons usually got there before the upper strata were accumulated. In other words, the lower levels are relatively earlier than the later strata. The deposition of a series of occupation levels or geological strata in order can be achieved by many processes: wind, water, earthquakes, and other factors. The fundamental principles of context in time and space are borrowed straight from geology, where observations of fossils and other phenomena in geological layers provide the framework of geological time.

Superposition is fundamental to the study of the stratigraphy of archaeological sites, for many settlements, such as desert caves in western North America or Mesopotamian mounds, were occupied more or less continuously for hundreds, even thousands, of years. Human occupation of any site results in the accumulation of all kinds of rubbish. Objects are lost and become imbedded in the ground. Buildings fall into disrepair and are leveled to make way for new ones. A flood may wipe out a village and deposit a thick layer of silt. A new village may rise on the same spot years later. The sequence of these superimposed occupation levels is carefully recorded as the excavation of a site proceeds. Of course, not all settlements were occupied several times. Single-occupation sites, even very temporary camps, are studied just as carefully.

The sequence of natural and humanly accumulated layers on an archaeological site is the basis for all stratigraphic observations in archaeology. But as Figure 5.1 shows, it is not only the carefully observed layers, but their detailed contents as well, that provide us with relative cultural chronologies. Each level in a settlement has its associated artifacts, objects that the archaeologist uses as indicators of technological, economic, social, or even religious change.

Figure 5.1 The principle of superposition. (a) A flourishing farming village 5,000 years ago. After a time, the village is abandoned and the huts fall into disrepair. The ruins are covered by accumulating earth and vegetation. (b) After an interval, a second village is built on the same site, with different architectural styles. This village in turn is abandoned; the houses collapse into piles of rubble and are covered by accumulating earth. (c) Twentieth-century people park their cars on top of both village sites and drop litter and coins that, when uncovered, reveal to the archaeologist that the top layer is modern. An archaeologist digging this site would find the modern layer is underlain by two prehistoric occupation levels, square houses were in use in the upper of the two, which is the later (law of superposition), and round huts are stratigraphically earlier than square ones here. Therefore, village 1 is earlier than village 2, but when either was occupied or how many years separate village 1 from 2 cannot be known without further data.

Artifacts and Relative Chronology

Manufactured artifacts are the fundamental data archaeologists use to study past human behavior. These artifacts have changed with passing time in radical ways. One has only to look at the humble stone chopper of the earliest humans and compare it with modern-day surgical instruments to get the point. Most artifact changes in prehistory are extremely small; minor changes in such characteristics as the shape, decoration, or lip angle of clay pots accumulate slowly as they lead ultimately to a vessel form that is hardly recognizable as originating from its ancestors.

The popularity of any artifact form is fleeting. Women's skirt lengths rise above the knee, then fall to mid-calf; clothing styles change from month to month. Recordings hit the Top 40 but soon pass into oblivion. Other artifacts have a far longer life. The crude stone flakes of the earliest humans were a major element in early **toolkits** for hundreds of thousands of years. People used candles for centuries before they turned to kerosene and gas lamps. But each has its period of maximum populari-ty, or frequency of occurrence, whether it lasts for millennia or only a few months. Archaeologists use **seriation techniques** to place artifacts in chronological order, on the assumption that the popularity of any artifact, be it a specific model of automobile, pottery types, stone artifact forms, or other objects, peaks at a specific moment in time. If we plot the frequencies with which these objects occur as a set of bars, they look like the hull of a battleship glimpsed from an aircraft (Figure 5.2). The center of the hull bulges outward amidships, where the armor is thickest, coinciding with the period of greatest popularity. This phenomenon is sometimes called the **battleship curve.** Thus, it is argued, when sites within a restricted geographic area contain simi-lar pottery and other artifacts at an equivalent rate of popularity, they are of approxi-mately the same age. If the samples are statistically reliable, a series of sites can be linked in a relative chronology, even though, without dates in years, one cannot tell when they were occupied.

A generation ago, archaeologists Edwin Dethlefsen and James Deetz tested this battleship-curve assumption against the changing decorative styles on dated grave-stones in New England colonial cemeteries. They found that the changing styles of death's-heads, cherubs, and urns succeeded one another in an almost perfect series of battleship curves. Because the dates of the gravestones were known from their inscriptions, the experiment could be conducted and tested within a precise chrono-logical context.

A series of archaeological sites may contain many different artifacts that appear and vanish over relatively short periods. By applying seriation, it is possible to place the different forms of artifacts in a series of relative chronologies, such as that from the *Tehuacán Valley*, Mexico, illustrated in Figure 5.3. Each occupation level of each site contains different proportions of each artifact form manufactured during that pe-riod. And once you have a sequence of changing artifact frequencies, it is possible to fit isolated, newly discovered sites into a relative chronology.

Cross-Dating

Seriation is effective for **cross-dating** sites as well. Let us assume that an English coin dating to A.D. 1825 is traded in a California Indian village. The coin falls onto a hut floor and is lost in the dust. In the 1990s, archaeologists find this dated coin in a strat-ified level of the ancient village. They know it was traded into the settlement *no ear-lier than its date of minting,* so the village was flourishing in, or after, 1825. They may find more sites with the same Indian artifacts in similar proportions—but no coins—a few miles away. When they seriate the finds, they will be able to cross-date the undat-ed settlements because their artifact frequencies are the same. This cross-dating tech-nique has been widely applied to central European prehistoric sites whose inhabitants

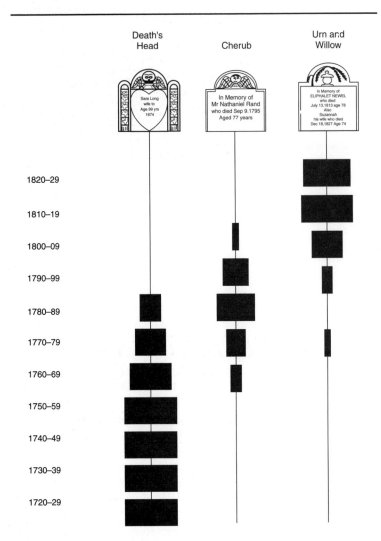

Figure 5.2 Seriation. The changing styles of New England gravestones, from Stoneham, Massachusetts, between 1720 and 1829, seriated in three styles. Notice how each style rises to a peak of maximum popularity and then declines as another comes into fashion. The cherub style shows the classic battleship curve. Each horizontal bar represents the percentage of a gravestone type at that date; for example, between 1720 and 1729 death's-heads were at 100 percent.

traded with literate civilizations in the Mediterranean basin, exchanging copper and other raw materials for ornaments and other luxuries whose age is known.

Absolute (Chronometric) Chronology

Figure 5.4 shows the chronological spans of the major methods used to date the past.

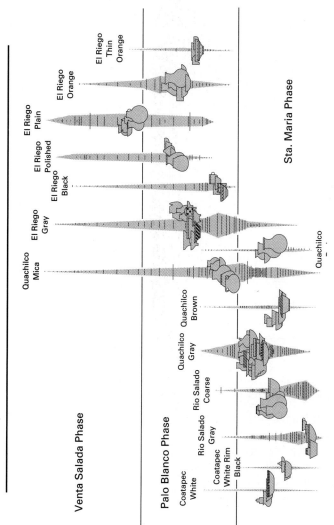

Figure 5.3 Seriation of pottery style from the Tehuacán Valley, Mexico, showing many sites ordered into a single sequence. Richard MacNeish classified the different pottery types at each site, then placed them in chronological order on the basis of periods of maximum popularity for each type. Here the battleship curve principle is used to develop a sequence of changing pottery forms, each site being "fitted" into the sequence on the basis of the percentage of each type represented.

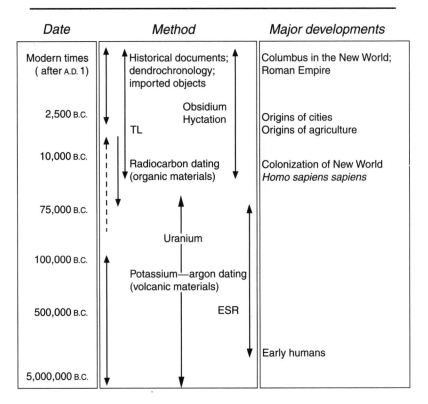

Figure 5.4 Major chronological methods in prehistory. Experimental methods eliminated for clarity.

Historical Records and Objects of Known Age

Historical records cover but the very smallest fraction of the human experience. King lists and genealogies in early Egyptian and Mesopotamian archives give us dates in years that go back to at least 3000 B.C. Recorded history starts in about 750 B.C. in the central Mediterranean, about 55 B.C. in Britain. The first historical records for the New World began with the Spanish Conquest, although the recently deciphered Maya script gives us invaluable information about Classic Maya civilization 1,500 years ago. Parts of Africa entered "history" in A.D. 1890.

Fortunately, the literate civilizations of three or four thousand years ago traded their products far and wide, so cross-dating is possible. The Egyptians traded fine ornaments to Crete; the Cretans sent wine and fine pottery to the Nile. When archaeologist Arthur Evans discovered Crete's Minoan civilization in 1900, he dated the Palace of *Knossos* by means of Minoan pottery fragments that had been excavated in faraway Egypt, in levels whose precise historical date was known. In recent years, German archaeologists have found brilliantly painted

Minoan friezes on the walls of *Avaris* in Lower Egypt, confirming earlier evidence for trading connections.

Coins and other imports of known age can be used to date buildings or refuse pits in which they were dropped centuries earlier. A bewildering array of dated objects are used by archaeologists dealing with the recent periods of prehistory. These include glass bottles and beads, seals, imported Chinese porcelain, even military buttons. Each of these objects has the advantage of its age being exactly known. Objects of known age, even such artifacts as barbed wire, beer and Coca-Cola bottles, and leather shoes, provide excellent dating evidence on historic sites of the past four or five centuries.

Tree-Ring Dating (Dendrochronology)

Everyone is familiar with the concentric growth rings that can be seen in the cross section of the trunk of a felled tree. These rings, formed in most trees, are of special importance to archaeologists in areas such as the American Southwest, where the seasonal weather changes markedly and growth is concentrated during a few months of the year. Normally trees produce two growth rings each year, which are formed by the cambium between the wood and the bark. Each year's growth forms a distinct ring that varies in thickness according to the tree's age and annual climatic variations. Weather variations in the Southwest tend to run in cycles of dry and wet years, which are reflected in patterns of thicker and thinner rings on the trees.

The tree-ring samples are taken with a borer from living or felled trees. The ring sequences from the borer are then compared to each other and to a master chronology of rings built up from many trees with overlapping sequences tied to a known terminal date. The patterns of thick and thin rings for the new sequences are matched to the master sequence and dated on the basis of their accurate fit to the master sequence. By using the California bristlecone pine, tree-ring experts have developed a master chronology over 8,000 years back into the past (Figure 5.5).

Tree-ring dating, usually called **dendrochronology,** can be practiced on long-felled wood beams to date the Indian pueblo buildings of which they were a part. Tree-ring experts have been able to develop an extremely accurate chronology for southwestern sites that extend back as long ago as 322 B.C. It was a difficult task, for they had to connect a prehistoric chronology from dozens of ancient beams to a master tree-ring chronology connected to modern times obtained from living trees of known age. The dates of such famed Southwestern sites as Mesa Verde and *Pueblo Bonito* (Figure 1.6) are known to within a few years because tree-ring chronologies are accurate to within a year. Such precision even allows the dating of individual rooms within single pueblos. So many tree-ring sequences now come from the Southwest that dendrochronologists can study drought cycles as they spread across the region, especially the great drought of A.D. 1276 to 1299, which caused the Anasazi people of the Four Corners region to disperse from their homeland (see Chapter 6).

Dendrochronology has been used in other areas of the world as well—in Alaska and the American Southeast, and with great success in Greece, Ireland, and Germany. The bristlecone pine is to the Southwest as oaks are to Europe. European tree-ring

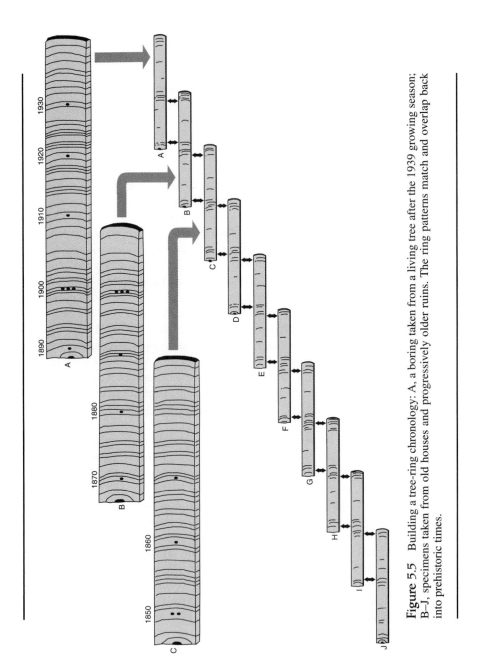

Figure 5.5 Building a tree-ring chronology: A, a boring taken from a living tree after the 1939 growing season; B–J, specimens taken from old houses and progressively older ruins. The ring patterns match and overlap back into prehistoric times.

experts have collected large numbers of tree-ring records from oaks that lived 150 years or so. By visual and statistical comparison they have linked living trees to farmhouse and church beams and to ancient trees found in bogs and prehistoric sites, providing a tree-ring sequence that goes back 10,021 years in Germany and 7,289 years in Ireland. Dutch tree-ring experts have even dated the oak panels used by old masters for backing their oil paintings as a way of authenticating paintings.

Tree-ring chronologies are exceptionally accurate and are now being applied in many areas of the world.

Radiocarbon Dating

Radiocarbon dating, developed by physicists J. R. Arnold and W. F. Libby in 1949, is the best known of all chronometric methods. Cosmic radiation produces neutrons that enter the earth's atmosphere and react with nitrogen to produce the carbon isotope carbon 14 (14C, or radiocarbon), which has eight rather than the usual six neutrons in its nucleus. With these additional neutrons, the nucleus is unstable and subject to radioactive decay. Arnold and Libby calculated that it took 5,568 years for half of the 14C in any sample to decay, the so-called **half-life** of 14C. (The half-life is now more accurately measured at 5,730 years.)

The 14C isotope is believed to behave just like ordinary carbon (12C) from a chemical standpoint. Together with 12C it enters into the carbon dioxide of the atmosphere. Because living vegetation builds up its own organic matter by photosynthesis and by using atmospheric carbon dioxide, the ratio of 14C to 12C in living vegetation and the animals that eat it is equal to that in the atmosphere. As soon as an organism dies, no further radiocarbon is incorporated into it. The radiocarbon present in the dead organism continues to disintegrate, so that after 5,730 years half of the original amount is left; after about 11,400 years, a quarter; and so on. Thus measuring the amount of 14C still present in plant and animal remains and emitting radiation enables us to determine the time that has elapsed since death. By calculating the difference between the amount of 14C originally present and that now present, and comparing the difference with the known rate of decay, we can compute the time elapsed in years. The amount of 14C in a fresh sample emits particles at a rate of about 15 particles per minute per gram of carbon. A sample with an emission rate of half that amount would be approximately 5,730 years old, the time needed for one half the original radioactive material to disintegrate (the half-life of 14C). When a 14C date comes from a laboratory, it bears a statistical plus or minus factor. For example, 3,600 ± 200 years (200 years represents one standard deviation) means that chances are 2 out of 3 that the correct date is between the span of 3,400 and 3,800. If we double the deviation, chances are 19 out of 20 that the span 3,200 to 4,000 is correct. *Radiocarbon dates should be recognized for what they are—statistical approximations.*

Radiocarbon samples can be taken from many **organic materials**: charcoal, burned bone, shell, hair, wood, or other organic substances. The samples themselves are collected with meticulous care from particular stratigraphic contexts so that an exact location, or a specific structure, is dated. For years, dating laboratories used a beta ray decay rate to date 14C samples. They now use **accelerator**

mass spectrometry (AMS), which allows radiocarbon dating to be carried out by direct counting of 14C atoms rather than by counting radioactive disintegrations. The samples required are so small that it is possible, for example, to date an individual tree ring.

Accelerator dating is especially useful for dating the amino acids from bone collagen, but one can date almost any material, even tiny wood fragments preserved in the haft sockets of metal spearheads, for example. This makes it possible, for example, to date an actual corncob in a Southwestern cave, a much better way of dating early agriculture than by merely using the principle of association to link a cob with a dated feature or isolated charcoal sample. AMS dating has revolutionized the dating of early agriculture in the Americas. For instance, researchers used conventional carbon dating to date the first appearance of maize farming in Mexico's Tehuacán Valley to at least 5000 B.C. AMS dates on actual early cobs show that maize cultivation dates to no earlier than about 2700 B.C. Dates from individual cereal seeds have dated agriculture on the banks of the Euphrates River in Syria to about 8800 B.C., centuries earlier than previously suspected.

The practical limits of radiocarbon dating are between 40,000 and 60,000 years. Researchers have tried detecting 14C atoms directly with a particle accelerator, a technique that would extend the limits of radiocarbon dating to as much as 100,000 years, although at present its limits, mainly because of contamination carried into soil by roots, are around 70,000 years.

When Arnold and Libby first developed radiocarbon dating they compared their 14C readings with dates from objects of known age, such as ancient Egyptian boats. These tests enabled them to claim that radiocarbon dates were accurate enough for archaeologists' purposes. But about 25 years later, just when archaeologists thought they at last had an accurate and reliable means for dating the past, some radiocarbon dates for dated tree rings of long-lived California bristlecone pines were published. They turned out to be consistently younger—for trees dating to before 1200 B.C. It turned out Libby had incorrectly assumed that the concentration of radiocarbon in the atmosphere has remained constant through time, so prehistoric samples, when they were alive, would contain the same amount of radiocarbon as living things today. But, in fact, changes in the strength of the earth's magnetic field and alterations in solar activity have considerably varied the concentration of radiocarbon in the atmosphere and in living things.

Fortunately, however, it is possible to correct 14C dates back to about 9000 B.C. by calibrating them with tree-ring chronologies, for dendrochronology provides very precise dates based, for early millennia, on European oaks. Some idea of the changes in accuracy of 14C dating over the past 10,000 years generated from tree-ring celibrations can be gathered from Figure 5.6. Calibration of dates earlier than 9000 B.C. is still at an experimental stage. Recently scientists have used a new, highly accurate technique based on the decay of uranium into thorium to date fossil coral near Barbados in the Caribbean and in the south Pacific. They compared these dates to radiocarbon results, and found that dates between 10,000 and 25,000 years ago have increasing margins of error, as much as 5,000 years in earlier millennia. Radiocarbon dates earlier than about 10,000 years ago must be treated as little more than approximations.

Radiocarbon Age	Calibrated age in years
A.D./ B.C.	
Tree-ring calibrations	
A.D. 1760	A.D. 1945
1505	1435
1000	1105
500	635
1	15
505 B.C.	767 B.C.
1007	1267
1507	1867
2007	2477
3005	3795
4005	4935
5005	5876
6050	7056
7001	8247
8007	9368
9062	9968

Calibrations based on Uranium/Thorium and AMS carbon 14 (Barbados)

AMS radiocarbon dates	Uranium Thorium calibration
7760 B.C.	9140 B.C.
8270	10,310
9320	11,150
10,250	12,285
13,220	16,300
14,410	17,050
15,280	18,660
23,920	28,280

(increasing differences after 25,000 B.C. [calibrated])

Calibrations based on tables in *Radiocarbon* 40 (3), 1998. It should be stressed that these calibrations are provisional, statistically based, and subject to modification, especially before 7,000 B.C.

Figure 5.6 Calibration of radiocarbon dates bases on tree-rings and uranium thorium dates from tropical corals.

Despite its chronological and technical limitations, radiocarbon dating is of enormous significance. Some 14C samples have dated African hunter-gatherers to more than 50,000 years ago and Paleo-Indian bison kills on the Great Plains to more than 9000 B.C. They have provided chronologies for the origins of agriculture and civilization in the New World and the Old. Radiocarbon dates are a means for developing a truly global chronology that can equate major events such as the origins of literate civilizations in such widely separated areas as China and Peru. The prehistory of the world from some 40,000 years ago up to historic times is dated almost entirely by the radiocarbon method.

Obsidian Hydration

Every archaeologist dreams of a dating method that gives accurate ages for durable artifacts like stone tools and potsherds. Obsidian hydration has potential for this purpose. Obsidian is a natural glass formed by volcanic activity, often used by the ancients for sharp-edged tools, mirrors, and ornaments. A freshly exposed obsidian surface absorbs water from its surroundings, forming a measurable hydration layer that is invisible to the human eye. The thickness of the hydration layer can be used to develop absolute and relative chronologies for stone tools, but little is still known about the effects of temperature changes and chemical compositions of soil on hydration. Obsidian hydration has been used successfully in widespread archaeological surveys around the Maya city at Copán, Honduras (see Chapter 11).

Thermoluminescence (TL) Dating

Another potentially important method, this time for dating fired clay and heated materials, is based on the fact that every material on earth receives a low level of radiation from the radioactive elements in the environment. Many solid materials store small fractions of this energy, which accumulates steadily over time. When the solid is heated, the stored energy is released and emits light, a phenomenon called **thermoluminescence**. The age of the sample comprises the length of time since the object was heated to a temperature higher than 3500 degrees C. TL has obvious applications for dating volcanic rocks and other geological formations, but can also be applied to humanly heated objects such as clay vessels, heat-treated stone artifacts, or fired bricks.

Samples are taken by crumbling an object such as a potsherd, or by drilling tiny holes. The laboratory measures the natural TL of the object with an alpha radiation counter, the rate at which the sample has been obtaining radiation from the environment (by monitoring the location where it was found), and the amount of TL produced by known amounts of radiation. All this assumes that the humanly manufactured object being tested has been heated to a sufficiently higher temperature, which is not always the case.

Thermoluminescence is claimed to have an accuracy of about ± 7 percent and is most commonly used to date pottery or clay-fired objects between 50 and about 20,000 years old. TL dates have also been applied to burnt flint and other siliceous toolmaking materials found in Stone Age rockshelters and burials, such as Neanderthal graves in Israel dating to more than 40,000 years ago. A related dating method uses laser technology to date the emissions from quartz and feldspar grains in archaeological layers. This optically stimulated luminescence (OSL) method can date sites in the 100- to 100,000-year range and is claimed to date the first settlement of Australia to as early as 60,000 years ago.

Although TL has been used to date such developments as the appearance of anatomically modern humans in southwestern Asia and early Australian colonization, most authorities agree that independent verification from radiocarbon or other approaches is advisable.

Electronic Spin Resonance (ESR)

ESR measures radiation-induced defects or the density of trapped electrons within a bone or shell sample without the need to heat them. This promising dating method is somewhat similar to TL and has the advantage of being nondestructive, being especially effective on tooth enamel, also bone, allowing investigators to date human fossil fragments up to about a million years old. ESR has important applications for the study of early human evolution and has already been used to date Neanderthal teeth in southwestern Asia.

Uranium Series Dating

Uranium series dating measures the steady decay of uranium into various daughter elements inside any formation made up of calcium carbonates, such as limestone or cave stalactites. Because many early human groups made use of limestone caves and rockshelters, bones and artifacts embedded in calcium carbonate layers can sometimes be dated by this method, using techniques somewhat similar to those used in radiocarbon dating. Uranium series dating is most effective when applied to sites between 50,000 and 1 million years old.

Fission Track Dating

Many minerals and natural glasses, such as obsidian, contain tiny quantities of uranium that undergo slow, spontaneous decay. The date of any mineral containing uranium can be obtained by measuring the amount of uranium in the sample, which is done by counting the fission tracks in the material, narrow trails of damage in the sample caused by fragmentation of massive energy-charged particles. The older the sample, the more tracks it possesses. Volcanic rocks are ideal for fission track dating, such as are commonplace at Olduvai Gorge and other early human sites. The volcanic level under the earliest hominid sites at Olduvai has been dated to 2.03 ± 02.8 million years, which agrees well with potassium-argon dates from the same location.

Potassium-Argon Dating

Potassium-argon dating has provided general chronologies for earlier prehistory. Geologists use this method to date volcanic rocks as early as 4 to 5 billion years old and as recent as 100,000 years before the present. Potassium (K) is one of the most abundant elements in the earth's crust, present in nearly every mineral. In its natural form, potassium contains a small proportion of radioactive 40K atoms. For every 100 40K atoms that decay, 11 percent become 40Ar (Argon), an inactive gas that can easily escape from its present material by diffusion when lava and other molten rocks are formed. As volcanic rocks form by crystallization, the concentration of 40Ar drops to almost nothing, but the decay of 40K continues, and 11 percent of every 100 40K atoms become 40Ar. It is possible therefore, using a spectrometer, to measure the concentration of 40Ar that has accumulated since the rock formed.

Many early archaeological sites, such as those at Olduvai Gorge, Tanzania, were formed during periods of intense volcanic activity. Dates have been determined for contemporary volcanic ashes, sometimes stratified above and below places where human tools and broken animal bones lie. Louis and Mary Leakey were able to determine potassium-argon dates for artifact and bone scatters at Olduvai, where early human fossils were found. The samples gave readings of about 1.75 million years. Even earlier dates have come from sites at *Hadar* in Ethiopia and *Laetoli* in Tanzania, both in East Africa, where volcanic materials associated with early human fragments have been dated by potassium-argon techniques to between 3 and 4 million years ago. Stone flakes and chopping tools have come from *Koobi Fora* in northern Kenya, dated to about 2.6 million years.

Potassium-argon dating is getting ever more accurate, and 1- to 4-million-year-old East African dates now have standard deviations in the 20,000- to 50,000-year range. Recent improvements in dating techniques have both reduced statistical errors and extended the range of potassium-argon dates into the past 100,000 years.

This array of absolute dating methods has developed a provisional chronology for world prehistory.

Space

Space—not the limitless space of the heavens, but a precisely defined location for every find made during an archaeological survey and excavation, and the subject of this chapter—is the second vital dimension of archaeological context.

Every archaeological find has an exact location in latitude, longitude, and depth measurement, which together identify any point in space absolutely and uniquely. (The universal transverse Mercator international grid system is often used as an alternative.) The telltale debris from stone toolmaking, heavy butchery tools and broken animal bones from a Plains bison kill site, carbonized loaves and clay ovens at an ancient Egyptian bakery: all tell stories of long forgotten human behavior in villages, houses, and workshops. All depend on the dimension of space. Spatial location is indispensable to archaeologists because it enables them to establish the distances between objects or dwellings, or between entire settlements, or between settlements and key vegetational zones and landmarks. Such distances may be a few inches of level ground between a fine clay pot and the skeleton of its dead owner, or 10 miles (16 km) separating two seasonal camps. A team of fieldworkers may record the distance measurements between dozens of villages that traded over hundreds of miles luxury goods such as seashells. The research teams who studied the hinterland of the great Maya city of Copán in Honduras located more than 2,500 outlying towns, villages, and small hamlets.

They used this spatial data to document the buildup and collapse of rural populations around the city between A.D. 400 and 1200.

When carrying out surface surveys or excavations, archaeologists use special methods to record the precise positions of artifacts, dwellings, and other finds. They tie in the position of each site to accurate survey maps so they can use the grid coordinates on the map to define the location precisely on the landscape. By using geographic positioning systems (see Chapter 11), they can combine their spatial data with environmental, topographic, and vegetational information in digitized databases, then examine changing settlement distributions over time. The same precision operates at the site level. When investigating an individual site, excavators lay out recording grids made up of equal squares over the entire site, using the grids or, more commonly, electronic measuring devices, to record the exact position of each object on the surface or in the trenches (see Figure 8.1 for a site grid). **Spatial analysis** is the analysis of spatial relationships both within sites and over much larger areas.

Space involves archaeologists in three directions of inquiry, described mainly in Chapter 11:

- The process of describing one's finds, of determining the cultural origins of artifacts. This procedure of ordering is described more fully in Chapter 9, where we discuss some of the arbitrary analytical devices that archaeologists use.
- Studying specific activities—economic, religious, social, technological— within a human settlement. These patternings may reflect the activities of a person, a household, or an entire community.
- The study of **settlement patterns**, the changing distributions of human settlement over ancient landscapes.

The Law of Association

Context in space is based on **associations** between artifacts and other evidence of human behavior around them. Let us say you find a beer can opener in a plowed field. An expert on such artifacts—and they can be found—usually can date your opener to within a few years of its manufacture by going to manufacturers' files or U.S. Patent Office records. But your beer can opener was an isolated find. No other signs of human activity were discovered nearby. How could you infer, if you were not a twentieth-century American, that the artifact was used for opening a can? But had you found the can opener in association with a dozen punctured beer cans of similar age, you could then infer the general activity that took place and you could draw some conclusions about the purposes for which the artifact in question was designed.

The law of stratigraphic association is based on the principle that an artifact is contemporary with the other objects found in the precise archaeological **horizon** (Figure 5.7). The mummy of Egyptian pharaoh Tutankhamun was associated with an astonishing treasury of household possessions and ritual objects. This association provided unique information on Egyptian life in 1323 B.C. The mummy alone would have been far less informative.

The law of association is of great importance when ordering artifacts in chronological sequences. Many prehistoric societies buried their dead with grave furniture—

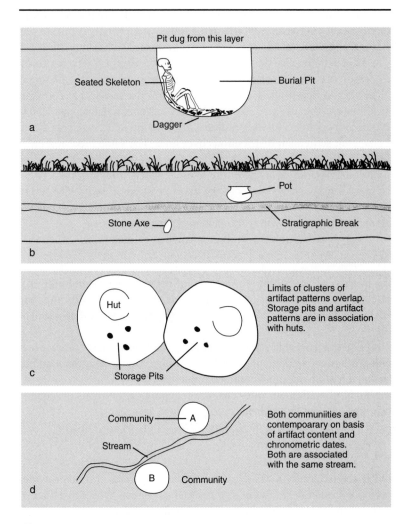

Figure 5.7 The law of association: (a) a skeleton associated with a dagger; (b) a pot and a stone ax, separated by a stratigraphic break, which are not in association; (c) two contemporary household clusters associated with each other; (d) an association of communities that are contemporary.

clay pots, bronze ornaments, seashells, or stone axes. In some cases, the objects buried with a corpse were obviously in use when their owner died. Occasionally, they may be prized heirlooms, passed down from generation to generation. Together they are an association of artifacts, a grave group that may be found duplicated in dozens of other contemporary graves. But later graves may be found to contain quite different furniture, vessels of a slightly altered form. Obviously some cultural changes had taken place. When dozens of burial groups are analyzed in this way, the associations and changing artifact styles may provide a basis for dividing the burials into different chronological groups (Figure 5.8).

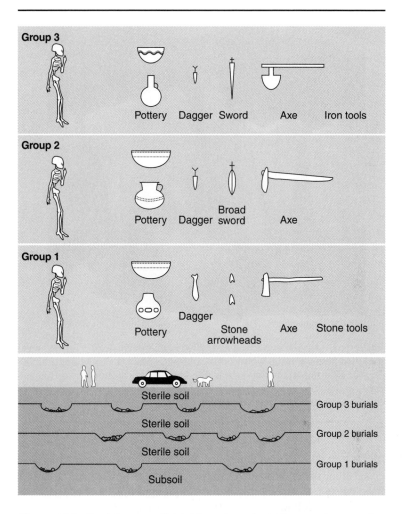

Figure 5.8   Burial groups divided into chronological groups by assessing associated artifacts. Group 1 burials contain no metal artifacts, but simple decorated shallow bowls that were made by all burial groups and show cultural continuity through time. The stone arrowheads of Group 1 are replaced by metal swords; daggers continue in use, made successively in stone, bronze, and iron. Continuity of artifacts is sufficient to place groups in sequence using the law of association; this grouping was in fact confirmed by stratigraphic observation, shown at the bottom.

Assemblages and Subassemblages

Human behavior can be individual and totally unique, shared with other members of one's family or clan, or common to all members of the community. All of these levels of cultural behavior should, theoretically, be reflected in artifact patterns and associations in the archaeological record. The iron projectile point found in the backbone of a British

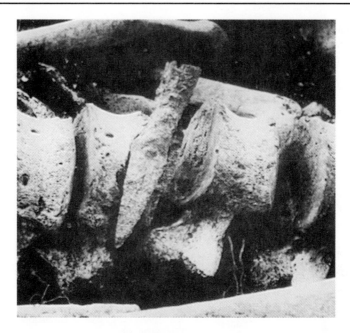

Figure 5.9   An iron arrowhead embedded in the backbone of a British warrior killed during a battle with Roman soldiers at Maiden Castle, England, in A.D. 43. This important Celtic Iron Age fortress was stormed by a Roman legion in that year, a battle reconstructed by British archaeologist Mortimer Wheeler from excavations at the fort entrance.

war casualty of A.D. 43 is the consequence of one person's behavior, but that behavior is clearly related to the common cultural behavior of the warrior's society (Figure 5.9).

Archaeologists use a hierarchy of units to group artifact associations, the lower levels of which are as follows (for higher units, see Chapter 9):

- **Subassemblages**   A collection of artifacts associated with a single individual. For example, a hunter uses a bow and arrows, which are carried in a quiver. An auto mechanic employs a tool kit of wrenches, screwdrivers, and gauges.
- **Assemblages**   Dissimilar subassemblages of artifacts—let us say, hunting weapons and baskets and also digging sticks used in collecting plant foods—occur in association. The artifacts together reflect in their patterning the shared activity of a group—an assemblage. This shared behavior is also reflected in the remains of houses—in the nonportable artifacts such as storage pits and hearths, inside and outside the house—and in community settlement patterns.

The distinction is straightforward. Some early Mexican villages consisted of groupings of square thatched houses. Each house contained subassemblages that reflected the behavior of individual males and females, subassemblages inferred from artifact associations and patternings. For instance, the Cerén houses have revealed evidence of female domestic activities: food preparation, cooking, and so on. The patterned household groups in the village—that is, the associations of those subassemblages and the features associated with them—make up the larger assemblage of human behavior in space that constitutes the entire community.

All scientific archaeology, whether survey, excavation, laboratory analysis, or sophisticated theoretical argument encompassing thousands of artifacts, is based on the two critical concepts—time and space—that make up archaeological context.

Summary

Western archaeologists think of the human past as having a linear chronology, in contrast with many other societies who believe human existence is governed by cyclical time scales. Archaeologists use two ways to date the past: (1) Relative chronology, the study of the chronological relationships among different sites, artifacts, occupation layers, and other features, is based on the principle of superposition. This principle, which originated in geology, states that the lower stratum is the earlier. Seriation techniques allow archaeologists to place artifacts in relative chronologies; large-scale climatic changes during the Ice Age provide a chronological framework for earlier prehistory; and (2) Absolute (or chronometric) chronology is the dating of the past in calendar years. Archaeologists use historical records and documents to date the past 5,000 years. For earlier times, they employ three major techniques: (1) Dendrochronology, tree-ring dating, uses the annual growth rates in oaks and other trees to date human societies in Europe, the American Southwest, and other areas back at least 8,000 years; (2) Radiocarbon dating, the measurement of the decay of radiocarbon isotopes, allows the dating of sites as early as 40,000 years ago, with dates calibrated by tree rings or coral reefs extending back to about 15,000 years ago; and (3) Potassium-argon dating, another isotopic dating method, is mainly used by geologists, but uses volcanic rocks to date early Stone Age sites and the origins of humankind some 3 to 4 million years ago.

Space in archaeology is the exact location of an archaeological find in latitude, longitude, and depth, which together identify any point in space absolutely and uniquely. Human behavior leaves patterns of artifacts in the archaeological record, which we study by spatial analysis. The context of space has close links to ancient human behavior. Archaeologists use this context by examining associations between artifacts and other evidence of human behavior.

6

Ancient Climate and Environment

Disc-wheeled cart used by Stone Age farmers at Klosterlund, Denmark, c. 3000 B.C.

> ... the Elysian Fields, where gold-haired Rhadamanthys waits, where life glides on in immortal ease for mortal man; no snow, no winter onslaught, never a downpour there but night and day the Ocean River sends up breezes singing winds of the West refreshing all mankind.
>
> Homer, *Odyssey* IV: 635–39

In 4500 B.C., a patch of woodland in northern England boasted of mature oaks, ash and elm trees, interspersed with occasional patches of open grassland and swamp. In 3820 B.C., some foragers set fire to the forest, to encourage fresh green shoots for feeding deer. Birch and bracken now appeared. About 30 years passed before the landscape was cleared even more. Judging from numerous charcoal fragments, fire swept through the undergrowth, leaving fine ash to fertilize the soil. Now wheat pollen and that of a cultivation weed named *Plantago lanceolata* appear. Fifty years of wheat farming ensued. These years saw only two fires, one after 6 years, the other 19 years after that. Then 70 years passed, when agriculture ceased and the land stood vacant. Hazel, birch, and alder became more common and oak resurged as woodland rapidly gained ground.

This scenario of brief clearance, slash-and-burn agriculture, then abandonment and regeneration was repeated at thousands of locations in ancient Europe in the early years of Stone Age farming. Over a few centuries, the natural environment of mixed oak forest was transformed beyond recognition by gardens and domesticated animals. Until a few years ago, we could only have guessed at these environmental changes. Today, fine-grained pollen analysis and other highly sophisticated methods allow the reconstruction of even short-lived climatic and environmental changes in the remote past.

Archaeology is unique in its ability to study culture change over very long periods of time. By the same token, it is a multidisciplinary science that also studies human interactions with the natural environment over centuries and millennia. Chapter 6 describes some of the ways archaeologists study long- and short-term environmental change from a multidisciplinary perspective.

Long- and Short-Term Climatic Change

Climatic change comes in many forms. The long cycles of cold and warm associated with the Ice Age occur on a millennial scale and have little more than long-term effects on human existence. For example, the existence of a low-lying land bridge between Siberia and Alaska during much of the late Ice Age may have allowed humans to forage their way from Asia into the Americas before 15,000 years ago, but the actual formation of the shelf that linked the two continents would have taken many centuries and human generations. Short-term climatic change, such as the floods or droughts caused by El Niño episodes or volcanic eruptions dumping ash into the atmosphere, are another matter. Memories of catastrophic famines and other events associated with such events would have endured for generations, for they had immediate impact on hundreds, if not thousands, of people. Through human history, people have developed strategies to deal with sudden climatic shifts, with drought, hunger, or unexpected food shortages. Humans have always been brilliant opportunists, capable of improvising solutions to unexpected problems caused by environmental change. Thus environmental reconstruction and climatic change are two major concerns for archaeologists wherever they work.

Geoarchaeology

Geoarchaeology, the study of archaeology using the methods and concepts of the earth sciences, plays a major role in reconstructing ancient environments, also long- and short-term climatic change. This is a far wider enterprise than geology and involves at least four major approaches:

- Geochemical, electromagnetic, and other remote sensing devices to locate sites and environmental features (Chapter 7).
- Studies of site-formation processes and of the spatial contexts of archaeological sites (Chapters 8 and 11), a process that includes distinguishing humanly caused phenomena from natural features.
- Reconstructing the ancient landscape by a variety of paleogeographic and biological methods, including pollen analysis.
- Relative and chronometric dating of sites and their geological contexts.

People are geomorphic agents, just like the wind. Accidentally or deliberately, they carry inorganic and organic materials to their homes. They remove rubbish, make tools, build houses, abandon tools. These mineral and organic materials are subjected to all manner of mechanical and biochemical processes while people live on site and after they abandon it. The controlling geomorphic system at a site, whatever its size, is made up not only of natural elements but of a vital cultural component as well. The geoarchaeologist is involved with archaeological investigations from the very beginning, and deals not only with formation of sites and with the changes they underwent during occupation but also with what happened to them after abandonment.

In the field, the geoarchaeologist is part of the multidisciplinary research team, recording stratigraphic profiles within the excavation and in special pits close by to obtain information on soil sediment sequences. At the same time, he or she takes soil samples for pollen and sediment analyses and relates the site to its landscape by topographic survey. Working closely with survey archaeologists, geoarchaeologists locate sites and other cultural features on the natural landscape using aerial photographs, satellite images, and even geophysical prospecting on individual sites. As part of this process, they examine dozens of natural geological exposures, where they study the stratigraphic and sedimentary history of the entire region as a wider context for the sites found within it. The ultimate objective is to identify not only the microenvironment of the site but also that of the region as a whole—to establish ecological and spatial frameworks for the socioeconomic and settlement patterns that are revealed by archaeological excavations and surveys.

Long-Term Climatic Change: The Great Ice Age

About 1.8 million years ago, global cooling marked the beginning of the **Pleistocene** epoch, commonly called the **Quaternary,** or more popularly, the Great Ice Age. It was remarkable for dramatic swings in world climate. On numerous occasions during the Pleistocene, great ice sheets covered much of western Europe and North America, bringing arctic climate to vast areas of the Northern Hemisphere. Scientists have identified at least eight major glacial episodes over the past 730,000 years, alternating with shorter warm periods, when the world's climate was sometimes warmer than today. The general pattern is cyclical, with slow coolings culminating in a relatively short period of intense cold, followed by rapid warming. For 75 percent of the past three quarters of a million years, the world's climate has been in transition from one extreme to another. We ourselves still live in the Ice Age, in a warm interglacial period. If the current scientific estimates are correct and humanly caused global warming does not interfere, we will probably begin to enter another cold phase in about 23,000 years.

No one knows exactly what causes the climatic fluctuations of the Ice Age, but they are connected with oscillations in the intensity of solar radiation and the trajectory of the earth around the sun. But such climatic changes are of great importance to archaeologists, for they form a long-term environmental backdrop for the early chapters of our past. Although almost no human beings lived on, or very close to, the great ice sheets that covered so much of the Northern Hemisphere, they did live in regions affected by geological phenomena associated with the ice sheets: coastal areas, lakes, and river floodplains. When human artifacts are found in direct association with Pleistocene geological features of this type, it is sometimes possible to tie in archaeological sites with the relative chronology of Pleistocene events derived from geological strata.

Deep-Sea and Ice Cores

CARL A. RUDISILL LIBRARY
LENOIR-RHYNE COLLEGE

Our knowledge of Ice Age climatic change comes from many sources, including geological strata such as glacial deposits and ancient high beach levels, and fossil animal bones from environmentally sensitive mammals as large as elephants and as small as mice. Such approaches have long provided a crude outline of Ice Age glaciations. But in recent years the study of deep-sea and ice cores have revolutionized our understanding of the Pleistocene by providing long sequences of constantly changing Ice Age climate from deep below the ocean floor and the heart of the Greenland ice sheet.

The world's ocean floors are a priceless archive of ancient climatic change. Deep-sea cores produce long columns of ocean-floor sediments that include skeletons of small marine organisms that once lived close to the ocean's surface. These planktonic foraminifera (protozoa) consist largely of calcium carbonate. When alive, their minute skeletons absorb organic isotopes. The ratio of two of these isotopes—oxygen 16 and oxygen 18—varies as a result of evaporation. When evaporation is high, more of the lighter oxygen 16 is extracted from the ocean, leaving the plankton to be enriched by more of the heavier oxygen 18. When great ice sheets formed on land during glacial episodes, sea levels fell as moisture was drawn off for continental ice caps. During such periods, the world's oceans contained more oxygen 18 in proportion to oxygen 16, a ratio reflected in millions of foraminifera. A mass spectrometer is used to measure this ratio, which does not reflect ancient temperature changes but is merely a statement about the size of the oceans and about contemporary events on land.

One can confirm climatic fluctuations by using other lines of evidence as well, such as the changing frequencies of foraminifera and other groups of marine microfossils in the cores. By using statistical techniques, and assuming that relationships between different species and sea conditions have not changed, climatologists have been able to turn these frequencies into numerical estimates of sea surface temperatures and ocean salinity over the past few hundred thousand years and produce a climatic profile of much of the Ice Age (Figure 6.1). These events have been fixed at key points by radiocarbon dates

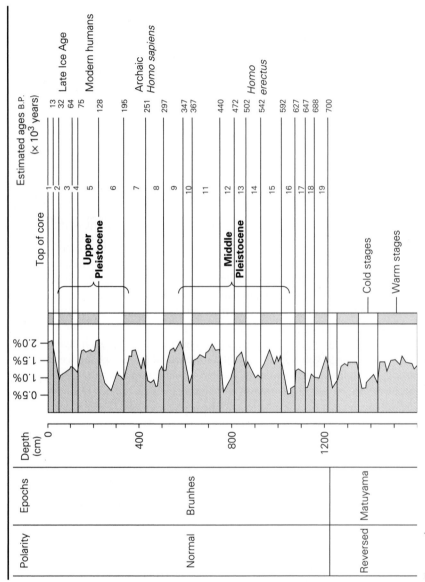

Figure 6.1 The deep-sea core that serves as the standard reference for the past 730,000 years comes from the Solomon Plateau in the southwestern Pacific Ocean. The Matuyama-Brunhes event occurs at a depth of 39.3 feet (11.9 m). Above it a sawtoothlike curve identifies at least eight complete glacial and interglacial cycles.

(see Chapter 8) and by studies of paleomagnetism (ancient magnetism). The **Matuyama-Brunhes** magnetic reversal of 730,000 years ago (when the world's magnetic field suddenly reversed) is a key stratigraphic marker, which can be identified both in sea cores and in volcanic strata ashore, where it can be dated precisely with potassium-argon samples.

Ice core studies are a comparatively recent development, but are now yielding increasingly accurate climatic portraits, especially of the later Ice Age and the past 10,000 years. They preserve records of annual snowfall going back far into the past. As the snow layers are buried deeper and deeper in a glacier, they are compressed into ice. The ice for winter and summer has different texture. Once researchers realized this, they were able to read ice cores like tree-ring samples, with very good resolution back for 12,000 years and improving accuracy back to 40,000 years. Ice cores have been especially useful for studying not so much the long-term fluctuations of Ice Age climatic change, but the short-term episodes of warmer and colder conditions that occurred in the middle of glaciations which had a profound effect on humanity. For example, scientists now suspect there were bursts of human activity in late Ice Age western Europe about 35,000 and 25,000 years ago, when conditions were relatively warm for short periods of time.

Ice and sea cores, combined with pollen analysis, have provided a broad framework for the Pleistocene, which is in wide use by archaeologists and worth summarizing here (Figure 6.2).

The Pleistocene Framework

The Pleistocene began about 1.8 million years ago, during a long-term cooling trend in the world's oceans. These millennia have been ones of constant climatic change. The Pleistocene is conventionally divided into long subdivisions.

Lower Pleistocene times lasted from the beginning of the Ice Age until about 730,000 years ago. Deep-sea cores tell us that climatic fluctuations between warmer and colder regimens were still relatively minor. These were critical millennia, for it was during this long period that humans emerged in Africa and spread from tropical regions into temperate latitudes in Europe and Asia.

The Middle Pleistocene began with the Matuyama-Brunhes reversal in the earth's magnetic polarity about 730,000 years ago, a change that has been recognized geologically not only in deep-sea cores, but in volcanic rocks ashore, where it can be dated by potassium-argon samples.

Since then, there have been at least eight cold (glacial) and warm (interglacial) cycles, the last cycle ending about 12,000 years ago. (Strictly speaking, we are still in an interglacial today.) Typically, cold cycles have begun gradually, with vast continental ice sheets forming on land—in Scandinavia, on the Alps, and over the northern parts of North America (Figure 6.3). These expanded ice sheets locked up enormous quantities of water, causing world sea levels to fall by several hundred feet during glacial episodes. The geography of the world changed dramatically, and large continental shelves were opened up for human settlement. When a warming trend began, deglaciation occurred very rapidly and rising sea levels flooded low-lying coastal areas within a few millennia. During glacial maxima, glaciers covered a full one third of the earth's land surface, and they were as extensive as they are today during interglacials.

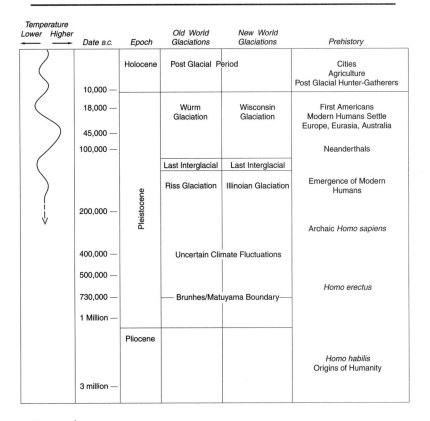

Figure 6.2   Provisional chronology and subdivisions of the Ice Age.

Throughout the past 730,000 years, vegetational changes have mirrored climatic fluctuations. During glacial episodes, treeless arctic steppe and tundra covered much of Europe and parts of North America, but gave way to temperate forest during inter-glacials. In the tropics, Africa's Sahara Desert may have supported grassland during interglacials, but ice and desert landscape expanded dramatically during dry, cold spells.

The Upper Pleistocene stage began about 128,000 years ago, with the beginning of the last interglacial. This period lasted until about 118,000 years ago, when a slow cooling trend brought full glacial conditions to Europe and North America. This Würm glaciation, named after a river in the Alps, lasted until about 15,000 years ago, when there was a rapid return to more temperate conditions.

The Würm glaciation was a period of constantly fluctuating climatic change, with several episodes of more temperate climate in northern latitudes (Figure 6.2). It served as the backdrop for some of the most important developments in human pre-history, notably the spread of anatomically modern *Homo sapiens sapiens* from the tropics to all parts of the Old World and into the Americas. Between about 25,000 and 15,000 years ago, northern Eurasia's climate was intensely cold, but highly variable. A series of brilliant Stone Age hunter-gatherer cultures evolved both on the open tun-

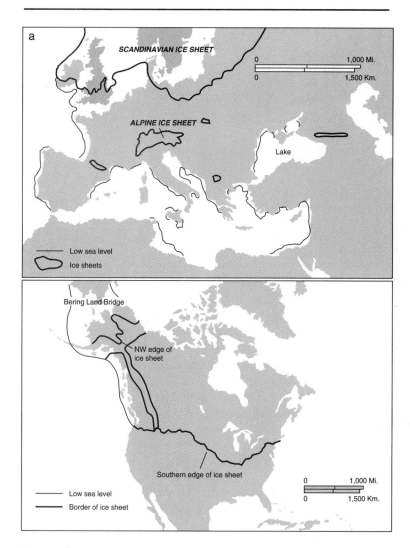

Figure 6.3   Distribution of major ice sheets in Europe and North America during the last Ice Age glaciation, and the extent of land exposed by low sea levels.

dra of central Europe and Eurasia and in the sheltered river valleys of southwestern France and northern Spain, cultures famous for their fine antler and bone artifacts and exceptional artwork.

The world's geography was dramatically different 18,000 years ago. These differences had a major impact on human prehistory—one could walk from Siberia to Alaska across a flat, low-lying plain, the Bering Land Bridge (Figure 6.4). This was the route by which humans first reached the Americas some time before 12,000 years ago. The low-lying coastal zones of Southeast Asia were far more extensive 15,000 years ago than they are now, and they supported a thriving population of Stone Age

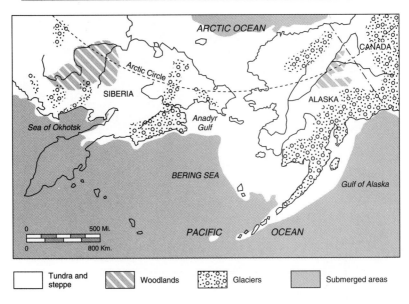

Figure 6.4   The Bering Land Bridge, as reconstructed by multidisciplinary research. Alaska finally separated from Siberia about 11,000 years ago as sea levels rose in response to warmer conditions.

foragers. The fluctuating distributions of vegetational zones also affected the pattern of human settlement and the course of human history.

Pollen Analysis

As long ago as 1916, Swedish botanist Lennart von Post used fossil pollen grains from familiar trees like birches, oaks, and pines to develop a sequence of vegetation change for northern Europe after the Ice Age. He showed how arctic, treeless tundra gave way to birch forest, then mixed oak woodland in a dramatic sequence of change that survived in pollen samples from marshes and swamps all over Scandinavia. Since then, **pollen analysis (palynology)** has become a highly sophisticated way of studying both ancient environment and human impacts on natural vegetation.

The principle is simple. Large numbers of pollen grains are dispersed in the atmosphere and have remarkable preservative properties if deposited in an unaerated geological horizon. The pollen grains can be identified microscopically (Figure 6.5) with great accuracy and used to reconstruct a picture of the vegetation, right down to humble grasses and weeds that grew near the spot where they are found.

Pollen analysis begins in the field. The botanist visits the excavation and collects a series of closely spaced pollen samples from the stratigraphic sections at the site. Back in the laboratory, the samples are examined under a very powerful microscope. The grains of each genus or species present are counted, and the resulting figures subjected to statis-

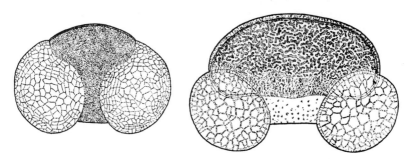

Figure 6.5   Pollen grains: left, spruce, right, silver fir. Both 340 times actual size.

tical analysis. These counts are then correlated with the stratigraphic layers of the excavation and data from natural vegetational sequences to provide a sequence of vegetational change for the site. Typically, this vegetational sequence lasts a few centuries or even millennia (Figure 6.6). It forms part of a much longer pollen sequence for the area that has been assembled from hundreds of samples from many different sites. In northern Europe,

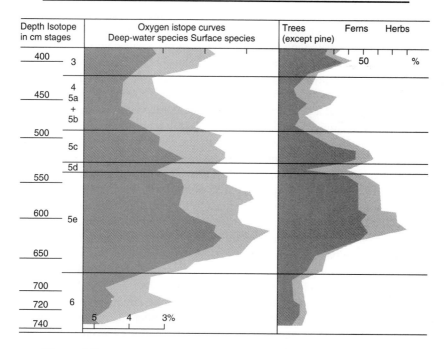

Figure 6.6   A long-term pollen sequence for the Ice Age from Spain (left) compared to oxygen-isotope curves taken from a deep-sea core in the nearby Bay of Biscay, showing the close correlation between the two.

for example, botanists have worked out a complicated series of vegetational time zones that cover the past 12,000 years. By comparing the pollen sequences from individual sites with the overall chronology, they can give a relative date for the site.

Palynology has obvious applications to prehistory, for sites are often found in swampy deposits where pollen is preserved, especially fishing or fowling camps and settlements near water. Isolated artifacts, or even human corpses (such as that of Tollund Man found in a Danish bog (Figure 4.6), have also been discovered in these deposits; pollen is sometimes obtained from small peat lumps adhering to crevices in such finds. Thus botanists can assign relative dates even to isolated finds that would otherwise remain undated.

Until recently, pollen analysts dealt in centuries. Now, thanks to much more refined methods and AMS radiocarbon dating, they can study even transitory episodes, such as the brief farming incident described at the beginning of this chapter. For example, dramatic falls in forest tree pollens at many locations in Europe chronicle the first clearance of farming cultures with almost decade-long accuracy—at a moment when characteristic cultivation weeds like *Plantago lanceolata*, already mentioned, appear for the first time. Southwestern archaeologists now have a regional pollen sequence that provides not only climatic information but also valuable facts about the functions of different pueblo rooms and different foods eaten by the inhabitants.

Identifying cultural activities from pollen archaeological sites can be extremely tricky, for the tiny grains can be transported to a site in many ways—by wind, water, rodents, even people bringing ripe fruit home. Sometimes, too, people use surface soil from neighboring areas, complete with its pollen content, to make a house floor. Some species like the sunflower have heavy pollen that can cling to ripe fruit. Such factors are likely to contaminate the pollen samples from many sites, unless one has other plant evidence, such as, say, squash rind or seeds, to confirm the palynological data.

Pollen analysis is providing new perceptions of Stone Age life at the height of the last glaciation in southwestern France, some 15,000 to 20,000 years ago (Figure 6.6). This was, we are told, a period of extreme arctic cold, when Europe was in a deep freeze, people subsisting off arctic animals and taking refuge in deep river valleys like the Dordogne and the Vézère, where some of the earliest cave art in the world has been discovered. In fact, pollen grains from the rockshelters and open camps used by Stone Age hunter-gatherers of this period paint a very different picture of the late Ice Age climate in this area. It is a portrait of a favored arctic environment in which the climate fluctuated constantly, with surprisingly temperate conditions, especially on the south-facing slopes of deep river valleys. Here, people used rock shelters that faced the winter sun, where snow melted earlier in the spring, within easy reach of key reindeer migration routes and of arctic game that wintered in the valleys. The vegetational cover was not treeless, as is commonly assumed, but included pine, birch, and sometimes deciduous trees, with lush summer meadows in the valley.

The late Ice Age was a period of continual, and often dramatic, short- and long-term climatic change. Some of these changes lasted millennia, bringing intervals of near-modern conditions to temperate Europe interspersed with much colder winters. Other cold and warm snaps extended over a few centuries, causing human populations to adapt to dramatically new conditions. Just like today, there were much shorter climatic episodes, which endured for a year or more, bringing unusually warm summers, floods, droughts, and other short-term events.

Short-Term Climatic Change: The Holocene

The last prolonged Ice Age glaciation ended about 15,000 years ago, when North American and European ice sheets retreated and the world entered a period of pronounced global warming. Then the great glaciers retreated, sea levels rose from 300 feet (91 m) below today's levels to near-modern heights, and vegetation patterns throughout the world changed considerably. Thus dawned the **Holocene** period (Greek: *holos*: recent), which saw massive global warming, sudden cold snaps, periods of warmer climate than today, and the appearance of both food production and civilization, also the Industrial Revolution. Many people believe this warming has been continuous and is reflected in the record warm temperatures of today. In fact, the world's climate has fluctuated just as dramatically as it did during the late Ice Age. Recent research is revolutionizing our knowledge of these changes, which started new chapters in human history, overthrew civilizations, and caused widespread disruption.

We can identify Holocene climatic changes from ice cores, sedimentary records in caves, tree rings, and pollen samples, with a chronological resolution that improves every year as analytical methods become ever more refined.

Centuries-Long Changes: The Younger Dryas and the Black Sea

At least three major cold snaps have cooled global temperatures since 11,000 years ago (Figure 6.7). The last of these was the so-called Little Ice Age, which lasted from A.D. 1400 to 1850. The earlier two of these cold intervals had major effects on the course of human history, which we can now assess thanks to new deep-sea core, ice core, and pollen researches.

The Younger Dryas lasted from 11,000 to 10,000 B.C. For some still little understood reason, global warming ceased abruptly, perhaps as a result of sudden changes in the warm water circulation in the Atlantic Ocean. Within a century or so, Europe again shivered under near Ice Age conditions as forests retreated and widespread drought affected areas like southwestern Asia. This catastrophic drought after centuries of ample rainfall may have been a major factor in the appearance of agriculture and animal domestication in areas like the Euphrates and Jordan River valleys, where dense forager populations had long subsisted off abundant food resources. What happened next has been documented by botanist Gordon Hillman with plant remains at the Abu Hureyra site (see Chapter 10). When the drought came, nut harvest yields plummeted, game populations crashed, and wild cereal grasses were unable to support a dense human population. So the foragers turned to cultivation to supplement their food supplies. Within a few generations, they became full-time farmers. The Younger Dryas–induced drought was not the only cause of agriculture, but the sudden climate change was of great importance.

The Black Sea was an enormous freshwater lake (often called the Euxine Lake) isolated from the Mediterranean by a huge natural earthen levee in the Bosporus Valley between Turkey and Bulgaria during the early Holocene. Four centuries of colder conditions and drought again settled over Europe and southwestern Asia between 6200 and 5800 B.C. Many farmers abandoned long-established villages and settled near the great lake and other permanent water sources. Deep-sea cores and pollen diagrams chronicle what happened next as the climate warmed up again after 5800 B.C. Sea levels resumed their inexorable rise toward modern high levels. Salt

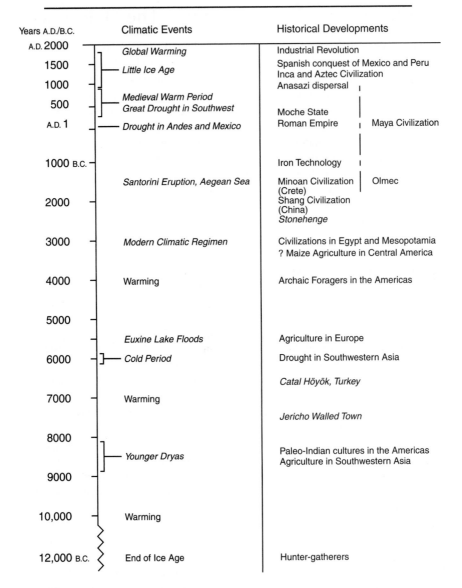

Figure 6.7 Major climatic and historical events of the Holocene. (This is, of course, a gross simplification of reality.)

Mediterranean waters climbed ever higher on the Bosporus levee. Then, in about 5500 B.C., the rising water breached the barrier. Torrents of salt water cascaded into the Euxine Lake 500 feet (150 m) below. Within weeks, the great waterfall had carved a deep gully and formed the narrow strait that now links the Black Sea to the Mediterranean. The former lake not only became a saltwater ocean, but rose sharply, flooding hundreds of agricultural settlements on its shores, perhaps with great loss of life. This long-forgotten event has recently been reconstructed from deep-sea cores taken in the Mediterranean, also in the Black Sea, which chronicle not only the cold snap and drought, but the sudden change in the now-drowned lake.

The Black Sea discoveries are so new that archaeologists still have to assess their full consequences. The flooding of the huge lake does coincide with the spread of farmers across temperate Europe from the Balkans. Some experts believe the environmental catastrophe and the spread of farming were connected, as people fled their once-fertile homelands.

Short-Term Climate Change: El Niño

We look back at the past through obscure mirrors, which become increasingly easy to use as we approach recent times. Our knowledge of Ice Age climatic change is necessarily on a grand scale, for, until recently, even ice cores did not attain the year-by-year resolution needed to track short-term shifts. Yet such sudden changes are the most important of all to human populations, who have to adjust constantly to unusual weather conditions—to droughts and floods, unusual heat and cold. The Younger Dryas and Black Sea drought and flood are centuries-long events that are short by geological and early prehistoric standards. We are only now beginning to understand their profound impact on ancient societies. As research into these, and other centuries-long events, has intensified, more scholars have played increasing attention to violent year-long episodes such as monsoon failures, volcanic eruptions, and, most important of all, El Niños.

Identifying ancient short-term climatic change requires extremely precise and sophisticated environmental and climatic evidence, much of it obtained from ice cores, pollen diagrams, and tree rings. Ice cores, in particular, are revolutionizing our knowledge of ancient climatic shifts, for they are now achieving a resolution of five years or less, which really allows the study of drought cycles and major El Niño events of the past.

El Niños like those in 1982–83 and 1997–98 grabbed world headlines and with good reason. Billions of dollars of damage came from drought and flood. California enjoyed record rains, Australia and northeast Brazil suffered through brutal drought, enormous wildfires devastated rain forests in Southeast Asia and Mexico. Once thought to be a purely local phenomenon off the Peruvian coast, El Niños are now known to be global events that ripple across the entire tropics as a result of a breakdown in the atmospheric and ocean circulation in the western Pacific. From the archaeologist's point of view, El Niños are of compelling interest, for they had drastic effects on many early civilizations living in normally dry environments, where flooding could wipe out years of irrigation agriculture in hours. Humanity was not that vulnerable to El Niños until people settled in permanent villages, then cities, when the realities of farming and growing population densities made it harder for them to move away from drought or flood (Figure 6.8).

A classic example of such vulnerability comes from the north coast of Peru, where the Moche civilization flourished around A.D. 400, ruled by powerful, authoritarian warrior-priests (see Figure 4.4). The Moche survived in one of the driest environments on earth by using elaborate irrigation schemes to harness spring runoff from the Andes in coastal river valleys. Everything depended on ample mountain floodwaters. When drought occurred, the Moche suffered.

The Quelccaya ice cap in the Cordillera Occidental of the southern Peruvian highlands lies in the same zone of seasonal rainfall as the mountains above Moche

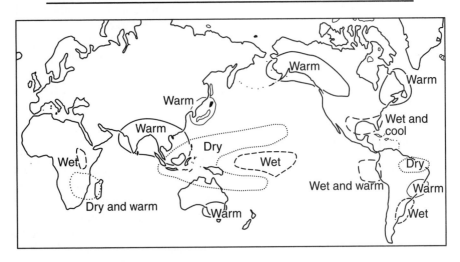

Figure 6.8   The worldwide effects of a strong El Niño, reconstructed on the basis of the 1982–83 event. We can assume that generally similar effects were experienced over the past 5,000 years.

country. Two ice cores drilled in the summit of the ice cap in 1983 provide a record of variations in rainfall over 1,500 years, and, indirectly, an impression of the amount of runoff that would have reached lowland river valleys during cycles of wet and dry years. In the southern highlands, El Niño episodes have been tied to intense short-term droughts in the region, also on the nearby *altiplano*, the high-altitude plains around Lake Titicaca. The appearance of such drought events in the ice cores may reflect strong El Niño episodes in the remote past. However, it is more productive to look at long-term dry and wet cycles.

The two ice cores, 508 and 537 feet (154.8 and 163.6 m) long, each yielded clear layering and annual dust layers that reflected the yearly cycle of wet and dry seasons, the latter bringing dust particles from the arid lands to the west to the high Andes, accurate to within about 20 years. The cores show clear indications of long-term rain-fall variations. A short drought occurred between A.D. 534 and 540. Then, between A.D. 563 and 594, a three-decade drought cycle settled over the mountains and low-lands, with annual rainfall as much as 30 percent below normal. Abundant rainfall resumed in 602, giving way to another drought between A.D. 636 and 645.

The 30-year drought of A.D. 563 to 594 drastically reduced the amount of runoff reaching coastal communities. The effect of a 25 or 30 percent reduction in the water supply would be catastrophic, especially on farmers near the coast, well downstream from the mountains. Moche society apparently prospered until the mid-sixth century's severe drought cycle. As the drought intensified, the diminished runoff barely watered the rich farming land far downstream. Miles of laboriously maintained irrigation canals remained dry. Blowing sand cascaded into empty ditches. By the third or fourth year, as the drought lowered the water table far below normal, thousands of acres of farmland received so weak a river flow that unflushed salt accumulated in the soil. Crops withered. Fortunately, the coastal fisheries still provided ample fish meal—until a strong El Niño came along without warning, bringing warmer waters and torrential rains to the desert and mountains.

We do not know the exact years during the long drought when strong El Niños struck, but we can be certain that they did. We can also be sure they hit at a moment when Moche civilization was in crisis, grain supplies running low, irrigation systems sadly depleted, malnutrition widespread, and confidence in the rulers' divine powers much diminished. The warmer waters of the El Niño reduced anchovy harvests in many places, decimating a staple both of the coastal diet and highland trade. Torrential rains swamped the Andes and coastal plain. The arid rivers became raging torrents, carrying everything before them. Levees and canals overflowed and collapsed. The arduous labors of years vanished in a few weeks. Dozens of villages vanished under mud and debris as the farmers' cane and adobe houses collapsed and their occupants drowned. The floods polluted springs and streams, overwhelmed sanitation systems, and stripped thousands of acres of fertile soil. As the water receded and the rivers went down, typhoid and other epidemics swept through the valleys, wiping out entire communities and eroding fertile soils. Infant mortality soared.

The Moches' elaborate irrigation systems created an artificial landscape that supported dense farming populations in the midst of one of the driest deserts on earth, where farming would be impossible without technological ingenuity. The farmers were well aware of the hazards of droughts and El Niños, but technology and irrigation could not guarantee the survival of a highly centralized society driven as much by ideology as pragmatic concerns. There were limits to the climatic shifts Moche civilization could absorb. Ultimately, the Moche ran out of options and their civilization collapsed.

We do not know how long El Niños have oscillated across the globe, but they have descended on Peru for at least 5,000 years. But a new generation of climatic researches from ice cores and other data show that short-term climatic shifts played a far more important role in the fate of early civilizations than once realized.

Tree Rings: Studying Southwestern Drought

Many ancient societies lived in environments with unpredictable rainfall, where agriculture was, at best, a chancy enterprise. The ancient peoples of the southwestern United States farmed their semiarid environment with brilliant skill for more than 3,000 years, developing an extraordinary expertise at water management and plant breeding. One central philosophy of modern-day Pueblo Indian groups surrounds movement, the notion that people have to move to escape drought and survive. Until recently, archaeologists did not fully appreciate the importance of movement in southwestern life and were at a loss to explain the sudden dispersal of the Anasazi people of Chaco Canyon and the Four Corners region in the twelfth and thirteenth centuries A.D.

Dendrochronologies for the Anasazi are now accurate to within a year, giving us the most precise time scale for any early human society anywhere. In recent years, the Laboratory of Tree-Ring Research at the University of Arizona has undertaken a massive dendroclimatic study that has yielded a reconstruction of relative climatic variability in the Southwest from A.D. 680 to 1970. The same scientists, headed by Jeffrey Dean, are now producing the first quantitative reconstructions of annual and seasonal rainfall, also of temperature, drought, and stream flow for the region. Such research involves not only tree-ring sequences but intricate mathematical expressions of the relationships between tree growth and such variables as rainfall, temperature, and crop yields. These calculations yield statistical estimations of the fluctuations in these variables on an annual and seasonal basis.

By using a spatial grid of 27 long tree-ring sequences from throughout the Southwest, Dean and his colleagues have compiled maps that plot the different station values and their fluctuations like contour maps, one for each decade. This enables them to study such phenomena as the progress of what Dean sometimes calls the "Great Drought" of A.D. 1276 to 1299 from northwest to southeast across the region. In 1276, the beginnings of the drought appear as negative standard deviations from average rainfall in the northwest while the remainder of the region enjoys above-average rainfall. During the next ten years, very dry conditions expand over the entire Southwest before improved rainfall arrives after 1299. This form of mapping allows close correlation of vacated large and small pueblos with short-term climatic fluctuations (Figure 6.9).

When the research team looked at the entire period from A.D. 966 to 1988, they found that the tree-ring stations in the northwestern region accounted for no less than 60 percent of the rainfall variance. In contrast, stations in the southeastern part of the Southwest accounted for only 10 percent. This general configuration, which persisted for centuries, coincides with the modern distribution of seasonal rainfall in the Southwest: predictable summer rainfall dominates the southeastern areas while the northwest receives both winter and summer precipitation. Winter rains are much more uncertain. When the scientists examined this general rainfall pattern at 100-year intervals from 539 to 1988, they observed that it persisted most of the time, even though the boundary between the two zones moved backward and forward slightly.

But this long-term pattern broke down completely from A.D. 1250 to 1450, when a totally aberrant pattern prevailed in the northwest. The southeast remained stable, but there was major disruption elsewhere. For nearly two centuries, the relatively simple long-term pattern of summer and winter rains gave way to complex, unpredictable precipitation and severe droughts, especially on the Colorado Plateau. The change to an unstable pattern would have had a severe impact on Anasazi farmers, especially as it coincided with the Great Drought of A.D. 1250 to 1299.

Why did this breakdown occur? Dean divides the relationship between climatic change and human behavior into three broad categories. Certain obvious stable elements in the Anasazi environment have not changed over the past 2,000 years, such as bedrock geology and climate type. Then there are low-frequency environmental changes—those that occur on cycles longer than a human generation of 25 years. Few people witnessed these changes during their lifetimes. Changes in hydrological conditions such as cycles of erosion and deposition along stream courses, fluctuations in water table levels in river floodplains, and changes in plant distributions transcend generations, but they could affect the environment drastically, especially in drought cycles.

Shorter term, high-frequency changes were readily apparent to every Anasazi: year-to-year rainfall shifts, decade-long drought cycles, seasonal changes, and so on. Over the centuries, the Anasazi were probably barely aware of long-term change, for the present generation and their ancestors enjoyed the same basic adaptation, which one could call a form of "stability." Cycles of drought, unusually heavy rains, and

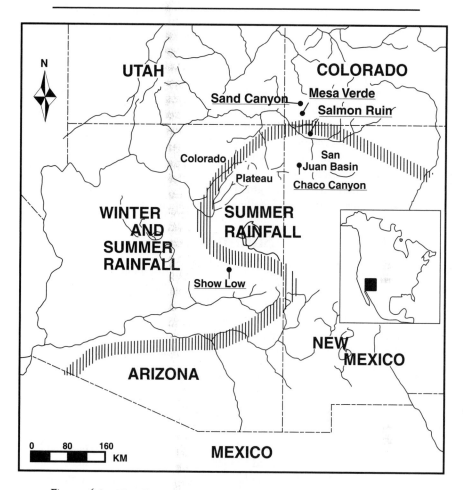

Figure 6.9   The climatic regimens of the American Southwest, showing the general configuration of rainfall across the region reconstructed with tree rings. The northwest receives both summer and winter rainfall, the southeast only predictable summer rainfall.

other high-frequency changes required temporary and flexible adjustments, such as farming more land, relying more heavily on wild plant foods, and, above all, movement across the terrain.

Such strategies worked well for centuries, as long as the Anasazi farmed their land at well below its carrying capacity. When the population increased to near carrying capacity, however, as it did at Chaco Canyon in the twelfth century, people became increasingly vulnerable to brief events like El Niños or droughts, which could stretch the supportive capacity of a local environment within months, even weeks. Their vulnerability was even more extreme when long-term changes—such as a half century or more of much drier conditions—descended on farming land already pushed to its carrying limits. Under these circumstances, a year-long drought or torrential rains could quickly destroy a local population's ability to support itself. So the people dispersed into other areas, where there was ample soil and better water supplies. Without question, the Anasazi dispersed from Mesa Verde and Chaco Canyon because drought forced them to do so. Unlike the Moche in distant Peru, they had the flexibility to move away.

The coming decades will see a revolution in our understanding of ancient environments and short-term climatic change as scientists acquire a closer knowledge both of climates in the past and of the still little known forces that drive the global weather machine. Like our predecessors, we still live in the Ice Age, which, some estimates calculate, will bring renewed glacial conditions in about 23,000 years time. So it is hardly surprising that, like our forebears, we have had to adjust to constant short-term climatic changes. And, as humanly induced global warming accelerates, these changes may become more frequent and violent, spelling danger for an overpopulated world.

Summary

The study of long- and short-term climatic and environmental change is of vital importance to archaeologists concerned with human societies' changing relationships with their surroundings. This chapter describes ways of studying such changes. Geoarchaeology is a multidisciplinary approach to the study of human adaptations that reconstructs ancient landscapes using such techniques as remote sensing and paleographic and biological methods such as pollen analysis. Deep-sea cores and ice drillings provide us with a broad framework of climatic change during the Pleistocene (Ice Age) that chronicle at least nine glacial periods during the past 730,000 years. The Pleistocene itself is divided into three broad subdivisions, the last of which coincides with the spread of modern humans across the world from Africa. The Holocene covers postglacial times and witnessed not only global warming, but at least three short periods of much colder conditions. The Younger Dryas brought drought and cold conditions and may have helped trigger agriculture in southwestern Asia. The catastrophic flooding of the Black Sea lake in about 5500 B.C. by salt water from the Mediterranean caused major population movements in Europe. Short-term events such as El Niños and southwestern droughts are studied with the aid of ice cores, geological observations, and tree rings, methods achieving increasing precision. We are now beginning to realize that short-term climatic change played a vital role in the rise and fall of many human societies.

7

Finding and Assessing Archaeological Sites

Spanish depiction of an Andean woman in highland Peru weaving with a backstrap loom. The pressure of her back tensions the wool.

Antiquities are history defaced, or some remnants of history which have casually escaped the shipwreck of time.

Francis Bacon, 1605

I will never forget the first time I went out in the field looking for Stone Age sites. We were walking through a dry river valley, where river gravels showed through the stunted dry season grass. My experienced companion walked with his eyes glued to the ground, picking up Stone Age scrapers without apparent effort. I moved at half his speed, puzzling over every piece, for I had not done this before. After half an hour we had hundreds of 100,000-year-old artifacts, collected from acres of gravel that had been sorted again and again by floodwaters. Artifacts from dozens of campsites had been mingled together in a hodgepodge of brown-colored artifacts and waste flakes. Suddenly, my companion bent down and picked up a broken flake. "That's the other half of a flake I collected in 1938," he declared. "Impossible," I replied. But he was right. When we got back to the museum, we opened the 1938 collection and the two pieces fitted together perfectly. It was a sobering lesson in the power and precision of an experienced archaeological eye. Since then, I have found many sites and artifacts on my own, but I am still in awe at my colleague's incredible memory.

How do you know where to dig? How do you find sites? Many people are amazed at how archaeologists seem to have an uncanny ability to choose the right place for their excavations. Part of this ability is having a good eye for landscape, a penchant for putting yourself in the shoes of the people you are seeking, and, yes, just plain old-fashioned common sense. However, formal survey methods play an important role in archaeological fieldwork, especially today when many projects are carried out under fast-moving cultural resource management projects. This chapter explores the ways in which archaeologists discover and assess archaeological sites, a fundamental part of field research.

The Process of Archaeological Research

There was a time when archaeologists concentrated most of their efforts on excavating single sites. They would choose a promising location, excavate it, and study the recovered artifacts without worrying too much about the environmental setting or the broader context of their excavation. Today, archaeologists think in terms of cultural and ecological systems, of interactions between humans and their natural environment. The focus has shifted toward regional studies, studies with specific, problem-oriented perspectives, and also toward formal **research design** (see Chapter 8). In many cases, excavation is the strategy of last resort, for, as every archaeologist knows, to dig a site is to destroy a finite record of the past.

Regional archaeology is a much more complex process than mere site investigation. Thus research problems, often involving entire teams of scholars from different disciplines, dictate the creation of systematic, detailed **research designs**. These designs are created through a formal process that acts as the driving mechanism for the entire research project. In a sense, a research design is like a flow chart, for it is created both to monitor the validity of research results and to maximize efficient use of money, people, and time.

A research design divides the research process into specific stages, each of which, in turn, is carefully designed to carry out certain functions. Together they form a sequence of investigation that divides the flow chart into stages—not that the stages necessarily follow one upon the other in close order. Several may be carried out simultaneously. The design may be a formal process, but it must be flexible and fluid enough to accommodate ever-changing circumstances in the field as well as individual needs. It must also accommodate the diverse needs of every participant in the project and bring together all relevant research for final publication. Archaeological research proceeds in the following general stages (Figure 7.1).

Design and Formulation

The problem is defined, its feasibility tested, and the entire background for the project is researched very carefully. Background library research is especially important because it provides an opportunity to refine research questions. The finished research design includes not only a definition of the research problem, but also a statement of specific goals, including sampling strategies to be used and specific hypotheses to be tested. It is also an accurate definition of the kinds of data the research team will be looking for to test its hypotheses. However, flexibility is essential if the research is not to be shackled too tightly.

Implementation

Fund-raising, an eternal problem for archaeologists, gaining permission for access to land and to excavate, acquiring equipment and a work force—all of these are important ingredients of the implementation stage.

Data Acquisition

Data acquisition is accomplished when field research takes place, and can be a regional survey or smaller scale project, or an excavation.

Processing and Analysis

Archaeological finds come in many forms—as artifacts, food remains, remains of houses, human skeletons, and so on. These finds are usually cleaned, identified, and cataloged in the field before packing for transport to the laboratory. Once back from the field, these data—including not only finds, but the detailed notes, drawings, and other recorded data acquired in the field—are analyzed. At this stage some specific materials, such as radiocarbon samples and pollen grains, are sent to specialists for analysis. Most laboratory analysis involves detailed artifact classification and study of animal bones and other food remains—the basis for the later interpretation of data (Chapters 9, 10).

Interpretation

Everything is brought together into an interpretative synthesis to answer the research questions posed in the original design. Anthropological and historical models usually provide the most consistent interpretations of the archaeological record (Chapter 13).

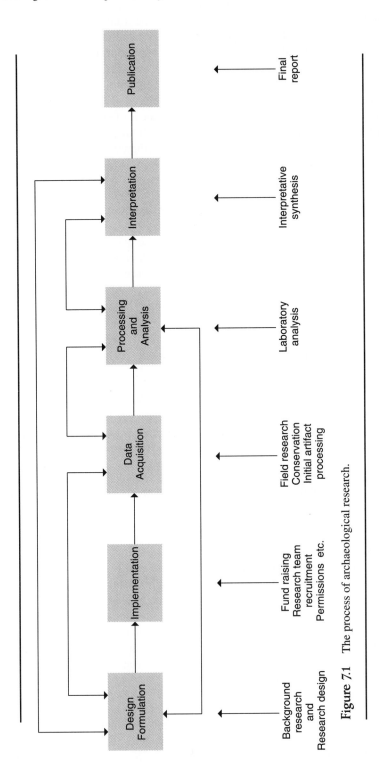

Figure 7.1   The process of archaeological research.

Publication

No research project is complete until the final results are published in a form accessible to other scholars. An unpublished site is effectively destroyed, not only by the excavations, but by the absence of any permanent record of the findings.

Only when the project is published and complete can the archaeologist move on to another project or use the results from this research design as a foundation for further inquiry in the same region. CRM contracts end with the completion of the final report on the project, usually a formal requirement of the contract.

Archaeological fieldwork has three stages, the first two of which are discussed in this chapter:

- *Finding archaeological sites.* The process of actually locating sites, which is either by accident or the result of deliberate archaeological survey.
- *Assessing the sites.* Nonintrusive archaeology, which involves recording the location of sites, surface finds, and sometimes electronic subsurface detection.
- *Archaeological excavation.* The investigation of the site by means of excavation (Chapter 8).

Increasingly, excavation is a strategy of last resort. Many important projects focus on survey and site assessment using surface data, to preserve the archaeological record.

Finding Archaeological Sites

Finding archaeological sites involves far more than merely locating a prehistoric settlement to dig. Some archaeological sites are so conspicuous that people have always known of their existence. The Pyramids of Giza in Egypt have withstood the onslaught of tourists, treasure hunters, and quarriers for thousands of years. The Pyramid of the Sun at Teotihuacán, Mexico, is another easily visible archaeological site (see Figure 11.3).

The eastern United States is dotted with hundreds of burial mounds and earthworks, which are easily distinguished from the surrounding countryside. One well-known early archaeologist simply hired a riverboat each summer and sailed along digging sites he saw on the riverbanks. Cemeteries may be marked by piles of stones, and the deep accumulations of occupation deposits at the mouths of rockshelters or caves or the huge piles of abandoned shells left by mollusk collectors are more readily located. Sites of this type are obviously simple to identify, and often have been known for centuries. For instance, in some parts of California ancient shell middens (shell heaps) are recognizable at a considerable distance by their gray soil and the stunted grass growth on them.

Most archaeological sites are far less conspicuous. They may consist of little more than a scatter of pottery fragments or a few stone tools lying on the surface of the ground. Other settlements may be buried under several feet of soil, leaving few surface traces except when exposed by moving water, wind erosion, or burrowing animals. Finding archaeological sites depends on locating such telltale traces of human settlement. Once the sites have been found, they have to be recorded, and surface collections must be made at each locality to assemble a general impression of the activities of the people who lived there.

Accidental discoveries of sites, spectacular artifacts, or skeletons have revealed whole chapters of the past. Cowboy George McJunkin was searching for a lost cow near Folsom, New Mexico, in 1909, when he noticed some sun-bleached bones projecting from the soil of a dry gully. He pried loose a few bones and a stone spear point and took them home with him. They lay around the ranch house for 17 years before they came to the attention of Jesse Figgins, director of the Colorado Museum of Natural History. Figgins identified the extinct bison bones at once and wondered if the animal had been killed by the owner of the stone spear head. Excavations at Folsom revealed more stone points directly associated with bison bones, the first such find in North America. From this chance discovery came direct proof that humans had hunted extinct animals in North America soon after the Ice Age, as early as 10,000 years ago (Figure 7.2).

The Cerén Maya village in San Salvador came to light when a bulldozer operator exposed a long-buried house mantled under feet of volcanic ash and completely invisible from the surface. Some boys out hunting rabbits in 1940 found the magnificent Ice Age paintings in Lascaux Cave in southwestern France when their dog became trapped in an underground chamber entered through a rabbit hole.

Dramatic finds have resulted from despoiling of the environment. Deep plowing and freeway and dam construction have led to the uncovering—and damaging—of priceless sites. When Mexico City's metro (subway) was constructed under the modern city, the 28 miles (45 km) of tunnels yielded a wealth of archaeological material. Mexico City is built on the site of the Aztec capital of Tenochtitlán, overthrown by Hernán Cortés in 1521. Little remains of the Aztec city on the surface today, but the contractors for the metro recovered 40 tons of pottery, 380 burials, and even a small temple dedicated to the wind god Ehecatl-Quetzalcoatl. The temple is now preserved on its original site as part of the Pino Suarez station of the metro system. All of the tunneling operations were under the supervision of expert archaeologists, who were empowered to halt construction whenever an archaeological find was made.

Even more dramatic was the accidental rediscovery of the great Templo Mayor in the heart of Mexico City. Modern construction activity revealed the most sacred shrine of Aztec Tenochtitlán, the temples of the gods Huitzilopochtli and Tlaloc. Mexican archaeologist Eduardo Matos Moctezuma's excavations subsequently unearthed at least five successive temples and many rebuildings going back to as early as A.D. 1390, if not earlier. The temple visited by Spanish conquistador Hernán Cortés had 114 steps, and a drum so loud it could be heard 6 miles (9.6 km) away. The conquistadors pulled it down to build a Catholic cathedral nearby. The abandoned shrines were forgotten until the 1970s.

Nature itself sometimes uncovers sites for us, which are then located by a sharp-eyed archaeologist looking for natural exposures of likely geological strata. Olduvai Gorge is a great gash in the Serengeti Plains of northern Tanzania. An ancient earthquake eroded a deep gorge, exposing hundreds of feet of lake beds that had been buried long before. These buried lake deposits have yielded early tool and bone concentrations dating back at least 1.75 million years. They would never have been found without the assistance of an earthquake and subsequent erosion. The Olduvai area is

Figure 7.2 Paleo-Indian projectile points found in association with the bones of extinct bison on the Great Plains of North America.

but one of many examples from all over the world where nature has revealed the incredible bounty of the past.

The fields of the Western world have yielded many caches of buried weapons, coins, smith's tools, and sacrificial objects, valued treasures that were buried in times of stress by their owners. For whatever reason, the owners never returned to recover their valuables. Thousands of years later, a farmer comes across the hoard and, if a responsible citizen, reports the find to archaeological authorities. If not, yet another valuable fragment of the past is lost to science.

Archaeological Survey

Archaeological survey means walking—a large-scale survey means lots of it, day after day, week after week, on carefully laid out transects that cross hill and dale. I always enjoy survey, for you develop a sense of the local landscape, meet all kinds of people, and get a unique impression of a place you might otherwise never encounter. And there is always the prospect of an important discovery. I have spent a month looking for Stone Age rockshelters in southwestern England and found no traces of human occupation whatsoever, returned from a week in southern Zambia with records of over 30 large mound villages, and walked in the Maya rain forest where you can see only a few yards on either side. Survey is fascinating because no two days are alike and the rewards can be immense.

An archaeological survey can vary from spending an afternoon searching a city lot for traces of historical structures to a large-scale survey over several years of an entire river basin or drainage area. In all cases, the theoretical ideal is easily stated: to record all traces of ancient settlement in the area. But this ideal is impossible to achieve. Many sites leave no traces above ground. And no survey, however thorough and however sophisticated its remote sensing devices, will ever achieve the impossible dream of total coverage. The key to effective archaeological survey lies in carefully designing the research before one sets out and in using techniques to estimate the probable density of archaeological sites in the region.

Archaeological surveys are most effective in terrain where the vegetation is burned off or sparse enough for archaeologists to be able to see the ground. In lush vegetation areas such as those of the American South, only the most conspicuous earthworks will show up. And, of course, thousands of sites are buried under housing developments, parking lots, and artificial lakes, which have radically altered the landscape in many places.

A great deal depends on the intensity of the field survey. The most effective surveys are carried out on foot, where the archaeologist can locate the traces of artifacts, the gray organic soil eroding from a long-abandoned settlement, and the subtle colors of rich vegetation that reveal long-buried houses. Plowed fields may display revealing traces of ash, artifacts, or hut foundations. Scatters of broken bones, stone implements, potsherds, or other traces of prehistoric occupation are easily located in such furrowed soil. Observation is the key to finding archaeological sites and to studying the subtle relationships between prehistoric settlements and the landscape on which they flourished.

Archaeologists have numerous inconspicuous signs to guide them. Gray soil from a rodent burrow, a handful of humanly fractured stones in the walls of a desert arroyo, a blurred mark in a plowed field, a **potsherd**—these are the signs they seek. After a few days, you learn to spot the telltale gray earth sent up by burrowing animals from village sites from some distance off. And often, information on possible sites is provided by knowledgeable local inhabitants, especially landowners who have an intimate knowledge of their own acreage.

There is far more to archaeological survey than merely walking the countryside, however. Such surveys can be of varying intensity. The least intensive survey is the most common: the investigator examining only conspicuous and accessible sites, those of great size and considerable fame. Heinrich Schliemann followed just this procedure when he located the site of ancient Troy at Hissarlik in Turkey in the 1870s. John Lloyd Stephens and Frederick Catherwood did the same when they visited Uxmal, Palenque, and other Maya sites in Mesoamerica in the early 1840s. Such superficial surveys barely scratch the archaeological surface.

A more intensive survey involves collecting as much information about as many sites as possible from local informants and landowners. Again, the sites located by this means are the larger and more conspicuous ones, and the survey is necessarily incomplete. But this approach is widely used throughout the world, especially in areas where archaeologists have never worked before.

Many more discoveries will be made if archaeologists undertake a highly systematic survey of a relatively limited area. This type of survey involves not only comprehensive inquiries among local landowners, but actual systematic on-site checking of those reports. The footwork resulting from the checking of local reports may lead to more discoveries. But, again, the picture may be very incomplete, for the survey deals with known sites and does not cover the area systematically from one end to the other or establish the proportions of each type of site known to exist in the region.

The most intensive surveys have a party of archaeologists covering a whole area by walking all over it, often in straight lines, with a set distance between them. Such surveys are usually based on carefully formulated research designs. The investigators are careful to check that their site distributions reflect actual settlement patterns rather than where archaeologists walked.

Some such surveys have thrown light on rural life in ancient Greece by identifying the locations of individual farmsteads and small villages. Without resorting to expensive and time-consuming excavation, the research teams have used surface finds, such as pottery, to provide dating evidence for the sites, and have thus been able to show changing patterns of settlement from prehistory to the present day. At the same time, these surveys have found evidence for ancient Greek farming practices. One key discovery was the so-called halo of artifacts that surrounds many sites. Some ancient cities have haloes extending over several square miles. They result from intensive manuring—the carting out of animal dung, night soil, and other organic wastes (including the accidental admixture of discarded pottery and other cultural material) and spreading them over the fields to increase fertility. Such an intensive agricultural practice is an indication of the high population density of many regions of Classical Greece. It was during this period, too, that extensive stone terraces were built on hillsides, again reflecting population growth and the need to increase agricultural productivity, in this case by creating new farmland.

What did the landscape of Classical Greece look like? A Stanford University research team carried out intensive field surveys in southern Greece of the southern Argolid at the eastern end of the Peloponnese. The researchers discovered several hundred archaeological sites of all periods and collected 45,000 ceramic pieces, mainly potsherds. Analysis of this huge body of material, coupled with study of soils and landscape, enabled them to chart changes in the settlement of the region from prehistory to the present day. The number of sites reached a peak during the fourth century B.C., when the area around the Classical town of *Halieis* became an important center of olive production, revealed by a combination of different kinds of evidence.

Rural settlements appear at this time on stony alluvium and lower hill slopes, areas that give poor cereal yields but are ideal for olives. Olives were probably grown on terraces built on the hillsides, indicating a more labor-intensive use of the landscape. Further evidence for the production of olive oil comes from oil presses found both at rural farmsteads and at Halieis itself. At the same time, cereal growing continued on the fertile and water-retentive deeper soils.

The importance of olive production on the fourth-century Plain of Argos in southern Greece may well be linked to political events in neighboring regions, notably the destruction of Athenian olive groves by Spartan forces during the Peloponnesian War (431–404 B.C.). Olive trees take many years to mature, and Athens would have been dependent on imported supplies for several decades. The Plain of Argos is geographically close to Attica and would have been well placed to supply that need. Thus the southern Argolid survey provides illustration of the intimate way in which rural fortunes may be linked to the politics of the wider world.

Clearly, most archaeological surveys can record only a sample of the sites in the survey area, even if the declared objective is to plot the position of every prehistoric settlement. Such has been the purpose of an ambitious survey of the Basin of Mexico, home of the Teotihuacán and Aztec civilizations of the past 2,000 years. The investigators have managed to chronicle the changing settlement patterns in the basin since long before Teotihuacán rose to prominence after A.D. 100 right up to the Spanish Conquest and beyond. But they would be the first to admit that they have recovered only a fraction of the basin's sites. For a start, most of the Aztec capital, Tenochtitlán, and its outlying suburbs lie under the foundations of Mexico City.

Sampling and Archaeological Survey

In the early days, archaeologists concentrated on conspicuous, easily found sites. Now, with so many sites endangered by all kinds of industrial development, they hurry to locate as many prehistoric locations as possible. Often, a survey is designed to make an inventory of archaeological sites in a specific area. When an area is to be deep-plowed or covered with houses, the burden of proof that archaeological sites do or do not exist in the endangered zone is the responsibility of the archaeologists. Time is often short and funds are very limited. The only way the archaeologists can estimate the extent of the site resource base is to survey selected areas in great detail, using formal sampling methods.

Sampling is the science of controlling and measuring the reliability of information through the theory of probability. Systematic and carefully controlled sampling of archaeological data is essential if we are to rely heavily, as we do, on statistical approaches in studying ancient adaptations to changing environmental conditions. Few modern archaeological surveys fail to make use of sampling, for many site distributions reflect the distribution of archaeologists rather than an unbiased sampling of the archaeological record. This bias applies particularly in vegetated areas like the eastern woodlands of North America, and the Mesoamerican and Amazonian rain forest, where the cover is so thick that even new roads are in danger of being overgrown within weeks. Sampling ensures a statistically reliable basis of archaeological data from which we can make generalizations about our research data. Such generalizations are often estimates of probability, which means they have to be based on unbiased data.

Sampling in archaeological survey typically can involve **element sampling**, where one selects arbitrary grid samples randomly over a large area. This is useful for estimating the densities of archaeological sites over a research area. Alternatively, **cluster sampling** governs a survey made up of arbitrary survey units defined by area, a sample of which are examined for inventories of archaeological remains. Any given sampling unit may contain a cluster of elements, a sample of sites, artifacts, or features, in which each sampling unit is a collection (cluster) of elements. Thus statistical population is made up of a number of clusters, each with a specific number of elements, which determine cluster size. This approach is useful when, for example, you want to examine the properties of individual sites, not of arbitrary units in a grid covering a research area. What is the proportion of sites in Mexico's Valley of Oaxaca, with seashells dating to 1000 B.C.? What is the average site area of settlements within the sampling area, and so on?

Formal sampling provides a means for generalizing from the sample survey areas to larger regions. The reliability of these vital generalizations is tested by routine statistical procedures. This approach to archaeological survey, often called *predictive modeling,* is a powerful weapon to counter the wholesale destruction of archaeological sites by industrial activity.

Archaeologists cannot stop the destruction of every threatened site. The best they can hope for is a chance to make decisions on which sites in the archaeological resource base are to be preserved, which will be excavated before destruction, and which will fall to destruction in the name of progress. More and more archaeology in North America is such cultural resource management, and results from efforts to conserve sites and to manage a diminishing resource base. CRM projects make intensive use of sampling surveys.

Remote Sensing

More and more archaeologists are relying on technology and elaborate instrumentation to help them discover the past. Many archaeologists are beginning to talk about *nondestructive archaeology,* the analysis of archaeological phenomena without excavations or collecting of artifacts, both of which destroy the archaeological record. The major methods in this approach are generally labeled **remote sensing.** These techniques include aerial photography, various magnetic prospecting methods, and side-scan radar.

Aerial Photography

The building of today's inventories of archaeological sites would never have been possible without aerial survey techniques. Aerial photography gives an overhead view of the past. Sites can be photographed from many directions, at different times of day, and at various seasons. Numerous sites that left almost no surface traces have been discovered by analyzing aerial photographs. Many earthworks and other complex structures have been leveled by plows or erosion, but their original layout shows up clearly from the air (Figure 7.3). The rising or setting sun can make large shadows, emphasizing the relief of almost vanished banks or ditches; the features of the site stand out in oblique light. Such phenomena are sometimes called *shadow sites.* I once had a chance to fly over southern England's chalk country two days after snow had mantled the rolling countryside. The ridges and hedgerows stood out sharply in the oblique light. So did the circular earthworks of Avebury, the standing stones casting long shadows in the chill winter sunlight.

In some areas, it is possible to detect differences in soil color and in the richness of crop growth on a particular soil. Such marks are hard to detect on the surface but often show up clearly from the air. The growth and color of a crop are greatly determined by the amount of moisture the plant can derive from the soil and subsoil. If the soil depth has been increased by digging features such as pits and ditches, later filled in, or because additional earth has been heaped up to form artificial banks or mounds, the crops growing over such abandoned structures are high and well nourished. The opposite is also true, where soil has been removed and the infertile soil is near the surface, or where impenetrable surfaces such as paved streets are below ground level and the crops grow less thickly. Thus a dark **crop mark** can be taken for a ditch or pit, and a lighter line may define a more substantial structure. Time and time again, I have walked over a plowed field with an aerial photograph and had great difficulty spotting the crop mark on the ground. But they are there if you look closely enough, photograph in hand.

Figure 7.3   A long-lost archaeological site revealed by dark crop marks.

Much of the world has been photographed from 24,000 feet (7,315 m) by military photographers. Such coverage has been put to use by archaeologists to survey remote areas such as the Virú Valley in Peru, where a team of archaeologists led by Gordon Willey plotted 315 sites on a master map of the valley. Many of the sites were stone buildings or agricultural terraces; others were refuse mounds that appeared as low hillocks on the photographs. By using aerial surveys, Willey saved days of survey time, for he was able to pinpoint many sites before going out in the field. When the settlements were visited, the fascinating story of shifting settlement patterns in Virú over thousands of years was made visible by a combination of foot survey and air photography.

Aerial remote-sensing devices of many types have become available in recent years to complement the valuable results of black-and-white photography. Infrared film, which has three layers sensitized to green, red, and infrared, detects reflected solar radiation at the near end of the electromagnetic spectrum, some of which is invisible to the naked eye. The different reflections from cultural and natural features are translated by the film into distinctive false colors. Vigorous grass growth on river plains shows up in bright red. Such red patterns have been used in the American Southwest to track shallow, subsurface water sources where springs were used by prehistoric peoples. The infrared data could lead the archaeologist to likely areas for previously undetected hunting camps and villages.

Aircraft and Satellite Imagery

In some areas, exuberant vegetation hampers archaeological surveys, especially in the Maya lowlands. For years, archaeologists have wondered how the Maya civilization managed to feed itself and have puzzled over the incompletely known distribution of its cities and ceremonial centers. Originally they believed the Maya population was supported by slash-and-burn cultivation, a *milpa* system still used today, in which people burn off and clear the forests, then cultivate the land for three or four years before leaving it fallow and moving on to virgin plots. The soils of the Maya lowlands, not particularly fertile, are vulnerable to soil erosion when cleared of vegetation and exposed to heavy rain. The Classic Maya population was far larger than such fields could support.

The best known source of aircraft-borne sensor imagery is Sideways-Looking Airborne Radar (SLAR), which senses the terrain on either side of an aircraft's path, with the instrumentation tracking the radar pulse lines in the form of images, whether or not clouds obscure the ground. A group of archaeologists, looking for a sensor system that would penetrate the dense forest cover of the Maya area, discovered an unexpected archaeological payoff in the imaging radar developed by NASA for spaceborne lunar sounders and in synthetic aperture radar. (The radar chosen for the Maya experiment was, in fact, developed for imaging the surface of the planet Venus.) On flights made over the Maya lowlands in 1978 and 1980, black-and-white and color infrared film were used to capture indications of archaeological sites and ancient landscape modifications. When the features discovered were plotted onto topographic maps, they revealed not only shadows of large mounds and buildings, but irregular grids of gray lines within swampy areas near known major sites. These lines were found to form ladder and lattice as well as curvilinear patterns, that very closely matched conventional aerial views of known canal systems in the Valley of Mexico and the lowlands. Ground surveys revealed that the Maya grew large food surpluses using large-scale swamp agriculture, developing field systems that are nearly invisible on the ground today.

Archaeology has even gone into space. **Satellite sensor imagery** is used for both military and environmental monitoring. The best known satellites are the LANDSAT series, which scan the earth with readers that detect the intensity of reflected light and infrared radiation from the earth's surface. The latest images pick up features only 90 feet (27 m) wide; the French SPOT satellites can work to within 60 feet (18 m). At a cost of up to $3,000 an image or even more, only the most well-heeled researchers can make free use of this revolutionary technology—and few archaeologists have access to that kind of money. The LANDSAT imagery offers an integrated view of a large region and is made up of light reflected from many components of the earth: soil, vegetation, topography, and so on. Computer-enhanced LANDSAT images can be used to construct environmental cover maps of large survey regions that are a superb backdrop for both aerial and ground reconnaissance for archaeological resources. These data are converted electronically into photographic images and mosaic maps, normally at a scale of about 1:1,000,000, too imprecise except for the most general of archaeological surveys. Aircraft and satellite scanner imagery will be more commonly used in archaeology, but the high cost will probably limit their application for the foreseeable future.

The space shuttle *Columbia* used an imaging radar system to bounce radar signals off the surfaces of the world's major deserts in 1981. This experiment was designed to study the history of the earth's aridity, not archaeology, but identified ancient river courses in the limestone bedrock 5 feet (1.5 m) or more below the Sahara Desert surface. All remote sensing is useless unless checked on the ground, so a team of geologists, including archaeologist C. Vance Haynes of the University of Arizona, journeyed far into the desert to investigate the long-hidden watercourses. About the only people to work this terrain were the World War II British Army and present-day Egyptian oil companies, the latter of which kindly arranged for a skip loader to be transported into the desert. To Haynes's astonishment, the skip-loader trenches yielded some 200,000-year-old stone axes, dramatic and unexpected proof that early Stone Age hunter-gatherers had lived in the heart of the Sahara when the landscape was more hospitable than today. The Haynes find is of cardinal importance, for African archaeologists now believe the Sahara was a vital catalyst in early human history that effectively sealed off archaic humans from the rest of the Old World. In later times, sub-Saharan Africa was isolated from the Mediterranean world until camel caravans opened up the desert in the first millennium A.D.

In a recent sensational discovery, LANDSAT satellite images and radar-based imagery helped NASA scientists identify virtually invisible 1,500- to 2,500-year-old tracks across the Rub al Khali, or "Empty Quarter" of the Arabian Peninsula. The ancient camel roads led archaeologists to the "lost city" of *Ubar*, once a major center of frankincense trade.

Geographic Information Systems

Radar imagery from space and other remote-sensing technologies are the high point of nonintrusive archaeology. They are at their best when combined with other remote-sensing data acquired from aerial photographs and such technologies as ground-pene-trating radar (see later, p. 134). Most remote-sensing methods rely on measuring the physical properties of the soil and anything on the surface. Optical satellite imagery and aerial photography measure reflections of light within the visible spectrum. Radar images do the same for the microwave portion of the electromagnetic spectrum, which is invisible to the human eye. Geographic Information Systems take all this data and provide integrated view of ancient landscapes.

Geographic Information Systems (GIS) are computer-aided systems for the collection, storage, retrieval, analysis, and presentation of spatial data of all kinds. GIS incorporates computer-aided mapping, computerized databases, and statistical packages, and is best thought of as a computer database with mapping capabilities. It also has the ability to generate new information based on the data within it.

GIS data comes from digitizing maps and from remote-sensing devices such as LANDSAT satellites, as well as manual entries on a computer keyboard. Sophisticated software packages allow the acquisition, processing, analysis, and presentation of data of many kinds. From the archaeological perspective, GIS has the advantage that it allows the manipulation of large amounts of data, especially useful for solving com-plex settlement analysis problems at places like the Roman towns of Pompeii, Italy, and *Wroxeter*, England (for Wroxeter, see Chapter 10). Satellites acquire environmen-tal and topographic information; the archaeological data can be added to the same database. Analyses that once took years can be done in minutes, even seconds. Now the archaeologist can examine, for example, the environmental potential of areas where no sites have been found to assess the overall distribution of sites within the environment.

GIS is fairly new to archaeology, and good examples of its application are still rare. Vincent Gaffney and Zoran Stancic used GIS for a regional survey of the island of Hvar off the Adriatic coast in the central Mediterranean. They created an environ-mental database for the island by covering it with a grid of 3.8 million 66-foot (20 m) units. Then they entered modern data on elevation, soils, geology, and microclimate. In the field, they visited and recorded every known archaeological site on the island from early farming villages to post-Roman settlements, entering the information into a computer database. They then combined this database with the GIS data for a series of studies on the extent of site territories, analysis of land use within the same territo-ries, and factors that affected site location. For instance, they were able to show that Roman villas were located near good agricultural soils (Figure 7.4). GIS also allows archaeologists to model different environmental scenarios and to study such problems as the ways in which different settlements controlled valuable land.

The Italian archaeologists responsible for Roman Pompeii, overwhelmed by an eruption of Vesuvius on August 24, A.D. 79, have used GIS technology to capture and interpret life in the town as it was 2,000 years ago, employing a computerized data-base of material excavated since 1862. They used an IBM computer to digitize archaeological maps and local terrain, to integrally link visual representations of the artifacts to both the detailed descriptions of each find from the city and to the loca-tions in which they were found. The thousands of computerized pictures of specific artifacts are linked to the maps to provide detailed insights into individual houses, rooms, and walls, the places where the finds were excavated. This "Neapolis" system with its 50 gigabytes of detailed information about Pompeii can be used to study such topics as the relationships between lifestyle and distribution of wealth, the spread of fashions and trends, or to correlate fresco motifs on house walls from one end of the

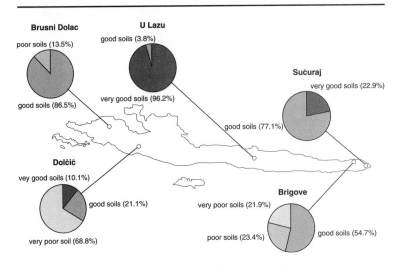

Figure 7.4   Roman sites on Hvar Island, Yugoslavia, with pie charts showing the proportions of soil types within catchment areas derived from GIS analysis.

town to the other. In this instance, GIS is used to understand relationships not readily perceived by the human mind, the myriad interconnections that tie works of art, buildings, and individual artifacts to an entire culture and community.

The most comprehensive North American GIS project is the National Archaeological Data Base, an on-line system that now contains over 100,000 records of archaeological reports. Any archaeologist with a telephone line or on an electronic mail system can now access this archive, which also provides comprehensive site distribution from many states and background environmental information through the Geographic Resources Analysis Support System (GRASS), the GIS system used by the National Park Service.

Assessing Archaeological Sites

Assessing the significance of an archaeological site without excavation has become increasingly important in recent years as the catastrophic damage done to the archaeological record hits crisis proportions. Thus surface recording and assessment, also subsurface detection methods, have assumed great importance.

Site assessment involves several processes:

- *Accurate mapping* of the site and recording its precise geographic location. It is not enough just to record a site on a map, even if this is a GIS record with background environmental data. Special forms are used to record location, unusual features, and information on surface features, landowner, and so on. The site is given a name and number, and any potential threats to the resource are noted. This form is the basis for an entry in any pertinent computer databases of archaeological sites.

- *Surface collection* of artifacts and other finds on the ground surface of the site.
- *Subsurface investigation using electronic detection methods.* These are used when the investigator suspects that significant features lie below the surface, both to acquire information and to form a basis for the research design.

Surface Collection

Controlled surface collection is a vital part of site assessment, for representative samples of artifacts from the modern ground surface can provide vital information on the age of the site and the various periods of occupation. For example, a pueblo site in the American Southwest might yield several forms of painted pottery, which, on the basis of stratigraphic observations elsewhere, can be placed in chronological order.

The same samples can sometimes be used to establish what activities took place on the site. A large sample of obsidian lumps and waste flakes might, for instance, be a clue that a quarry once flourished at the location. By plotting surface finds on a grid laid out over the site, the investigators can sometimes establish which areas of the site were most densely occupied and would be most productive for excavation. They may also reveal the presence of important structures below the surface.

Surface deposits can yield valuable information on artifact distributions and other phenomena lying underground. For this reason, surface collections form an important part of any archaeological survey, especially one that seeks to establish the limits of an ancient city, or different housing areas, such as was the case at Maya Copán or Roman Wroxeter.

Many archaeologists distrust surface collections, arguing that artifacts are easily destroyed on the surface and can be displaced from their original positions. But this viewpoint neglects a fundamental archaeological truth. *All* archaeological deposits, however deep, were once surface layers, subject to many of the same destructive processes as those outcropping on the surface today. In fact, with controlled surface collection involving random, or some other, sampling technique, present land surfaces can yield much valuable information on artifact distributions or other phenomena found underground, provided, of course, they have not been subjected to strip mining, deep plowing, or other catastrophic modifications.

With carefully controlled surface collection, and a clear understanding of the relationship between surface finds and those found below the ground, accurate site assessments are often possible. The large-scale survey of the hinterland of Copán relied heavily on surface collecting to identify sites large and small and to assess their significance (see Chapter 10).

Subsurface Detection Methods

All archaeologists dream of a new and revolutionary method that will enable them to find out what is underground without the labor of excavation! Thanks to radar and other electronic devices, modern technology shows promise of actually achieving this elusive goal. Ken Weeks and a team of fellow Egyptologists have embarked on a long-term project to map all of the royal tombs in Thebes's Valley of Kings. They have used a hot-air balloon, X rays, and sonic detectors to map subterranean features and hidden chambers in royal tombs. The team recently discovered a long-lost tomb with many subterranean chambers built for the sons of the great New Kingdom pharaoh Ramses II.

The excavations at the Maya village of Cerén in San Salvador offer an instructive example of a coordinated use of geophysical methods to locate subsurface features. The site was buried under up to 16 feet (5 m) of volcanic ash and was first located by a chance bulldozer cut. Obviously, it was not economical to bulldoze large areas, so Payson Sheets consulted a geophysicist, who recommended deploying a portable seismograph, a ground-penetrating radar, and a resistivity meter. The survey started with the seismograph, which records shock waves passing through the earth. Instead of the usual dynamite, Sheets struck a steel plate set in the soil with a hammer, recording the resulting waves with a set of 12 sensitive microphones. Buried hut floors conducted shock waves faster than the surrounding ash, and the seismograph did indeed locate some structures, but, designed as it was for detecting huge geological anomalies, the results were somewhat haphazard.

Next, he turned to **ground-penetrating radar**, using an instrument developed for studying **permafrost** melting along the Alaskan oil pipeline. To eliminate all background vibration, he enlisted the services of an oxcart. The oxcart driver simply drove slowly and steadily along a carefully marked straight line. The machine itself sent microwave energy deep into the soil and detected it as it was reflected back. The subsurface stratigraphy was recorded on special paper and revealed strong reflectors, some of which turned out to be the clay surfaces of hut floors covered by ash (Figure 7.5a). Using a drill rig, Sheets then tested some of the anomalies. Some were the result of eroded and redeposited volcanic ash. Others were large structures, but the radar was unable to detect smaller features, although it may be able to do so when the data is digitized and the original ground surface is mapped.

Finally, Sheets turned to a **resistivity survey** meter to measure the variations in the resistance (resistivity) of the ground to electric current. For instance, stone walls or hard pavement retain less dampness than a deep pit filled with soft earth or a silt-filled ditch. These differences can be measured accurately with a resistivity meter, which records the resistivity "contours" across a grid of squares laid out on the site. Sheets expected the Cerén house floors would conduct electricity better than the surrounding ash, for they are constructed of dense fired clay. His researchers recorded measurements along a grid over the site and fed the data into a laptop computer. The three-dimensional software revealed interesting double-peaked anomalies, which, when tested with a drill rig, turned out to be large prehistoric structures (Figure 7.5b).

Thus a combination of geophysical methods provided an effective and economic way to locate subsurface features at Cerén—at a fraction of the cost that would have been needed to bulldoze away acres of ashy overburden.

Nonintrusive archaeological survey is the most vital of all field research. Without adequate surveys and efforts at resource management, the future of archaeology in some parts of the world, especially North America and western Europe, would be in grave doubt. There simply would be nothing left to explore.

Summary

Archaeological fieldwork consists of finding, assessing, and excavating archaeological sites. Many sites come to light by accident during construction work or other modern activity, or as a result of natural phenomena such as earthquakes. Archaeological

(a)

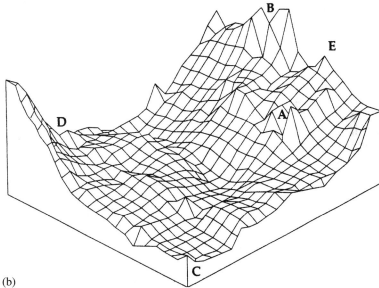

(b)

Figure 7.5   (a) Remote sensing at Cerén, San Salvador. Ground-penetrating radar slung behind an oxcart. (b) A three-dimensional computer plot of a resistivity survey at the Maya village at Cerén, San Salvador. The anomalies resulting from different electrical resistance show up as sharp peaks (A to E), of which A and B have been investigated and shown to be prehistoric structures.

surveys locate and record sites within specific areas, using carefully formulated research designs, remote-sensing techniques such as aerial photography or even satellite imagery, and, above all, observation on foot on the ground. Formal statistical sampling methods play an important role in survey work as a basis for estimating the site resource base in a specific region. They provide a statistically reliable basis of archaeological data for making generalizations about site distributions. Increasingly, archaeologists record sites with computer-aided mapping methods, known as Geographic Information Systems (GIS). GIS allows the researcher to manipulate large amounts of data during complex analyses of ancient settlement patterns using sites, also environmental and topographic data. Site assessment involves mapping, surface collection, and subsurface investigation with electronic devices like ground-penetrating radar and resistivity meters. Such approaches were highly successful at the Cerén Maya village in El Salvador, where volcanic ash mantles an entire farming settlement.

8

Excavation

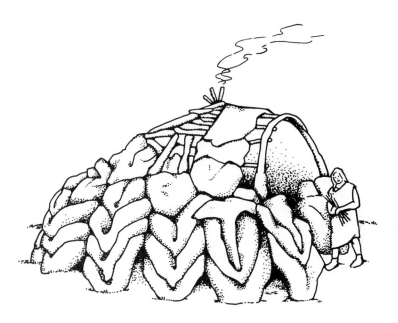

Reconstruction of a mammoth bone dwelling at Mezhirich, Ukraine, c. 18,000 years ago.

A mere hole in the ground, which of all sights is perhaps the least vivid and dramatic, is enough to grip their attention for hours at a time.

P.G. Wodehouse, *A Damsel in Distress* (1919)

We all have dreams of digging into a mysterious, undisturbed tomb. Then, suddenly, a sealed door. You break down the door and find yourself in an undisturbed, gold-strewn sepulcher that puts Tutankhamun's burial chamber to shame. But in reality modern archaeological excavation is a precise, slow-moving process, working with trowels and brushes, often without a spectacular find, from one day to the next. In this chapter we describe some of the basic principles of excavation and many excavation problems that archaeologists can encounter in the field. Realize, though, that each site presents distinctive challenges and requires modification of the basic principles enumerated here.

Planned Excavation: Research Design

The first principle of excavation is that digging is destructive. As archaeologist Kent Flannery once remarked, we are the only scientists who murder their informants (our sites) when we question them! The archaeological deposits so carefully examined during a dig are destroyed forever. Site contents are removed to a laboratory, permanently divorced from their context in time and space in the ground. And this is a radical difference from other disciplines: a chemist can readily recreate the conditions of a basic experiment, a biographer can return to the archives to reevaluate the complex events in a politician's life, but an archaeologist's archives are destroyed during the dig. All that remains from an excavation are the finds from the trenches, the unexcavated portions of the site, and the photographs, notes, and drawings that record the excavator's observations for posterity. One of the tragedies of archaeology is that much of the available archaeological data have been excavated under far from scientific conditions. Our archives of information are uneven at best. Increasingly, the ethics of archaeology research require absolutely minimal excavation consistent with acquiring essential scientific information.

The treasure hunter ravages a site in search of valuable finds and keeps no records. Archaeologists demolish sites as well, but with a difference: they create archives of archaeological information that document contexts for the objects they take back to the laboratory with them. Although they have destroyed the site forever, they have created a data bank of information in its place, the only archive their successors will be able to consult to check their results. Archaeologists have serious responsibilities: to record and interpret the significance of the layers, houses, food remains, and artifacts in their sites, and to publish the results for posterity. Without accurate records and meaningful publication of results, an excavation is useless. Many CRM investigations in North America are now funded under contracts that require prompt reporting, even if only for limited circulation.

A generation ago, an archaeologist's first inclination was to dig sites to solve problems. Nowadays, there is increased awareness that excavation destroys irreplaceable evidence of the past, and we dig only when we must. Anyone who excavates without serious attention to record keeping and all of the other processes of excavation is committing vandalism of an unforgivable kind.

At the core of every modern archaeological excavation lies a sound research design, a design that very often has a regional rather than a specific site focus (Chapter 3). The research design is developed to answer specific questions and to acquire maximum information with minimum disturbance of finite archaeological resources. It is, of course, a flexible, ever-changing plan, modified as hypotheses are tested, proved wrong, validated, or refined as a result of knowledge acquired in the ongoing excavation.

The design extends beyond the excavation itself. The end products of even a month's excavation on a moderately productive site are boxes upon boxes of potsherds, stone tools, animal bones, and other finds that have been cleaned, sorted, and bagged in the field. Rolls of drawings and stacks of computer disks hold valuable stratigraphic information. So do slides, photographs, and hundreds of pages of field notes compiled by excavation staff as the long days of toil continue. At the same time, radiocarbon and soil samples are collected for later analysis. Freshwater shells and charcoal fragments are packed for shipment to specialist investigators. It takes a minimum of six months to analyze the notes and finds from a month's excavation. The dozens of boxes, hundreds of notebook pages, and megabytes of computer data contain a vast array of data that must be collated to reconstruct what happened at the site. It follows, then, that the excavation research design is constantly reevaluated to determine the future course of the dig and to monitor the long months of analysis and interpretation that follow. The days when a site was dug simply because it "looked good" are long gone.

The organization of even a moderate-sized excavation requires careful planning at the implementation stage of the research design. One classic example of such planning comes from the Midwest. Illinois archaeologists James Brown and Stuart Struever spent many field seasons in the 1970s excavating the *Koster* site in the lower Illinois River Valley. Here, at least 12 human occupations are represented at one site, the earliest of which dates to before 5100 B.C. Koster is a deep site, probably abandoned before A.D. 1000 after generations of Indians had settled at this favorable locality. It offered Brown and Struever a unique opportunity to examine the changing cultures of the inhabitants over more than 6,000 years. But the organizational problems were enormous. Koster is more than 30 feet (9 m) deep, with each of the 12 cultural horizons separated from its neighbor by zones of sterile soil. Brown and Struever were fortunate in that they were able to treat each occupation level of this large site as an entirely separate digging operation.

The archaeologists had two options. One was to dig small test trenches and obtain samples of pottery and other finds from each stratigraphic level. But this approach, although cheaper and commonly used, was inadequate for the problems to be investigated at the Koster site. The excavators were interested in studying the origins of agriculture in the lower Illinois Valley. Brown and Struever therefore decided to excavate each living surface on a sufficiently large scale to study the activities that had taken place there. This procedure would enable them to examine minute economic changes. Thus the emphasis in the Koster excavations was on isolating the different settlement types that lay one on top of the other.

In developing the Koster research design, Brown and Struever needed to control a mass of complex variables that affected their data. They had to invent special procedures to ensure the statistical validity of their excavations. In order to acquire immediate feedback on the finds made during the excavations, they organized an elaborate data-processing system that sorted the animal bones, artifacts, vegetable remains, and other discoveries on location in the field. The tabulated information on each sorted find was then fed by remote access terminal to a computer many miles away. Within a few days, the excavators had instant access to the latest data from the dig. This system meant that overall research design could be modified while an excavation was still in progress (Figure 8.1).

The Koster site is a fine example of elaborate research design that uses complex computer technology. The dig employed dozens of people each field season. Most excavations operate on a far smaller scale, but the ultimate principles are the same: sound research design, very careful recording of all data, and scientifically controlled excavation. The Koster excavation was designed, like all good digs, to solve specific research problems formulated in the context of a sound research design.

Types Of Excavation

People commonly ask the same questions when they visit an excavation. How do you decide where to dig? What tools do you use? Why are your trenches in this shape? How deep do you excavate? Every site differs in its complexity and special problems, but here are some general principles.

You can decide where to dig on a site by the simple, arbitrary choice of a spot that has yielded a large number of surface finds or one where traces of stone walls or other ancient structures can be seen above ground. When Richard Daugherty dug the Ozette

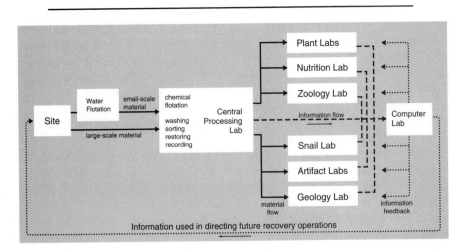

Figure 8.1　Organization of the Koster excavation.

site on the Washington coast, he began by digging through the place where the largest occupation sequence seemed to be. Why? He needed to obtain as complete a cultural sequence as possible. The logical way to do so was to dig through the deepest part of the site. There was, of course, no guarantee that his trench would penetrate to the earliest part of the whale hunters' site. But his choice was a practical way to start attacking the fundamental questions of when and for how long the whale hunters lived at Ozette. Similar decisions have been made at thousands of other sites all over the world.

Sampling

In these days of high digging costs, archaeologists rely more heavily on statistical sampling than their predecessors did. Sampling is used in digging shell heaps or dense accumulations of occupation debris containing thousands of artifacts. Obviously, only a small sample of a large garbage heap can be dug and analyzed. To ensure validity of the statistical samples, some form of unbiased sampling must be used to choose which part of a site is to be dug.

Sampling is the "science of controlling and measuring the reliability of information through the theory of probability." Sampling techniques allow us to ensure a statistically reliable basis of archaeological data from which we can make generalizations about our research data. Most archaeologists make use of **probabilistic sampling,** a means of relating small samples of data in mathematical ways to much larger **populations.** The classic example of this technique, commonly used in the disciplines of statistics and statistical theory, is the political opinion poll, testing national feelings from tiny samples, perhaps as few as 1,500 people. In archaeology, probabilistic sampling improves the likelihood that the conclusions reached from a survey or excavation on the basis of the samples are relatively reliable.

The use of formal sampling techniques in archaeology is still in its early stage. Simple **random sampling** is quite commonly used, for example, when an archaeologist wishes to obtain an unbiased sample of artifacts from an ancient shell mound. One can arrive at this result by laying out a rectangular grid of squares on a site and then selecting the squares to be dug by using a table of random numbers. The excavated samples are thus chosen at random, rather than on the basis of surface finds or other considerations.

Stratified sampling, whereby the investigator uses previous knowledge of an area, such as its topographic variation, to structure further research, enables one to sample some selected units intensively, others less thoroughly. Archaeological sampling, based as it is on descriptive and inferential statistics, is a complex subject. I urge you to consult the references at the back of this book.

Site Testing

In these days of subsurface radar technology and sophisticated geomorphological studies, site testing has become more sophisticated than it was even a few years ago. However, a number of testing approaches amplify such data or are used as stand-alone ways of deciding whether a site is worth further investigation or to establish its date, function, or type of occupation. Such methods are especially important on CRM projects.

Augurs and other forms of borers can be used to explore archaeological deposits, especially hydraulic corers, which provide column samples of subsurface layers and allow one to follow conspicuous or distinctive strata over considerable distances, even if they are buried far beneath the surface.

However, the **test pit** remains the most useful way of obtaining preliminary information on stratigraphy and culture history in advance of larger-scale excavation. Some test trenches are small control pits, dug carefully as a way of anticipating subsurface stratigraphy and occupation layers. Such excavations are reference points for planning an entire dig. More often, test pits are laid out in lines and over considerable distances to establish the extent of a site, basic stratigraphy in different areas. Sometimes their locations are selected by statistical means, at others on the basis of surface finds or exposed features. Kent Flannery once called such trenches "telephone booths," an apt description of small cuttings placed to acquire highly specific information.

Shovel pits are a variation on the test pit theme, usually used in surface survey to trace occupation deposits. They are little more than a small hole dug with a shovel a few inches below the surface.

Vertical Excavation

The layout of small digs is determined not only by surface features, density of surface finds, or sampling techniques, but by available funds as well. Most excavations are run on a shoestring, so small-scale operations have to be used to solve complex problems with minimal expenditure of time and money. Some of the world's most important sites have been excavated on a small scale by **vertical excavation,** digging limited areas for specific information on dating and stratigraphy (Figure 8.2). Vertical trenches can be used to obtain artifact samples, to establish sequences of ancient building construction or histories of complex earthworks, and to salvage sites threatened with destruction. The small trenches are often dug in areas where the deposits are likely to be of maximal thickness or where important structures may be found. Much vertical excavation consists of long cross sections cut across mounds, buildings, or other structures designed to establish their chronology and architectural sequence.

Vertical excavation comes into its own in small sites such as caves and rockshelters, where space is limited and the excavators have to cope with hidden boulders from ancient rock falls and other such obstructions. Sometimes the deposits spill out from the cave itself to the steep slope in front of the site, necessitating the use of a long, stepped vertical cutting, as was the case at the *Klasies River Cave* in South Africa, which records some of the earliest activities of *Homo sapiens sapiens* in tropical Africa. Vertical excavation is also important when investigating the banks and ditches of such sites as Roman forts or Iron Age encampments like Maiden Castle in Europe, and is widely used when investigating Adena and Hopewell burial mounds in North America.

Figure 8.2 Vertical excavation on a British Iron Age hill fort and its fortifications.

Area (or Horizontal) Excavation

Large-scale excavations are normally used to uncover wider areas of a site. These **horizontal,** or **area, excavations,** used to uncover house plans and settlement layouts, are expensive (Figure 8.3). As a general rule, the only sites that are completely excavated are very small hunter-gatherer camps, isolated structures, and burial mounds. With larger settlements, all one can do is excavate several portions of the site in order

Figure 8.3   Area excavation of an Iroquois longhouse near Onondaga, New York. The small stakes indicate positions of house wall posts; placement of hearth areas and support posts can be seen inside the walls. The Iroquois Nations dominated much of the North American Northeast in the centuries before Europeans arrived. Many settlements comprised close groupings of fortified longhouses.

to sample areas representative of the entire settlement. Again, modern archaeological ethics require minimal horizontal excavation consistent with the carefully controlled objectives of the investigation.

Area excavations expose large, open areas of ground to a depth of several feet. A complex network of walls, houses, or abandoned storage pits may lie within the site. Each of these ancient features relates to other structures, a relationship that must be carefully recorded if the site is to be interpreted correctly, as was the case at the Koster site. Horizontal excavation exposes large parts of a site, but the excavator is confronted with the problem of maintaining stratigraphic control from one side of the trench to the other. Many area excavations are organized on grid systems, which allow walls (often called balks) to be left between adjoining squares.

Horizontal excavation is highly effective with small hunter-gatherer sites, such as the artifact-and-bone scatters at Olduvai Gorge and other early human sites in East Africa, where the position of every stone flake and animal bone is recorded in place. Such an approach also works well with complex structures like Iroquois longhouses, which survive as complexes of decayed wooden postholes buried under a few inches of topsoil. Such structures were often expanded, rebuilt, or sited on top of another, resulting in a jigsaw of posthole patterns that can only be deciphered with a large area excavation. Perhaps the most remarkable horizontal excavations are those of historic gardens, among them King Henry VII's private garden at Hampton Court by the River

Thames in London. Archaeologist Brian Dix located long-vanished flower beds, paths, and other features with a huge area excavation that exposed the entire buried garden, which was then reconstructed for modern visitors.

Large open area excavations require accurate recording over considerable distances, made much easier when the position of houses and finds can be recorded with a **total data station**, an electronic distance measuring device with recording computer that records data which can be downloaded into laptop computers at the end of the day's work.

Any form of horizontal excavation is expensive, even if earthmoving machinery is used to remove sterile overburden, but it provides a unique overall, horizontal view of human occupation or entire human settlements obtainable in no other way.

There are numerous variations on the vertical and horizontal excavation theme, depending on the circumstances of the dig, the funding available, and the time available. In these days of tightly scheduled CRM excavations, a combination of excavation methods is used to acquire and record the maximum amount of information in the most cost-effective manner possible while maintaining high scientific standards. Some of the most complex excavations are conducted underground, such as those in London deep under high-rise buildings and in subway stations (Figure 8.4).

Figure 8.4   Excavations under a highrise building in the heart of the City of London show the complexities of modern urban archaelogy

Digging, Tools, and People

How do you do the digging? Much depends on the type of site you are excavating. A huge burial mound on the Ohio River may be more than 20 feet (6 m) deep. Much of the sterile deposit covering the burial levels is removed with earthmoving machinery, picks and shovels. But as soon as the archaeologists reach layers in which finds are expected, they dig with meticulous care, removing each layer in turn, recording the exact position of their finds upon discovery. Smaller caves or cemeteries are excavated centimeter by centimeter. The earth surrounding the finds is passed through fine screens so that tiny beads, fish bones, and myriad small items can be found.

Excavation is in part a recording process, and accuracy is essential. The records will never be precise unless the dig is kept tidy at all times. The trench walls must always be straight. Why? So you can record the layers you are digging and follow them across the site. Surplus soil is dumped well away from the trenches so it does not cascade into the dig or have to be shifted when new areas are opened. The excavation is a laboratory and should be treated as such.

All archaeological digs are headed by a director, who is responsible both for organizing the excavation and for overseeing the specialists and diggers. Many larger digs involve a team of specialist experts who work alongside the excavators. When digging the famous Late Bronze Age site of about 1100 B.C. at *Flag Fen* in eastern England, archaeologist Francis Pryor worked with a timber expert, a palynologist, soil scientists, experts on ancient metallurgy and mammal bones, even specialists in prehistoric beetles. The only way to study this complex site was to develop a team approach that looked at the site in a broad environmental setting. A really large excavation in Mesopotamia or Mesoamerica can involve dozens of people—specialist archaeologists, a team of resident experts in other fields including an architect, graduate student trainees, and volunteer or paid workers who do much of the actual excavation. In Chapter 14, we describe some of the ways in which you can obtain digging experience.

The traditional symbols of the archaeologist at work are the shovel and the triangular-bladed bricklayer's trowel. In fact, archaeologists use many digging tools in their work. Earthmoving machinery, once despised, has become a necessity in these days of high costs and rapid-moving CRM excavation driven by contractor's deadlines. In the hands of an expert operator, a front loader or bulldozer or backhoe with toothless bucket are remarkably delicate implements for removing sterile soil and surprisingly thin slivers of overburden. On occasion, earthmoving equipment has been used to excavate sites doomed in the face of road construction. The right piece of equipment is capable of removing even thin arbitrary levels of a site with soft deposits, which are then passed through screens to recover the artifacts in them. Meanwhile, the archaeologists focus on hand excavation of important features. The difference in scale is impressive, for a hand excavator only removes about 27 square feet (2.5 sq. m) of deposit a day, whereas a mechanical device in skilled hands can excavate as much as 530 cubic feet (15 cu. m) in the same time.

Despite widespread use of mechanical earthmovers, most excavation still proceeds by hand. Picks, shovels, and long-handled spades carry the brunt of the heavy work. But the most common archaeological tool used in North America is the diamond-shaped trowel with straight edges and a sharp tip. With it, soil can be eased from a delicate specimen or an unusual discoloration in the soil can be scraped clean. Trowels are used for tracing delicate layers in walls, clearing small pits, and other exacting jobs. They are rarely out of the digger's hand.

Household and paint brushes often come in handy, the former for soft, dry sediments and for cleaning trenches, the latter for freeing fragile objects from the soil. Even fine artists' brushes have their uses—cleaning beads, decaying ironwork, or fine bones. Enterprising archaeologists visit their dentists regularly, if only to obtain regular supplies of worn-out dental instruments, which make first-rate fine-digging tools! And so do 6-inch (15 cm) nails ground to different shapes. A set of fine screens for sifting soil for small finds, several notebooks and graph paper, tapes, plumb bobs, surveyors' levels, and a compass are just a few of the items that archaeologists need to record their excavations and process their finds. Increasingly, laptop computers and electronic recording equipment are part of the archaeologist's field kit because they provide fast, accurate ways of recording features, finds, and stratigraphy.

Recording

No dig is worth more than its records. The excavation notebooks provide a day-to-day record of each trench, of new layers and significant finds. Before any trench is measured out, the entire site is laid out on a grid of squares (Figure 8.5a). Important finds, or details of a house or a storage pit, are measured in on the site plan by simple three-dimensional measuring techniques or with an electronic recording instrument (Figure 8.5b). It is information from your records, as well as the artifacts from the dig, that form the priceless archive of your excavation. If the records are incomplete, the dig is little better than a treasure hunt.

Stratigraphic Observation

The laws of superposition and association lie at the very core of archaeology, for they provide the context of archaeological finds in time and space. The layers of archaeological sites, be they natural or humanly formed, form much quicker than geological levels, but they are still subject to the same law of superposition. Thus the excavated stratigraphic profiles through an archaeological site represent a sequence of layers that have formed through time. Stratigraphic observation is the process of recording, studying, and evaluating stratified layers in archaeological sites, layers that were deposited horizontally, but are studied in the vertical (time) dimension.

Stratigraphic observation involves not only recording the layers, but confirming that they do, in fact, represent a sequence in time. Many factors can disturb stratified layers. For instance, rabbits can burrow through soft earth, or later occupants of a house dig into underlying layers to construct storage pits, build foundations, or even bury the dead. This is where the law of association comes in, for the artifacts associated with stratified, undisturbed archaeological layers can then be placed in a relative chronology, and, if radiocarbon samples are dated from one or more layers, perhaps in an absolute one as well (Figure 8.6). Thus accurate stratigraphic observation is the cornerstone of all excavation, for it provides the context for the studies of artifacts and human behavior that are the central goals of all excavation.

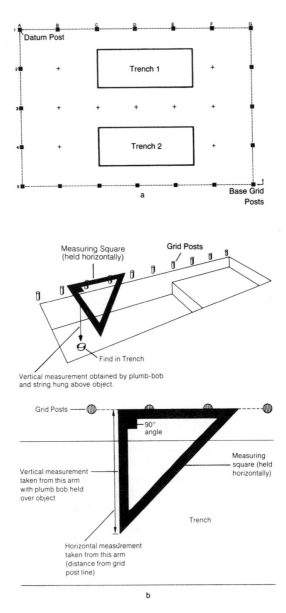

Figure 8.5 (a) Two trenches laid out with a grid. (b) Three-dimensional recording of the position of an object using the grid squares.

Reading a stratigraphic profile is an art, for you have not only to record the layers, but to interpret them as well, taking account both of the natural formation processes as well as of human activities. This means watching for the subtle color changes resulting from the decay of adobe brick on pueblo sites, the thin lines of

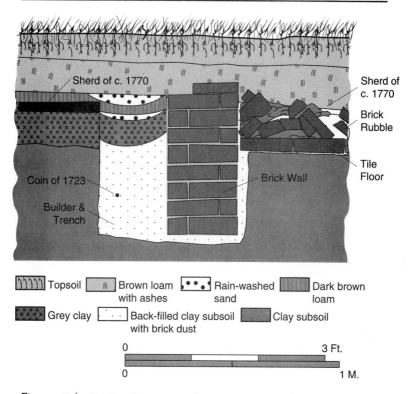

Figure 8.6 Dating the construction and the destruction of a building at Colonial Williamsburg by its associated artifacts. Judging from the coin of A.D. 1723, the builder's trench for the stone wall was dug no earlier than 1723, and the building fell into ruin before 1820.

hearths used for a short time, whose edges have spilled down a slight slope, and the loosely packed outline of a rabbit burrow used and abandoned many centuries ago. Often the changes are so subtle that they appear only as a slight color change or a minute difference in the texture of the soil. Only patience results in an accurate interpretation of a stratigraphic profile—looking at the trench wall in different lights, at dawn, or in the oblique light of evening, wetting down dry strata with a fine water spray, even looking at the wall from below. All these tricks and many others help you interpret complex stratigraphic jigsaw puzzles, even on small sites.

Let us now turn from general principles to some specific excavation problems that will give you an insight into the multitude of challenges awaiting fieldworkers. As we indicated in Chapter 3, archaeological sites, in all shapes and sizes, are the basis for all field investigations. All contain traces of human activity, in the form of artifacts, structures, and food remains. Archaeologists most commonly classify sites by their functions, that is to say, by the activities that took place within them. It is no coincidence that these various site categories present different excavation problems.

Excavation Problems

Open Campsites and Villages

Small sites, often little more than scatters of artifacts, that were once places where specific tasks were performed, are probably the most common archaeological sites. However, the most obvious and most interesting locations are habitation sites, places where people have lived and carried out many activities. Hunter-gatherers have occupied temporary camps for short periods since the earliest millennia of prehistory. Where preservation conditions are good, archaeologists can sometimes identify such settlements, represented by concentrations of stone artifacts and broken animal bones, as well as the stone foundations of long-abandoned brush shelters. Such concentrations have been found in the Great Basin of the American West, in the arctic North, and also in sub-Saharan Africa.

Many hunter-gatherer camps are hard to identify from the surviving archaeological record (Figure 8.7). The same is not true of later farming villages, which were usually occupied longer, resulting in the accumulation of considerable quantities of occupation debris as well as substantial house foundations. In about 7800 B.C., the inhabitants of the Abu Hureyra village in Syria's Euphrates Valley dwelt in a tiny settlement of square, mudbrick houses with courtyards, separated by narrow alleyways. The house foundations and numerous animal bones, as well as other artifacts, enabled excavator Andrew Moore to trace the extent and nature of the settlement. Iroquois farmers in the northeastern United States built substantial wood and bark longhouses, which were occupied over several generations and constantly modified (Figure 8.3). The decayed postholes from the walls provide an excellent record of Iroquois dwellings, often clustered in close juxtaposition in palisaded settlements.

Caves and Rockshelters

Cave people, complete with clubs, long hair, and brutish manners, are one of the popular stereotypes of newspaper cartoonists. Caves and convenient rocky overhangs did indeed serve as human dwellings from very early times, but were by no means the only home bases used by hunter-gatherers. The Stone Age Cro-Magnon people of southwestern France, famous for their rock art, occupied great rockshelters and caves in the deep river valleys of the Dordogne during the late Ice Age, between about 32,000 and 12,000 years ago. The *Danger* and *Hogup* caves in Utah reflect thousands of years of hunter-gatherer occupation. The dry environment of the desert preserved wood objects and basketry as well as minute details of economic life. And the dry caves of Tehuacán Valley in south-central Mexico provide a unique history of how maize cultivation developed in the New World (Chapter 10).

Cave and rockshelter excavations are some of the hardest digs to carry out successfully. The ground below cliff overhangs usually consists of ash and other debris piled up through successive human occupations. Sterile soils may interrupt this sequence of habitation, representing periods when the site was abandoned. Excavating such complicated sequences is slow and meticulous work. The trenches are usually restricted by the size of the shelter. Each hearth and small occupation layer has to be isolated from the others during excavation.

Figure 8.7   Site FxJj50, Koobi Fora, an early hominid site in the East Turkana area of northern Kenya, where human artifacts and animal bones date to about 2.3 million years ago.

Many cave and rockshelter excavations deal purely with dating and stratigraphy, but others are more ambitious. When Hallam Movius dug the *Abri Pataud* rockshelter in southwestern France, he had to record at least six layers of human occupation dated to between 40,000 and 19,000 years ago, extending through more than 20 feet (6 m) of stratified deposit. The site was excavated following a coordinated master plan that involved not only archaeologists but botanists, geologists, and other specialists as well. Movius was able to record minute changes in tool types as well as many details of the changing hunting and gathering practices of Abri Pataud's inhabitants.

Mound Sites

Occupation mounds (often called **tells** in the Near East) are common in many parts of the world. Mound sites result when the same site is occupied for centuries, even thousands of years. Successive generations lived atop their predecessors' settlements. The result is a gradual accumulation of occupation debris, which, when excavated, provides a complicated picture of occupation levels. Even a small mound can cost a fortune to excavate, simply because the lowest levels are so deeply buried below the surface. A huge mound such as that of Ur in Mesopotamia, or even a relatively small mound like *Tepe Yahya* in Iran, can be sampled only by large trenches that cut into the sides of the mound in a series of great steps, or by very large-scale excavation indeed, using a combination of vertical and area trenches (Figure 8.8).

Figure 8.8   Tepe Yahya, Iran, a typical Near Eastern city mound, or tell. The stepped trenches of the excavation can be seen in the slope of the mound. Tepe Yahya is famous as a center of international trade in fine soapstone vessels that traveled as far as India and Mesopotamian cities.

There is far more to excavating an occupation mound than merely stripping off successive layers. So many natural and artificial processes, ranging from wind erosion to human activity, can change the stratigraphy of a site of this type that each presents a challenging new excavation problem.

Burial mounds such as those used by Bronze Age people in Britain or the Hopewell folk of eastern North America present complex excavation problems, often requiring total excavation. In many cases, the mounds were built in stages or the dead were buried in them at different times, long after the identity of the original occupants was forgotten. A generation ago, such mounds were often excavated completely, exposing the ancient land surface. Today, very carefully placed vertical trenches are most commonly used, with excavation being used only to answer specific questions. For example, at *Easton Down* near Avebury in England, archaeologist Alisdair Whittle excavated part of a communal burial mound to acquire pollen and mollusk samples that showed the mound had been erected on open grassland.

Earthworks and Forts

Many peoples—Iron Age peasants in western Europe, Maori warriors in New Zealand, Hopewell Indians in Ohio—built extensive earth fortifications to protect their settlements and sacred places. The Ohio earthworks enclose large areas of ground, but no one knows exactly why such earthworks were undertaken. To excavate them would require both vertical excavation to record cross sections across the earthworks, and area investigation to uncover the layout of the structures built inside the earthworks. Such excavations were indeed carried out on the great prehistoric fortress

Figure 8.9   The Iron Age hill fort at Maiden Castle, Dorset, England; its extensive earthworks were excavated by Mortimer Wheeler.

at Maiden Castle, England, many years ago. The massive earthworks of Maiden Castle were stormed by a Roman legion in A.D. 43. By careful excavation and use of historical data, the excavator Mortimer Wheeler was able to provide a blow-by-blow description of the battle for the fortress (Figure 8.9):

> For a space, confusion and massacre dominated the scene. Men and women, young and old, were savagely cut down, before the legionaries were called to heel and the work of systematic destruction began. . . . That night when the fires of the legion shone out (we may imagine, in orderly lines across the valley), the survivors crept forth from their broken stronghold, and in the darkness buried their dead. (1943:310).

Shell Middens

Shell **middens**—vast accumulations of abandoned shells, fish bones, and other food remains—are common in many coastal areas of the world. Remarkable results can be attained by studying these dense heaps, especially in reconstructing prehistoric diets (Chapter 9). The excavation problem is twofold: first, to identify the stratified levels in the middens, and second, to obtain statistically reliable samples of food remains and artifacts from the deposits. Most shell midden digs use random sampling, described very briefly earlier, which employs vertical trenches or test pits. Some midden excavations unfold on a larger scale. We illustrate an example of an area excavation on a shell midden at *Galatea Bay* in New Zealand (Figure 8.10), where much information on ancient diet was found by using a carefully laid-out grid of trenches. The excavation of a shell midden is mostly rather unspectacular, for the detailed statistical results come from laboratory analysis of artifacts rather than from actual digging. The Galatea Bay excavation provided detailed information on the

Figure 8.10 An exemplary area excavation of a shallow shell midden at Galatea Bay, New Zealand. This site was occupied in the second millennium A.D.

ways the inhabitants utilized different communities of shellfish, such as oysters of various sizes, through time.

Ceremonial and Other Specialist Sites

Some of the world's most famous archaeological sites are ceremonial centers, such as the pyramids of Giza in Egypt or the Maya ceremonial center at Copán, Honduras. Many ceremonial sites are enormous, and, like occupation mounds, present great difficulties for the excavator. Teotihuacán in the Valley of Mexico is, of course, far more than a ceremonial center (see Figure 11.3). It was a great city as well, which flourished from 200 B.C. to as late as A.D. 750. Discovering the true significance of the site has involved not only extensive area excavation designed to help reconstruct pyramids and major buildings, but sophisticated mapping and surface survey combined with small-scale excavation. René Millon and other archaeologists have mapped more than 12.5 square miles (32 sq. km) of Teotihuacán in a survey program combined with excavation. Years of fieldwork have shown the founders of the great city laid it out on a grid pattern that was followed or centuries. The Pyramids of the Sun and Moon were the original focus of the city, until an unknown but charismatic leader built a palace complex, marketplace, and temple to the Feathered Serpent god Quetzalcoatl in the so-called Cuidadela complex some distance away.

The Acropolis complex at Copán provided an extraordinary challenge to a team of American and Honduran excavators (see Figure 3.4). Fortunately for science, the Copán River had exposed the layers of the temple complex. The diggers were able to tunnel into the center of the sacred buildings in an attempt to decipher the history of successive temples built at the same sacred location. No less than 2 miles (3.2 km) of tunnels now burrow under the Acropolis. Tunneling offers a unique three-dimensional view of a building's history, aided in the case of Copán by deciphered Maya glyphs that record the history of the city's ruling dynasty. The excavators have managed to link individual temples buried in the heart of the Acropolis to different rulers between about A.D. 400 and 800.

Artifact patternings play a vital role in interpreting ceremonial centers, trading sites, quarries, and other specialized sites. Do these patterns reflect long-distance trading activity in, say, copper ornaments or seashells? Are marine stingray spines, which are present in ruins appearing to be shrines built hundreds of miles inland, artifacts of great religious significance in Mexico? Questions like these can be answered only by careful studies of spatial associations.

Burials and Cemeteries

The golden mask of the pharaoh Tutankhamun, the refrigerated bodies of Siberian horsemen and women from the Russian permafrost, dessicated mummies of humble folk from northern Chile: human burials are the stereotypic finds of archaeology, reflecting humanity's abiding concern with the afterlife. The earliest human burials were left by Neanderthal peoples more than 70,000 years ago. Most human societies have paid careful attention to funerals and burials ever since. Burials were deposited with simple or elaborate grave furniture designed to accompany its owner to the afterlife. People have buried their dead in isolated, shallow graves within their settlement, under hut floors, in special cemeteries, in caves, as cremated remains in jars, and in vast burial mounds. Some burials consist of the body alone; others lie with a few beads or a handful of clay pots (Figure 8.11). Royal personages were often buried in all their glory: Shang kings in China with their chariots; the rulers of early Ur, Mesopotamia, with their entire court; Maya nobles with their prize treasures; the *Moche* lords of Sipán in Peru in their full golden regalia.

By studying a group of burials from one cemetery, it may be possible to distinguish different social classes by the grave furniture buried with the remains. The common people may take nothing with them; merchants or priests may be buried with distinctive artifacts associated with their status in society. The *Adena* and Hopewell peoples of North America were much concerned with the afterlife during their heyday 2,000 years ago. From the distribution of the burials and cemeteries in their burial mounds, and from the cult objects and ornaments associated with the skeletons, it may be possible to gain some insights into the social organization of Adena and Hopewell societies (Chapter 12). And, of course, burials are a fruitful source of information on personal ornamentation and appearance, too, for people were (and still are) often buried in the clothes and ornaments they wore in life. The physical characteristics of the skeletons themselves can provide valuable data on age, nutrition, sex, disease, and medicine.

French archaeologists led by Françoise Dunand have excavated more than 700 skeletons from a cemetery at *Duch*, a remote Egyptian village in the Libyan Desert west of the Nile River occupied between 100 B.C. and A.D. 400. At least 5,000 people lived in the village during its heyday. The inhabitants of this obscure settlement are better known medically today than they were in their lifetimes. The excavators

Figure 8.11 A Classic Maya communal tomb at Gualan in the Motagua Valley, Guatemala.

cleaned the skeletons in place, then X-rayed them with a portable machine hooked up to an on-site generator. They developed a clinical description of each body and took samples of hair, nails, and skin before placing them in well-protected tombs. This field research gave an extraordinary portrait of the Duch people. They were of Mediterranean physical type, slender and between 5 feet 4 inches and 5 foot 1 inch (1.62 to 1.54 m) tall. They had pale skin and dark hair like many ancient Egyptians and an average life span of about 38 years if they survived infancy. Many of them suffered from osteoarthritis and scoliosis as a result of hard agricultural labor and carrying heavy loads. More than two thirds of the skeletons showed clear signs of malnutrition at some point in their lives. Human skeletons and mummies are the dispassionate medical records of the past that reveal the consequences of years of inadequate diet and backbreaking work.

How do you excavate a burial? Whether digging a large cemetery or a lone burial, each skeleton and its associated grave, ornaments, and grave goods are considered a single excavation problem. Each burial is exposed as a unit that has both internal associations with its accompanying goods and external associations with other burials in the same and other levels. The first step is to identify the grave, either by locating a gravestone or a pile of stones, or from the grave outlines, which may appear as a discoloration in the surrounding soil. Once the grave outlines have been found, individual bones are exposed. The main outline of the burial is traced first. Then you uncover the fingers, toes, and other small bones. You leave the bones in place and take care not to displace any ornaments or grave furniture associated with them. Once the skeleton is exposed and fully cleaned where it lies, the layout of the burial and grave furniture is recorded by drawings and photographs before the skeleton is lifted bone by bone or encased in a cocoon of plaster of paris and metal strips (Figure 8.11).

Reburial and Repatriation

Burial excavation may seem very romantic. In reality it is not only technically demanding, but raises important ethical questions as well. For years, archaeologists casually dug up Indian burials and other prehistoric graves all over the world, some of them even of people of known tribal or historical identity. Now both Australian Aborigines and Native Americans, among others, are objecting strenuously to excavation and destruction of ancient burial grounds—and with good reason. Why should their ancestors be dug up and displayed in museums, they argue. Many surviving communities retain strong emotional and religious ties with their ancestors, and excavation of their remains flies in the face of their religious beliefs. There are now demands for reburial of human remains stored in museums, especially of those that can be documented to have direct historical links with modern Native American groups.

The Native American Grave Protection and Repatriation Act (NAGPRA) of 1990 establishes two main requirements. First, all federal agencies and museums receiving federal funds are required to inventory their holdings of Native American human remains and associated funerary objects. They must also develop written summaries for religious objects not found in graves, sacred artifacts, and what are called "objects of cultural patrimony" that are in the collections they control. This inventorying process, which will take years to complete, also requires that agencies and museums establish, as best they can, whether their individual holdings have cultural affiliation, or, in the case of skeletons, lineal descendants with living Native American groups. If they do establish such relationships, they are required to notify the relevant Native American organization about the existence of the materials and to offer to repatriate them.

The second requirement protects all Native American graves and other cultural objects found within archaeological sites on federal and tribal land. This requirement encourages the in situ preservation of archaeological sites, or at least those parts of them that contain graves. It also requires anyone carrying out archaeological investigation on federal and tribal lands to consult with affiliated or potentially affiliated Native Americans concerning the treatment and disposition of any finds, whether made during formal investigations or by accident.

NAGPRA is having a profound effect on the way in which American archaeologists go about their business, for it mandates a level of consultation and concern for Native American rights that is far greater than has been the norm in the United States. This is quite apart from the scientific impact on the study of ancient Native American populations. The Native American Rights Fund estimates that as many as 600,000 Native American human skeletons may be in museums, historical societies, universities, and private collections.

The signing of the 1990 act came after years of controversy that pitted, and still pits, Native Americans against scientists. The archaeologists and anthropologists point out that revolutionary new research techniques are beginning to yield a mine of new information about prehistoric North Americans. To rebury the database for such research would deprive science, and future generations of Americans, of a vital resource, they argue. Others, including some archaeologists, respond that this is an ethical and moral issue, and such considerations should outweigh any potential scientific gains.The Native Americans feel deeply about repatriation for many complex reasons, if nothing else because they are concerned about preserving old traditions and values as a way of addressing current social ills.

Furious controversy sometimes surrounds newly discovered burials, like the recent case of a 9,000-year-old skeleton unearthed at Kennewick, Washington, where local Native American groups claimed ownership. This claim pitted them against the Bureau of Land Management, and the case is still in the courts, with no easy resolution in sight.

There will be no quick resolution of the repatriation issue, however promptly and sensitively archaeologists and their institutions respond to Native American concerns and comply with the provisions of the 1990 act. Only one thing is certain—no archaeologist in North America, and probably elsewhere, will be able to excavate a prehistoric or historic burial without the most careful and sensitive preparation. This involves working closely with native peoples in ways that archaeologists have not imagined until recently. Nothing but good can come of this.

Summary

The process of archaeological research, including excavation, begins with the formulation of a comprehensive research design. The design is then implemented; data are acquired in the field through survey or excavation and then processed and analyzed in the laboratory. Interpretation using anthropological and historical models is followed by final publication. The research design is developed to answer specific questions and to acquire the maximum information with minimal disturbance of the finite archaeological record. Excavation itself is a meticulous process of recording both finds and their context in time and space. Vertical and test excavations are used to test and study stratigraphic sequences. Horizontal excavations uncover large areas of a site, for example, an entire Iroquois longhouse. Stratigraphic recording is based on the principle of superposition, with care being taken to distinguish natural and humanly caused disturbances, such as animal burrows or garbage pits. The chapter reviews the distinctive excavation problems associated with various types of archaeological sites, among them habitations, caves and rockshelters, burials, and shell middens. Special problems surround human burials, which, in North America, are subject to stringent regulations surrounding their reburial and repatriation.

9

Analyzing the Past: Technology

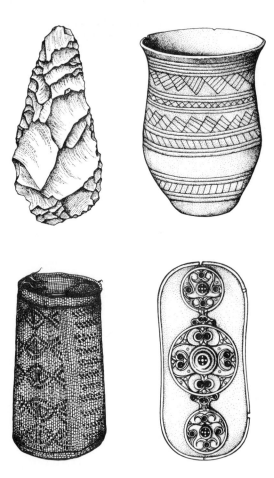

From left top clockwise: Acheulian Hand Axe, British Bronze Age Beaker, Celtic Shield, North American Basket.

Order is Heav'n's first law.

Alexander Pope, *An Essay on Man*

Fresh air, modest (sometimes hectic) exercise, the potential of spectacular discoveries, a constant stream of challenging stratigraphic problems—nearly all archaeologists enjoy excavation or survey work most of all. They dread the moment of truth when they return to base with truckloads of stone tools or potsherds and confront an uncomfortable reality: most of the work still lies ahead and much of it is the routine work of sorting and artifact classification. I vividly remember once returning from the field with a 3-ton truckload of potsherds and animal bones from a densely occupied African village. We piled dozens of cartons in a corner of the laboratory. As I looked over the pile, I suddenly realized that I would hardly see the open air for months!

For all its wearing routine, the classification of artifacts and the study of ancient technology, discussed in this chapter, is both challenging and fascinating.

Back from the Field

Archaeologists spend much more time in their laboratories than they do excavating and surveying. They must, for the finds from even a brief excavation can take months to sort, clean, label, classify, and analyze. The field crew returns from the dig with truckloads of boxes and bags of unsorted stone tools, pot fragments, broken animal bones, and other finds. Cartons contain precious human skeletons and rows of radiocarbon and soil samples for specialists to examine. It can take some days simply to organize these piles of boxes in the laboratory before the real work begins. Then, once the tables are clear, the long work starts of describing and ordering all of the finds from the dig.

The laboratory crew—on academic projects, usually graduate students and undergraduates working under supervision; on CRM, usually professional employees—begins by sorting all of the finds into very broad categories. They send soil and radiocarbon samples off to experts. They separate animal bones, seeds, and other food remains from manufactured artifacts and hand them over to those members of the team who are skilled in identifying such finds. The researchers sort the manufactured artifacts into broad classes, separating pot fragments from stone implements, metal tools from shell beads, and so on. They check the labeling of every bag and box. Properly marked containers must specify the three-dimensional unit of space and time in which the materials were found, often recorded with bar codes (see Figure 8.5). Only then is everything ready for basic classification and ordering of the manufactured artifacts. In this chapter we describe some of the ways in which archaeologists tackle these complex tasks.

Classification, Taxonomy, and Systematics

Our attitude toward life and our surroundings involves constantly classifying and sorting massive quantities of data. We classify types of eating utensils: knives, forks, and spoons; each type has a different use and has a separate compartment in the kitchen drawer. We group roads according to their surface, finish, and size. A station wagon is classified separately from a truck. As we classify artifacts, lifestyles, and cultures, we make choices among them. Most Westerners eat rice with a fork, but the Chinese and other Asian people use chopsticks, and still others have decided a spoon is more suitable for that purpose. There are myriad choices. Cultural usage rather than functional pragmatism often dictates the final decision.

Everyone "classifies" because doing so is a requirement for abstract thought and language. Archaeological classification is something quite different, for classification is used as a research tool. All classifications used by archaeologists follow directly from the problems they are studying. Let us say that a researcher is studying changes in pottery designs over a 500-year period in the Southwest. The classification he or she uses will follow not only from what other people have done, but also from the problems being studied. How, and even what, archaeologists classify stems directly from the research questions they ask about the data.

Taxonomy is a system for classifying materials, objects, and phenomena used in many sciences, including archaeology. The taxonomies of biology, botany, geology, and some other disciplines are highly sophisticated and often very rigid systems that were created in the nineteenth century and early in the twentieth. Many are now dated by today's sophisticated standards. In contrast, archaeology has built its own taxonomy of specialist terminologies and concepts, often along cultural lines. British archaeologists often refer to "cultures," North American scholars to "phases" (see p. 176), and the French to "civilizations." Each term has basically the same meaning, but the subtle differences stem from diverse cultural traditions and from field situations.

Systematics is essentially a way of creating units that can be used to categorize things as a basis for explaining archaeological or other phenomena. It is a means for creating units of classification within a scientific discipline. Biologists classify human beings within a hierarchy of classification constructed by Carl Linnaeus in the eighteenth century. They group human beings in the *kingdom* Animalia, in a classificatory hierarchy that passes through the *class* Mammalia, ending with the *subspecies Homo sapiens sapiens*. This biological classification consists of empirically defined units, each precisely described and related to the others. Archaeologists use systematics in much the same way, but their classifications are closely related to the problem being studied.

The Objectives Of Classification

As we have stated, classification in archaeology depends on the problem being studied, but it has four fundamental objectives:

1. *Organizing data into manageable units.* This step is part of the preliminary data-processing operation, and it commonly involves separating finds on the basis of raw material (stone, bone, and so on) or separating artifacts from food remains. This preliminary ordering allows much more detailed classification later on.
2. *Describing types.* By identifying the individual features (attributes) of hundreds of artifacts or clusters of artifacts, the archaeologist can group them by common attributes into relatively few types. These types represent patterns of separated associa-

tions of attributes. Such types are economical ways of describing large numbers of artifacts. Which attributes are chosen depends on the purpose of the typology.

Artifact types (sometimes called archaeological types) are based on criteria set up by archaeologists as a convenient way of studying ancient tool kits and technology. They are a useful scientific device that provides a manageable way of classifying small and large collections of prehistoric tools and the by-products from manufacturing them.

3. *Identifying relationships between types.* Describing types provides a hierarchy that orders the relationships between artifacts. The relationships stem, in part, from the use of a variety of raw materials, manufacturing techniques, and functions.

These three objectives are used a great deal in culture-historical research (see Chapter 13). Processual archaeologists may use classification for a fourth objective:

4. *Studying assemblage variability in the archaeological record.* These studies are often combined with middle-range research on dynamic, living cultural systems (see Chapter 4).

Typology

Typology is a system of archaeological classification based on the construction of types. It is a search for structure among either objects or the variables that define these objects, a search that has taken on added meaning and complexity as archaeologists have begun to use computer technology and sophisticated statistical methods.

Originally, archaeological typology involved dividing up objects and variables arbitrarily. I remember sitting in a Cambridge archaeological laboratory many years ago and learning the basics of stone tool classification. Our instructor laid out a series of Acheulian hand axes in front of us, magnificent specimens from the gravels of the Thames River (see Figure 4.3). He divided them into different categories. "These are pointed axes, these ovates (oval-shaped), these ovates with twisted edges, these linguate, with tongue-shaped ends," he declared. One of us pointed out that some of the axes in the pointed category were far from ideal examples of the form; in fact, one or two were distinctly oval. "They are pointed hand axes," pronounced our instructor firmly, brooking no disagreement. The arbitrariness of his classifications was just like that used by a stamp collector classifying postage stamps. It was as if prehistoric hand axes were all standardized productions turned out by an impersonal stone flaking machine. We lost the opportunity to examine the underlying patterns of human design and behavior, which is what interests archaeologists more than mere classification.

Typology enables archaeologists to construct objectively defined units of analysis that apply to two or more samples of artifacts, so these samples can be compared objectively. These samples can come from different sites, or from separate levels of the same site. Typology is classification to permit comparison.

Archaeological Classification

As we have emphasized, archaeological classification is the ordering of data according to shared characteristics. But how do archaeologists go about this organizing?

Typology is based on the archaeologist's "concept of types," a subject of great controversy in archaeology. On a formal level, a **type** can be defined as a group or class of items that is internally cohesive and separated from other groups by one or more discontinuities. Most now argue that types are identified by combinations of attributes that distinguish and isolate one artifact type from another. In the final analysis, the idea is to organize data in such a way as to reveal continuities and breaks between groups of artifacts that display internal cohesion and are isolated from other such groups.

Attributes are the physical characteristics used to distinguish one artifact from another. As archaeologists work out their typologies, they find themselves examining hundreds of individual fragments, each of which bears several distinctive attributes (Figure 9.1). Every commonplace artifact we use has such attributes. The familiar glass beer mug has a curved handle that extends from near the lip to the base, often fluted sides, a straight, rounded rim, and dimensions that are set by the amount of beer it is intended to contain. It is manufactured of clear, relatively thick glass (the thickness can be defined by precise measurement). You can find numerous attributes on any human artifact, be it a diamond ring or a prehistoric pot. For example, a collection of 50 potsherds lying on a laboratory table may bear black painted designs; 8 have red panels on the neck, 10 are shallow bowls, and so on. An individual potsherd may come from a vessel made of bright red clay that was mixed with powdered seashells so the clay would fire better. It may come from a pot with a thick rim made by applying a rolled circle of clay before firing, and a crisscross design cut into the wet clay with a sharp knife during manufacture. Each of the many individual features is an attribute, most of which are obvious enough. Only a critically selected few of these attributes, however, will be used in classifying the artifacts. (If all were used, then no classification would be possible: each artifact would be an individual object identified by an infinite number of attributes.) Thus the archaeologist works with only those attributes considered most appropriate for the classificatory task at hand.

A number of broad groups of attributes are in common use:

- *Formal attributes* are features such as the shape of the artifact, its measurable dimensions, and its components. Normally, they are fairly obvious.
- *Stylistic attributes* include decorations, color, surface finish, and so on.
- *Technological attributes* are those covering the material used to make an artifact and the way it was made.

The selection of attributes and the entire process of archaeological classification involves many hours in the laboratory, working with large numbers of artifacts that are laid out on tables and examined individually. Today the archaeologist relies heavily on quantitative methods for both describing and comparing artifacts, and for recording and manipulating attribute data. A discussion of these approaches lies beyond the scope of this short book. Attribute-based classifications of artifacts are based on large numbers of attributes, selected by the classifier and usually coded on a computer. Statistical typologies are often derived from attribute clusters, the archaeologist using statistically derived attribute clusters as a way of dividing artifact collections into categories. This approach gives researchers an insight into the most important artifact clusters; however, many different criteria can affect such clustering. For example, a classification of bronze swords based on blade dimensions results in a

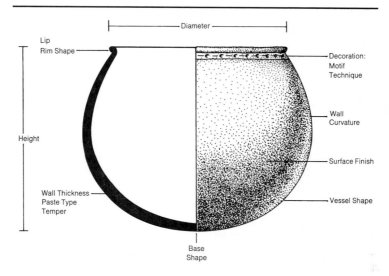

Figure 9.1 Some common attributes of a clay vessel. Specific attributes that could be listed for this pot are concave shoulder, dot and drag decoration, mica temper, round base, and thickness of wall at base.

very different clustering from one based on the sources and composition of the copper and tin used to fabricate them. Other quantitative approaches, outside the scope of this book, work with entire artifacts. They calculate the similarities between all possible pairs of objects in a collection to produce hierarchies of different artifact clusters.

In the final analysis, quantitative methods enable archaeologists to organize artifact data in intelligent, efficient, and replicable ways, allowing them to discern possible patterns that relate to past human behavior. These same techniques also allow them to evaluate the reliability of their inferences objectively and to make inferences about the interrelationships between different variables in attribute counts. As such, they are an invaluable aid to artifact classification.

Archaeological Types

All of us have feelings and reactions about any artifact, whether it is a magnificent wood helmet from the Pacific Northwest coast (Figure 9.2), or a simple acorn pounder from the southern California interior. Our immediate instinct is to look at and classify these and other prehistoric artifacts from our own cultural standpoint. That is, of course, what prehistoric peoples did as well. The owners of the tools that archaeologists study classified them into groups for themselves, each one having a definite role in their society. We assign different roles in eating to a knife, fork, and spoon. Knives cut meat; steak knives are used in eating steaks. The prehistoric arrowhead is employed in the chase; one type of missile head is used to hunt deer, another to shoot birds, and so on. The use of an artifact may be determined not only by convenience and practical considerations, but by custom or regulation. The light-barbed spearheads used by some Australian hunting bands to catch fish are too fragile for dispatching kangaroo; with the special barbs, an impaled fish can be lifted out of the water. Women made baskets and pots in most African and American Indian societies, which have division of labor by sex; each has formed complicated customs, regulations, and taboos, which, functional considerations apart, categorize baskets and pots into different types with varying uses and rules in the culture (Figure 9.3).

Furthermore, each society has its own conception of what an artifact should look like. Until recently, Americans have generally preferred larger cars, Europeans smaller ones. These preferences reflected pragmatic considerations of road width and longer distances in the New World, and also differing attitudes toward traveling. Many Americans still think their car is a reflection of prestige and social standing. To these people, style changes, aluminum wheel designs, turbos, and other niceties are important. But we all think a car should have a color-coordinated interior to look "right." The steering wheel is on the left, and it is equipped with turn signals and seat belts by law. In other words, we know what we want and expect an automobile to look like, even though minor design details change as do the length of women's skirts and the width of men's ties.

Figure 9.2 Tlingit carved wood helmet from the Northwest coast, classified as a **natural type** when found in an archaeological context. This artifact would obviously be classified as a helmet from the perspective of our cultural experience. The Tlingit subsisted off foraging, sea mammal hunting, and fishing, and enjoyed one of the most complex hunter-gatherer societies on earth. (Height, 9 inches; width, 10 inches [23 cm, 25 cm].)

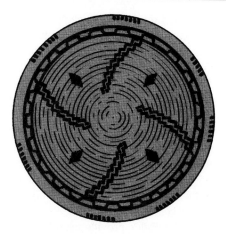

Figure 9.3   This Chumash parching tray is a good example of the difficulties of archaeological classification. This finely made basket was produced by the Chumash Indians of southern California by weaving plant fibers. The design was formed in the maker's mind by several factors, most important of which is the tremendous reservoir of learned cultural experience that the Chumash have acquired, generation by generation, through the several thousand years they lived in southern California. The designs of their baskets are learned, and relate to the feeling that such and such a form and color are "correct" and traditionally acceptable. But there are more pragmatic and complex reasons, too, including the flat, circular shape that enables the user to roast seeds by tossing them with red embers. Each attribute of the basket has a good reason for its presence—whether traditional, innovative, functional, or imposed by the technology used to make it. The band of decoration around the rim is a feature of the Chumash decorative tradition and occurs on most of their baskets. It has a rich red-brown color from the species of reed used to make it. The steplike decoration was dictated by the sewing and weaving techniques, but the diamond pattern is unique and the innovative stamp of one weaver, which might or might not be adopted by other craftspeople in later generations. The problem for the archaeologist is to measure the variations in human artifacts and to establish the causes behind the directions of change, and to find what these variations can be used to measure. This fine parching tray is a warning that variations in human artifacts are both complex and subtle.

The Chumash hunter-gatherers occupied the Santa Barbara Channel region of southern California. So bountiful was the local terrestrial and marine environment that they were able to live in permanent villages, some housing as many as 1,000 people. They were ruled by chiefs and enjoyed a complex ritual and social life.

Archaeologists have a different problem. They have to devise archaeological types that are appropriate to the research problems they are tackling, an extremely difficult task. In archaeology, a type is a grouping of artifacts created for comparison with other groups. This grouping may or may not coincide with the actual tool types designated by the original makers.

A good example comes from the world-famous Olduvai Gorge site in East Africa, where Louis and Mary Leakey excavated a series of cache sites used by very early humans, *Homo habilis*. Mary Leakey studied the stone tools and grouped them in the *"Oldowan tradition,"* a tradition characterized by jagged-edged chopping tools and flakes. Her classifications were based on close examination of the artifacts, and the idea that the first human tool kit was based on crude stone choppers soon became archaeological dogma (Figure 9.10b). Recently, Nicholas Toth of Indiana University has taken a radically different approach to classifying Oldowan artifacts. He has spent many hours not only studying and classifying the original artifacts, but also learning Oldowan technology for himself, fabricating hundreds of artifacts identical to those made by *Homo habilis* nearly two million years ago. His controlled experiments have shown that *Homo habilis* was not using chopping tools at all. The primeval stone workers were more interested in the sharp-edged flakes they knocked off lumps of lava for cutting and butchering the game meat they scavenged from predator kills. The "chopping tools" were, in fact, just the end product of knocking flakes off convenient lumps of lava and not artifacts at all.

Controlled experiments like Toth's provide useful insights into how prehistoric peoples thought of the raw materials they used, and how they used them to manufacture the tools they needed. Toth and other experts are now trying to study the telltale patterns of edge wear on the cutting edges of Oldowan flakes; the scars left by working fresh bone as opposed to hide or wood, for example, are highly distinctive. With controlled experimentation and careful examination of edge wear, they hope to achieve a closer marriage between the ways in which the first humans used stone tools and the classifications devised by the archaeologist hundreds of thousands of years later.

Everyone agrees that types are clusters of attributes or clusters of objects. Although patterns of attributes may be fairly easy to identify, how do archaeologists know what is a type and what is not? Controversy surrounds this issue. Should they try to reproduce the categories of pot that the makers themselves conceived? Or should they just go ahead and create "archaeological" types designed purely for analytical purposes?

The archaeologist constructs typologies based on the recurrence of formal patterns of physical features of artifacts. Many of these formal types have restricted distributions in space and time, which suggests they represent distinctive "styles" of construction and/or tasks that were carried out in the culture to which they belong. For example, the so-called Chavín art style was widespread over much of northern highland Peru between 900 and 200 B.C. The characteristic jaguar, snake, and human forms of this art are highly characteristic and were copied over a wide area. Chavín art, and the characteristic styles associated with it, had a specific role in Peruvian society of the time (Figure 9.4). Archaeologists tend to use four "types of types" (descriptive, chronological, functional, and stylistic), which we describe briefly here; in practice they are rarely separated one from another, for experts tend to draw this kind of information from more general classifications of artifacts.

Descriptive types are the most elementary descriptions, based solely on the form of the artifact—physical or external properties. The descriptive type is used even when the use or cultural significance of the object or practice is known. For example, the excavations at Snaketown in Arizona revealed a "large basin-like depression," a mysterious feature that also turned up at other *Hohokam* sites in the Southwest. This descriptive type was subsequently proven to be a ball court, and so the noncommittal

Figure 9.4 A Chavín carving on a pillar in the temple interior at Chavín de Huantar, Peru. This reconstruction makes the temple walls seem more regular and the background more open than they actually were. The distinctive motifs exhibit the style of Chavín art spread throughout highland and coastal Peru, marking an interval termed the Chavín "horizon" that cuts across many local sequences.

descriptive classification was abandoned in favor of a functional one that defined the structure's role in Hohokam culture.

Descriptive types are commonly used for artifacts from early prehistory, when functional interpretations are much harder to reach (Figure 9.5). For instance, the famous prehistoric stone circles found throughout Britain are usually classified as just that, because we have no idea what their purpose was, except for a general impression that they had a ritual and symbolic function.

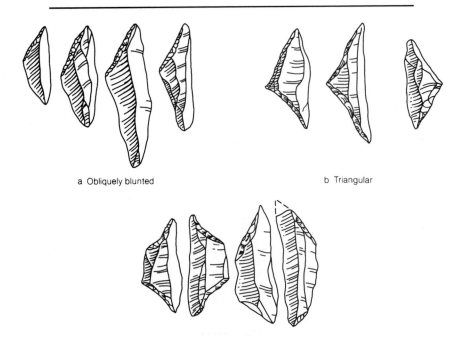

a Obliquely blunted   b Triangular

Figure 9.5 Ten-thousand-year-old **Mesolithic** artifacts from Star Carr, England (shown actual size). You can classify these as follows: *Descriptive type,* geometric stone tools; *Chronological type,* Mesolithic microliths (from the Greek "small stone"), Star Carr forms; *Functional type,* microlithic arrowhead barbs.

Chronological types are defined by form, but are time markers. They are types with chronological significance. Like descriptive types, they are part of a culture's inventory as reflected in the archaeological record, but are widely used to distinguish chronological differences. For example, on the Great Plains of North America, *Clovis* and *Folsom* points were used for short periods of prehistoric time, the former in about 10,950 B.C. and somewhat earlier. Projectile points have long been used as chronological markers in North American archaeology. Pottery is probably the most common form of chronological type, for the clay, decoration, and so on, change, and are shown to be significant historical indexes.

Chronological types are defined in terms of attributes that do show change over time. When the archaeologist compares artifacts known to be of different ages, certain attributes are observed to be different, so he or she uses them to define the types. Chronological types figure prominently in southwestern archaeology, and were used by Alfred Kidder in his classic excavations at *Pecos,* New Mexico, in the 1920s.

Functional types are based on cultural use or role rather than on outward form or chronological position. The same artifacts can be treated as functional or descriptive types. You can classify an assemblage in broad categories: "wood," "bone," "stone," and so on. But a functional classification can be adopted equally as well: "weapons," "clothing," "food preparation," and so on.

Ideally, functional types should reflect the precise roles and functional classifications made by the members of the society from which they came. Needless to say, such an objective is virtually impossible to achieve because of incomplete preservation and lack of written records. Many artifacts—for example, the polished stone ax, the bow and arrow, or the atlatl, the prehistoric throwing stick—were in use for thousands of years, indeed right into modern times. In many cases like these, it is easy to tell what an artifact was used for. However, we have no means of visualizing the complex roles that some artifacts played in prehistoric society or of establishing the restrictions placed on their use by the society (Figure 9.6). The famous "Venus" female figurines made by Stone Age hunter-gatherers in Europe about 25,000 years ago have often been assumed to be part of an elaborate fertility cult, but, in fact, we have no means of knowing what functional and symbolic role they played in these societies (see Figure 12.6).

Stylistic types are best exemplified by items such as dress, because style is often used to convey information by displaying it in public. The Aztecs of central Mexico lived in a ranked society where everyone's dress was carefully regulated by sumptuary laws (regulations governing dress codes) (Figure 9.7). Thus a glance at the noble in the marketplace could reveal not only his rank but the number of prisoners he had taken in battle and many other subtle facts. Even the gods had their own regalia and costumes that reflected their roles in the pantheon.

Stylistic types can be expected, theoretically at any rate, to have a structure entirely different from that of functional ones. As such, they are not used often in archaeological classification, except when historical records are available. The approach is much debated.

What do Assemblages and Artifact Patternings Mean?

For generations, archaeologists studying culture history classified artifacts into assemblages, associations of tools that were thought to be contemporary. This approach assumed that human culture had evolved through the millennia. Thus artifact assemblages were merely traces of contemporary cultural "species" that extended far back into prehistory. This "organic" view of culture history saw assemblages of artifacts as distinct categories, like organic species, which did not modify their form from one context to the next. The organic approach assumed that a specific cultural tradition leads to only one characteristic type of industry in the archaeological record, an industry circumscribed in time and space. The organic view of the past is a highly organized scheme, rather like the medieval "chain of being" in early biology, where every living thing had its place in the general scheme of things.

American archaeologists have generally preferred a more "cultural" perspective, making considerable use of data on artifacts and other culture traits known to have been used by living societies in North America. The observation of these data has shown a strong correlation between the distributions of distinctive cultural forms and different environments. For example, plank houses and an elaborate canoe technology are characteristic of the peoples of the Pacific Northwest coast, where readily split cedar and other trees flourished in abundance. In contrast, desert peoples in the Great Basin lived in much more transitory settlements of brush shelters and houses using a

PASTE

Tempering Grit, diameters ranging from − 0.5 to 2.0 mm. The appearance and composition (quartz, mica, and a little feldspar) suggest that the tempering material is a decomposed granite.

Texture Medium to coarse.

Hardness 3.0–4.0.

Color Tan to dark gray; exterior surfaces often heavily carboned.

FORM

Overall shape Jars with collared rims, constricted necks, rounded shoulders, and rounded bottoms.

Lip Rounded, occasionally thickened by the addition of a small bracing fillet on the exterior surface.

Rim All the rims are collared. The collars range from 24 to 55 mm. in height. Interior and exterior profiles are more or less parallel to each other, forming a straight or concave plane which extends downward and outward from the lip. The lower edge of the collar is marked by a fairly abrupt shoulder which forms the junction between the collar and the low curved neck. The bottom of the collar is sometimes scalloped. Below the neck, the vessel wall turns outward toward the shoulder. These rims might be contrasted with the rims of the Foreman types by describing them as Z-rims rather than S-rims, since the surface is flat or concave rather than convex.

Neck A relatively low, constricted zone below the shoulder of the rim.

Shoulder Rounded.

Base Rounded.

HANDLES One sherd has a short tablike lug extending down from the lower edge of the collar in the same plane as the face of the collar itself. Two others have fractured areas which seem to indicate the presence of loop handles running from the base of the rim collar to the shoulder of the vessel.

SURFACE FINISH Bodies simple stamped, some with extensive plain areas. The stamping on one of the restored vessels is vertical. Necks are plain or brushed vertically; interior surfaces are plain.

DECORATION The decoration is confined to the rim and lip. It is preponderantly cord impressed. Patterns consist of a series of horizontal lines, or a series of interlocking triangles filled alternately with horizontal and diagonal cord impressions. The cord-impressed zone is sometimes bordered by a series of punctations. Two pieces were decorated with diagonal broad-trailed lines, and one was plain except for a series of punctations at the base of the rim.

REMARKS A number of the pieces assigned to Colombe Collared Rim at the Phillips Ranch site show a considerable similarity to some Lower Loup sherds from Nebraska. The most striking difference is in the incised decoration on the Nebraska pieces and the predominantly cord-impressed decoration on the Phillips Ranch rims.

FROM: D. J. Lehmer, *Archaeological Investigations in the Oahe Dam Area, South Dakota, 1950–51*, Bureau of American Ethnology, Bulletin 158, 1954.

Figure 9.6 An archaeologist's type description of a pottery type from South Dakota, "Colombe Collared Rim." This description appears exactly as it was published in 1954 by D. J. Lehmer. This example illustrates the detail required for type description. (Do not be dismayed if you do not understand some of the technical terms used; they are irrelevant to the main discussion of types in this text.)

Figure 9.7   Aztec warriors wearing elaborate uniforms signifying different ranks, awarded according to the number of captives taken in battle. From the Aztec document known as the Codex Mendoza.

highly portable tool kit that was adapted to a mobile desert lifeway. It is all very well to say that such correlations were true of historic times, but what about earlier prehistory? Can we say that artifact assemblages from the Great Basin dating to 5,000 years ago reflect similar adaptations, similar social groups? Were conditions different in the past from today—can modern artifact patternings be used as a basis for interpreting ancient behavior?

Some archaeologists, among them Lewis Binford, have attacked this problem by studying living hunter-gatherer societies. Binford spent time among the Nunamiut caribou hunters of northern Alaska. There he learned that the only way to understand a living society's subsistence and material culture is to conceive of all of their sites as part of a larger system. The Nunamiut had residential sites and other kinds of sites used for specialized purposes. Thus, he argued, archaeologists have to identify the specific function of each site they examine, then fit the sites into a much larger, overall pattern of land use.

Archaeology's basic unit is the site; the artifacts in it are part of an assemblage pattern that reveals the different activities which took place there. If archaeologists want to understand the dynamics of cultural systems like that of the Nunamiut in the past, they have to study and interpret prehistoric living conditions, using such classificatory devices as typology, tool frequencies, and the relationships between tool debris and finished artifacts, as just some of their methods of doing so. Thus the role of classification in archaeology is shifting away from "organic" viewpoints that see artifacts and cultures as finite in time and space, to new means of problem-oriented classification that concentrate not only on individual tools, but on entire assemblages and their patternings.

However, the data for interpreting these patterns must finally come from sources other than stone tools or potsherds. In other words, classification alone is meaningless unless the classifications are interpreted in terms of other data. And here is where the study of contemporary societies—middle-range research—is coming into its own (Chapter 4). Artifact classifications are still carried out for the most part with approaches meant for reconstructing culture history, formulations of time and space that owed much to functional classifications of artifacts based on common sense. At the same time, however, new explanatory frameworks based on theories of cultural evolution are providing new explanations of the past. They are designed to account for the structure and change that everyone can see in the archaeological record of the ages, phenomena that are far more dynamic and ever-changing than implied by the more rigid classifications of earlier scholars.

Robert Dunnell and other theorists have pointed out that these new explanatory frameworks render it unimportant when a new element in human culture such as, say, the plow, was invented or first appeared. What matters is how and why it becomes accepted and visible in the archaeological record. The challenge for the archaeologist is to devise new methods for classifying artifacts that enable us to identify processes of cultural evolution in the archaeological record. Research into this most fundamental of problems is still in its infancy.

Units Of Ordering

Recall from Chapter 6 that an assemblage is the diverse group of artifacts found together that reflects the shared activities of a community. This assemblage was found in a single site. Recall, too, that the site is the fundamental **unit** for all stratigraphic studies in archaeology. Units of ordering are universal in archaeology, but there are significant differences between those used in the Americas and the Old World, which are glossed over here for space reasons. For example, Old World archaeologists refer to components as "industries" and to phases as "cultures." In general, Americanist terms are emphasized here (Figure 9.8).

Components and Phases

Many archaeological sites, such as the Olsen-Chubbuck site in Colorado, consist of a single assemblage of artifacts and a single component—another **archaeological unit.** A **component** is a physically bounded portion of a site that contains a distinct assemblage, which serves to distinguish the culture of the inhabitants of a particular level. Sites that were occupied many times, like Hogup Cave in Utah, visited repeatedly over a period of more than 9,000 years, contain many components, each of them distinguished by assemblages that separate them in time and space from other components at the same site. The social equivalent of the archaeologist's component is the community.

Once the research team's analysis is completed, they may find they have only one component to deal with. If the site was occupied several times, they might have two or

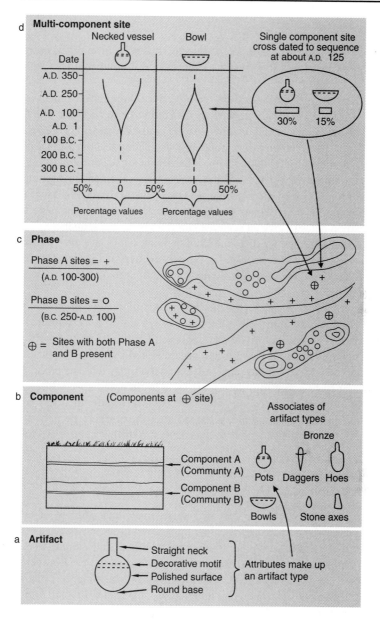

Figure 9.8 Archaeological units in use. (a) Patterns of attributes form an artifact type. (b) Cross section through a hypothetical archaeological site with two stratified components. The two components are radiocarbon dated to between 250 B.C. and A.D. 100 and between A.D. 100 and 350, respectively. Our artifact type is a diagnostic vessel in Component A, the later one. The total artifact content from the site is the assemblage. (c) Now the archaeologists have studied dozens of sites in their archaeological region, which consists of an estuary with an offshore island. Higher ground with pine forest overlooks the estuary. When they plotted site distributions, they found that the earlier, Phase B sites were distributed on the higher ground, and the later components were established near the shore where shellfish were abundant. Only three sites contain both components, stratified one above the other. The two distributions are distinctive, both phases defined in space and time, forming a local sequence. (d) At the four 2-component sites, the archaeologists seriated the pottery types and other artifacts and obtained distinctive battleship curves. Then they were able to fit other sites into the same sequence by cross-dating.

three. How do they compare these components with those from other, nearby sites? And how do they develop a sequence of occupation levels and cultures for their local area?

When all of the artifact collections from the local area have been analyzed and classified to everyone's satisfaction, they are ordered in space and time with the aid of stratigraphic observations, seriation, cross-dating, and radiocarbon or tree-ring dates. In Chapter 5, we described both seriation and cross-dating techniques that place artifacts in chronological order with the help of battleship curves and dated components. Figure 5.3 shows how the Tehuacán Valley archaeologists joined ten sites into a local sequence, a chronological ordering built up from several multicomponent sites and some single-component settlements within the area. They were also able to obtain some radiocarbon dates to give an accurate chronology for the sequence.

When the team studied the distribution of their sites, they discovered that two different dated components were repeated at settlements over a considerable area. These were so well dated and precisely distributed in time that two phases in the sequence could be identified.

A **phase** is a cultural unit represented by like components on different sites or at different levels of the same site, although always within a well-defined chronological bracket. The characteristic assemblage of artifacts of the phase may be found over hundreds of miles within the area covered by a local sequence. Many Old World archaeologists use the term **culture** in the same sense as phase. Both are concepts designed to assist in ordering artifacts in time and space. Phases or cultures usually are named after a key site where characteristic artifacts are found. The *Acheulian* culture, for example, is named after the northern French town of St. Acheul, where the stone hand axes so characteristic of this culture are found (see Figure 4.3).

Larger Archaeological Units

After many seasons' work, the research team may have studied several local sequences and may be able to describe their finds in a wide context such as that of the dozens of local sequences within the southwestern United States. Some characteristic art styles or artifacts, such as the Chavín art that flourished in Peru between 900 and 200 B.C., spread over considerable distances, perhaps representing the popularity of a new set of religious beliefs, which originated at Chavín de Huantar in the Andes mountain foothills (Figure 9.4).

Archaeologists sometimes use the term **horizon** to cover such phenomena, where a number of phases in neighboring areas contain rather general cultural patterns in common. The term **tradition** describes a lasting artifact type, assemblages of tools, architectural styles, economic practices, or art styles that last much longer than one phase or even the duration of a horizon. A single toolmaking tradition may continue in use while the many cultures that share it develop in entirely different ways. A good example of a tradition is the so-called paleoarctic tradition of Alaska that originated at least as early as 8500 B.C. and lasted for several thousand years. Perhaps the most renowned larger archaeological units are those identified by the Danish archaeologist Christian Jurgensen Thomsen in 1807. His Stone Age, Bronze Age, and Iron Age technological labels are still in wide use.

Ancient Technologies

The artifacts that people have manufactured throughout their long history have enabled them to augment their limbs and extend their use of the environment. The technological achievements of humanity over the past two-and-a-half million years have been both impressive and terrifying. Today, we can land an astronaut on the moon, transplant human hearts, and build sophisticated computers. Yet, in the final analysis, our contemporary technologies have evolved in a direct, albeit branching, way from the first simple tools made by the earliest human beings. These evolving, and sometimes very durable, technologies have survived in the archaeological record and provide one of the primary sources of information on the past.

Stone, bone, clay, fiber, metal, shell, textiles, skin, hair, and hide, and also wood were the main raw materials used by our forebears. Of these, metal ores require smelting, a technology that came into use in southwestern Asia about 5,000 years ago, and in the Americas within the past 2,000 years. Bone, fiber, and inorganic materials like hide do not survive well, so it is no coincidence that stone and fired clay have attracted the most archaeological interest and provide the foundation for classification of many prehistoric cultures.

Unfortunately, space precludes us from discussing all of these important technologies here. Bone tools, for example, were often made by cutting bone and antler into long strips with stone tools, then fashioning these blanks into spear points and harpoons. Some astonishing wood artifacts have survived under waterlogged conditions (Figure 4.7), not only finished artifacts but the waste products. Specialists have been able to identify the timbers used, even the complete woodworking techniques, and also the methods used to conserve forests and make hedges. For more information on these technologies, also basketry and textiles, see the Guide to Further Reading at the end of this book (Figure 9.9). Here we focus on the most durable and most commonly studied tool kits.

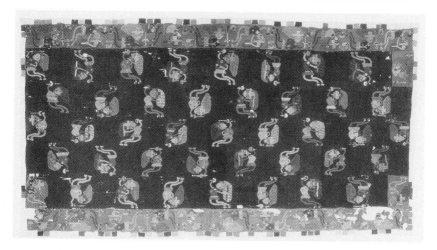

Figure 9.9   Cotton funerary textile from the Paracas Peninsula, Peru, dating to c. 300 B.C.

Stone

Stone tools were the earliest artifacts, little more than simple sharp-edged flakes struck off lava lumps by the simple expedient of knocking one stone against another. Over the ensuring millennia, people exploited almost every possibility afforded by rocks suitable for making tools of all kinds—axes, borers, choppers, knives, scrapers, and delicate spearheads. The manufacture of stone tools is a **reductive, or subtractive, technology,** for stone is acquired, then shaped by removing flakes until the desired form is achieved. Their making depends on the property of **conchoidal fracture,** characteristic of many crystalline rocks such as flint or obsidian. Such stone breaks in a predictable way when struck vertically, producing characteristic fracture patterns and cores or flakes, which allow an archaeologist to identify the rock as humanly modified, and as an artifact (Figure 9.10).

For millennia, people did little more than fracture rock with another stone. Eventually, they began making tools flakes on both sides, like the Acheulian hand ax

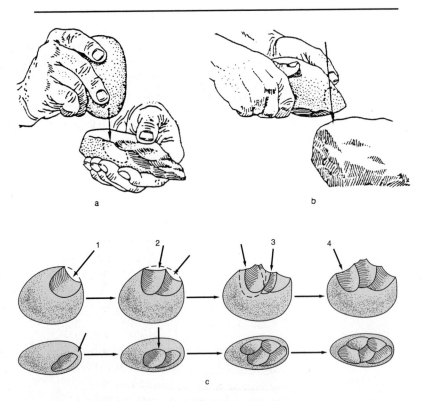

a

b

c

Figure 9.10   The earliest stoneworking techniques: (a) Using a hammerstone. (b) A variant on the hammerstone, striking a core against a stone block, the so-called anvil technique. (c) The earliest stone tools were made by a simple method. The top row shows the side view: First, two flakes were struck off (1 and 2); second, the stone was turned over, and two more flakes were removed (3); third, a fifth flake completed the useful life of the core (4). The bottom row shows the process from above.

(Figure 4.3), eventually turning to bone, a softer hammer, to make thinner and better finished tools. After about 100,000 years ago, *Homo sapiens sapiens* used more sophisticated technologies that produced specialized artifacts such as spear points and scrapers designed for specific purposes. These technologies culminated in the use of punches to prepare dozens of fine parallel-sided **blades,** thin, often parallel-sided blanks used to make a wide variety of small tools such as chisel-shaped gravers for working bone and antler. Some of the finest stoneworking dates from more recent times. The Predynastic Egyptians made superb ceremonial knives. Ancient Native Americans made delicate projectile points, shaping them with small billets of bone or antler and pressure techniques (Figure 7.2). By this time, many human societies produced diminutive stone artifacts designed as arrow barbs and used for other specialized purposes (Figure 9.5).

Lithic analysis, the study of stone tools, is based not only on the identification of attributes and types, but on actual reconstructions of the reductive technology used to make them. This requires refitting of actual cores and waste flakes found in excavations, a painstaking task that can produce remarkable results, like identifying the work of individual stone workers, some of whom may be left handed. Lithic experimentation, the actual replication of stone technologies, has long been part of experimental archaeology (Chapter 4), and the study of the edge wear on long-discarded tools under microscopes combined with actual experiments has produced evidence for cutting hide, meat, and bone. Some artifacts have even produced trace elements of organic residues such as blood still clinging to the cutting edges of butchery tools.

Lithic analysis is not just the study of artifacts, it is the understanding of what the implements mean in terms of human behavior.

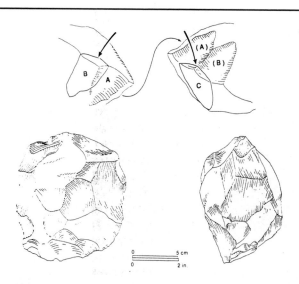

Figure 9.10 *(continued)*   Making Oldowan bifaces. *Top,* a simplified picture of the process required for bifacial flaking. *Bottom,* a large Oldowan discoid-like artifact from Chesowanja, East Africa, in plan and side views. The stoneworker used this bifacial technique but did not fashion the biface along a long axis, as later humans did.

Clay

From the earliest times, people used containers of all kinds, such as animal skins, bark trays, gourds, and ostrich eggshells. Then, in about 8000 B.C., the *Jomon* people of Japan started making baked clay containers, an innovation that took hold in southwestern Asia before 6000 B.C., and in the Americas after 2500 B.C.

Clay containers have the advantage of being both durable and long lived, which is why they are such an important part of the archaeological record. They served as water and storage containers, as cooking and drinking vessels. Their shape, style, and form have been the basis for thousands of archaeological analyses. Prehistoric artisans created their pieces individually, using the simplest of technology, but attaining astonishing skill in shaping and adorning their pots (Figure 9.11). They selected their clay with great care, pounded it and prepared it to a fine consistency, then built up their pots in a variety of ways, most commonly by building up long coils of clay, or by using a mold, or, in later times in the Old World, by using a potter's wheel. The outside surface was smoothed with the hands, sometimes painted with a wet clay solution, then dried before being burnished, decorated, and fired. As with other artifacts, the making of clay vessels was circumscribed by all manner of social and other variables, which are almost impos-

Figure 9.11   Pueblo Indian woman making pots using the coil method.

sible to discern from conventional archaeological analysis. Such analyses focus on the form, function, style, and technology of the vessel. The latter includes studies of the fabric and clay paste, using such techniques as neutron activation analysis and X-ray diffraction to study what has been called "ceramic ecology," the interaction of resources, local knowledge, and style that led to finished clay vessels. Some pioneer spectrographic analyses have even identified the powdered residues adhering to the interiors of ancient vessels, as was the case of a wine storage jar from Iran dating to 4000 B.C.

Metals and Metallurgy

Metals were familiar phenomena to ancient peoples in the form of rocks in their environment. Perhaps their color, luster, and weight made them attractive to use as ornaments. Eventually, people realized that native copper and other rocks could be formed into tools by a sequence of hammering and heating. But only eight metals—arsenic, copper, gold, iron, lead, mercury, tin, and silver—were worked before the eighteenth century A.D.

The earliest metal tools were made in southwestern Asia by 6000 B.C. by cold hammering copper into simple artifacts. Copper tools were commonplace by 4000 B.C., but the real revolution came after 3000 B.C. when smiths learned how to alloy the metal with arsenic, lead, or about 10 percent tin to produce tough-edged bronze tools and weapons. By 2500 B.C., practically every kind of metallurgical phenomenon except hardening of steel was known (Figure 9.12), by which time Chinese smiths were using clay molds to produce highly sophisticated three-legged cauldrons and other ceremonial vessels. Ironworking appeared in southwestern Asia in about 1500 B.C., and was in widespread use by 1000 B.C., a utilitarian and abundant metal ore ideal for making farming tools and weapons (Figure 9.13).

The analysis of metal artifacts again involves conventional classificatory techniques, but now relies heavily on technological researches. Again, spectrographic analyses provide clues as to the sources of raw materials. For example, we know that the copper ingots from the fourteenth-century B.C. Uluburun shipwreck off southern Turkey came from Cyprus (see Figure 11.8). Chemical examination of copper and iron slags and of smelting furnaces can provide valuable information on ancient metallurgical processes. Archaeologists have sat alongside and watched as traditional smiths in Africa and elsewhere recreate ancient smelting and manufacturing techniques. They record furnace temperatures and other arcane details as a means of better understanding the techniques used in the remote past. The ultimate purpose of the technological analyses is to reconstruct the entire process of metal tool production from the mining of the ore to the production of the finished artifact.

The study of ancient technologies is one of the foundations of all archaeological research. In Chapter 3, we introduced the notion of cultures and cultural systems. Under this rubric, it follows that the study of artifacts and technology may involve only one aspect of the cultural system, but as we also see in Chapters 10 to 12, it also implies a great deal about the rest of the culture.

Figure 9.12 Gold beaker with decoration hammered into relief from the reverse side, also turquoise inlay, attributed to Chimu goldsmiths from coastal Peru, c. A.D. 1200.

Summary

Archaeologists rely heavily on formal classification systems in their analyses of artifacts. Archaeology has its own taxonomy (classification system) for classifying artifacts and cultural units. This allows the organizing of data into manageable units and more detailed classification into artifact types using the individual features of artifacts, or clusters of tools. Describing types provides a hierarchy that orders the relationships between artifacts and allows archaeologists to study assemblage variability in the archaeological record. Typology is a system of archaeological classification based on the construction of types to permit comparisons from different levels and sites. Types are distinguished by combinations of artifact features (attributes) that serve to distinguish one object from another. Statistical methods play an important part in manipulating attribute clusters, and permit researchers to discern patterns that

Figure 9.13   Celtic Iron Age helmet from the bed of the River Thames in London, 8.07 inches (20.5 cm) at the base. A fine example of skilled metallurgy.

relate to past human behavior. They use descriptive types, chronological types, functional types, and stylistic types, defined in this chapter. Archaeologists commonly use arbitrary archaeological units, such as components, phases (cultures), horizons, and traditions, also defined in this chapter, for studying larger cultural phenomena. The chapter also reviews the major technologies of ancient times, including stone, wood, metal, and bone.

10
Subsistence

San rock painting from the Drakensburg Mountains, South Africa.

There was a noise, and behold a shaking, and the bones came together, bone to his bone. And when I behold, lo, the sinews and the flesh came up upon them, and the skin covered them above, but there was no breath in them.

Ezekiel 37:7–8

How did ancient peoples make their living? The old stereotype of Stone Age hunters pursuing large game animals like saber-toothed tigers and living off orgies of frenzied meat consumption vanished generations ago. We now know that plant foods and fish were vital components in many ancient diets, and ancient Native Americans had an astounding knowledge of potentially cultivable native plants. Reconstructing ancient subsistence is a painstaking process, involving days of analysis of animal bones broken into tiny fragments and highly specialized research into tiny plant seeds recovered with sophisticated sampling machines.

In some ways, studying ancient subsistence is archaeological detective work at its best. Astoundingly detailed information about prehistoric foraging and agriculture can come from the tiniest of clues such as fish scales and seed impressions in clay pots. But, as always, these triumphs of detection form part of a larger concern, a search for answers to fundamental questions. For example, when studying prehistoric subsistence, the archaeologist seeks to answer many fundamental questions, among them the role of domestic animals in a mixed farming economy. How important was fishing to a shellfish-oriented population living by the ocean? Was a site occupied seasonally while the inhabitants concentrated on, say, bird snaring to the exclusion of all other subsistence activities? What agricultural systems were used? How was the land cultivated? In this chapter we review some of the ways we seek the answers to these and related subsistence questions.

Evidence for Subsistence

The archaeological evidence for prehistoric subsistence consists of artifacts and food remains. How much survives depends, of course, on preservation conditions on the site. All too often the evidence for ancient diet is incomplete. Stone axes or iron hoe blades may give an indication of hunting or agriculture, but they hardly yield the kind of detail archaeologists need. Many artifacts used in the chase or for agriculture were made from such perishable materials as bone, wood, and fiber (Figure 10.1).

Figure 10.1   A reconstructed stone ax used by early Danish farmers for forest clearance in about 4000 B.C. Such artifacts tell us little about prehistoric economic practices.

Food remains themselves survive very unevenly. The bones and teeth of larger mammals are the most common subsistence data, but careful excavation often reveals remains of such small animals as birds, fish, and frogs as well as invertebrates, such as beetles. Plant remains are very perishable and usually are underrepresented, despite the development of sophisticated field recovery methods.

Ancient Diet

The ultimate aim in studying prehistoric food remains is not only to establish how people obtained their food, but to reconstruct their actual diet. An overall picture of prehistoric diet requires, of course, constructing a comprehensive list of food resources available to the people within that particular environment and then answering questions such as these: What proportion of the diet was meat? How diverse were dietary sources? Did the principal diet sources change from season to season? Was food stored? Were some foods more desirable than others? These and many other questions can be answered only from composite pictures of prehistoric diet reconstructed from many sources of evidence.

Just occasionally, however, it is possible to gain insights into actual meals consumed thousands of years ago. The stomach of Tollund Man, whose body was buried and preserved in a Danish peat bog, contained the remains of finely ground porridge made from barley, linseed, and several wild grasses (see Figure 4.6). No meat was found in his belly. The Ice Man from the European Alps, described in Chapter 12, died hungry: scientists could not determine what he last ate. However, his bones showed clear signs of malnutrition from famines in his 9th, 15th, and 16th years. Ancient digestive tracts also yield informative waste products. Human excrement (**coprolites** or feces) found in dry caves in the United States and Mexico has been analyzed microscopically. The inhabitants of *Lovelock Cave* in the central Nevada desert were eating bulrush and cattail seeds, as well as Lahontan chub from the waters of nearby Humboldt Lake. These fish were eaten raw or roasted over a fire. One coprolite contained the remains of at least 51 chub, calculated by a fish expert to represent a total fish weight of 3.6 pounds (1.6 kg). The same people were eating adult and baby birds, as well as water tiger beetles. Human feces from Texas caves near the mouth of the Pecos River have been subjected to pollen analyses so precise that the investigators established the sites to have been occupied regularly during the spring and summer months for 1,300 years between 800 B.C. and A.D. 550.

Although coprolite studies are a promising source of dietary information, the food remains from most sites are far too incomplete to allow more than a very general impression of diet. Research using the ratio between two stable carbon isotopes—12C and 13C in animal tissue—has enabled scientists to establish the diet of prehistoric populations as they switched from wild foods to a predominantly maize diet. Carbon is metabolized in plants through three major pathways: C4, C3, and by Crussulacean acid metabolism. The plants that make up the diet of animals have distinct C13 values. Maize, for example, is a C4 plant. In contrast, most indigenous temperate flora in North America is composed of 3C varieties. Thus a population that shifts its diet from wild vegetable foods to maize also will experience a shift in dietary isotopic values. Because C13 and C12 values do not change after death, researchers can study archaeological carbon from food remains, humus, and skeletal remains to gain insight into ancient diet.

For example, a detailed bone chemistry analysis of adult burials from *Grasshopper Pueblo* in east-central Arizona shows the great potential of this approach. Joseph Ezzo was able to show that between A.D. 1275 and 1325, males had greater access to meat and cultivated plants, and females had greater access to wild plants. Between 1325 and 1400, both men and women ate virtually the same diet, one in which meat and wild plant foods were less important. This may have resulted from a combination of social and environmental factors: increased population, drought cycles, and use of marginal farming land, which compelled the Grasshopper people to live on agricultural products. The people responded to food stress by increasing storage capacity, reducing household size, and eventually by moving away.

The stable carbon isotope method has been used to study the diet of prehistoric Northwest Coast populations in British Columbia. Forty-eight samples from prehistoric human skeletons from 15 sites along the coast revealed a dietary reliance of about 90 percent on marine sources, a figure much higher than crude ethnographic estimates. The same data suggest that there has been little dietary change along the British Columbia coast for the past 5,000 years, which is hardly surprising, given the rich maritime resources of the shoreline.

Isotopic analysis offers great promise. Recent research has focused on nitrogen isotopes that allow researchers to distinguish between marine and freshwater and terrestrial food sources, an approach of importance when investigating changeovers from more land-based diets to marine ones, an important issue in ancient California. Isotopic tests also allow research into child weaning practices, dietary changes over the life of an individual, even mobility from one area to another, identified by studying the bone chemistry of burials in royal graves and cemeteries (sacrificial victims, for example, could come from a different area).

Animal Bones

Broken animal bones can tell us a great deal about ancient hunting, herd management, and butchery practices. One can identify mammal species from their skeletal remains. Unfortunately, however, most animal bones found in archaeological sites are highly fragmentary. Until recently, researchers assumed they were in such small fragments because the inhabitants slashed to ribbons every carcass they butchered. But research on modern predator kills and controlled experiments on butchered animals, mainly in Africa, have shown that a great many complex and little-understood forces act on bones found in archaeological sites long after they are dropped where archaeologists find them. Weathering as bones decay in the open air, compaction of the sediments in which they are buried, chemistry of the soil, even treading by animals can break up bones and help determine which parts of the body survive and which do not. Add to these accidents the butchering activities of the prehistoric inhabitants, and you have an archaeological jigsaw puzzle to piece together (Figure 10.2).

Generally speaking, the older the archaeological site, the more daunting it is to study postdepositional forces. The problem is particularly confusing at locations such as Olduvai Gorge or Koobi Fora in East Africa, where hominids chewed and cut bones more than two million years ago—and probably scavenged their meat from predator kills in the bargain. On more recent sites, one finds that people often utilized the carcasses they butchered to the maximum. Every piece of usable meat was stripped by the inhabitants from the bones of even the smallest animals or the larger mammal portions brought back to the settlement. Sinews were made into thongs. Skins became clothing, containers, or even part of a shelter. Even the entrails were

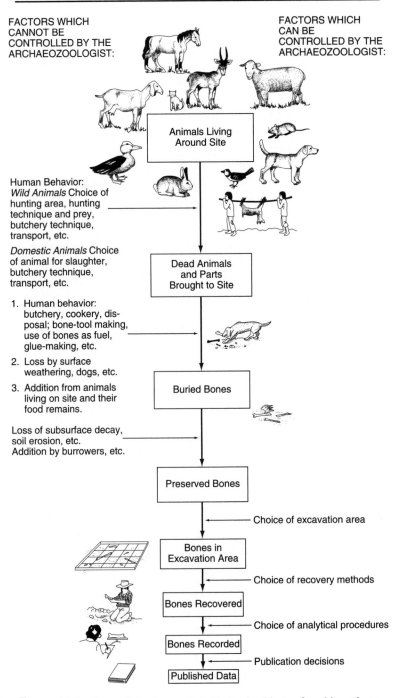

FACTORS WHICH CANNOT BE CONTROLLED BY THE ARCHAEOZOOLOGIST:

FACTORS WHICH CAN BE CONTROLLED BY THE ARCHAEOZOOLOGIST:

Animals Living Around Site

Human Behavior:
Wild Animals Choice of hunting area, hunting technique and prey, butchery technique, transport, etc.

Domestic Animals Choice of animal for slaughter, butchery technique, transport, etc.

Dead Animals and Parts Brought to Site

1. Human behavior: butchery, cookery, disposal; bone-tool making, use of bones as fuel, glue-making, etc.

2. Loss by surface weathering, dogs, etc.

3. Addition from animals living on site and their food remains.

Loss of subsurface decay, soil erosion, etc.
Addition by burrowers, etc.

Buried Bones

Preserved Bones

Choice of excavation area

Bones in Excavation Area

Choice of recovery methods

Bones Recovered

Choice of analytical procedures

Bones Recorded

Publication decisions

Published Data

Figure 10.2   Some of the factors that affect animal bones found in archaeological sites. On the left are factors over which the archaeologist has no control; on the right, those that can be controlled.

eaten. The hunters smashed the bones themselves to get at the marrow or for manufacture into arrowheads or other tools. Animal bones were fragmented by many domestic activities, quite apart from trampling underfoot and scavenging by dogs and carnivores. Thus one has the formidable task of identifying from tiny, discarded fragments the animal that was hunted or kept by the site's inhabitants and the role the animal played in the economy, diet, and culture of the community.

Faunal Analysis (Zooarchaeology)

Most animal bone collections consist of thousands of scattered fragments from all parts of a site. Occasionally, however, a kill site, perhaps from prehistoric bison kills on the Great Plains or the big game slaughtered by Stone Age hunters in East Africa, provides a chance to reconstruct the hunters' activities in more detail. Apart from such unusual finds, most collections have to be sorted out in the laboratory simply to give a general impression of hunting and stock-raising techniques at the site. The goal of **zooarchaeology**—the study of animal bones found in the archaeological record—is to reconstruct the environment and behavior of ancient peoples as thoroughly as animal remains allow. But the study of such bones is complicated by the natural and humanly induced processes that operate on organic remains as they lie on or in the ground. The study of this transition by animal remains from the **biosphere** is known as **taphonomy.**

Taphonomy involves two related forms of research: observing recently dead carcasses as they are gradually transformed into fossils and studying fossil remains with the knowledge gained from these observations. The crux of the zooarchaeologists' difficulty is their subject: a collection of animal bones, the part of the fossil assemblage that is actually excavated or collected. This fossil assemblage in turn consists of the body parts that survive in the archaeological record, an assemblage very different from the original community of live animals which once populated the natural environment in their "natural" proportions. Animal bone analysis involves two fundamental problems: First, estimating the characteristics of a fossil assemblage from a collected sample, a statistical problem; and second, inferring what the original bone assemblage was like before it became a fossil, a taphonomic problem (Figure 10.2).

Researchers begin by isolating the diagnostic fragments. Often only a few bones are identifiable to the species level. One 3,000-year-old central African hunter-gatherer settlement yielded only 2,128 identifiable fragments out of 195,415 bones! The actual identifications are made by comparing such diagnostic body parts as teeth, jaws, horns, and some limb bones with modern animal skeletons (Figure 10.3). This procedure is not as easy as it sounds. Domestic sheep and goats have skeletons that are almost identical to those of their wild ancestors, the bones of the domestic ox closely resemble those of the African buffalo, and so on. But accurate identifications are vital, for they provide answers to many questions. Are both domestic and wild animals present? If so, what are the proportions of each group? Were the inhabitants concentrating on one species to the exclusion of all others? Are any now-extinct species present?

Comparing Bone Assemblages

Having identified the animals present, how do you compare the proportions of different species from one site to those from another? The work is fraught with difficulty because it is almost impossible to infer the once-living population from the surviving bones.

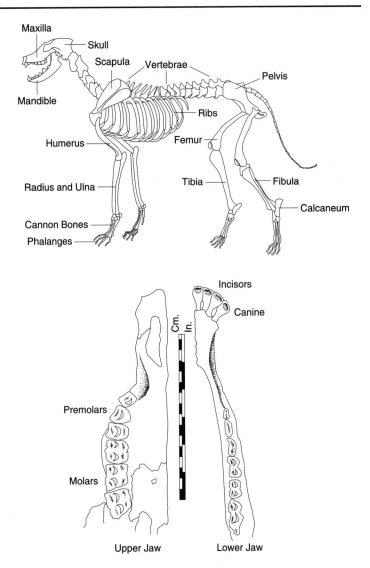

Figure 10.3   At the top, a dog skeleton with the most important body parts labeled from the bone identification point of view. At the bottom, a domestic ox jaw seen from below (upper jaw) and above (lower jaw). Notice the characteristic cusp patterns of molars and premolars that grow as the beast gets older.

Zooarchaeologists therefore apply two measures of specimen abundance to study the relative abundance of species:

- The *Number of Identified Specimens (NISP)* is a count of the number of bones or bone fragments. This assay has obvious disadvantages because it is easy to overestimate one species at the expense of another, especially if its bones are cut into small fragments. The NISP has some limited use in conjunction with:

- The *Minimum Number of Individuals (MNI)*, a count of the number of individuals necessary to account for all of the identifiable bones. This count is based on careful inventories of individual body parts (e.g., jaws). The MNI is a much more accurate estimate of the number of animals present in a collection. For example, Joe Ben Wheat used the thousands of bison skulls from the Olsen-Chubbuck site to estimate that the hunters killed no less than 190 animals.

Using these two counts together brackets the actual number of animals present in a bone sample, but the figure is still only an approximation, even when used with sophisticated computer programs.

Species Abundance and Cultural Change

Climatic change rather than human culture was probably responsible for most long-term shifts in abundance of animal species during the great Ice Age. Some changes in the abundance of animals in bone collections, however, must reflect human activity—changes in the way in which people exploited animals.

Zooarchaeologist Richard Klein has studied two coastal caves in South Africa, *Klasies River* and *Nelson's Bay* caves, to document such changes. The Klasies River cave on the Cape coast was occupied by "Middle Stone Age" hunters from about 130,000 to about 70,000 years ago, during a period of progressively colder climate. The people took seals, penguins, and shellfish and lived off the eland, a large antelope. The nearby Nelson's Bay cave was occupied by "Late Stone Age" people, after 20,000 years ago. These people took not only dangerous or elusive land mammals such as the Cape buffalo, but birds and fish, both quarries requiring some skill to hunt or take successfully.

Did these changes between the two sites reflect cultural change or climatic differences? Were eland more abundant in earlier times, or just easier to hunt? Klein examined the tool kits from each cave, and found that Middle Stone Age artifacts were large spear points and scrapers, but the later Nelson's Bay people used bows, arrows, and an elaborate tool kit of small, more specialized tools. This more specialized tool kit allowed the Nelson's Bay groups to hunt more dangerous and tricky quarry with great success. Therefore, eland were less common prey later not because of climatic change, but because other animals were hunted, too. Then, too, in later times the population was larger. Klein suggests the growth from his examination of the limpet and tortoise shells from both sites. The Nelson's Bay specimens are smaller, as if these creatures were allowed to grow larger in earlier millennia when fewer people were there to exploit them.

Game Animals

A collection of game animals yields a wealth of information about the great variety of mammals that ancient hunters killed with astonishingly simple weapons. North American paleo-Indian bands used game drives, spears, and other weapons to hunt herds of now-extinct big game. Twenty thousand years ago, big-game hunters on the banks of the Dnieper and Don rivers in western Russia cooperated in pursuing mammoth and other arctic mammals. They cached supplies of game meat to tide them over the long, bitterly cold winters, which lasted more than eight months.

When the identified game animal bones are counted, one species may appear to dominate. Some hunters concentrate on one or a few species, whether from economic necessity, convenience, or cultural preference. They may take hundreds of bison in fall, when they are fat from summer forage, and kill the minimum in spring, when the animals are in poor condition after the harsh months. Even with these differences taken into account, the figures can be misleading, for many societies restrict the hunting of particular animals. Others forbid males or females to eat certain species, although others may be consumed by everyone. The !Kung San of the Kalahari today have complicated personal and age- or sex-specific taboos to regulate their eating habits. No one may eat all of the 29 game animals regularly taken by the San. Indeed, no two individuals have the same set of taboos. Such complicated restrictions are repeated with innumerable variations in other hunter-gatherer societies. The simple dietary figure of, say, 40 percent white-tailed deer and 20 percent wild geese may, in fact, reflect much more complex behavioral variables than mere concentration on two species.

Domesticated Animals

Domestic animal bones present even more difficulties. Owners can affect their herds and flocks in many ways—by selective breeding to improve meat yields or to increase wool production, and by regulating the ages at which they slaughter surplus males and old animals. All domesticated animals originated from wild species with an inclination to be sociable, a characteristic that aided close association with humans.

Animal domestication may have begun when a growing human population needed a regular food supply to support a greater density of people per square mile. Wild animals lack many characteristics valuable in their domestic relatives. Wild sheep have hairy coats, but their wool is unsuitable for spinning. The ancestors of oxen and domestic goats produced milk for their young but not enough for human consumption. People have selectively bred wild animals for long periods to enhance special characteristics. Often the resulting domestic animals can no longer survive in the wild.

The history of domestic animals must be written from fragmentary animal bones found in sites occupied by prehistoric farmers. The difference between domestic and wild animal bones is often so small that it may be next to impossible to tell the two apart. From a single jaw, no one can tell a domestic sheep or goat from a wild one. Archaeologists have to work with large numbers of animals, studying changing body sizes and bone characteristics as the animals undergo selective breeding. Early southwest Asian domestic sheep are smaller and display less variation in size than their wild relatives. Even then, it is, according to the Scriptures, "difficult to tell the sheep from the goats."

Prehistoric peoples hunted game animals for food, used their hides for garments and tents, and their stomachs for bags. Domesticated animals provided meat and were used for plowing, for riding, or for their milk. Establishing such practices from fragmentary animal bones is difficult, involving close study of both the age of slaughtered animals and the ways in which they were butchered.

Just as with comparing different assemblages, the problem is turning figures and percentages into meaningful interpretations of human behavior. Research such as Lewis Binford's studies of Alaskan caribou hunters has provided valuable information for such approaches (see Chapter 4).

Determining the sex and age of an animal may provide a way of studying the hunting or stock-raising habits of those who slaughtered it. Many mammal species vary considerably in size and build between male and female. With species such as the North American bison, researchers can often distinguish male from female by bone sizes, but the determination is much more difficult with animals where the size difference is less.

Teeth and the **epiphyses** (joints) at the end of limb bones are most commonly used to establish the ages of prehistoric animals. In almost all mammals, the epiphyses fuse to the limb bones at adulthood, so one can immediately establish two categories of animals: immature and fully grown. Teeth and complete jaws are a more accurate way of establishing animal age. Teeth provide an almost continuous guide to the age of an animal from birth to old age. With complete jaws one can study immature teeth as they erupt. Large numbers of them enable archaeologists to count with some accuracy the proportions of immature and very old animals with heavily worn teeth.

Richard Klein has used the height of tooth crowns to study the age of mammals taken by Stone Age hunters at Klasies River and Nelson's Bay caves in South Africa. He has identified two "mortality distributions" that apply to prehistoric and living animal populations.

A **catastrophic age profile** is stable in size and structure and has progressively fewer older individuals. This is the normal distribution for living antelope populations (Figure 10.4). If a group of hunters drives a herd over a cliff, you will find a distribution like this, for they are not being discriminating in their hunting.

An **attritional age profile** shows underrepresentation of prime-age animals relative to their abundance in living populations, but young and old are overrepresented. This profile is thought to result from scavenging or simple spear hunting.

The eland tooth profiles at both Klasies River and Nelson's Bay were close to the catastrophic profile, and so Klein argued that they were hunted in mass game drives. In contrast, the more formidable Cape buffalo displayed an attritional profile, as if the hunters had preyed on immature and old beasts over long periods.

These interpretations are fine at a general level, but it is much harder to draw more specific conclusions. Lewis Binford's Nunamiut caribou hunters from Alaska direct much of their hunting activities toward obtaining meat for winter consumption. In the fall, they pursue caribou calves to obtain clothing. The heads and tongues of these young animals provide meat for the people who process the skins.

The fragmentary bones in an occupation level are the end product of the killing, cutting up, and consumption of domestic or wild animals. To understand the butchery process, the articulation of animal bones must be examined in the levels where they are found, or a close study made of fragmentary pieces. Rarely is an entire kill site preserved, like the famed *Olsen-Chubbuck* bison kill in Colorado, where at least 190 bison were driven to their death, then dismembered, more than 8,000 years ago. Archaeologist Joe Ben Wheat showed that for several days the hunters camped by their prey as they dismembered the uppermost bison in the confused heap of dead animals before them. When they had eaten their fill and dried enough meat to last them a month or more, they simply walked away and left the rotting carcasses. Archaeologists found the articulated and butchered skeletons thousands of years later.

Interpreting butchery techniques is a complicated matter, for many variables affect the way in which the carcass is dismembered. Toughness of hide, available

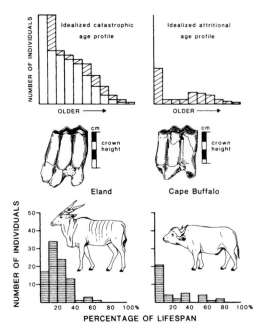

Figure 10.4   Idealized mortality data based on molar crowns of two common South African mammals, the eland and the Cape buffalo. Left, idealized catastrophic age profile. Right, idealized attritional age profile (for explanation, see text).

tools, size and portability of the animal, and potential use for skins and horn are a few of the variables. The only way to interpret body parts in this context is by understanding in detail the cultural system that generated them. The herders, finding a constant surplus of males beyond their breeding requirements, may castrate some of these animals and then use them for riding and for dragging carts or plows. But even with some insights into the cultural system and excellent bone preservation, it is frequently hard to interpret the meaning of butchering techniques.

So many factors affect the counts of identified bones from any collection of animal remains that one must interpret the fragments in the context of artifact patterns, site-formation processes, and all other sources of data potentially bearing on the behavior of the people who killed the animals.

Plant Remains

Gathering and agriculture are almost invariably unrepresented in most sites because the tiny seeds and other vegetable remnants that result from such activities as food storage, grinding, and harvesting are among the most fragile of all archaeological remains. Except for occasional burned seeds found in hearths or storage pits, the vegetable remains from human feces, and grain impressions in clay pot walls, much evidence for prehistoric gathering and agriculture comes from dry sites, where preservation conditions are almost perfect (Figure 10.5a). However, the development of sophisticated **flotation** techniques in recent years has enabled archaeologists to recover large samples of tiny plant remains from settlements in every kind of environment imaginable, including moist environments like those at Koster in Illinois.

Flotation methods are used both in the field and in the laboratory. With this technique, water or chemicals are used to free tiny seeds from the soil (Figure 10.5b). The freshly excavated earth is poured into a container and sinks slowly to the bottom while the light seeds float to the surface. Some botanists prefer to collect soil samples in the field, then process them in the laboratory, where they can work with samples that have not been screened or treated in any other way, giving them a random sample for statistical purposes. Armed with statistical samples of plant remains, **paleobotanists,** experts on ancient plants, can not only determine what people ate and used, but can trace the beginnings of domestication of native plants. Sometimes they can give clues as to the uses of different structures by establishing the abundance of different seeds around them, or even establish what seasons of the year a site was occupied, but such analyses are very difficult and in their infancy.

Flotation methods have revolutionized the study of plant remains, for they provide large seed samples that can be studied with statistical methods. At the *Ali Kosh* mound in Iran, Kent Flannery and Frank Hole thought that plant remains were scarce. Then they used flotation methods and recovered 40,000 seeds from the trenches. In recent years, botanists have obtained literally pints of seed samples from the early farming village at Abu Hureyra in Syria, samples so complete that botanist Gordon Hillman has been able to chronicle major shifts in plant gathering preferences over more than 3,000 years. When Abu Hureyra was a small foraging settlement before 8800 B.C., the people relied heavily on acorns and other nut crops in nearby forests. But as the forests retreated in the face of dry conditions, the people turned to wild cereal grasses, which they soon domesticated to provide extra food supplies.

Much of our knowledge of early major food crops such as wheat, barley, and maize has come from dry caves. Richard MacNeish assembled a continuous sequence of human occupation in the Tehuacán Valley in Mexico for the period 10,000 years ago to the Spanish Conquest. He dug more than a dozen open sites and caves, all so dry that they yielded 80,000 wild plant remains and 25,000 specimens of domestic corn. MacNeish was able to identify diminutive maize cobs in several caves, which have been AMS dated to about 2700 B.C., the earliest maize agriculture yet recorded in the Americas. These early maize cobs were no more than 0.78 inch (2 cm) long, but later ones were far larger. Unfortunately, MacNeish was unable to identify the original wild ancestor of Tehuacán maize, probably the native grass teosinte.

Farmers modify the landscape around them by grazing their herds and by clearing forests. Simple, shifting cultivation techniques required new garden acreage every season. Each time cultivation required more cleared woodland, drastic environmental changes were triggered. Few people have ever tried to assess how profoundly early agricultural economies affected the world environment. Pollen analysis has provided remarkable evidence of how early farmers cleared natural environments for their fields. Many European marches chronicle a sudden moment when dense oak forest suddenly gives way to an open landscape in which grass pollens predominate. The sudden change often coincides with the appearance of domesticated cereal grain pollens, also with characteristic, but inconspicuous weeds that are found in cultivated fields, such as a grass named *Plantago lanceolata*.

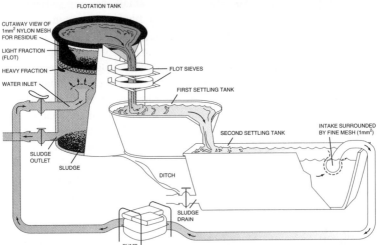

Figure 10.5   Recovering evidence for gathering and agriculture. (a) A grain impression preserved on a clay pot fragment from an early farming site in eastern England (approximately 2.2 inches [5.6 cm] diameter). (b) Model of a water flotation device for recovering plant remains using recycled water, developed by British botanist Gordon Hillman. The lightest remains float to the surface and are caught in special sieves. The heavier material sinks and is trapped in light nylon mesh.

This early clearance activity dramatizes how little we know about prehistoric agriculture and gathering, simply because the archaeological evidence is so hard to recover. For example, the !Kung San, present-day inhabitants of the Kalahari Desert in southern Africa, know of at least 85 edible seeds and roots. Most of the time they eat but 8 of these. The rest of the vegetable resource base provides a reliable cushion for this foraging population in times when key vegetable foods are scarce. Such people have a buffer against famine that many farmers with their cleared lands, much higher population densities, and crops that rely on regular rainfall rarely enjoy. Is a farming life really to be preferred? A few studies of the skeletons of early farming populations show how malnutrition due to food shortages was commonplace in many areas.

Birds, Fish, and Mollusks

Bird bones, although very informative, are often neglected at the expense of larger mammal remains. As long ago as 1926, Hildegarde Howard studied a large bird bone collection from an Indian shell midden on the eastern shores of San Francisco Bay. The inhabitants had hunted many waterbirds, especially cormorants, ducks, and geese. When Howard looked more closely at the bones, she found that all of the geese were migrant winter visitors that frequent the Bay Area between January and April. Nearly all the cormorants were immature specimens, birds about 5 to 6 weeks old. What time of the year had the Indians occupied the site, she wondered. Howard consulted present-day records pertaining to when cormorants hatch and used these to estimate what time of year the earlier inhabitants must have eaten the young cormorants. Based on these records, she estimated the cormorants had been killed about June 28. She then determined the Indians must have lived there once in the winter and a second time in the early summer.

Fishing, like bird hunting, became more important as people began to specialize in different lifeways and adapt to highly specific environments. Evidence for fishing comes from both artifacts and fragile fish bones, which, when they survive, can be identified with considerable accuracy.

Freshwater and ocean fish may be caught with nets or basketlike fish traps. Indians who lived on the site of modern Boston in about 2500 B.C. built a dam of vertical stakes and brush. When the Atlantic tides rose, fish were directed into gaps in the dam and trapped in huge numbers. Barbed fish spears and fishhooks are relatively common finds in some archaeological sites, but such artifacts tell us little about the weight of fishing in prehistoric subsistence. Did the people fish all year or only when salmon were running? Did they concentrate on coastal species or venture far offshore in large canoes? Such questions can be answered only by examining the fish bones themselves.

The Chumash Indians of southern California were remarkably skillful fishermen, who went far offshore in plank canoes to fish with hook and line, basket, net, and harpoon. It was no surprise when the fish bones found on archaeological sites at Century Ranch, Los Angeles, included not only the bones of such shallow-water fish as the leopard shark and California halibut, but the remains of albacore, ocean skipjack, and large rockfish, species that occur in deep water and can only be caught there. Early Spanish accounts speak of more than 10,000 Indians living in the Santa Barbara area of California alone, a large population indeed. Archaeology has shown that this maritime population was able to exploit a very broad spectrum of marine resources.

Fishing, with its relatively predictable food resources and high protein potential, allows much more sedentary settlement than other forms of hunting and gathering. The Northwest Coast Indians enjoyed a very rich maritime culture based on ocean fishing and salmon runs that enabled large numbers of people to live in one area for long periods and to build permanent dwellings.

Shellfish from seashore, lake, or river supplied a good portion of the prehistoric diet for many thousands of years. Freshwater mollusks were important both to California Indians and to prehistoric people living in the southeastern United States. Most mollusks have limited food value and so great quantities are needed to feed even a few people. One estimate for 100 people's mollusk needs for a month runs as high as 3 tons. In all probability, mollusks were more a supplemental food at set times of the year than a staple. They were simply too much effort to collect in sufficient quantity.

Even sporadic collecting led to rapidly accumulating piles of shells (shell middens) at strategic points on lake or ocean shores, near rocky outcrops or tidal pools where mollusks were commonly found. Shell midden excavations in California and elsewhere have yielded thousands of shells, which are counted, identified, and also measured to check for size changes. When Claude Warren sampled a shell midden near San Diego, California, he found five major species of shellfish commonly exploited by the inhabitants. The earliest shellfish collectors concentrated on the bay mussel and oysters, both of which flourish on rocky shores. But by 4000 B.C., the lagoon by the shell middens had so silted up that mud-loving scallops and Venus shells were now collected, for the earlier species were unable to flourish in the new, sandy environment. Soon afterward, however, the lagoon became clogged and the shellfish collectors moved away, never to return. And their abandoned seashells told the story of the changing environment around the sites.

Both fresh- and saltwater shells were widely used as prehistoric ornaments. Gulf Coast shells were bartered over enormous distances of the southeastern and midwestern United States to peoples who had never seen the ocean. Sometimes such ornaments could assume incredible prestige value. When nineteenth-century explorer David Livingstone visited Chief Shinte in central Africa in 1855, he found him wearing two seashells that had come 1,000 miles (1,609 km) inland from the distant East African coast. The chief told him that two such shells would buy a slave; five, a large ivory elephant tusk. Small wonder that enterprising merchants were trading china replicas of these shells in central Africa half a century later.

Rock Art

Sometimes prehistoric rock art gives vivid insight into subsistence activities of long ago, such as hunts and fishing expeditions. Hunter-gatherers and fishing cultures have left behind paintings of their daily life on the walls of caves and rockshelters. In recent years, South African archaeologist David Lewis-Williams and others have used oral traditions and nineteenth-century ethnographies to develop interpretations of some of the rituals depicted in the paintings. However, the art has a valuable role to play in the interpretation of subsistence activities. Careful examination of these paintings can take us back centuries and millennia to the time when the people were killing

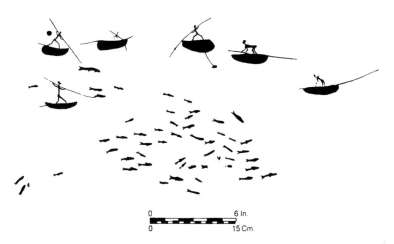

Figure 10.6 The fishing scene from Tsoelike rockshelter, Lesotho, southern Africa.

the animals whose bones lie in occupation deposits under the observer's feet. Many details of weapons, domestic equipment, and hunting and fishing methods can be discerned in these vivid scenes.

The Stone Age paintings of southern Africa have long been known not only for their representations of important symbolic rituals in hunter-gatherer life, but also for their depictions of life in prehistoric times. At Tsoelike River rockshelter in Lesotho, southern Africa, paintings show fishermen assembled in their boats (Figure 10.6). They have cornered a shoal of fish that are swimming around in confusion. Some boats have lines that seem to be anchors. The fishermen are busy spearing their quarry. Another famed scene depicts a peacefully grazing herd of ostriches. Among them lurks a hunter wearing an ostrich skin, his legs and bow protruding beneath the belly of the apparently harmless bird. One can only wonder if his hunt was successful.

The artists painted big-game hunts, honey collectors, women gathering fruit, cattle raids, even red-coated British soldiers. Scenes like these take us back to hot days when a small group of hunters pursued their wounded quarry until it weakened and collapsed. The hunters, having stalked their prey for hours, relax in the shade as they watch its death throes. Then they settle down to butcher the dead animal before carrying the meat and skin home to be shared with their group. Few artifacts survive from scenes such as these, but the objective of reconstructing ancient subsistence patterns is to recreate, from the few patterned traces that have survived in the soil, just such long days in the sun.

Summary

Archaeological evidence for subsistence comes from artifacts and food remains, with animal bones forming the most common source of information. Reconstructing entire diets is much harder, for the proportions of different foods in the diet have to be established. Bog corpses, human feces, and stable carbon isotope analysis provide invaluable information on ancient diets. Fragmentary animal bones broken up for food (zooarchaeology) provide information on hunting and herding, requiring careful analysis of the minimum numbers of species present and counts of the minimum number of individuals.

Zooarchaeology can sometimes provide information on hunting preferences, butchery, seasonal occupation of camps, and on early domesticated animals, also animal husbandry. Wild and domesticated plant remains can be studied in carbonized seed form, or as imprints in clay pot walls, but flotation methods provide much larger statistical samples for analyses of changing foraging and farming practices. AMS radiocarbon dating allows researchers to date individual seeds or cobs, providing new information on the origins of food production. Birds, fish remains, and shellfish are invaluable sources on seasonal occupation and intensive foraging in many parts of the world.

11

Settlement and Trade

Monkey-like Maya scribe gods paint a codex. From a Late Classic Maya vase.

In the temple alone are as many as 1523 columns. What means of transport, what a multitude of workmen, must this have required, seeing that the mountain out which the stone is hewn is thirty miles distant!

Henri Mouhot on Angkor Wat, Cambodia, 1860

"The murmur and hum of their voices could be heard more than a league [three miles] away . . ." Conquistador Bernal Diaz marveled at the great market in the heart of the Aztec capital, Tenochtitlán, in 1519. The Spaniards wandered among throngs of buyers and sellers, at least 20,000 of whom flocked to the marketplace daily. They were impressed by the orderliness of the stalls and its cleanliness. Every kind of merchandise had a separate quarter. Dealers in gold, silver, semiprecious stones, feathers, and other exotics sold goods from every corner of the Aztec empire. You could buy capes, chocolate, dogs, foodstuffs of every kind, even ice from high on the slopes of the mountains. A dozen judges sat in shifts in a large hall, presiding over the orderliness of the market. Inspectors wandered through the crowds checking for price gouging or false measures. A standardized pricing system was based on staple commodities such as cacao beans, cotton cloths, and small T-shaped pieces of copper. Tenochtitlán's market was a hub of a vast pre-Columbian empire held together by force, trade, and tribute.

The next two chapters widen our focus, away from single sites and artifacts to the broader compass of ancient societies and the ways in which they interacted with one another. This first chapter examines ways in which archaeologists study ancient settlement patterns and trading; Chapter 12 discusses more human interactions, between individuals and groups, also the study of religious beliefs.

The tool kits and food remains found in archaeological sites reflect their inhabitants' material culture and subsistence activities. Hunter-gatherers tend to have portable tool kits, manufactured for the most part from organic materials that do not survive well in archaeological sites (see Figure 4.10). Many of their sites are temporary camps. Rarely can the archaeologist look at the patterning of artifacts and food remains in such camps, for many are gone forever. But the more sedentary farmer settles much longer in one spot and is confronted with much more elaborate annual tasks. The farmer has to store each year's food surplus, too, an activity that immediately adds complexity to a farming settlement. Substantial houses, storage pits, cemeteries, threshing floors, cattle enclosures—all of these can be elements in even a small farming village.

Archaeologists study patterning in such structures as houses and storage pits just as thoroughly as they study artifacts and food remains. They also analyze distributions in time and space of different communities and relationships between them. These activities are classified as **settlement archaeology,** which reveals the many ways in which individual communities relate to one another—through trade, religious beliefs, and social ties, among others. Settlement archaeology research requires a combination of common sense, careful mapping and survey combined with fine-grained excavation, and, often, high-technology science.

Settlement Patterns

Settlement archaeology is part of the analysis of human interactions with, and adaptations to, the natural and social environment. The houses and villages of a prehistoric society, like the artifacts and food residues by their hearths, are part of the settlement pattern. This pattern involves relationships among people who decided—for practical, political, economic, ideological, and social reasons—to place their houses, settlements, and religious structures where they did. Settlement archaeology also allows us to examine the relationships between different communities, and trading networks, ways in which people exploited both their environment and social organization. By studying settlement patterns, we have a chance to examine the intangible factors that caused culture change in ancient times.

For instance, the Chumash Indians of southern California lived on the islands and shores of the Santa Barbara Channel, where ocean upwelling nourished one of the richest inshore fisheries on earth. Seven hundred years ago, this rich bounty of marine resources allowed the Chumash to live in densely populated, permanent settlements with as many as 1,000 inhabitants. The most important of these villages clustered at sheltered spots on the coast with good canoe landings, kelp fisheries close offshore, and sea mammal rookeries within easy reach. If you find a series of coastal Chumash settlements in sheltered positions that protect them from the southeastern storms of winter, you can reasonably assume there were sound, practical reasons behind the site distribution. Within the village itself, we know that a complex variety of social, economic, and even personal factors dictated the layout of houses in relation to one another.

At another level, an entire village or city may reflect a society's view of their world and the cosmos. The ancient Mesoamericans placed great emphasis on lavish public ceremonies set in the heart of large ceremonial centers. Fifteen hundred years ago, great lowland Maya cities like Copán and Tikal were replicas in stone and stucco of the layered Mesoamerican spiritual world of the heavens, the living world, and the underworld (Figure 3.4). Their pyramids were sacred mountains, the doorways of the temples atop them the sacred openings by which the ruler, as intermediary with the spiritual world, traveled to the Otherworld up and down the *Wacah Chan*, the symbolic World Tree that connected the layers of the Maya universe. A thousand years later, the vast plaza of the Aztec capital, Tenochtitlán, stood at the center of the ancient Mexica world. When Spaniard Hernán Cortés and his conquistadors climbed to the summit of the great temple of the sun god Huitzilopochtli and the rain god Tlaloc in 1519, they stood at the axis of the Aztec universe. The four quarters of the Aztec world radiated from a temple so sacred that pyramid after pyramid rose at the same location.

The relationship between an individual and the landscape can be as complex as that of an entire society. A central African farmer once showed me his land, a patchwork of small gardens, some intensely cultivated, others lying fallow as the soil regenerated after years of use. I saw just land until he pointed out the subtle signs of regenerating soil, different kinds of grasses to be eaten by his cattle in the weeks ahead, the flowering nut trees that would come into harvest at the end of the wet season. The landscape came alive, a quilt of gardens, plants, and animals protected by his ancestors, who were now the spiritual guardians of the land. My friend's relationship to his surroundings was a "landscape of memory," built from generations of his own and his predecessors' experience.

Settlement archaeology is about these many layers of dynamic relationships, some of which are near impossible to discern without the careful use of analogy with

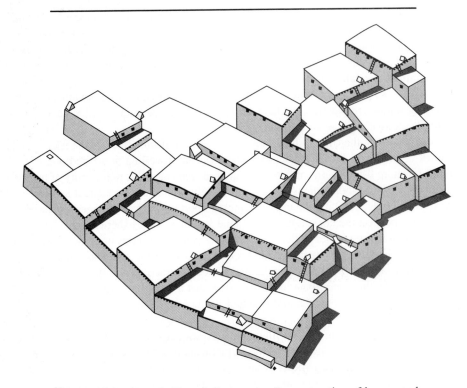

Figure 11.1   Households and Community. Reconstruction of houses and shrines from the town of Çatalhöyük, Turkey, in about 6000 B.C. The close juxtaposition of houses provided insulation against climatic extremes and protection against enemies. Çatalhöyük was an important farming center, and owed much of its importance to trade in fine-grained obsidian, which was mined nearby. In its heyday, it was one of the largest human settlements in the world.

living societies. For working purposes, many archaeologists divide these layers of relationship into a loose hierarchy of three general levels—households, communities, and distribution of communities (Figure 11.1).

Households

The eruption came as a sudden rumble that shook the Maya village at the end of the day 1,400 years ago, just as everyone was finishing their evening meal. An underground fissure less than a mile away had erupted with little warning. Clouds of ash and gasses darkened the sky. The villagers fled for their lives, leaving their dirty dishes behind them. Within a few days, the tiny hamlet and its surrounding fields lay under 15 feet (4.5 m) of ash.

About 1,400 years later, a bulldozer operator leveling the ground for grain silos accidentally uncovered the corner of a thatched hut mantled in ash. The Maya village at Cerén, El Salvador, is an extraordinary archaeological treasure, a prehistoric settlement frozen in time (Figure 4.8). Archaeologist Payson Sheets has plotted the contents of entire Cerén houses. One household lived in a complex of four buildings: a kitchen, a workshop, a storehouse, and a residence where the inhabitants socialized, ate, and slept. Sheets and his colleagues found grindstones still standing on forked sticks that elevated them above the ground, even a well-tended garden by the storehouse with three species of medicinal herbs, each plant standing in its own mound of soil. A nearby field held ridges of young maize plants 8 to 15 inches high, typical August growth in this environment.

The Cerén excavations reveal humble Maya households going about their daily business, their artifacts preserving by chance the one moment in the day when men, women, and children were all together for the evening meal. Archaeological sites like Cerén are archives of human interactions, where patterns of artifacts, food remains, and other material finds provide vital information on ancient human behavior. Few sites have the exceptional preservation found at Cerén, but many contain informative patternings of artifacts that reflect activities of all kinds.

When Kent Flannery and his students excavated farming villages in the Valley of Oaxaca, Mexico, dating to between 1350 and 850 B.C., they not only uncovered and recorded the one-room, thatched, pole-and-mud houses, but plotted the associated artifact patterns as well. They carefully distinguished between the house with its contents and the cluster of household storage pits, graves, and garbage heaps that lay nearby. Flannery plotted household features very carefully and identified areas where special activities took place from the specialist tool kits—for bead making and obsidian toolmaking—associated with them. Every household obtained, processed, and stored food, although the types of food consumed by each varied. Some Oaxacan households also spent much time making stone tools or ornaments. These specialist activities presumably supplied the needs of the community as a whole. In this Mexican example, and in all studies of individual structures, the artifacts and activities associated with them are just as important to the archaeologist as the design and layout of the structure itself.

We should never forget that households are chronicles of human interactions, communities even more so. Archaeological sites, whether small hunting camps, humble farming villages, or vast cities, are archives of human interaction. People lived and died in these places. They grew up, got married, had children, quarreled with neighbors. These daily interactions, between men and women, rich and poor, traders and their customers, slaves and masters, come down to us in the form of distinctive artifact patternings and community settlement patterns. The anonymous testimony of artifacts from individual houses, from neighborhoods, palaces, and temples, reveals the full, and often unsuspected, diversity of ancient human communities.

Households require slow-moving area excavation, so that the exact position of every artifact, features such as hearths or pits, and the tiniest of food remains like seeds and broken animal bones can be recorded electronically and photographically before anything is lifted from the dwelling. Sometimes, I have managed to identify the activities of different individuals while still excavating the house floor: stoneworking activity surviving as a scatter of stone tools and the waste flakes and cores used to make them, butchering of a rabbit by a cluster of broken bones. More often, however, the database in the laboratory computer is the best source of information, allowing you, for example, to call up the position of every potsherd of a certain style, or all ox forelimb bones. It is then that you discern unexpected associations, subtle signposts to long-forgotten domestic activities, or even of children playing. Short of a burial or a house belonging to a known historical individual, this is about as close as you can get in archaeology to individuals as opposed to households. This type of excavation is invaluable when studying male and female roles, or the cultural diversity of a household revealed by distinctive artifacts

Like a shipwreck on the seabed, a well-excavated ancient house can be a sealed capsule of a moment in the past, which can be read by an expert like a book.

Communities

Every household member interacts with other members of the household and with individuals in other households within the community. And entire households interact with other households as well. Once we begin to look at a community of households, new complexities enter the picture. The first is permanency of settlement, which is affected primarily by the realities of subsistence and ecology. How long San forager camps in Africa's Kalahari Desert are occupied is determined by availability of water, game, and vegetable foods near the site; the camp moves at regular intervals. In contrast, the farmers of Çatalhöyük, a Turkish farming settlement of 6000 B.C., lived in the same crowded village of mud houses separated by narrow alleys for many centuries, because they were anchored to their nearby fields (Figure 11.1).

In such small communities, family and kin ties were of overwhelming importance, affecting the layout of houses, household compounds, and groups of dwellings. By mapping and analyzing artifact patterns and house inventories, you can sometimes find traces of different residential clusters within a single community. Kent Flannery and a University of Michigan research team used such data plots to find at least four residential wards (barrios) within the rapidly growing village of San José Mogote, which flourished in Mexico's Valley of Oaxaca after 1350 B.C. A trash-filled erosion gully separated each cluster of square thatched houses from its neighbors.

Small communities, like cities, are never static entities. People's children grow up, marry, and start new households nearby. Houses burn down or collapse, so new dwellings take their place. As often happened with Iroquois villages in the American Northeast, a settlement would outgrow its fortifications, then erect an extended palisade to protect new houses (Figure 8.3). The study of an ancient community is a study of constant interactions between individuals, **household groups,** and members of the settlement discerned through the careful study of **activity areas** (places where individuals carried out specific tasks like food preparation) and artifact patternings.

The behaviors and interactions of people living in much larger communities like cities are also reflected in artifact patternings and in the settlement pattern of the city as a whole. Whereas economic and environmental realities often affect the siting of a smaller community, more complex factors such as religious authority come into play with ancient cities. For example, the city of *Eridu* in southern Iraq was the largest human settlement on earth in 4000 B.C. Eridu lay close to the Euphrates River, with easy access to the wider world of the Persian Gulf. Perhaps 5,000 people clustered in the crowded precincts of the city, at first, little more than an agglomeration of villages of close kin or specialist artisans living close to one another for mutual protection and economic interest. They lived in the shadow of the great mudbrick *ziggurat* temple-mound of the god Enlil, a veritable artificial mountain that reached toward the wide heavens above (Figure 11.2). Eridu's temple was the highest point in the flat country-side for many miles around, a symbol of an intensely sacred place favored by the gods. Compelling political and religious factors helped determine the site of Eridu, the chosen city of Enlil. Like many other ancient cities, this oldest of human cities was a symbolic center of the universe, the holiest place on earth.

The largest community settlement pattern ever investigated systematically is that of Teotihuacán, where René Millon has mapped dozens of residential compounds, a market, and vast ceremonial structures (Figure 11.3). He even found special quarters where foreigners from Oaxaca and lowland Veracruz on the Gulf of Mexico—revealed by their distinctive architecture and pottery—lived for centuries in an alien city. Millon sought the answers to many questions. What social classes existed in the city? What specialist crafts were practiced and where? How many people lived at Teotihuacán at different periods? The only way to answer such questions was to map the entire city and make comprehensive surface collections and test excavations to give an overall picture of the total settlement pattern.

Thanks to the mapping project data, we know that teeming neighborhoods of single-story, flat-roofed, rectangular apartment compounds complete with courtyards and passageways lay beyond the enormous ceremonial precincts of the city. Narrow alleyways and streets about 12 feet (3.6 m) wide separated each compound from its neighbors. Each housed between 20 and 100 people, perhaps members of the same kin group. Judging from artifact patternings, some sheltered skilled artisans, families of obsidian and shell ornament makers, weavers, and potters.

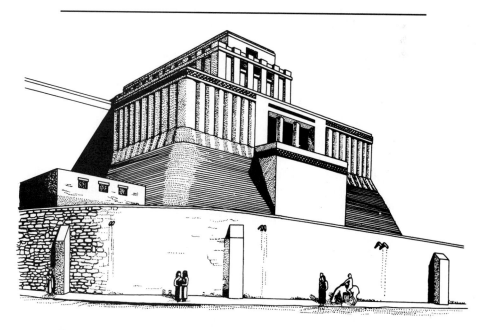

Figure 11.2 A reconstruction of the *ziggurat* temple at Eridu, Iraq.

Figure 11.3   Pyramid of the Sun, Teotihuacán, Valley of Mexico. The pyramid and other structures at Teotihuacán formed the core of a vast prehistoric city. The great mass of the pyramid was designed as part of a setting for grandiose public ceremonies, which were a common feature of Mesoamerican religious beliefs. Teotihuacán was a city conceived on a grand scale, its ceremonial precincts designed to give the visitor a sense of the power of the gods and the forces of the spiritual world.

What was life like inside Teotihuacán's anonymous apartment compounds (barrios)? Mexican archaeologist Linda Manzanilla has investigated one such complex close to the northwest edge of Teotihuacán, searching for traces of different activities within the complex. The stucco floors in the apartments and courtyards had been swept clean, so Manzanilla and her colleagues used chemical analyses of the floor deposits to search for human activities. She developed a mosaic of different chemical readings, such as high phosphate readings where garbage had rotted, and dense concentrations of carbonate from lime (used in the preparation of both tortillas and stucco) that indicated cooking or building activity. Manzanilla's chemical plans of the compound are accurate enough to pinpoint the locations of cooking fires and eating places where the inhabitants consumed such animals as deer, rabbits, and turkeys. She was able to identify three families of about 30 people who lived in three separate apartments within this community inside a much larger community. Each apartment had specific areas for sleeping, eating, religious activities, and funeral rites.

Teotihuacán's barrios have revealed intense interactions between people who knew one another well, and between these tight-knit communities and the wider universe of the city itself. Walking along one of the cleared streets, you can imagine passing down the same defile 1,500 years earlier, each side bounded by a bare, stuccoed compound wall. Occasionally, a door opens onto the street, offering a view of a shady courtyard, of pots and textiles drying in the sun. The street would have been a cacophony of smells and sounds—wood smoke, dogs barking, the monotonous scratch of maize grinders, the soft voices of women weaving, the passing scent of incense.

Distribution of Communities

No human being has ever lived in complete isolation, for even the smallest hunter-gatherer family group has at least fleeting contacts with neighboring bands at certain times of the year. But as human societies become more complex and settlements more lasting, intercommunity relationships become much more complicated. Different settlements depend more and more on one another for essential raw materials (salt or copper ore) and for specialist products (stone knives, religious ornaments, and the like). Growing villages might split into two settlements that, although separated in space, still maintain close ties of kinship. Human settlement patterns are not just site dots on maps. They are complex and constantly changing networks of human interaction, of trade, religion, and social ties, of differing adaptations of local environmental challenges.

For years, the study of community distributions depended on large-scale archaeological surveys that combined aerial photographs with months of systematic foot survey on the ground. Such studies began with the development of a classification of archaeological sites in a region. Each of these site types has a relationship to others, the total distribution of all site types making up a settlement pattern. Each site type is defined by the characteristic structures, artifact patterns, food remains, and small finds therein. These definitions provide us with a way to organize the sites into a hierarchy of successive levels of settlements (Figure 11.4). For instance, the Maya city of Copán was a major ritual and trade center, the seat of an important kingdom. A hierarchy of secondary centers, small towns, villages, and tiny hamlets lay throughout the city's territory, each dependent on one another, and each with a well-defined position in the hypothetical pyramid of human settlement. Trading and the payment of tribute played a major role in linking the different layers of this and other settlement hierarchies in the ancient world. So did the availability of food and other resources within the immediate vicinity of a settlement. Eric Higgs of Cambridge University developed a method known as **site catchment analysis**, which inventories resources within different radiuses of sites that is an effective way of defining where people obtained food and other commodities from (see Figure 11.5a and b).

William Sanders and a large research team from Pennsylvania State University surveyed the entire Valley of Mexico, center of the Aztec civilization, in the 1970s. They compiled distribution maps of every known archaeological site and plotted them against comprehensive environmental data, with dramatic results. Sanders showed how the population of the Basin ebbed and flowed over many centuries, with the rise and fall of the great city of Teotihuacán in the first millennium A.D.

The most dramatic changes came some centuries later when the growing Aztec capital, Tenochtitlán, achieved overwhelming dominance. By the end of the

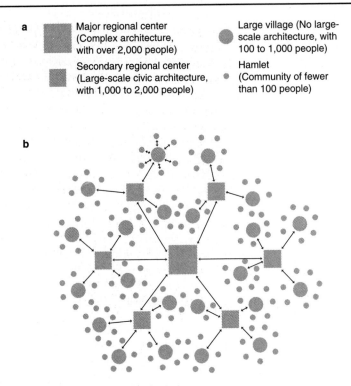

a Major regional center (Complex architecture, with over 2,000 people)

Secondary regional center (Large-scale civic architecture, with 1,000 to 2,000 people)

Large village (No large-scale architecture, with 100 to 1,000 people)

Hamlet (Community of fewer than 100 people)

b

Figure 11.4   A site hierarchy in Mesoamerica. (a) Simplified hierarchy of site types. (b) Hypothetical site hierarchy on the ground, with the major regional center serving secondary centers spaced at regular intervals. These in turn serve larger villages and their networks of hamlets.

fifteenth century A.D., the imperial capital housed at least 200,000 people, living in dense residential areas now buried under the concrete jungle of Mexico City. The concentration of sites nearby was such that Sanders estimated at least 400,000 city and country dwellers occupied a 230 square mile (370 sq. km) zone of foothills, plains, and lake bed areas near the capital. He calculated that about a million people lived within the confines of the Basin of Mexico at the time. Tenochtitlán was a magnet to outlying populations. Its very presence skewed the entire settlement pattern of the Basin. So many people lived there that the Aztecs now farmed every local environment in the region, to ensure there was enough food to go round.

Tenochtitlán stood at the center of an organized landscape, created by ambitious rulers who thought nothing of creating about 25,000 acres (10,000 ha) of highly productive swamp gardens in the southern part of the Basin alone. Over less than two centuries, the local settlement pattern changed from a patchwork of small states and major centers to a highly centralized agricultural landscape capable of meeting the basic food needs of at least half a million people.

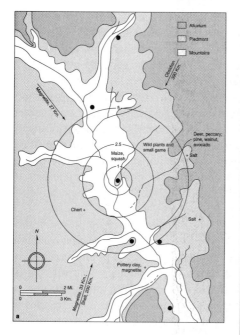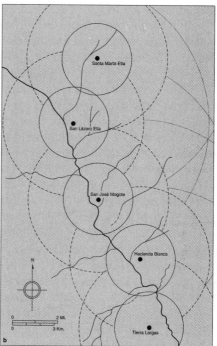

Figure 11.5   (a) A simple example of site catchment analysis, not using GIS, from the Valley of Oaxaca, Mexico. The inhabitants of this farming village, occupied between 1150 and 850 B.C., obtained their basic agricultural needs within a radius of less than 1 to 3 miles (1.6–4.8 km). (b) Common minerals and seasonal plant foods were found within the 3-mile (4.8 km) circle, game meat and construction materials within a 9-mile (14.4 km) radius. When plotted on a map, the inner circles for each settlement did not overlap, but the wider ones, where minerals were obtained, did. It was here that each community set up seasonal camps to share resources. (Radii in kilometers.)

Few settlement patterns show such dramatic changes as those in the Basin of Mexico. Sanders was a pioneer in combining environmental and archaeological data in settlement archaeology, but his project was unsophisticated by the standards of some of today's projects, which rely on high technology to integrate field surveys with a wide variety of spatial data.

Geographic Information Systems and Roman Wroxeter, England

Virconium Cornoviorum, the Roman town at present-day Wroxeter near Shrewsbury in west-central England, was the fourth largest urban center in Roman Britain. Wroxeter started as a legionary camp in A.D. 60, then became a town 30 years later, flourishing until the fifth or sixth century. Most Roman towns lie under modern cities like London or York. Fortunately for archaeologists, much of Wroxeter is in open country. For more than a century, generations of excavators investigated the major public buildings and commercial zone of the town. They used aerial photographs and surface collections of potsherds and other artifacts to plot the general outlines of the settlement and to develop a detailed chronology of its buildings.

However, these simple approaches could not answer fundamental questions about the history of a once-strategic military gateway into neighboring and unconquered Wales. Many Roman forts and camps lie close to the town. What impact did these army encampments have on the rural population? What were the consequences of the Roman conquest on local Iron Age farmers? Archaeologist Vince Gaffney and an international team of researchers have combined the powerful technology of Geographic Information Systems (GIS) with aerial photographs and ground survey to provide some answers (for GIS, see Chapter 7).

The Wroxeter archaeologists could draw on a massive archive of aerial photographs of the surrounding countryside, taken under every kind of weather condition imaginable over more than half a century. They located over 40 farming enclosures and the remains of a once-extensive field system. The researchers "warped" digital images of the aerial photographs onto Britain's national map grid, turning the images into GIS maps so accurate a fieldworker can measure and interpret such features as the Roman street grid at Wroxeter itself with margins of error as small as 3 feet (1 m) (Figure 11.6).

The Wroxeter project is unusual in that the archaeologists working on the ground have the ability to manipulate all available archaeological data on the screen before they go into the field. The fieldworkers rely heavily on volunteers, who are recording the Roman town's topography by taking measurements every 33 feet (10 m). A magnetometer survey combined with ground penetrating radar has revealed hitherto unknown buildings on the edge of the town. For generations, experts on Roman Britain had called Wroxeter a carefully planned "garden city," with parks and open spaces. GIS and remote sensing has revealed a less well-organized community with uncontrolled expansion at its margins as it drew people from the surrounding countryside.

The Wroxeter data is so complete that you can even explore the dynamic, ever-changing settlement pattern on the World Wide Web. Your computer leads you through three-dimensional images of a long-vanished Roman town. Within a few years, Wroxeter's archaeologists will be able to answer questions about changing patterns of supply and demand. By assuming the town was the economic hub of the surrounding area, they will be able to show how mass-produced pottery from remote sites flowed through the region along an existing infrastructure of roads, tracks, and rivers accessible through the GIS database.

Population

Settlement patterns across a landscape evolve in response to three broad variables: environmental change, interactions between people, and shifts in population density. Of these three, population is the hardest to study.

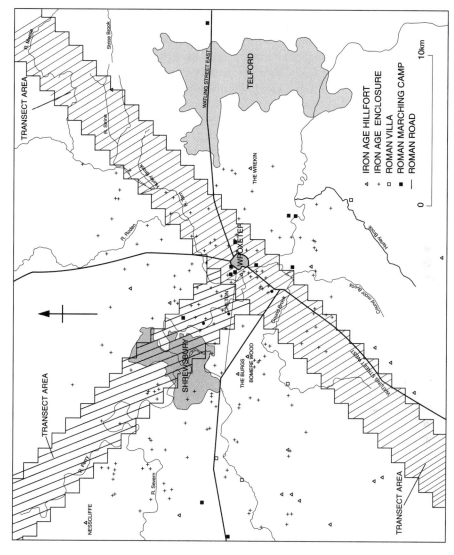

Figure 11.6 GIS data derived from many sources, including generations of aerial photographs provided the background data for the survey of Roman Wroxeter's hinterland. The map shows the Roman city and outlying sites, also the three transects walked by archaeologists on the ground. Wroxeter is unique among Roman towns in Britain in not being buried under a modern city, which makes it unusually important for settlement studies.

Population growth was not a major factor in human history until after the Ice Age, which ended about 10,000 years ago. No question, however, that growing population densities were a major factor in the development of agriculture in southwestern Asia in about 9000 B.C., and in the appearance of the first cities and civilizations about 6,000 years later. In the case of farming, much drier conditions, diminished supplies of wild plant foods, and many more mouths to feed turned many hunter-gatherer groups in the Jordan Valley and modern-day Syria into sedentary farmers within a few centuries. Unfortunately, estimating population densities is often little more than guesswork. Despite attempts to develop censuses from house counts and refuse accumulation, most population estimates are little more than guesses. For instance, one estimate places the population of Britain in 11,000 B.C. at about 10,000 people; another, the average population of early states in southern Iraq at about 17,000.

Nevertheless, changing population distributions are of great importance, for there is a clear cause-and-effect relationship between population and the potential *carrying capacity* and productivity of agricultural land. As populations grow, goes one popular argument, so people try to collect or produce more food, perhaps by developing highly efficient ways of fishing or hunting, or by turning to agriculture. Like the ancient Egyptians, farmers may face the challenge by developing large-scale irrigation systems capable of producing several crops a year and feeding many more people.

Population, then, is a critical variable in settlement archaeology, as William Sanders and his colleagues showed with the rapid growth of the Aztec capital in the Basin of Mexico. Although Sanders's population estimates were little more than highly informed guesses, he was able to show a dramatic rise over several centuries. Such general trends are of great interest, for they enable us to monitor large-scale processes like the rise or fall of an entire civilization.

Trade and Exchange

Humans obtain food by exploiting the natural environment. Many hunter-gatherer societies were self-sufficient in their dietary needs. They used only the raw materials within their regular territory. But many societies, especially after the invention of agriculture, were no longer self-sufficient. They needed access to a much wider range of raw materials and finished artifacts, many of which they obtained by trading with neighboring communities.

Trade has been defined as the "mutually appropriative movement of goods between hands." People make trade connections and create **exchange systems** that handle trade goods when they need to acquire goods and services which are not available to them within their own site catchment area. The movement of goods need not be over any great distance, and it can operate internally, within a society, or externally, across cultural boundaries. Trade always involves two elements: the goods and commodities being exchanged and the people doing the exchanging. Thus any form of trading activity implies both procurement and handling of tools and raw materials and some form of social system that provides the people-to-people relationships within which the trade flourishes. Not only raw materials and finished objects, but also ideas and information, were passed along ancient trade routes.

Trade appears in the archaeological record in the form of exotic objects discovered in sites miles away from their point of origin. For instance, the Indians of the

Lake Superior region obtained copper from natural outcrops near the lake. They traded the precious metal over thousands of miles, as far away as Ohio. In Mesoamerica and southwestern Asia, one well-known trade commodity was obsidian, fine volcanic glass widely prized for making knives, ornaments, and mirrors. In Mesoamerica, obsidian was traded in regional networks through informal trading relationships that gradually became more and more organized as new local rulers began to control the valuable trade.

Studying Ancient Trade

In the early days of archaeology, such exotica were deemed sufficient to identify trade, even what were loosely called "influences" or even "invasions." Today, however, studies of prehistoric exchange are far more sophisticated, owing to two major developments. The first is a new focus throughout archaeology on cultural process and on regional studies. The second is the development of a wide range of scientific techniques that are capable of describing the composition of certain types of raw material and even of identifying their sources with great precision.

Obtaining evidence of long-distance trade involves far more sophisticated inquiry than merely plotting the distribution of distinctive artifacts hundreds of miles away from their place of manufacture. Research into the sources of raw materials is sometimes called **characterization** (or sourcing), because it involves identifying the characteristic properties of the distinctive raw materials used to fashion, say, stone axes. We should stress the word *distinctive,* for the essence of these methods is that we are able to identify the specific source with great accuracy. For example, obsidian from Lipari Island off Sicily was traded over a wide area of the central Mediterranean, an obsidian with highly specific characteristics that show it came from Lipari and nowhere else. Analytical methods include microscopic examination of thin sections of stone axes or potsherds that use trace element analysis and other methods to source raw materials and identify constituents in pottery clays or metal artifacts.

Trace element analysis employs a variety of techniques such as neutron activation analysis and X-ray spectrometry. All of them produce tables of individual elements, for example, antimony, lead, tin, and so on. Matching such tables with sources is extremely difficult and requires a careful research strategy, usually involving multivariate statistics and several elements. Some spectacular results have been obtained, especially with obsidian. For instance, we now know that obsidian from the Admiralty Islands in the Bismarck Archipelago in the southwestern Pacific was traded no less than 1,860 miles (3,000 km), as far as Vanuatu in Micronesia and 2,200 miles (3,500 km) to Borneo in the west.

In the 1960s, Colin Renfrew and others used **spectrographic analysis** to identify no fewer than 12 early farming villages that had obtained obsidian from the Ciftlik area of central Turkey (Figure 11.7). This pioneer study showed that 80 percent of the chipped stone in villages within 186 miles (300 km) of Ciftlik was obsidian. Outside this "supply zone," the percentages of obsidian dropped away sharply with distance, to 5 percent in a Syrian village and 0.1 percent in the Jordan Valley. If these calculations were correct, each village was passing about half of its imported obsidian further down the line. Obsidian has proved an ideal raw material for monitoring prehistoric exchange and for developing new theoretical approaches to early trade,

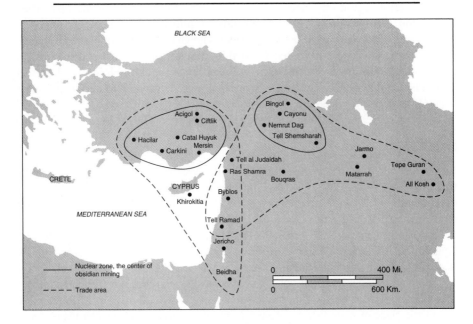

Figure 11.7   Obsidian trade in the eastern Mediterranean region. **Sourcing** studies reveal that early farming communities in Cyprus, Anatolia, and the Levant obtained their obsidian from two sources in central Anatolia. Meanwhile, villages like Jarmo in the Zagros Mountains and Ali Kosh far to the southeast relied on sources in Armenia. Settlements like Çatalhöyük in Anatolia were so close to obsidian sources that they probably collected their own supplies. More than 80 percent of their stone artifacts are made of the material. Obsidian tools are much rarer down the line, the further one travels from the source.

based not only on single sites but also on studies of entire regions. For example, we now know of no fewer than nine **Neolithic** and Early Bronze Age obsidian "interaction zones" between Sardinia and Mesopotamia, each of them linked to well-defined sources of supply.

The use of source data enables us to conceive of exchange on a regional basis. The ultimate research goal is to identify the exchange mechanisms that distributed the obsidian or other material within each interaction zone. Prehistoric quarries, such as those in Greece, Mesoamerica, and Australia, are potentially valuable sources of information on the exchange of exotic materials. Archaeologist Robin Torrence studied the Aegean obsidian trade and found that the exchange was noncommercial and noncompetitive in 5000 B.C.: the prehistoric stoneworkers visited quarries and prepared material for exchange with minimal concern for economical use of the raw material. On the island of Melos, for example, the visitors simply quarried what they wanted and left. There is no evidence of specialized production.

Artifact distributions and characterization techniques have helped provide a unique portrait of prehistoric trade from a Bronze Age shipwreck at Uluburun, off southern Turkey. The heavily laden ship was sailing westward from the eastern Mediterranean in 1305 B.C. when it was shattered on the jagged rocks of Uluburun, near Kas. It sank in 151 feet (48 m) of water. Archaeologists plotted the exact position of every timber, every item of the ship's equipment and cargo, before lifting any artifacts from the seabed. They found the ship was laden with 6 tons (6,096 kg) of copper ingots, probably mined in Cyprus, also with tin ingots and artifacts (Figure 11.8). The tin may have come from southern Turkey. Canaanite jars from Palestine or Syria held olives, glass beads, and resin from the terebinth tree, used in religious rituals. The ship's hold contained Baltic amber that probably reached the Mediterranean overland, ebonylike wood from Africa, elephant and hippopotamus ivory, and ostrich eggshells from North Africa or Syria. Egyptian, Levantine, and Mycenaean daggers, swords, spearheads, and woodworking tools lay aboard, and sets of weights, some fashioned in animal forms. There were costly glass ingots, Mesopotamian cylinder seals, a Mycenaean seal stone, even a gold cup and parts of a tortoiseshell lute. The ship carried Egyptian scarabs, dozens of fishing weights, fishhooks, and 23 stone anchors, vital when anchoring in windy coves. Even the thorny burner shrub used to pack the cargo was preserved.

By using find distributions from land sites and a variety of sourcing techniques, archaeologists George Bass and Cemal Pulak have reconstructed the anonymous skipper's last journey. He started his voyage on the Levant coast, sailed north up the coast, then crossed to Cyprus and coasted along the southern Turkish shore. The ship called at ports large and small on its way west along a well-traveled route that took advantage of changing seasonal winds, to Crete, some Aegean islands, and perhaps to the Greek mainland. The skipper had traversed this route many times, but on this occasion his

Figure 11.8   Excavations on the Uluburun ship, southern Turkey.

luck ran out and he lost his ship, the cargo, and perhaps his life on Uluburun's pitiless rocks. From the archaeologist's perspective, the Uluburun shipwreck is a godsend, for it allows us to fill in many details of an elaborate trade network that linked the eastern Mediterranean with Egypt, the Aegean, and Greece more than 3,300 years ago.

Types of Trade

Gift giving is a common medium of exchange and trade in societies that are relatively self-supporting. The exchange of gifts is designed primarily to reinforce a social relationship, both of an individual and of a group as a whole. The gifts serve as gestures that place obligations on both parties. This form of trade is common in New Guinea and the Pacific, was widespread in Africa during the past 2,000 years, and in the ancient Americas as well. Perhaps the most famous example is that of the *kula* ring of Melanesia in the southwestern Pacific. An elaborate network of gift exchanges passes shell necklaces in one direction, arm shells in the other. They are passed as ceremonial gifts from one individual to another, in gift partnerships that endure for decades. These gift exchanges enjoy great prestige, yet serve as a framework for the regular exchange of foodstuffs and other more day-to-day commodities. This sporadic interaction between individuals and communities reduced people's self-sufficiency and eventually made them part of a larger society who depended on one another not only for basic commodities but also for social purposes.

Reciprocity, the mutual exchange of goods between two individuals or groups, is at the heart of much gift giving and barter trade. It can happen year after year at the same place, which can be as humble as someone's house. Such "central places" become the focus of gift giving and trade. When a village becomes involved in both the production of trade goods and their exchange with other communities, it probably will become an even more important center, a place to which people will travel to trade.

Redistribution of trade goods from a central place throughout a culture requires some form of organization to ensure that the redistribution is equitable. A redistributive mechanism may be controlled by a chief, a religious leader, or some form of management organization. Such an organization might control production of copper ornaments, or it might simply control distribution and delivery of trade objects. Considerable social organization is needed for the collection, storage, and redistribution of grain and other commodities. The chief, whose position is perhaps reinforced by religious power, has a serious responsibility to his community that can extend over several villages. His lines of redistribution stretch out through people of lesser rank to the individual villager. A chief will negotiate exchanges with other chiefs, then redistribute the exotic materials and objects he or she obtains to individual households.

Markets are both places and particular styles of administering and organizing trade that encourage people to set aside one place for trading and relatively stable, almost fixed prices for staple commodities. Markets are normally associated with more complex societies. No literate civilization ever developed without strong central places, where trading activities were regulated and monopolies developed over both sources of materials and trade routes themselves. Successful market trading required predictable supplies of basic commodities and adequate policing of trade routes. It is significant that most early Mesopotamian and Egyptian trade was riverine, where policing was easier. When the great caravan routes opened, the political and military issues—tribute, control of trade routes, and tolls—became paramount. The caravan, predating the great empires, was a form of organized trading that kept to carefully defined routes set up and maintained by state authorities (Figure 11.9). The travelers moved along these set routes, looking neither left nor right, bent only on delivering and exchanging imports and exports. Markets were, and still are, places for gathering information from people living at a considerable distance. In West Africa, Fulani cattle herders spend much time hanging around markets, not because they are idling away time, but because they are acquiring valuable information about grazing grass and water supplies.

The study of ancient trade is a vital source of information on social organization and the ways in which societies became more complex. Trade itself developed a great complexity, in both goods traded and the interactions of people involved. Colin Renfrew has identified no fewer than ten types of interaction between people that can result from trading, ranging from simple contact between individuals to trading by professional traders, such as the *pochteca* of the Maya and the Aztec, who sometimes acted as spies.

Figure 11.9   A camel caravan. Caravans were traditionally neutral in the wider political world because they carried commodities essential to widely separated peoples. The domestication of the camel in southern Arabia, and the development of saddles for both fighting and carrying loads on their backs, revolutionized both desert travel and commerce in southwest Asia at about the time of Christ. Those who bred camels and controlled caravan routes acquired great political power. The famous city of Petra in present-day Jordan was one major caravan terminus.

In Chapter 12, we move from trade to other forms of human interaction, between individuals and groups, and examine some of the ways in which archaeologists study social organization and the religious beliefs that often underpin such organization.

Summary

Many factors determine settlement patterns, including environment, economic practices, and technological skills. Settlement archaeology is part of the study of human interactions with, and adaptations to, the natural and social environment. There are three basic levels of human settlement: the single building, the arrangement of such buildings in the community, and the distribution of such communities against the landscape. Both site catchment analysis and GIS play important roles in studying the relationships between hierarchies of different sites located in ancient landscapes. Exchange systems were used by ancient societies to acquire goods and services from outside their own site catchment areas. Trade appears in the archaeological record in the form of such exotic objects as seashells far inland or metals far from their original sources. A variety of characterization, or sourcing, techniques allow archaeologists to identify the specific sources of some raw materials like copper and obsidian, thereby allowing them to study ancient trade routes. These methods include spectrographic and neutron activation analysis, also artifact distributions. Much ancient trade depends on reciprocity, the mutual exchange of goods between two individuals, and the redistribution of trade goods from a central place throughout a culture. Such exchange differs from markets, which were places for administering and organizing trade, found in more complex societies.

12

The Archaeology of Society

Vase painting of two Moche warriors fighting. Coastal Peru, c. A.D. 400.

Sad fragility of human things! How many centuries and thousands of generations have passed away, of which history, probably, will never tell us anything. . . . How many distinguished [people]—artists, sovereigns, and warriors—whose names were worthy of immortality, are now forgotten, laid to rest under the thick dust which covers these tombs!

Henri Mouhot, 1860

In September 1991, German mountaineers Helmut and Erika Simon made their way around a narrow gully at 10,530 feet (3,210 m) near Hauslabjoch in the Italian Alps. Erika suddenly spotted a brown object projecting from the ice and glacial meltwater in the bottom of the gully. At first she thought it was merely a doll, but soon identified the skull, back, and shoulders of a man with his face lying in water. She had stumbled across the casualty of a 5,000-year-old mountain accident. The first police on the scene also assumed the man was a climbing victim. A unique archaeological find became corpse number 91/619 on the local coroner's dissection table. Within days, the authorities realized the body was very old and called in archaeologist Konrad Spindler of the University of Innsbruck, Austria. Local archaeologists organized a dig at the site, which was already under 2 feet (0.6 m) of snow. They used a steam blower and a hair dryer to recover parts of a grass cloak, leaves, tufts of grass, and wood fragments. By the end of the excavation, they had established that the man, now nicknamed "Otzi the Ice Man," had deposited his ax, bow, and backpack on a sheltered ledge. He had lain down on his left side, his head on a boulder, perhaps taking shelter from rapidly deteriorating weather in the small gully. Judging from his relaxed limbs, the exhausted man had gone to sleep and frozen to death a few hours later. For 5,000 years, Otzi's body lay in the gully, which protected his corpse as a glacier flowed overhead.

Otzi the Ice Man is the earliest European to survive as an identifiable individual, one of the few people of the past to come down to us so well preserved that we know almost more about him than he knew himself—his injuries, his diseases, his parasites. This remarkable discovery comes as somewhat of a jolt, because we come face to face with a once-living person, who laughed and cried, worked, and played, loved, hated, and interacted with others.

For all the hi-tech, late twentieth-century wizardry of modern archaeology, we must never forget that archaeologists study people, not just artifacts, food remains, and culture change. This chapter, "The Archaeology of Society," moves from the general to the particular. We use artifacts and other material remains to look behind the facades of ancient societies, at social organization and religious beliefs, and, above all, at the complex interactions between groups and individuals that are at the very heart of all human societies.

Individuals

The Innsbruck University research team called on the latest archaeological and medical science to conserve and study the 47-year-old man. Within a few weeks, five AMS radiocarbon dates dated Otzi's body to between 3350 and 3150 B.C. Biological anthropologists estimated his height as about 5 feet 2 inches (1.6 m) and took DNA samples that showed his genetic makeup was similar to late Europeans. Otzi's stomach was empty, so he was probably weak and hungry at the time of death. He also suffered from parasites. Smoke inhaled while living in small dwellings with open hearths had blackened his lungs as much as those of a modern-day smoker. Otzi had endured prolonged malnutrition in his 9th, 15th, and 16th years. His hands and fingernails were scarred from constant manual labor. He had groups of tattoos—mostly parallel vertical lines—on his lower back, left calf, and right ankle.

On his last day alive, Otzi wore a leather belt that held up a loincloth. Suspenders led from the belt to a pair of fur leggings. He wore an outer coat of alternating stripes of black and brown animal skin, also an outer cape of twisted grass, just like those still worn in the Alps a century ago. Otzi's bearskin cap fastened below his chin with a snap. On his feet he wore bearskin and deerskin shoes filled with grass held in place by a string "sock" (Figure 12.1)

Figure 12.1   A reconstruction of Otzi the Ice Man wearing a grass cloak and carrying his weapons.

Otzi was a self-sufficient man on the move. He carried a leather backpack on a wooden frame, a flint dagger, a copper-bladed axe with wooden handle, and a yew longbow and skin quiver filled with 14 arrows. His equipment included dry fungus and iron pyrite for fire lighting and spare arrowheads.

Today, Otzi lives in a special freezer that replicates glacial conditions. Scientists are still puzzling over the reason why he was so high in the mountains. A few wheat seeds lodged in his fur garments tell us he had recently been in a farming village. Some wild seeds come from a valley south of the Alps, as if he climbed from the Italian side. Was he a shepherd caught out at high altitude? Had he fled to the mountains to escape a family feud, or was he simply hunting wild goats? Nearly 150 scientists have collaborated on the Otzi project, but the circumstances of his death remain a complete mystery.

Groups

The relationships between individuals, their own households, communities, and society at large express themselves in all manner of tangible and intangible ways. There are relationships between people and communities that are expressed by gift exchanges, as well as through kin ties and reciprocal obligation. Then there are the issues of division of labor, of ever-changing roles of men and women from one generation to the next. Many such relationships are intangible, in the sense that they cannot be identified readily in the archaeological record, except in indirect ways.

As individuals, we all live in constant contact with other people: family members, kin, fellow community members, and people from many different groups. Our lives are those of interaction and constant negotiation with others, hedged in by kin rules, personal relationships, and social distinctions between individuals. Archaeologists study three important phenomena that reflect such interactions: social ranking; relationships between individuals, households, communities, and the wider society; and social diversity (ethnicity).

Social Ranking

Rare and unusual artifacts, be they exotic seashells, gold necklaces, or obsidian mirrors, have been signs of rank for thousands of years, proclaiming the status of those who own or wear them. Generally speaking, the more complex the society, the more great wealth, such as hoards of buried gold ornaments or fine drinking vessels, was concentrated in a few hands. Wealth and power became synonymous: witness the elaborate palaces and public buildings of Mycenean rulers in Greece or the richly decorated Sumerian temples in Mesopotamia.

As was the case with great Maya ceremonial centers like Tikal and Palenque in Mesoamerica, many such structures were built as important symbolic statements of political, social, and religious power. Copán, for example, is a symbolic model of the Maya spiritual world, complete with sacred mountains, trees, and caves (see Figure 3.4). The Temple of the sun god Amun at Karnak, Egypt, was a powerful statement of divine kingship, adorned with paintings and statues of great pharaohs and of the gods. Accompanying hieroglyphs and small details of royal costume provide constant, symbolic reminders of royal power and divine-given authority (Figure 12.2).

Figure 12.2 An Egyptian ruler in the presence of the scribe god Thoth at Karnak, Thebes, Egypt. Such depictions of Egyptian pharaohs were designed to validate the divine authority of the king.

Evidence of social ranking can sometimes be inferred from buildings and community layout. Teotihuacán shows every sign of having been an elaborately planned city, with special precincts for markets and craftspeople, and the houses of the leading priests and nobles near the Avenue of the Dead, which bisected the city (see Figure 11.3). In instances like this, it is easy enough to identify the houses belonging to each class in the society, both by their architecture and by the distinctive artifacts found in them.

Human burials are the most important source of information about prehistoric social organization and ranking. For instance, the Egyptian pharaoh Khufu expended vast resources on building his pyramid and mortuary temple at Giza (see Figure 2.1). Thousands of laborers moved more than 2.3 million limestone blocks weighing from 2.5 to 15 tons to build his pyramid during his 23-year reign.

Sometimes the differing status of burials may indicate that a society was rigidly ranked. When Leonard Woolley excavated the Early Dynastic royal burials of Ur in Mesopotamia, he found a great cemetery containing 1,850 graves. Sixteen of them stood out by virtue of their remarkable grave furniture. The royal tombs were sunk into the earlier levels of the mound, and a sepulcher consisting of several rooms was erected in the middle of a huge pit. The royal corpses were decked out in a cascade of gold and semiprecious stone ornaments, gold and silver ornaments were placed next to the biers, and several attendants were slaughtered to accompany the dead (Figure 12.3). Once the royal sepulcher was closed, the entire court filed into the grave pit, drank poison, and lay down to die in correct order of protocol. Woolley was able to identify the different rankings of the courtiers from their ornaments. In contrast to all this luxury, the average person was buried in a matting roll or a humble coffin.

In the New York/Albany region of northeastern North America there are numerous sites where Dutch traders lived in the early years of colonization. Wampum beads and belts were widely used as a medium of exchange for beaver pelts and other commodities throughout an enormous area extending over the St. Lawrence Valley. Distributions of wampum manufacturing sites and beaver traders' settlements are adding new dimensions to historical accounts of the region.

Figure 12.3   A reconstruction of the burial ceremony at the Royal Cemetery at Ur. The ranked members of the court stand in their assigned places, the grooms tending their wheeled carts.

Ethnicity and Inequality

For the most part, archaeologists have focused their attentions on two broad topics. Culture historians have described long-lasting cultural traditions in many parts of the world, and cultural ecologists and advocates of processual archaeology have studied the ever-changing relationships between human societies and their natural environments.

In recent years, however, a small number of scholars have used archaeology's unique perspective to study ethnic diversity, and what is sometimes called "the archaeology of inequality": the ways in which people have exercised economic and social power over others. Despite a few studies that are now focusing on the importance of social ranking and the political power of kings and nobles, almost no archaeologists have studied the phenomenon of resistance to overwhelming social and political power and the archaeology of ethnic minorities.

Elites have used many tactics to exercise power over others, everything from gentle persuasion to divine kingship, precedent, economic monopolies, and naked force. Perhaps most important of all are the ideologies of domination. The ancient Maya lords built great ceremonial centers with towering pyramids and vast plazas that were symbolic models of the Maya universe. It was here that the ruler went into a shamanistic trance, communicating with the gods and ancestors in lavish public ceremonies. Everything validated the complex relationship between the living and the dead, between ruler and commoner, displayed in lavish, pointed metaphors that confirmed the divine power of the supreme lords.

Political and social power are extremely heterogeneous phenomena that are exercised in many forms. From the archaeologist's point of view, what is fascinating is using material objects like pottery to study how people negotiated their social positions and resisted the submergence of their own culture. Artifacts offer a unique way of examining the history of the many communities that kept no written records, but expressed their diverse feelings and cultures through the specific artifacts and commodities they purchased and used.

The classic studies of such resistance are coming from the southern states, where the earliest Africans to reach North America brought their own notions of religion, ritual, and supernatural power to their new homes. "The guinea negroes had sometimes a small inclosure for their god house," wrote one Florida plantation owner in 1839. Historical records rarely refer to such shrines, but archaeologists have found blue beads and other charms at many slave sites in the North American Southeast. Black African slaves arrived in North America with cultural values and a worldview radically different from that of their masters. Slave plantations were part of much wider and very complex networks that linked planters to other planters, planters to slaves, and slaves to slaves on other plantations. Despite oppressive conditions, African Americans maintained their own beliefs and culture, which they melded over the generations with new ideas and material innovations from their new environment. They believed that their culture, their way of living, everything from cuisine to belief systems, was the best way.

African spiritual beliefs in all their variety were highly flexible, and were often responses to outside influences, whether political, religious, or economic. Thus existing spiritual beliefs adapted readily to the new American environment, adopting new artifacts or modifying existing ones over the generations. For example, archaeologists working at Thomas Jefferson's Monticello estate in Virginia have recovered crystals, pierced coins, and other ritual artifacts from Mulberry Row, where his slaves resided. Traditional practitioners were operating in a hostile environment, so they were careful to disguise their activities. At the Levi Jordan cotton and sugar plantation in south Texas, archaeologists Kenneth Brown and Doreen Cooper excavated a cabin occupied by an African American healer-magician. The cabin yielded animal bones, iron spikes, and other artifacts that were part of the paraphernalia of a traditional West African healer. To the African American workers on the plantation, these objects had a symbolic meaning that was not revealed to outsiders. It was for this reason that none of the healer's tools in trade bore any telltale symbolic decoration that might reveal their true purpose.

African Americans were disfranchised from white people in their own villages and slave quarters to the point that their masters and mistresses may well have been more like parts of their environment than key players in their social lives. In South Carolina and Georgia, slaves even spoke a distinctive African American language. Children growing up in this culture used material objects like earthen bowls that were made by members of this culture and heard stories of magic and religious chants that were important ways of establishing African American identity, of maintaining ideological power and molding values. Although many slaves may not have resisted their inferior, white-bestowed social status on a day-to-day basis, they ignored European-American culture in favor of their own and rejected an ideology that rationalized their enslavement.

Leland Ferguson has documented this resistance in South Carolina, where, in 1740, blacks outnumbered whites by almost two to one, and one half of that majority was African born. Here, as elsewhere along the South Atlantic coast, African women arrived with a knowledge of pot making that they used to fashion domestic wares in their new homes. Their distinctive unglazed earthenware products occur in slave quarters, on plantations, and in cities (Figure 12.4). Once considered Native American pots that had been traded to slaves, these "Colono wares" were the product of complex demographic and cultural forces that resulted from interactions between blacks and whites, and between both of them and Native Americans. Ferguson found that what he calls the "container environment" of South Carolina consisted of wood, basketry, and earthenware manufactures broadly similar to those of the slaves' African homeland. Ferguson believes that African American eating habits were much the same as those of West Africa and radically different from those of the European-Americans around them. Colono ware is remarkably similar over a large area, made by people living in an ethnic environment where reciprocal relationships with one another were of vital importance, and where there were strong ties to ancestral African culture. It was, says Ferguson, an unconscious resistance to slavery and the plantation system. The development of southern culture, he concludes, was a long process of quasi-political negotiation. And what is exciting is that we can use archaeology to look at the early stages of this complex process of negotiation from both sides.

Another fascinating chronicle of ethnic resistance comes from an archaeological investigation of the route taken by a small group of northern Cheyenne when they broke out of Fort Robinson, Nebraska, on January 9, 1879. They fought a running battle with the garrison, across the White River, up some bluffs, and into open country,

Figure 12.4   Colono ware vessel.

where it took the military 11 days to capture them. This much is beyond controversy, but the route that the Cheyenne took out of the river valley is disputed. According to military accounts, the escaping party moved up an exposed sandstone ridge to reach the bluffs. This exposed route was illogical, indeed foolhardy, for there was a full moon. Cheyenne oral traditions insist on another route to the bluffs through a well-protected drainage that offered excellent cover from pursuing riflemen. Archaeologists from the University of South Dakota Archaeology Laboratory investigated the escape routes with the collaboration of local Cheyenne representatives. They used random shovel testing and metal detectors to search for spent bullets in three areas—two drainages and the exposed ridge mentioned in military accounts. The survey recovered no bullets from the exposed ridge, but did find them in the drainages, thereby confirming the oral account of the Cheyenne Outbreak.

This may seem like a footnote to modern history, but it is important to remember that the Outbreak has become a classic story of the American West in white eyes, immortalized by John Ford's movie *Cheyenne Autumn*. This film tells the story from the victors' perspective, and is a form of moral tale of the Old West. Now oral tradition and archaeology have shattered part of the myth, telling the story from the Indian perspective in circumstances where science has helped fashion a mosaic of the recent past that is the historical truth rather than a myth.

The most compelling studies of ethnic minorities and their resistance to social domination come, at present, from the United States, from historical sites where written records amplify the archaeological record in important ways. As so often happens, methodology developed on historical sites will ultimately be applied to prehistoric situations. What, for example, was the lifeway of slaves and workers in ancient Egypt? We know from excavations in workers' quarters at the Pyramids of Giza that many laborers lived harsh lives, suffered from malnutrition, and had very short life expectancy. Such excavations raise many questions about the relationships between the rulers and the ruled. Archaeology, with its rich potential for studying the mundane and the trivial, the minutest details of daily life, is an unrivaled tool for the dispassionate study of social inequality and ethnicity.

Gender

For more than two-and-a-half million years, men and women have interacted, negotiated with one another, and shared the responsibilities of life and survival. Yet archaeologists have paid little attention to the study of gender and changing interactions between the sexes in the past. In part, this is because of a disinterest in the subject, but also because the archaeological record has been seen as anonymous and archaeologists have been more concerned with explaining general processes of culture change than with the archaeology of individual people. Only recently have archaeologists turned their attention to the complex issue of gender and gender relations, a promising avenue of new research.

Gender is not the same as sex, which refers to the biological male or female. Gender is socially and culturally constructed. Gender roles and relations acquire meaning in culturally and historically meaningful ways. This means that gender is a vital part of human social relations and a central issue in the study of ancient human societies.

The expression of gender varies, and has always varied, from society to society, and through time. Some archaeologists, like Margaret Conkey and Joan Gero, write of "engendering archaeology," an attempt to reclaim men and women in nonsexist ways in the past. This goes much further than merely demonstrating that pots were made by women, stone projectile points by men, or trying to identify women's activities in the archaeological record. The archaeology of gender deals with the ideology of gender, with roles and gender relations—the ways in which gender intersects with all aspects of human social life. How are roles and social relationships constructed? What contributions did men and women make to ancient societies? An engendered archaeology uses a wide diversity of archaeological methods and approaches to find how out gender "works" in ancient societies, to unravel its cultural meanings.

The most promising approaches use science to study male/female roles. The Abu Hureyra farming village in Syria, described in Chapter 10, is one of the earliest known agricultural settlements in the world. In about 9000 B.C., the inhabitants switched from hunting and foraging to growing cereal crops. For hours on end, the Abu Hureyra women would labor on their knees, grinding grain for the evening meal, as the monotonous scraping sound echoed through the settlement. Biological anthropologist Theya Molleson studied the many skeletons found under the Abu Hureyra houses and soon found out the people were remarkably healthy, except for bone deformities caused by arduous and repetitive tasks. Then she noticed some adolescents had enlarged portions on their neck vertebrae, the result of carrying heavy loads. She also identified many knee bones with bone extensions on their articular surfaces, the result of repeated kneeling for long periods of time. Many female skeletons also had stressed low back vertebrae, enlarged toe joints, and gross arthritic conditions of the big toe.

Molleson was puzzled by these deformities, until one of her colleagues visited Egypt and noticed that kneeling supplicants on the walls of ancient temples always had their toes curled forward. The only activity at Abu Hureyra that could produce the same effect was kneeling in front of the stone grinding querns found set into the house floors. Intrigued, Molleson now reconstructed the grinding process. The grinder put grain on the quern and gripped the grinding stone with both hands. He or she then knelt with the toes bent, pushing the stone forward, arms turning inward as the stone reached the end of the quern. At the end of the stroke, the upper body was almost parallel to the floor. Repeated every day, such a back-and-fro movement would cause backbone damage identical to those on the skeletons, also placing bending stress on the knee and hip joints, and eventually causing arthritic conditions in the toes, conditions found in the Abu Hureyra bones. Theya Molleson is virtually certain that women and girls suffered repetitive-stress injuries because they shouldered the laborious task of preparing food.

The Engendered Past

To engender the past means focusing not only on major material achievements like metallurgy or pot making, or on ancient environments, but also on interpersonal relations and the social dynamics of everyday activity. These are the activities that take up most of people's daily lives—hunting, gardening, preparing meals, building houses, and so on. But gender also impacts on trade, craft specialization, state formation, religion, and ritual—to mention only a few major human activities.

Gender research in archaeology is concerned not just with women, but with people as individuals and their contributions to society. Archaeologist Elizabeth Brumfiel has studied Aztec women, who were expert weavers. Indeed weaving was a fundamental skill for an Aztec noblewoman (Figure 12.5). However, she points out that to characterize them merely as weavers ignores the vital links between weaving, child rearing, and cooking (to mention only a few women's tasks) and the wider society in which the women lived. For instance, the population of the Valley of Mexico rose tenfold during the four centuries before the conquest, a striking testimony to the success of the Aztec household economy. Women wove textiles and the capes that were the badges of social status in Aztec society. Their woven products were vital to the enormous tribute system on which Aztec civilization depended. Cotton mantles even served as a form of currency. Cloth was a primary way of organizing the ebb and flow of goods and services that sustained the state.

Brumfiel shows that the Aztec household and the roles of women were much more varied than those attributed to them by early Spanish observers. Furthermore, the skills of cooking and weaving were important political tools, ways of maintaining

Figure 12.5   An Aztec woman teaches her daughter how to weave. From the *Codex Mendoza*, one of the few surviving Aztec codices.

social and political control. Thus, she argues, the idealization of these skills in both Aztec folklore and schooling developed because women were makers of both valuable goods and of people. It was they who assured the continuity of Aztec kin groups. More simplistic views of Aztec life mask the dynamic and highly adaptive role that women played in this remarkable civilization.

Gender studies are still in their infancy, and based, for the most part, on extrapolations from ethnoarchaeological and ethnological data. The Sausa are maize and potato farmers who live in highland Peru's northern Mantaro Valley. Before the Inka took control in about A.D. 1460, the Sausa lived in local population groups of several thousand people. Their conquerors, anxious to increase maize production, dispersed them into small village settlements. Archaeologist Christine Hastorf was interested in the changing social dynamics resulting from the Inka conquest. How did women's social position change as a result of the new conditions? She approached this question by using two different avenues—the distribution of food remains in excavated settlements compared with those in modern house compounds, and dietary evidence obtained by stable isotope analyses of male and female skeletons from ancient Sausa villages.

In Andean households, women are responsible for food preparation and storage. Hastorf studied the relationship between the distribution of plant remains in dwellings and compounds, and the behavior of men and women in that household. For example, in households with male heads, she found the most diverse plant forms in kitchen areas, and fewer crop seeds elsewhere in the compound where other activities took place. In contrast, a household with a female head had concentrations of crop seeds not only in the kitchen area but on the patio, as if there were different constraints acting on the preparation and food consumption.

Next, Hastorf plotted the distribution of crop seeds in pre-Hispanic compounds. The pre-Inka structures date from a time when maize was less common and of great sacred value. The inhabitants of every dwelling used and consumed a wide range of plant foods, including maize, potatoes, and many legumes. Maize occurred mostly in patio areas. It was here, argues Hastorf, that such communal activities as beer making took place, a commodity that was a vital part of ritual, social, and political meetings. A later Inka-period compound yielded fewer potatoes and much more maize. Here the processing of corn was more concentrated, with little burning of corn, as if more of it was consumed as beer. Hastorf wonders if the dense and restricted distribution of maize in the later compound might reflect more intensified processing of corn by women. They were now living under Inka policies that sought a constant rise in maize production, regular taxation in the form of labor and produce, and, therefore, more restricted, intensified roles for women in support of male activities.

Hastorf now turned her attention to male and female skeletons found in the compounds, and to staple carbon isotope analysis. As carbon is passed along the food chain, the carbon composition of animals, including humans, continues to reflect the relative isotopic composition of their diet. The plants that make up the diet of humans have distinct carbon 13 values: by studying the archaeological carbon from food remains and skeletal remains, one can study dietary changes.

Hastorf also studied the stable isotopes in bone collagen extracted from Sausa skeletons. She found pre-Inka diets were the same for men and women, mainly one of quinoa and tubers, with some maize. These similar values suggest that beer was shared between men and women. Then the Inka entered Sausa society. The 21 skeletons (12 males, 9 females) from these centuries reveal a higher consumption of maize, but half of the male diets were much richer in maize than those of the women. Hastorf believes this reflects changed social conditions under Inka rule. The women were processing much more maize into beer, which was consumed not by everyone, but by a relatively small proportion of the males in the community. The dietary differences reflect a changed political climate in which the Sausa, once small groups, were now incorporated into a larger political sphere, which depended on men becoming involved in far more gatherings, rituals, and obligatory tasks, when beer was consumed. The women worked harder, but their position outside the home was more restricted under the Inka regime.

As the Hastorf example shows, gender research will be a marriage between modern high-tech science and good old-fashioned archaeological observation. This will give us the potential to go far beyond the material, to probe the subjective and the gender driven, even, as Hastorf shows, the ways in which men and women adapt to changing circumstances. This kind of meticulous research with its concerns for the changing dynamics of ancient society offers great promise for the future.

Wider Society: Prestate and State Societies

Human society has changed dramatically since the first appearance of modern humans in Africa more than 100,000 years ago. Much effort has gone into deciphering the complexities of ancient social organization, the most successful approaches being those that use broad evolutionary frameworks. These provide a general outline for tracing human social organization from the first simple family structures of the earliest humans to the highly complex state-organized societies of the early civilizations.

All theories of cultural evolution are based on the premise that human societies have changed over long periods of time and that the general trend throughout prehistory has been toward a greater complexity of human culture and social institutions. This does not mean, of course, that all human societies have evolved in a linear, ladderlike way, as Victorian anthropologists once believed. Cultural change has proceeded, and still proceeds, in many directions. If there is a general trend over time, it is toward increasing social and political complexity.

Furthermore, this trend toward greater complexity has manifested itself in remarkably similar ways in terms of political and social organization. Many archaeologists take this broad similarity into account by grouping early human societies into two broad, arbitrary categories: prestate societies and state-organized societies.

Prestate societies are small-scale societies based on the community, band, or village. They vary greatly in their degree of political integration, and can be divided into three groupings.

Bands are autonomous and self-sufficient groups that usually consist of only a few families. They are egalitarian, with leadership coming from experience and the personal qualities of particular individuals rather than from inherited or acquired political power.

Tribes are egalitarian like bands, but with more social and cultural organizations. They have developed kin-based social mechanisms to accommodate their more sedentary lifestyle, to redistribute food, and to organize some communal services. Some more complex hunter-gatherer societies—for example, the North American Pacific Northwest coast groups—can be classified as tribes; however, most were associated with village farming.

Chiefdoms are societies headed by individuals with unusual ritual, political, or entrepreneurial skills, and are often hard to distinguish from tribes. Society is still kin based, but is more hierarchical, with power concentrated in the hands of powerful kin leaders responsible for the redistribution of resources. Chiefdoms tend to have higher population densities and to display signs of social ranking, reflected in more elaborate material possessions for leading individuals. Chiefdoms vary greatly in their elaborateness, but reached a high level of sophistication in Hawaii, Tahiti, and among the Mississippian people of the Midwest and South after A.D. 1000.

Many researchers now question the general utility of the band-tribe-chiefdom classification, on the grounds it is too rigid and of limited application. At a general level, prestate societies are remarkable for their small-scale social and political organization, although the degree of complexity can vary dramatically, from a few families to an elaborate chiefdom extending over an entire Pacific Island.

State-organized societies *(civilizations)* operate on a large scale, with centralized social and political organizations, class stratification, and intensive agriculture. They have complex political structures, many permanent government institutions, and are based on notions of social inequality, the assumption that privilege will reside in the hands of a few individuals. State-organized societies are synonymous with the early urban civilizations—those of the Sumerians, ancient Egyptians, Maya, and others—that were governed by supreme rulers with absolute powers (Figure 2.1). These preindustrial civilizations, founded on social inequality and maintained by the labor of thousands, were the precursors of the industrial civilizations of later history.

The absolute power of early Egyptian pharaohs or Maya lords came from their perceived supernatural powers, which were embedded in compelling, often recited ideologies. Pyramids, plazas, and temples provided the settings for lavish public ceremonies, where the ruler would appear before his subjects as drums played, chants were sung, and incense rose into the sky. Sacred places were the settings where civilization was validated. They provide one way for archaeologists to decipher the religious beliefs of our forebears.

Religious Beliefs

An anonymous scholar wrote cynically that "religion is the last resort of troubled archaeologists." At one time archaeologists were inclined to call any object they could not identify "ritual." Obviously, some important sites were of religious significance. The Pyramid of the Sun at Teotihuacán is one, Stonehenge is another. Some of the earliest religious objects in the world are the so-called Venus figurines made in Europe 25,000 years ago (Figure 12.6).

Some evidence for religious rituals comes from burials. The Neanderthal peoples of western Europe may have deliberately buried their dead of 70,000 years ago with a variety of goods. Hundreds of Adena and Hopewell burial mounds dot the landscape of the Midwest, holding the graves of thousands of leaders and lesser personages, each buried with distinctive grave furniture, some with elaborate, highly prestigious

Figure 12.6 A Venus figurine head from Brassempouy, France. Two-thirds actual size.

Figure 12.7   The Great Serpent Mound, built by the Mississippian people as a ceremonial earthwork.

artifacts such as mica and copper ornaments. The building of the Hopewell mounds was carried out step by step as the dead were deposited on an earthen platform that was later covered with a large mound. The famed Great Serpent Mound in Ohio is a later ceremonial earthwork whose exact religious significance still escapes us (Figure 12.7).

Many prehistoric societies enjoyed highly organized religions that were reflected in widely distributed and characteristic art styles. The Olmec art style of Mexico was carried over thousands of square miles of highlands and lowlands after 1000 B.C. Olmec art's snarling jaguar and human motifs coincide with distinctive religious beliefs that may have linked large and small communities all over Mexico.

Most societies' religious beliefs were interpreted and maintained through regular religious rituals conducted at specific times of the year, as at harvests and plantings. These regular ceremonies were vital to the elaborate organization of newly emerging complex societies. The predictable yearly round of religious life gave society an orderly framework for redistributing food, disposing of surplus cattle, accumulating wealth, and other economic functions. The long-term effects of these new, unifying religious beliefs were startling.

Between 1150 and 850 B.C., Mesoamerican society began to undergo rapid transformation. Administrative and religious authority came together in the hands of leaders of a newly ranked society, with specialists and a hierarchy of settlements. This organization contrasted with the dispersed villages of earlier times. More elaborate public buildings appeared as temples and monumental buildings began to reflect individual communities' common involvement in public works. In Mesoamerica and elsewhere, the ultimate sacred beliefs and rituals of a society are linked to the processes of social and environmental change that act upon it.

Studying Religion

In recent years, many researchers have turned to ethnohistorical and historical records to decipher ancient religious beliefs. Only a few years after the Spanish Conquest of Mexico, missionary Fray Bernardino de Sahagun (c. 1499–1590) laboriously recorded a mass of information about Aztec life and civilization from Indian survivors of the Conquest. In his great work, *A General History of the Things of New Spain*, he described not only early Aztec history, but minute details of Indian religion, even Aztec philosophy and poetry. Modern scholars are interpreting his writings and discovering that Aztec religious beliefs were at least as sophisticated and complex as the Catholic beliefs that replaced them.

David Lewis-Williams is an expert on the prehistoric rock art in southern Africa mentioned earlier, an art tradition painted on the walls of caves and rockshelters for thousands of years until Europeans came in the eighteenth and nineteenth centuries A.D. This art depicts animals, hunters during the chase, scenes of camp life and religious ceremonies, as well as complex signs and symbols (Figure 12.8). No painters survived into this century, but Lewis-Williams dug into early oral traditions of the paintings collected by nineteenth-century investigators, who also recorded some of the San oral traditions about the paintings. His research has enabled him to evaluate some of the paintings of eland and other animals in their ancient symbolic context. The paintings were integral to the symbolic world of the San, a world intimately tied to the animals they hunted.

David Friedel and Linda Schele's work on Maya cosmology is a fine example of this type of research. They have used changes in Maya images and hieroglyphs to study the meaning of symbols associated with political power. For example, the religious symbolism of Maya society in 100 B.C. was based on the passage of Venus as morning and evening star with the rising and setting of the sun. The people of any Maya community could identify and verify their cosmos simply by observing the sky. As time went on, Maya cosmology was expanded and elaborated. Initially, the names of rulers were not recorded publicly. Perhaps such permanent verification on public monuments was not yet deemed necessary. After A.D. 200, Maya rulers followed a quite different strategy. They legitimized their rule through genealogies, public ceremonies, and monuments—much art was commissioned as part of this process of legitimizing rulers, who claimed identity with gods in the Mayan cosmos. Friedel and Schele believe that the metaphor of the twin ancestors—Venus and the sun—provided a potent image for lateral blood ties between lineages, communities, and everyone who believed in the same myths. Because twins are of the same womb and blood, so the Maya are all of common ancestry and blood.

This Maya research shows that we should never think of religion and ritual in isolation but rather as integral to social organization, economic life, and political systems. The ideas and beliefs, the core of all religions, are reflected in many aspects of

Figure 12.8 A San rock painting from South Africa, interpreted with the aid of oral traditions. Shaman-hunters are performing a trance dance. Their elongated bodies convey the sense of being stretched out that is felt by people in altered states of consciousness. Dots along the spine of the central figure depict what the San describe as a "boiling," as supernatural power rises up the spine and "explodes" in the head. The power is derived from certain animals like the eland, depicted to the right.

human life, especially in art and architecture. Every society has its own model of how the world is put together, its own ultimate beliefs. These sacred propositions are interpreted for the faithful through a body of theology and rituals. The rituals are more or less standardized religious acts often repeated at regular times of the year—harvests, plantings, and other key times. Others are performed when needed: marriages, funerals, and the like. Some societies, such as those of the ancient Egyptians and the Maya, made regular calendars to time religious events and astronomical cycles. These regular ceremonies performed important functions not only in integrating society but also in such activities as redistributing food, controlling population by infanticide, and dispersing surplus male cattle in the form of ritually accumulated wealth.

Religious experiences are predominantly emotional, often supernatural and awe inspiring. A religion operates through sanctified attitudes, values, and messages, an ethic that adds a sacred blessing, derived from the ultimate sacred propositions of the society, to elicit predictable responses from the people. Such predictability, sparked by directives from some central religious authority, ensures orderly operation of society. In time, as in Mesopotamia, that authority can become secular as well. The institutions and individuals associated with these messages can become sanctified, for they are associated with the sacred propositions that lie at the heart of the society's beliefs. As societies become more complex, so does the need for a stable framework to administer the needs of the many increasingly specialized subgroups that make up society as a whole.

Religious beliefs are intangible and survive only in the form of temples, ritual paraphernalia, and art. Viewed in isolation, the study of ancient religion seems a hopeless task—if archaeological finds are the only source of information available. But if one views religion and ritual as integral to a society and closely tied to all other aspects of its activities, there is some hope that we may be able to look at ritual and religious artifacts in the context of a society as a whole.

One example comes from the Valley of Oaxaca, Mexico. Between 1400 and 1150 B.C., modest temples appear in local villages, built on adobe and earth platforms. Rare conch-shell trumpets and turtle-shell drums traded from the coastal lowlands were apparently used in public ceremonies in such buildings. Clay figurines of dancers wearing costumes and masks that make them look like fantastic creatures and animals, as well as pottery masks, also appear at the same time (Figure 12.9). So does another religious artifact, the stingray spine imported from the Gulf of Mexico, used in personal self-mutilation rituals of bloodletting. The Spanish described how the Aztec nobles would gash themselves with knives or with fish and stingray spines in religious acts of mutilation that were penances before the gods. Thus, argued archaeologist Kent Flannery, there were three levels of religious ceremony: personal bloodletting; dances run by kin groups, which cut across household lines; and public rituals in ceremonial buildings, involving a region wider than one village.

Figure 12.9 Four figures grouped deliberately to form a scene, found buried beneath a house of about 1200 B.C. at San José Mogote, Oaxaca, Mexico.

The study of prehistoric religion depends heavily on the study of sacred artifacts and temples and on careful research design. The most effective way to study such intangibles as social organization or religious beliefs and rituals is to consider them as integral to a society, closely tied to all other aspects of its activities. The rituals that ensured the continuity of religious belief are reflected in architecture and art, and the presence or absence of sacred artifacts in the archaeological record may reveal valuable information on prehistoric religion, provided that research designs are carefully made.

In these and other ways, archaeologists are trying to unravel the complex and little-understood symbolic world of the ancients. The task will never be easy and requires large data sets, excellent preservation, and sophisticated theoretical approaches. Australian historian Inga Clendinnen, the author of a superb book on the Aztecs, calls us "Ahabs pursuing our great white whale." She writes aptly, "We will never catch him . . . it is our limitations of thought, of understandings, of imagination we test as we quarter these strange waters. And then we think we see a darkening in the deeper water, a sudden surge, the roll of a fluke—and then the heart-stopping glimpse of the great white shape . . . there on the glimmering horizon."

We must now turn our attention to another pressing problem in archaeology—the relationship between the archaeological record and our own ever-changing world.

Summary

Humans spend their lives interacting with one another as individuals and as groups. This chapter explains how archaeologists study such interactions, beginning with individuals, then groups. In studying social organization, archaeologists use exotic artifacts and human burials to identify social ranking, by examining the differences in wealth and ornamentation. They use distinctive artifact patterns, historic documents, and symbols of political and religious power to study social ranking and ideologies of domination, also resistance to power. Important studies of African American societies in the southern United States have shown how many such communities maintained their beliefs and culture for many generations. In recent years, some archaeologists have analyzed gender relations in ancient societies, using artifacts, monumental architecture, and the changing status of women as revealed through artifacts and changing food patterns. Archaeologists define several broad levels of sociocultural evolution in prehistory, which provide a general framework for tracing human organization through time. Prestate societies include bands, tribes, and chiefdoms, small-scale societies that vary greatly in their degree of political integration. State-organized societies, the preindustrial civilizations, operate on a large scale, with centralized social and political institutions and social classes. Religious beliefs can sometimes be discerned from traditional histories, also from art traditions, and through the decipherment of early scripts, such as Maya glyphs. Such beliefs were integral to all societies and are best studied with careful research designs.

13
Explaining the Past

The gods Horus and Seth joined by a knot made up of the heraldic plants of Upper and Lower Egypt: a symbolic representation of the unity of Ancient Egypt, c. 1928 B.C.

Academics in universities are often theorists, intoxicated by theory or haunted by it. To the field-worker, their theories compete and multiply like insects in a hot-house, the dominant species being variously social, processual, analytical, behavioural, cognitive, structural, symbolic, or contextual, each with its own plumage and coterie.

M.O.H. Carver, 1989

W e have now described many of the ways in which archaeologists reconstruct the past—the planning of research, the acquisition and analysis of archaeological data, the construction of culture histories, and the reconstruction of ancient lifeways. There remains one objective of archaeology—the explanation of culture change. This chapter examines some of the ways in which archaeologists approach the study of cultural process.

Interpretation of Culture History

The ordering of archaeological data is a descriptive process. It highlights the patterning and regularities in archaeological data. The concepts and units of culture historical studies are devices used to organize data as a preliminary to studying culture change. These classificatory units put artifacts and other culture traits into a time and space context by using distribution maps, stratigraphy, seriation and cross-dating, and chronometric dating methods.

Culture history is a sound way of describing the past, but it is of minimal use for explaining variability in the archaeological record. It is based on inductive research methods, the development of generalizations about a research problem that are based on numerous specific observations, and on a normative view of culture. This assumes that abstract rules govern what a culture considers normal behavior.

The normative view of culture is a descriptive one, one that can be used to describe culture during one particular time period or throughout time. Archaeologists base it on the assumption that surviving artifacts, such as potsherds, display stylistic and other changes that represent the changing norms of human behavior through time.

So far we have dealt with components, phases, and other units as phenomena in isolation. We have assumed that the artifacts they contain reflect gradual, evolutionary change in human society. But the archaeological record does not invariably reflect an orderly and smooth chronicle of culture change. A radical new artifact inventory may suddenly appear in components at several sites while earlier tool kits suddenly vanish. The economy of sites in a local sequence may change completely within a century as the plow revolutionizes agricultural methods. Such changes are readily observed in thousands of local sequences all over the world. But how did these changes come about? What processes of cultural change were at work to cause major and minor alterations in the archaeological record? A number of descriptive models have been formulated to characterize culture change—some cultural, others noncultural. Several involve internal change, others external influence. These descriptive models include inevitable variation and cultural selection, invention, diffusion, and migration.

Inevitable Variation and Cultural Selection

Inevitable variation is somewhat akin to the well-known phenomenon of genetic drift in biology. As people learn the behavior patterns of their society, inevitably some differences in learned behavior appear from generation to generation, which, although minor in themselves, accumulate over a long time, especially in isolated populations. The snowball effect of inevitable variation and slow-moving cultural evolution can be detected in dozens of prehistoric societies. The great variation in Acheulian hand ax technology throughout Europe and Africa between a million and 150,000 years ago may be in part the result of the effects of inevitable variation.

Inevitable variation often results from isolation, a very low density of humans per square mile. It should not be confused with broad trends in human prehistory that grew over long periods. For example, the more and more complex burial rituals in the Adena and Hopewell cultures of the American Midwest between 500 B.C. and A.D. 300 probably resulted from trends toward greater complexity in religious beliefs and rituals as well as from political and economic organization over a long time, and not from isolation.

Inevitable variation is also quite different from what happens when a society recognizes that certain culture changes or inventions may be advantageous. Perhaps, many hunter-gatherer societies deliberately took up cultivating the soil once they saw the advantages it gave neighboring peoples, who had already adopted the new economies.

Invention

Invention is the creation or evolution of a new idea. Many inventions, such as new social institutions or religious beliefs, leave no trace in the archaeological record. But some innovations are reflected in new types of surviving artifacts, such as the plow or the iron ax. If an invention such as plowing is sufficiently useful to be attractive to more than a few people, the new idea or a product of the idea spreads widely and often rapidly.

By tracing, from their place of origin, the distribution of such distinctive artifacts as plowshares, archaeologists have studied ways in which inventions spread. The earliest occurrence of iron making was in northern Turkey about 1500 B.C. Iron tools first appear in the archaeological record of Europe and Egypt very much later. Because the earliest presently known and dated iron artifacts occurred in Turkey, we can say that iron making may have been invented there.

In the early days of archaeology, people assumed that metallurgy and other major inventions were invented in only one place—in many cases southwestern Asia. These innovations then spread all over the world as other societies realized how important the new ideas were. But as the importance of environment and adaptation in the development of human culture have become better understood, this simple view of invention has been rejected. We now know agriculture developed quite independently in southwest and southeast Asia, Mesoamerica, and the Andean area. Complex adaptive processes occurred in all of these areas. Scholars now try to identify the many interacting factors that caused people to modify their lifestyles to adopt food production. The genius of humanity was that it recognized opportunities when they came along and adapted to new circumstances.

The issue is not to discover who first cultivated corn but rather to study the dozens of major and minor alterations in human culture that were the result of adaptive changes over time.

Diffusion

The spread of ideas, over short or long distances, is termed *diffusion*. Ideas can be transmitted in many ways other than by the movements of entire societies or communities. Regular trade between neighboring villages or more distant peoples results in the exchange not only of goods but of ideas as well, especially when much of this trade is conducted reciprocally. Reciprocity implies a two-sided relationship in which both parties exchange goods, services, and, of course, ideas. Ideas such as a new religious belief are transmitted from individual to individual and ultimately from group to group. But neither the exchange of ideas nor that of technological innovations necessarily involves actual movements of people. Even the spread of material objects and abstract ideas can have a quite different effect in a new area. For instance, the Hopi Indians of the Southwest received American trade goods but still retained their own culture, trading objects but rejecting the ideas of an alien culture.

Let us say that a new type of painted pot is invented in one village in A.D. 1400. The advantages of this new vessel are such that villagers 10 miles (16 km) away learn about it at a celebration a year later. Within ten years, their potters are making similar receptacles. In a short time the pot form is found commonly in villages 10 miles (16 km) farther away. Half a century later, communities in a 50-mile radius are making the now well-established vessel design. If we put this stirring tale on paper, we end up with the cone effect shown in Figure 13.1. The cone effect is the type of distribution we study when identifying diffusion in the archaeological record.

Archaeologically, diffusion is difficult to identify unless one can use very distinctive artifacts obviously of common origin to demonstrate that the artifacts were

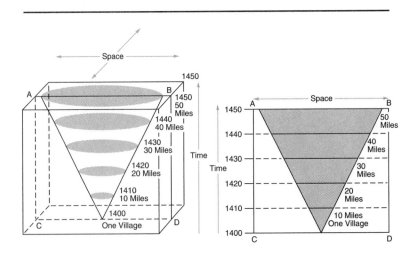

Figure 13.1   The spread of a culture trait in time and space: the cone effect.

invented in only one place, and trace the distribution of the artifact in space and time from its origin point to neighboring areas. To do so means establishing that the tool was first made in one place and other sites nearby later (Figure 13.1). Instances of diffusion in prehistory are common. A classic example is the Chavín art style of Peru, which diffused widely over the lowlands from a homeland in the highlands, where it appeared about 900 B.C.

Migration

Migration takes place when entire societies deliberately decide to expand their sphere of influence. English settlers moved to North America, taking their own culture with them. Spanish conquistadors occupied Mexico. Migration involves not only the movement of ideas but a mass shift of people that results in social and cultural changes on a large scale. A classic prehistoric migration was that of a group of Polynesians who deliberately voyaged from the Society Islands to Easter Island and New Zealand, where they settled. In each case, new land masses were found by purposeful exploration, then colonized by small numbers of people who moved to an uninhabited island.

These types of mass migration were rare in prehistoric times. They would be reflected in the archaeological record by totally new components and phases or by skeletons of a totally new physical type. To be proved, the migration would have to show up as new complexes in the cultural sequence at many neighboring sites. A second type of migration is on a smaller scale, when a group of foreigners move into another region and settle there as an organized group. A group of Oaxacans did just that at Teotihuacán in the Valley of Mexico. When René Millon mapped the whole of this remarkable city, he found a concentration of distinctive Oaxacan artifacts in one residential area. This Oaxacan colony flourished for centuries in an alien city. In this and many other cases, the immigrants adopted some features of the host culture but retained their own cultural identity.

There are other types of migration, too. Slaves and artisans are often unorganized migrants, sometimes taking new technological devices with them. Great warrior migrations, like those of Zulu regiments in South Africa in the early nineteenth century, can cause widespread disruption and population shifts. Such migrations leave few traces in archaeological sites. Within a few generations, the warriors settle down and adopt the sedentary life of the conquered. Only a few new weapon forms reveal the presence of strangers.

Noncultural Models

Culture change triggered by alterations in the natural environment is an integral part of culture history. Earlier noncultural models tended to be simple, stating, for example, that agriculture began in southwestern Asia when population pressure caused game and plant food shortages, causing people to turn to farming instead. However, the most recent research in archaeology has focused heavily on specific details of the relationship between environment and prehistoric cultures. The complex models that are emerging from this research show that earlier explanations were far too general to explain these ever-changing environment–culture relationships.

Great amounts of data obviously are needed to identify invention, diffusion, or migration in the archaeological record. The identification of these classic cultural processes is largely a mechanical, descriptive activity because the artifacts used, be they stone axes, pots, or swords, are considered in isolation and not as an element of the cultural system of which they are part. The explanation of culture change requires more sophisticated research models, based on the notion that human cultural systems are made up not only of many complex interacting elements—religious beliefs, technology, subsistence, and so on—but that these cultural systems also interact with the natural environment and other complex systems.

Processual Archaeology

Processual archaeology is based on deductive research methodology that employs research design, formulation of explicit research hypotheses, and testing of these against basic data. Its methods are cumulative; that is, initial hypotheses are designed which propose a working model to explain culture change. These hypotheses are tested against basic data and some are discarded; others are refined again and again until the factors that affect cultural change are isolated in highly specific form.

The processual approach is firmly based on culture history and data obtained from inductive research. It must be, for the chronological and spatial frameworks for prehistory come from such investigations. The difference between the processual and systems-ecological approaches lies in the orientation of the research. Processual archaeologists rely on deductive strategies, formulate testable hypotheses, and then gather data to test them. Very often, however, the initial hypotheses are based on data derived from inductive culture history.

The Systems-Ecological Approach

Deductive research is extremely valuable for the study of the past, provided that realistic account is taken of the uniqueness of archaeological data. In many respects, the numerous theoretical problems archaeologists are grappling with are the same as those encountered by biologists working on change in living organisms. It is for this reason that evolutionary theory is playing an increasingly important part in archaeology.

The most common processual approach deals with the ways in which cultural systems function, both internally and in relation to external factors such as the natural environment. The systems-ecological approach involves three basic models of cultural change: systems models, which are based on general systems theory; cultural ecology, which provides complicated models of the interaction between human cultures and their environment; and multilinear evolution, which is a theory of the cumulative evolution of culture over long periods through complex adaptations to the environment. It is, as archaeologist Kent Flannery (1976: 16) once put it, "the search for the ways human populations (in their own way) do the things that other systems do."

General systems theory came to archaeology from other sciences and has caused archaeologists to think of human cultures as open systems, regulated in part by external stimuli. This general concept is most applicable to human cultures that interact intimately with the natural environment. Systems theory is little more than a general concept in archaeology, with the advantage that it frees us from having to look at only one agent of culture change, such as migration or diffusion. It allows us to focus instead on relationships between different components of a cultural system and between a cultural system and its environment.

Cultural ecology is a means of studying human culture that gives a picture of the way in which human populations adapt to, and transform, their environments. Human cultural systems have to adapt to other cultures and to the natural environment. Indeed, so many factors influence cultural systems that the processes by which cultural similarities and differences are generated are not easy to understand. Cultural ecologists see human cultures as subsystems interacting with other major subsystems, among them the biotic community and the physical environment. Thus the key to understanding cultural process lies in the interactions among these various subsystems.

Effective subsistence strategies and technological artifices are the cornerstones of any society's successful adaptation to its environment. But social organization and religious beliefs are important in ensuring cooperative exploitation of the environment as well as technological cooperation. For instance, religious life provided an integrating force in many societies, not least among them the Maya of Mesoamerica and the Sumerians of Mesopotamia. There are obvious difficulties in studying the interactions between people and their environment, especially when preservation conditions limit the artifacts and other data available for study. Fortunately, however, artifacts and other elements of the technological subsystem often survive. Because technology is a primary way in which different cultures adapt to their environment, detailed models of technological subsystems allow archaeologists to obtain a relatively comprehensive picture of the cultural system as a whole.

Multilinear cultural evolution is a branching, cumulative process that results from cultural adaptations over long periods. Multilinear evolution recognizes that there are many evolutionary tracks, the differences resulting from individual adaptive solutions. Thus cultural adaptations are complex processes that are fine-tuned to local conditions, with long-term cumulative effects. These adaptations can be studied on a large and small scale by a systems-ecological approach. Multilinear cultural evolution, then, is the vital integrative force that brings systems theory and cultural ecology together into a closely knit, highly flexible way of studying and explaining cultural process.

The systems-ecological approach produces very complex interpretations of major developments in prehistory—for example, the origins of literate civilization in southwestern Asia. Early theories invoked single causes, such as population pressure, the invention of irrigation agriculture, even warfare or trade, as the ultimate single causes, prime movers if you will, of civilization. Systems-ecological models argue that a whole series of important variables with complex interrelationships and variations caused the emergence of civilization. Under this rubric, the rise of civilization should be thought of as a series of interacting and cumulative processes that were triggered by favorable cultural and ecological conditions, which continued to develop cumulatively as a result of continuous positive feedback.

For example, farming communities were established in the low-lying Mesopotamian delta between the Tigris and Euphrates by at least 5700 B.C. These settlements triggered three processes that set up critical feedback relationships: slow but steady population growth within the delta, increased specialization in food production by different groups within society, and a demand for and acquisition of raw materials from outside the delta region. Each of these processes set off feedback reactions that became more and more complex as time went on. A need for more fields to feed more people, more centralized planning and administration, larger and more densely populated settlements that took up a minimum of agricultural land, irrigation farming, and finally an administrative elite that controlled people's access to resources—all were complex reactions to long-term processes of cultural change.

Postprocessual Archaeology

Archaeology is based on the optimistic belief that knowledge about human societies has accumulated gradually, through rational inquiry modeled on the hard sciences and mathematics. This notion of cumulative science and knowledge is vital to understanding the convoluted history of archaeological theory since the 1960s.

In the 1960s and 1970s, archaeologists were talking about a so-called new archaeology, a revolutionary approach to the past that promised to overcome the many limitations of the archaeological record. In fact, this new archaeology, usually called processual archaeology, has failed to deliver on many of its promises. Processual archaeology has emphasized subsistence and settlement patterns, animal bones, plant remains, and ancient population distributions, topics covered extensively in this book. Its many practitioners embraced methodological rigor and interpreted the past in terms of cultural systems, with a strong emphasis on material objects. Many of its once new tenets are part of today's mainstream archaeology. Back in the 1960s, Lewis Binford and others believed that processual archaeology would allow researchers to investigate all aspects of human experience, including intangibles such as beliefs. But eventually, many discouraged processual archaeologists dismissed religion, ideology, and human ideas as marginal to the central enterprise of studying subsistence and settlement.

Inevitably, there was a reaction against the materialist processual approach, which seemed to dehumanize the past in a quest for processes of cultural change. During the late 1970s and 1980s, more researchers began thinking about the entire spectrum of human behavior—the development and expression of human consciousness, religion and belief, symbolism and iconography, as part of a more holistic archaeology. Thus was born *postprocessual archaeology,* a sometimes violent antidote to its predecessor, in general terms a reaction against the relatively anonymous processual approach that emphasized cultural processes over people and individuals.

Postprocessual archaeology is a loosely defined term that covers several, often aggressively expressed intellectual developments that often parallel the postmodernist schools of thought in literature and anthropology. As British archaeologist John Bintcliff has pointed out, a subdiscipline of archaeology, archaeological theory, has unfolded not in a cumulative manner, but by a process of almost total renewal every ten years or so. In each case, the leading proponents of the new approach write off the previous paradigm as useless and introduce new concepts, often derived from attractive theoretical approaches developed in other disciplines, and not in archaeology itself. Postprocessualism is no exception, representing a long period of theoretical instability in the 1970s and 1980s, which saw some archaeologists, notably British scholar Ian Hodder, turning to spatial analysis, then structuralism and postmodernism. Almost without exception, the new approaches arrive within archaeology via what Bintcliff (1991: 277) calls "a novel bibliography of intellectual traditions [from other academic disciplines] likely to be esoteric and unpalatable to their predecessors—who 'write themselves out' of the debate by failing to read the new sacred texts." Very often, their original authors, in, say sociology, have never thought about archaeology in their lives! With such constant renewal going on, there is often very little debate or even dialogue between people who adhere or have developed new theoretical approaches. Very often, their predecessors are too busy testing their own laboriously developed approaches in the field.

For all its constantly shifting paradigms, postprocessual archaeology has made three positive, and important contributions.

First, meaning is more important than materialism. No longer can we interpret the past in terms of purely ecological, technological, and other material considerations. Culture is interactive. In other words, people are actors who create, use, and manipulate their symbolic capabilities to make and remake the world they live in.

Second, archaeologists must critically examine their social responsibilities, looking beyond their specialties to the broader aims of the discipline, and to issues of moral and emotional involvement with the past in contemporary society. How does the public interact with the past?

Third, many perspectives on ancient society have been neglected, among them those of women, ethnic minorities, and what are often called "the people without history," anonymous, often illiterate commoners.

Considerable debate surrounds the third of these issues, for some archaeologists believe that their interpretations of the past are Eurocentric and culturally biased, making them unacceptable to those whose history they claim to study. In other words, they are imposing their culture and view of the past on others such as Australian Aborigines and Native Americans, who may have entirely different perspectives. The controversy is still unresolved, but there is no question that archaeologists will have to work closer with those they study in the future, or they are in real danger of becoming marginalized as a source of history. One helpful approach considers the archaeologist as a form of "active mediator" between the present and the past. The debate continues.

Cognitive-Processual Archaeology

Some postprocessual approaches offer promise when combined with the best of processual archaeology, with its empirical data collection and rigorous data description, and meticulous analyses of archaeological sites and their ecological contexts.

People are like actors, interacting with their culture—this concept is the major difference in approach between archaeologists using a materialist approach to the past and those who are concerned with symbolic meaning, structure, and the rules that once governed society. After intensive debate, the beginnings of a theoretical consensus is emerging, under the broad label of cognitive-processual archaeology.

The *Oxford English Dictionary*, the ultimate arbiter of the English language, even for Americans, defines cognition as "The action or faculty of knowing taken in its widest sense, including sensation, perception, conception, etc." From an archaeological perspective, the term **cognitive archaeology** covers the whole spectrum of human behavior, especially religion and belief, also the development and expression of human consciousness. Since the very early days of archaeology, researchers have been concerned with ancient religion, belief, and expression, the subject matter of cognitive archaeology, what has sometimes been called the "archaeology of mind." How can one define cognitive archaeology? Is it possible to study human cognition from the material remains of the archaeological record, even if we cannot afford to ignore it? Some of the best minds in archaeology are debating these questions and attempting to create a cognitive-processual approach, which creates a new framework for archaeology, drawing on both old and new models and methods. This is an important exercise because the archaeology of the 1990s is built on solid scientific foundations, not hermeneutics, interpretive approaches that allow insight to play a key role. That is the approach used by those who believe ancient civilizations lie under Antarctic ice or that astronauts from outer space founded Maya civilization. Thus cognitive-processualists never claim they can establish what people thought, but they can give insights into how they thought.

Cognitive archaeology covers all of the human past, but can be divided into two broad areas of concern. One involves the study of the cognitive facilities of early hominids and archaic humans, the relationships between toolmaking and cognitive abilities, the origins of language, and the social contexts of early human behavior. The other covers the past 40,000 years, the cognitive aspects of such major developments as the origins of food production and civilization. British archaeologist Colin Renfrew considers the challenge for cognitive archaeology to be establishing how the formation of symbolic systems in, say, the Near East or early Mesoamerica, molded and conditioned later cultural developments, for example, Mayan civilization. He considers humans use symbols in about six ways: design and planning, measurement and social relations (using symbols to structure and regulate interpersonal behavior), for representation, and mediating between the human and supernatural worlds. He also believes the reason that cognitive archaeology has been neglected is because it lacks a coherent methodology. This methodology may emerge from the convergence of such diverse fields as cognitive psychology, artificial intelligence, computer simulation, and cognitive archaeology itself. But this convergence, and the potential intellectual leap forward that might result, will not occur until archaeologists interested in human cognition develop a rigorous and explicit methodology that will substitute for many of the simplistic generalizations which masquerade under the label "postprocessual archaeology."

Archaeologists Kent Flannery and Joyce Marcus have long been interested in cognition. Their earliest work was an attempt to understand ancient Zapotec subsistence behavior in Mexico's Valley of Oaxaca by taking into account what early Spanish accounts told of local Indian cosmology. They believe this kind of approach, which makes use of critically analyzed historical documents and other sources, to be productive, as opposed to the inspired speculation so common in the 1980s. Flannery and Marcus (1993: 263) consider cognitive archaeology not to be the study of epiphenomena, but "the study of all those aspects of ancient culture that are the product of the ancient mind." This includes cosmology, religion, ideology, iconography, and all forms of human intellectual and symbolic behavior. They also firmly state that effective cognitive archaeology depends on rigorous research methods. Thus it can only be used when the body of supporting data is rich. Otherwise, it becomes (1993: 264) "little more than speculation, a kind of bungee jump into the Land of Fantasy." In practical terms, and for obvious reasons, cognitive archaeology is usually most effective when historical records are available to amplify the archaeological record, as they are when working with archaeological evidence and Maya inscriptions.

Under this approach, cognitive archaeology has considerable limitations. All cultures have a theory of the universe in which they live. Their cosmology, like that of Western civilization based on modern astronomy, constitutes a theory of the origin of the universe, defines space and time, and can provide a structure for religion and ideology.

Many cultures, among them ancient Greek and Maya, envisage a cosmos inhabited by supernatural beings, another link to religious beliefs. Although cosmology can have a strong influence on both settlement and subsistence, as, for example, in cases where certain aspects of the environment such as pristine forest may be held sacred, it is difficult, if not impossible, to reconstruct cosmology from animal and plant remains alone.

Religious beliefs provide ethics and values, often within the framework of a quest for the values of an ideal life. A well-defined worldview links cosmology and religion, the latter providing the rituals and practices that help the worshipper attain the ideal. Clearly, these ethics and values can have a powerful effect on human behavior, even on such pragmatic areas of life as obtaining food and trading. Religion can provide a powerful catalyst for social and political change, as was the case, for example, when Buddhist merchants brought their religion to Southeast Asia and changed the course of history by providing the spiritual inspiration for a series of brilliant kingdoms, like those of the Khmer of Cambodia.

Kent Flannery and Joyce Marcus believe that one approach to reconstructing ancient religions is to construct models from ethnohistoric sources, then to isolate temples, artifacts, art styles, and other cultural elements that can be identified archaeologically. These are studied in their cultural context, and the observed archaeological remains compared with the model from ethnohistoric documents. Ideology is a product of society and politics, "a body of doctrine, myth, and symbolism associated with a social movement, an institution, class, or group of individuals, often with reference to some political or cultural plan, along with the strategies for putting the doctrine into operation" (Flannery and Marcus, 1993: 266). For example, any archaeologist concerned with the appearance of ranked, as opposed to egalitarian, societies is studying fundamental changes in ideology, simply because egalitarian societies tend to have leveling mechanisms that prevent one individual or a group from attaining superior rank. Again, these changes can only be documented by a judicious use of historical analogies and artifacts.

For instance, in the Valley of Oaxaca, many village farming communities functioned without any apparent ranking between 1400 and 1150 B.C. Between 1150 and 850 B.C., the first artistic depictions of supernatural lineage ancestors appear. Some may represent the earth, others the sky, in the form of lightning or a fire serpent. Some form of hereditary social ranking seems to accompany the new art. Then the Zapotec state came into being, with a powerful elite ruling from Monte Alban, a tiny minority associated with depictions of sky and lightning, while earth and earthquake symbols fade into obscurity. It is as if those who rose to prominence were associated with lightning's descendants, in an ideological shift where hereditary social inequality is condoned for the first time.

Iconography offers another fertile avenue for cognitive archaeology, the analysis of the way ancient peoples represented religious, political, ideological, or cosmological objects or concepts in their art. Again, ethnohistory and history provides vital background for the interpretation of the archaeological record, for without such information one is engaged in little more than guesswork. Such studies, based very often on intuition and "aesthetic sense," reflect the author's personality more than reality.

Olga Linares used a rigorous cognitive approach in a little known 1977 study of ideology and high-status cemeteries in central Panama. Using sixteenth-century Spanish eyewitness accounts of local Panamanian chiefdoms engaged in constant warfare and raiding, and detailed information on local animal species, Linares studied graves and the associated flamboyantly polychrome vessels found in them. They were open pots designed to be seen from above, where mourners could see the animal motifs painted on them. Sometimes the pots were apparently so valuable that they were exhumed from one grave and put in another. Ethnohistorical accounts mentioned that the highly competitive chiefs vied constantly for leadership and prestige, painting and tattooing their bodies with badges of rank and bravery. Each group of warriors wore different symbols that associated them with their leader. They went to their graves with helmets, weapons, other military paraphernalia, and painted pottery. Linares noticed that the art styles rarely depicted plants, but many animal species, motifs that commemorated qualities of aggression and bravery. Crocodiles, large felines, sharks, stingrays, scorpions, even poisonous snakes were the animals that were dangerous and symbols of bravery. They often appeared on clay vessels, and sometimes parts of their bodies, like shark's teeth and stingray spines, were buried with the dead. In contrast, prey species and animals with soft parts like, say, monkeys, were largely ignored by the artists. Thus the cognitive world of the Panamanian chiefdoms used carefully selected animals to communicate the qualities most admired in chiefs and warriors.

Such researches are highly effective, if they use established analytical techniques and draw on information from many sources. Cognitive archaeology reaches a high degree of refinement when document aided, as is the case with the Aztec civilization of Mexico or the Inka of the Andes. But earlier societies, like, for instance, the first farming societies of the Near East with their female figures and plastered human skulls, offer much greater challenges. It is all too easy to call each female figure a "fertility figurine" and to talk of ancient Mother Goddesses, when there is, in fact, no scientific basis for such conclusions.

Cognitive archaeology is no shortcut, but an approach to cosmology, religion, ideology, and iconography based on rigorous analysis and data from many sources. It is a theoretical perspective that offers enormous promise for the future, and a far cry from entire ideologies reconstructed from the orientation of a building or a single carving.

All of the postprocessual approaches to the past are reactions to the feeling that modern archaeology has become too dehumanized, too divorced from its proper role in modern society. In a sense, this is a process of archaeologists becoming more critical of their own place in the unfolding intellectual development of Western scholarship.

The Future

Where does the future lie? The answer can only be that archaeologists are uncertain. Clearly, both evolutionary theory and ecology will be important in the study of cultural change and the birth of complex societies. Many archaeologists find evolutionary theory useful, so one future direction of archaeological theory will lie in reconsidering the applications of evolutionary theory to archaeology.

The most useful evolutionary perspective in archaeology, concerned as it is with change through time, is one that focuses on individuals as dynamic persons, constantly adjusting their behavior as their social and physical environments alter. These same individuals are people capable of creative thinking, a uniquely human characteristic. Thought is a driving force in cultural change, in decision making and learning, in the process of adaptation. There are, of course, limits on human knowledge—problems we cannot cope with, processes of comprehension that are beyond us, mistakes we can make through mental confusion. These limits place a premium on cooperation between individuals in the solving of problems, such as finding a way to kill large numbers of bison at one time.

This form of evolutionary archaeology will involve developing new methodologies that integrate evolutionary ecology and human psychology and ways of relating short-term individual behavior to the inevitably generalized data from the archaeological record. Many new and sometimes arcane approaches will characterize the next generation of evolutionary archaeology, everything from computer simulations to cost-benefit analysis. In many ways, the biologist and the archaeologist are facing the same problem: How do forms, whether living or cultural, emerge and stabilize?

The Archaeology of Constraints

"Archaeology is a curious social science, since archaeologists are unable either to observe human behavior or to learn about human thoughts at first hand from their primary data," writes Canadian archaeologist Bruce Trigger (1991: 551). Therein lies the crux of current theoretical debates. Trigger and others believe that the processual approach may give us a better understanding of what archaeologists know, but this is useless without a better comprehension of what human behavior produced the archaeological record.

Today, many archaeologists believe there was much greater variation in human behavior than processual archaeologists have allowed for. In other words, human behavior is less orderly than many cultural evolutionists would like us to believe, yet not entirely random, as some postprocessual scholars assume. There are sufficient regularities in cultural developments in different regions, such as, for example, in the development of agriculture and village life in the Near East and Mesoamerica, to suggest that recurrent operations of cause and effect do result in the evolution of similar forms of behavior in widely separated areas. There is much we do not know about the nature of cultural and social systems. Does a change in one subsystem affect all others, as many archaeologists assume? It is by no means certain that this is the case.

Humans never adjust to the physical world as it really is, but to this same world as they perceive it through their own cultural conditioning. Thus the human ability to reason and adjust cultural perceptions plays an essential role in the ways in which people interact with one another and with the environment. In other words, the post-processualists are right in recognizing that the human mind plays an important role in all aspects of human behavior.

Unfortunately, although materialist approaches tell us much about ancient life, and how economy and material culture influenced political, social, and intellectual life, we still have an inadequate knowledge of the constraints that influence human behavior. Bruce Trigger says (1991: 567) we should view human behavior as "the product of interaction between the ability of individual human beings to foresee at least some of the consequences of what they do and the sorts of constraints on human behavior, both physical and imagined, that such calculations must take into account."

These constraints can be external. Processual archaeologists have made important studies of the ecological, technological, and economic constraints that act on human societies: witness important research into changes in settlement patterns in the Basin of Mexico and on the rise of Mesopotamian civilization. But many noneconomic and nonecological factors also influence human behavior. So do actual physical limitations of the human body and the nature of our brains. So instead of saying that the environment is responsible for cultural change, one can argue that it constrains human behavior. Finally, general systems research has shown convincingly that there are only a limited number of alternative ways to process information and make decisions. This limits the number of social and political organizations that are viable for human societies. For instance, decision making by consensus, so typical of small-scale societies, only works well in groups of 300 people or fewer. Some form of coercion is essential when more than 1,500 people live in the same group.

In general terms, the larger the scale of the society, the more complex and bureaucratized the institutions that regulate it. There are only a limited number of viable social and political structures that human societies can adopt, which accounts for the striking similarities in general organization between, say, Sumerian and Maya civilization in different corners of the world.

Internal constraints also operate on our behavior. These include knowledge, beliefs, values, and other culturally conditioned habits, all of them different in each culture. Yet some of them are shared by cultures flourishing thousands of miles apart. For instance, two widely separated cultures may develop bronze metallurgy, which is based on a common body of technological know-how, but the cultural context of that knowledge is radically different, as it was, say, in the Shang civilization of China and Moche culture in coastal Peru (Figure 13.2). Some symbols, like the common practice of elevating chiefs or kings on a dais, or associations between rulers and the sun, have developed in many places. That does not mean they are connected, as early diffusionists would have argued, but simply reflect more or less uniform operations of the human mind.

According to this perspective, human cultures are historical phenomena shaped by both external and internal constraints. Our ability to use our imaginations, to make calculated decisions, plays a significant part in streamlining any form of innovation. Our culture has a store of ideas and social values that channel and restrict innovation. In other words, information transmitted from one generation to the next provides most of the knowledge that an individual has to deal with ecological and social realities. Each generation reworks this information and its accompanying cultural constraints to reflect the realities of their own circumstances, a process that transformed human societies and at times led to new social institutions.

Figure 13.2 Moche gold ear ornament in hammered gold. The warrior wears a turquoise tunic and holds a detachable war club. He wears an earplug, minute bells on his belt, and carries a removable circular shield. Every part of this intricate ornament had intense symbolic meaning in Moche society.

Cultural traditions provide guidance for coping with the environment, a force that can operate against innovation, and a body of intellectual information that is changed constantly from one generation to the next. They are as important as ecological factors in influencing human behavior. Under this approach, the individual is the one who has perception, who takes steps to make changes. So external and internal constraints on human behavior are equally important, and complement each other throughout human history. Ecological and other external factors can be culturally mediated, but they operate independently of human actions, which makes them susceptible to understanding in terms of evolutionary theory and other such generalizations. Cultural traditions, the internal constraints, are far more idiosyncratic, far more haphazard. This makes it difficult to impose evolutionary order on human history, for, despite external constraints, much cultural change is contingent on ever-changing circumstances and cultural traditions. Human culture's open-ended capacity for further elaboration creates a need for order to make its diversity understandable. By studying individual cultural traditions, archaeologists can explain the distinctive features of cultures in ways that evolutionists and cultural ecologists can never hope to.

Bruce Trigger believes that archaeologists should try to explain the past in terms of constraints. There are those of a natural order, such as environment, technology, and limitations placed on social organization by the cultural system. Such general factors can best be explained through applications of middle-range theory and ethnoarchaeological data. This research should be combined with inquiries into cultural meanings, using refinements of the direct historical method that employ documents, archaeology, linguistics, and oral traditions to provide cultural meaning for the generalizations of middle-range theory. Archaeological understandings of all the constraints that have shaped ancient societies will vary considerably from one culture to another. Although the direct historical method can take us back many millennia, there are many societies, like, for example, those of the European Cro-Magnons of 20,000 years ago, that will always be known to us mainly from the perspective of external constraints. This does not mean, of course, that archaeologists despair of ever understanding the behavior of very early human societies. It is simply that they have a lively perception of the limitations of archaeological data. At the same time, they are striving to make archaeology more human centered than the kind of impersonal science that characterized much of earlier processual archaeology.

The debate over a new, more human-centered archaeology has barely begun, but we can predict that more all-encompassing approaches to the past will replace the somewhat polarized viewpoints so characteristic of the discipline today.

Summary

Chapter 13 is concerned with the explanation of culture change. Culture history is descriptive archaeology, based on inductive research methods, the development of generalizations based on numerous specific observations, and on a normative view of culture. Culture historians use five descriptive models to characterize culture change: inevitable variation, cultural selection, invention, diffusion, and migration. The processual approach to culture change uses inductive research and is most commonly concerned with the ways in which cultural systems function. This systems-ecological approach uses systems models, cultural ecology, and multilinear evolution to produce complex interpretations of such developments as the origins of agriculture. In recent years, many archaeologists have reacted against the materialist processual approach and have focused on the entire spectrum of human behavior. Such reactions form the complex field of postprocessual archaeology, which emphasizes the importance of individuals and groups in cultural change, including women and minorities, and also the role of the modern-day archaeologist as an interpreter of the past. In recent years, a synthesis between processual and what is sometimes called cognitive archaeology has begun to develop, which combines scientific approaches with studies of human consciousness, religion, and belief. The debate over a new, more human-centered archaeology is in its infancy, as now polarized viewpoints develop into new, more all-encompassing approaches.

14

Archaeology Tomorrow

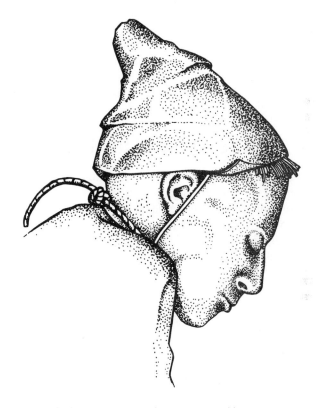

The head of Tollund man, Denmark, c. 2,000 years old.

I fell in love with Ur, with its beauty in the evenings, the ziggurat standing up. . . . I enjoyed the workmen, the foremen, the little basket-boys, the pickmen—the whole technique and life. The lure of the past came up to grab me. To see a dagger slowly appearing, with its gold glint, through the sand was romantic. The carefulness of lifting pots and objects from the soil filled me with a longing to be an archaeologist myself.

Agatha Christie (1977)

A rchaeology tells us the remarkable story of the human past, from its very beginnings on the East African grasslands more than two-and-a-half million years ago right up to the time, some 5,000 years ago, when state-organized societies emerged in Egypt and Mesopotamia, and far beyond. This sophisticated science is, in a real sense, an integral part of twentieth-century life, for it gives us unrivaled perspectives on evolving humanity over more than two-and-a-half million years, and proves that all of us humans are part of a single, if diverse, family. The lessons it teaches us about ourselves are of vital importance to everyone in an ever more complex and diverse world. Yet archaeology is in crisis, threatened by a tidal wave of destruction and looting of the finite archives of the past, a past that offers a unique cultural identity to much of humankind.

The Future of the Past

Anthropology tells a story of human biological and cultural evolution that climaxes in urban civilization and the extraordinary diversity of the modern world. However, the very emergence of civilization has hastened the evolution of new, much larger, global societies. Scores of societies are now linked by common religious beliefs, political ideologies, or remarkable heights of technological achievement. Our own Western society, with its ability for instant communication and its capacity to feed more people than ever before, has reached out to the farthest corners of the world in search of new economic and spiritual domains to conquer. The results for many societies have been traumatic.

The Polynesians encountered the Western world in the eighteenth century A.D. A hundred years later, they were a shadow of their previous selves, exploited and missionized almost to death. Millions of American Indians perished from exotic diseases brought by Europeans, in epidemics that spread in advance of actual foreign settlement. Few bands of Australian Aborigines retain even a part of their millennia-old culture. The alternatives for the members of these societies were extinction or assimilation into a culture where they were, at best, second-rate citizens. Only in the 1960s and 1970s have some of them been able to stand on their own feet again, as newly independent groups or nations trying to reestablish their identity in a much-changed world.

Nationalism can be seen as one of the major historical trends of recent decades. It is manifested in new nations and in ethnic minorities that have begun an ardent search for their own historical identity. Alex Haley's *Roots* rightly caused a sensation when it recounted how Haley found his ancestry in West Africa. For many people, such oral traditions were lost in the enormous adjustment their societies have made in the past century. Thus archaeology remains the primary source of historical data about the Australian Aborigines, the Tahitians, the American Indians, and hundreds of other societies. Many of these peoples have their own views of their history, distinctive worldviews and cultural traditions that are radically different from those of Western archaeologists. We must respect these viewpoints, but the fact remains that coming generations may develop a passionate interest in their past, available to them only through archaeology. Thus it is our responsibility to conserve sites belonging to these cultures for the future. If asked whether archaeology has any use, we need only point to the huge gaps in world history that confront us—if any sites are left to excavate.

The breathtaking pace of agricultural and industrial development in recent years has taken a massive toll on the past. Thousands of American Indian sites have been destroyed by flooding behind hydroelectric dams, by deep plowing and strip mining, and by thousands of acres of urban development and freeway construction. Pothunters, too, have taken their toll. We may be the last generation of Americans to see many undisturbed archaeological sites. Charles McGimsey of the University of Arkansas has estimated that few untouched sites remain in his state. Probably fewer than 3 percent undisturbed sites of all prehistoric periods that originally existed are left in Los Angeles County. Despite many newly passed laws regarding antiquities, which mainly protect sites on federal land, there is a real danger that archaeology in North America is doomed. The finite resource base of sites is being eroded with little thought for the information these priceless archives contain. It is genocide, not of the living, but of the dead.

The popular interest in archaeology still revels in ancient mysteries, the excitement of discovery, and buried treasure. Many people regard archaeology as a luxury with no relevance for understanding of humankind. It is a means for gratifying their urge to possess things. Projectile points, Maya pots, and bronze swords look good on a mantel shelf or in a museum display case. So great is the demand for such treasures that a flourishing antiquities market has grown up to satisfy our greed. Archaeological sites have been destroyed for commercial ends ever since the eighteenth century. The early collections of the Metropolitan Museum of Art in New York and many other major museums were very often accumulated by purchase of looted objects handled by large-scale dealers in the past. Today's prices are astronomical. So much damage has been done that more and more museums and wealthy collectors are competing for fewer and fewer finds. Entire Inca cemeteries and Maya ceremonial centers have been decimated in search of salable objects. Many sites in the American Southwest had been ravaged beyond repair by the early years of this century.

Almost nothing can be, or has been, done about the illegal trade in antiquities. Unscrupulous collectors and some museums do not care, the dealers do not care, and the treasure hunting supports whole villages of poor farmers in many countries. Worst of all, the public as a whole is disinterested. Despite highly sophisticated conservation movements in the United States, archaeology still lies outside the mainstream of environmental activism in this country and elsewhere. This is surprising, for archaeological sites are an integral part of the modern environment that we seek to conserve. In the case of North America, this may be because most Americans do not feel a direct cultural and emotional link to the sites and artifacts of the American Indian. This is unfortunate, for archaeology is the study of the human past, not the Indian past, the American past, or the Egyptian past.

Cultural resource management (CRM)—the informed careful preservation and management of the past for future generations—is of vital importance. CRM is mandated by a variety of federal and state laws on publicly owned lands, and for private lands where government funds are used for development. Substantial sums of taxpayers' money are spent on CRM every year, to the point that most archaeologists now work in this field rather than in academia, as was the case half a century ago.

It cannot be stressed too strongly that vandalizing an archaeological site destroys it forever, thereby depriving all humanity of a priceless part of our collective cultural heritage. The future of archaeology lies in everyone's hands. Despite this obvious fact, people destroy archaeological sites without realizing it or because they consider them useless (Figure 14.1).

Archaeology and You

How can you become involved in archaeology? Are there career prospects as an archaeologist? What can a layperson do to help save the past? There are many ways to become involved.

Thousands of archaeologists work in the United States. Many teach in universities and colleges, some in high schools. Others head up archaeological departments of national, city, state, or local museums all over the country or direct state archaeological surveys. Archaeologists work for the National Park Service, the Bureau of Land Management, and other federal and state agencies. Others support themselves by part-time teaching or working independently for private companies undertaking contracts on federal projects or for companies seeking cultural resource management services.

The research interests of these archaeologists range from early Indian settlements on the North American Plains to historical sites in New England, from theoretical models of early agriculture to computer simulations of ancient settlement patterns. One can find almost more specialties than archaeologists. And many of America's archaeologists work overseas—in Africa, Europe, Mesoamerica, Peru, and even farther afield.

In the 1960s, nearly all archaeologists were university or college teachers, or worked in museums. In a recent study of American archaeologists, Melissa Zeder of the Smithsonian Institution has chronicled a dramatic shift in archaeological employment. Only 35 percent of American archaeologists are now academics. Eight percent labor in museums, and 23 percent work for federal, state, or local government, many in purely administrative functions. The fastest growing segment of archaeological employment is in the private sector. In 1997, 18 percent of all American archaeologists worked for private consulting firms engaged in environmental monitoring and cultural resource management. The number increases every year. Anyone wanting to become an archaeologist is wise to contemplate the private sector as a career option.

The Zeder study shows archaeology is changing rapidly from a purely academic discipline into a profession with strong roots in both government and private business. This is because the past is under siege from industrial civilization in the form of deep plowing and mining, industrial development, road construction, and the inexorable expansion of huge cities—not to mention looters and pothunters, who think nothing of ravaging sites for valuable finds they can sell. Increasingly, archaeologists are managers rather than professors, supervising a precious and rapidly vanishing resource: the human past. The pith-helmeted professor of yesteryear is the cultural resource manager of today. An image further removed from Indiana Jones is hard to envision.

You can find someone who will teach you almost any type of archaeology you want, above or below ground, under the water, even in the air. If, however, you plan a

Figure 14.1   Two possibilities for the future of the past.
Top: Removal of the Abu Simbel temples was an international effort at rescue archaeology. Here, the face of Ramses II is lifted to the new location of the Great Temple.
Bottom: Pothunters at work do irreparable damage to a site. Compare this scene of devastation with the excavations illustrated in Chapter 7.

career on the professional and administrative sides of archaeology, you will find specialized graduate training harder to find, as few schools offer a Ph.D. in nonacademic specialties like conservation.

Most archaeological jobs, whether in a college, museum, or university, demand a minimum of a master's degree, most often a doctorate as well. The doctorate is a research degree requiring comprehensive seminars, courses, and field training in graduate school and then a period of intensive fieldwork that, when written up, forms the dissertation, which is submitted to a committee of examiners. The average doctoral program takes about seven years to complete. Once you have the degree, you still have to find a job as a faculty member or museum officer somewhere. And that, in these days of great numbers of Ph.D.s searching for jobs, is not easy. Many archaeologists with doctorates have put their academic training to practical use by joining private CRM firms, where they learn additional management and legal compliance skills on the job. Fascinating and challenging long-term careers await those who want to move out of the academic sector. The opportunities to become involved in all aspects of archaeology from working with the public and Native American groups to intense project management in the field proliferate every year—for well-qualified and thoroughly trained graduates.

The M.A. degree normally takes one or two years of graduate work and gives you broad, general training in the basic methods and theory of archaeology as well as world prehistory, with some specialization in a local area or in cultural resource management. The degree is satisfied by courses and seminars. You may have to write a library thesis as well and obtain some digging experience. M.A. qualifications offer open-ended opportunities in cultural resource management or local archaeology, especially in government and the private sector which is where the greatest job potential now lies. Various universities and colleges do offer certification programs for people interested in contract, conservation archaeology, work for which no Ph.D. is required. Consult your professors about such opportunities.

There is a constant demand for people with some hands-on archaeological experience for CRM projects, which offer basic employment in the field or laboratory for people with B.A.s in archaeology, but few people treat this kind of work as a career.

Anyone who considers becoming a professional archaeologist must have a superior academic record with in-depth coverage of anthropology and archaeology. A course average of "A" is a minimal requirement for entrance to good graduate schools. Some field experience on a dig or survey is also necessary, as is strong and meaningful support from at least two qualified archaeologists willing to write letters of recommendation. As for attitude, a passion for the past and strong motivation to become an archaeologist are musts, and, for the Ph.D., a specific research interest. An archaeologist who thrives on hard work, and who can tolerate some discomfort, a mass of detail, and long hours of routine laboratory work, will be a happy one. An interest in teaching and a moral commitment not to collect artifacts for profit or personal gain are the remaining prerequisites on this formidable list. If the list sounds rigorous, remember that archaeologists of the next generation have the future of the past in their hands.

Let us say you do want to become an archaeologist. Which graduate school should you apply to? You should choose your school according to your specific interests. It is wise to apply to more than one department and to make sure first that your faculty advisers really support your application.

Many people want to gain digging experience whether they intend to go to graduate school or not. The best way to learn is to take a course in field methods, then volunteer to dig for a period on a summer excavation. Details of digs are normally posted on anthropology department bulletin boards or at local museums. Alternatively, take a general introductory course in archaeology, then go to a field school. Many university-sponsored field schools offer academic credit for your participation. Such summer programs are well worth the time, for they combine lectures and seminars with actual digging and laboratory experience. And the camaraderie of such digs can be a memorable experience.

Some people venture farther afield and join an excavation overseas for some weeks. Cheap flights have made Europe readily accessible. By contacting such organizations as the Council for British Archaeology in York, England, it is possible to obtain details of excavations in progress where volunteers are needed. Bear in mind that very few digs in this country or overseas pay you to be an excavator. At the costly end of the spectrum are package travel tours that take students to such faraway places as Israel to dig and learn archaeology under close supervision. These tend to be expensive experiences, often of variable academic quality. But whatever type of dig you choose, an excavation experience is a good way of testing your commitment.

An undergraduate degree in archaeology is insufficient qualification for a job in the field. But good undergraduate training can give you a perspective on archaeology that will be with you for the rest of your life. There are many ways to enjoy archaeology as a layperson. You can join a local archaeological society, participate in excavations and volunteer museum programs, and keep an eye on endangered sites in your community. The background in archaeology you take with you into later life will enable you to see famous sites all over the world as an informed visitor, to enjoy the achievements of the ancients to the full.

Above all, you can influence the ways in which other people think about, and behave toward, archaeological sites and accidental discoveries. And your contacts with former instructors and other professional archaeologists may help you prevent damage to important, undisturbed sites.

This book may be the only experience you have with archaeology. We hope it has given you some insight into how archaeologists reconstruct the human past. But how can you help save the past for future generations? How should responsible people live with the finite resources of prehistory? Here are some important ethical guidelines:

- Treat every archaeological site and artifact as a finite resource that, once destroyed, can never be replaced.
- Report all archaeological discoveries to responsible archaeological authorities (archaeological surveys, museums, university or college departments, government agencies).
- Obey all laws relating to archaeological sites.
- Never dig a site without proper training or supervision.
- Never collect archaeological finds from any country for your private collection or for profit. If you must collect, collect reproductions.
- Respect modern and prehistoric Indian burial grounds and sacred sites. They have deep spiritual significance.

Is there a future for the past? Yes, if we want one. It is up to all of us.

Summary

Chapter 14 summarizes the great crisis of destruction that faces archaeology as inexorable industrial activity and often uncontrolled looting threatens the finite resources of the archaeological record. We stress that the future of archaeology lies in everyone's hands, a record of the past which represents our common and collective cultural heritage. Most careers in archaeology are either in academic life, teaching in colleges or universities, in museums, or in the professional resource management side of archaeology, which is expanding rapidly. A Ph.D. degree is required for a position in a research university and many colleges; an M.A. opens up many opportunities in cultural resource management. The chapter ends with an explicit statement on archaeological ethics to which all of us should adhere.

Sites and Cultures Mentioned
in the Text

These brief descriptions give some background on prehistoric sites and cultures mentioned in the text; they are not meant to be precise definitions. Ask your instructor for more information and references if you need them. Some sites mentioned in passing are not included in the list if their significance is self-evident.

Abri Pataud, France   Large rockshelter near the Vezère River in the Dordogne region of southwestern France, occupied by Neanderthal and Cro-Magnon hunter-gatherers between about 50,000 and 19,000 years ago.

Abu Simbel, Egypt   Ancient Egyptian temple erected by Ramses II in Nubia, c. 1250 B.C. The site with its seated figures of the pharaoh was moved to higher ground to prevent its flooding by Lake Nasser in 1968 at a cost of $40 million.

Acheulian   Widespread early Stone Age culture named after the town of St. Acheul in northern France. The Acheulian flourished in Africa, western Europe, and southern Asia from before a million years ago until less than 100,000 years before the present. The Acheulians made many types of stone artifacts, including multipurpose butchering hand axes and cleaving tools.

Adena, Ohio   Distinctive burial cult and village culture in the Ohio Valley of the Midwest. It flourished between about 700 B.C. and A.D. 200 and was remarkable for its long-distance trading and distinctive burial cults expressed in large earthworks and mounds.

Ali Kosh, Iran   Early farming site on the Deh Luran plain in Iran, where evidence for cereal cultivation was found by flotation techniques. The site dates to as early as 7500 B.C.

Avaris, Egypt   Palace and trading site in Lower Egypt celebrated for its Minoan (Cretan) wall paintings, evidence of trade between Egypt and Crete in about 1500 B.C.

Benin, Nigeria   West Africa state ruled from the city of Benin from before A.D. 1400 to modern times.

Cerén, San Salvador   Maya village buried by an unexpected volcanic eruption in A.D. 684. The ash mantled the village so completely that complete household inventories, even crops, are preserved in the archaeological record.

Cerro Palenque, Honduras   Terminal Classic Maya center dating to after A.D. 900.

Chichén Itzá, Mexico   Post-Classic Maya ceremonial center in the northern Yucatán dating to c. A.D. 1100.

Clovis   Paleo-Indian culture that flourished in North America, and perhaps further afield, about 8950 B.C. and somewhat earlier.

Colonial Williamsburg, Virginia   Reconstruction of Virginia's first capital city, carried out partly with the aid of archaeological research.

Copán, Honduras   Classic Maya city, A.D. 435 to 900.

Danger Cave, Utah   Long visited desert cave in the western United States, occupied sporadically by Archaic foragers from c. 9,000 B.C. to recent times.

Duch, Egypt   Egyptian desert village of the first millennium B.C, famous for its cemeteries.

Eaton Down, England   Long barrow, built as a communal sepulcher by Stone Age farmers, c. 2500 B.C.

Eridu, Iraq   Early city in the Mesopotamia delta that boasted of a major temple as early as 4000 B.C. One of the earliest cities in the world.

Flag Fen, England   Late Bronze Age field system and ceremonial center in eastern England dating to c. 1100 B.C., famous for its wooden artifacts and timber posts and trackways.

Folsom   Paleo-Indian culture that flourished on the North American Plains after 9000 B.C.

Galatea Bay, New Zealand   Important shell midden site, about 500 years old, in New Zealand's North Island, famous for exemplary excavation methods and data recovery.

Giza, Egypt   The Pyramids at Giza were built in the desert near Cairo during Egypt's Old Kingdom, around 2550 B.C. The Great Pyramid is 481 feet (146.6 m) high and covers 13.1 acres (21 ha).

Grasshopper Pueblo, Arizona   Important Pueblo site occupied in the fourteenth and fifteenth centuries A.D.

Hadar, Ethiopia   Region of Ethiopia where hominid fossils dating to as early as four million years ago have been found.

Halieis, Greece   Classical town of the fourth century B.C. Famous for its olive oil.

Harappan civilization, Pakistan   Urban civilization based on the Indus Valley that flourished from before 2500 B.C. to 1500.

Herculaneum, Italy   Roman town destroyed by an eruption of Mount Vesuvius in A.D. 79.

Hissarlik, Turkey   Site of Homeric Troy in northwestern Turkey, which was an important Bronze Age city during the second millennium B.C.

Hogup Cave, Utah   Dry cave in the Great Basin occupied from c. 9000 B.C. until recent times, famous for its excellent dry preservation of organic artifacts like fiber sandals.

Hohokam, Arizona   Southwestern cultural tradition that originated as early as 300 B.C. and lasted until A.D. 1500. The Hohokam people were farmers who occupied much of what is now Arizona. Their cultural heirs are the Pima and Papago Indians of today.

Hopewell, Ohio   Between 200 B.C. and A.D. 600, the "Hopewell Interaction Sphere" flourished in the Midwest. Hopewell religious cults and distinctive burial customs were associated with an art tradition that spread far and wide through long-distance trading connections.

Inyan Ceyaka Atonwan, Minnesota   Historic Dakota Indian settlement occupied in the early nineteenth century A.D.

Jomon tradition, Japan   Japanese cultural tradition dating from before 8000 B.C. until about 300 B.C., remarkable for its early manufacturing of pottery and complex hunter-gatherer culture.

Karnak, Egypt   Site of the temple of the ancient Egyptian sun god Amun, which reached the height of its glory in the New Kingdom, c. 1500 B.C.

Khorsabad, Iraq   Palace of Assyrian King Sargon, eighth century B.C.

Klasies River Cave, South Africa   Middle Stone Age cave, occupied c. 120,000 to 100,000 years ago, which yielded fossil and cultural evidence for very early modern humans.

Knossos, Crete   Palace and shrine complex in northern Crete, which started life as a small village in about 6000 B.C. and became the major center of Minoan civilization, being finally abandoned in the late second millennium B.C.

Koobi Fora, Kenya   Location on the eastern shores of Lake Turkana in northern Kenya, where the earliest traces of human culture have been found, dating to more than 2.5 million years ago.

Koster, Illinois   From before 7000 B.C. until less than 1000 years ago, hunter-gatherers and later farmers settled at this location on the Illinois River to exploit the fertile river bottom. The site is unusual for its long stratigraphic sequence of Archaic and Woodland settlements and abundant food remains.

Kourion, Cyprus   Small Roman port in southwestern Cyprus in the eastern Mediterranean overwhelmed by a great earthquake early on the morning of July 21, A.D. 365. Excavations at the village have revealed many details of a long-forgotten disaster.

Laetoli, Tanzania   This East African site yielded the earliest hominid footprints, potassium-argon dated to more than 3.5 million years ago.

Lascaux Cave, France   Painted cave of the Magdalenian culture of southwestern France dating to about 15,000 years ago.

Lovelock Cave, Nevada   Desert site in the far West occupied as early as 7000 B.C. Located near a desert marsh, it has yielded minute details of prehistoric desert adaptations over a long period.

Mesa Verde, Colorado   Deep canyon area famous for its Anasazi pueblos, notably the Cliff Palace, which reached their heyday in the twelfth century A.D.

Moche civilization   Coastal state in northern coastal Peru, which reached its height after A.D. 400.

Mycenae, Greece   Major palace of the Mycenaean civilization, c. 1500 B.C. famous for its royal graves and beehive tombs.

Neanderthal, Germany   Cave that yielded the first Neanderthal skull (named after the site) in 1856.

Nelson's Bay, South Africa   Late Stone Age coastal cave in southeastern Africa occupied c. 5000 B.C.

Nimrud, Iraq   Assyrian city, the biblical Calah.

Nineveh, Iraq   Assyrian capital, famous for the palace of King Assurbanipal in the seventh century B.C.

Nippur, Iraq   Sumerian city in southern Iraq, c. 2800 B.C., celebrated in archaeological circles for its clay tablet archives.

Olduvai Gorge, Tanzania   Stratified lake beds with associated artifact scatters and kill sites, also early hominids, dating from slightly before 1.75 million years ago up to 100,000 years before present.

Olmec   One of the earliest lowland Mexican state-organized societies, Olmec culture flourished from around 1500 B.C. to 500 B.C. Olmec people traded widely, had a distinctive art tradition that depicted humanlike jaguars and both natural and supernatural beings, and developed many of the religious traditions that were to sustain the Maya and other Mesoamerican civilizations such as Teotihuacán.

Olsen-Chubbuck, Colorado   An 8,000-year-old bison kill site on the North American plains that revealed many details of Paleo-Indian hunting and butchering techniques.

Olympia, Greece   Site of the Olympic Games in the northern Peloponnese, c. 400 B.C.

Ozette, Washington   Coastal settlement in Washington State occupied for at least 1,000 years by ancestors of the present-day Makah Indians. Ozette suffered disaster two centuries ago when houses were buried by mud slides and preserved in perfect condition for archaeologists to investigate in the 1970s.

Palenque, Mexico   Classic Maya city and ceremonial center, which reached its height in the mid-first millennium A.D.

Pecos, New Mexico   Anasazi pueblo in the Southwest that was occupied for much of the past 2,000 years, and provided the first stratigraphic sequence for southwestern prehistory as a result of A. V. Kidder's excavations.

Port Royal, Jamaica   Waterside settlement in Jamaica partially submerged by an earthquake on June 7, 1692, once famous for its pirates and freebooters.

Pueblo Bonito, New Mexico   Anasazi pueblo first constructed about A.D. 850 and in its heyday in the twelfth century A.D.

Sand Canyon, Colorado   Anasazi pueblo in the Four Corners region of the Southwest occupied in the twelfth century A.D.

Shang Civilization   Early Chinese civilization that flourished from as early as 2700 B.C., when the Xia dynasty arose in the north. The Shang dynasty rose to power around 1766 B.C. and ruled until 1122 B.C. Its rulers occupied a series of capitals near the Yellow River, the most famous being Anyang, occupied around 1400 B.C.

Sipán, Peru   Site of four spectacularly adorned warrior priest graves of the Moche civilization, c. A.D. 400.

Star Carr, England   Postglacial hunting site in northeast England dating to about 9200 B.C., remarkable for the bone and wooden artifacts recovered from a small birchbark platform at the edge of a small lake.

Stonehenge   Stone circles in southern Britain that formed a sacred precinct as early as 2700 B.C. and remained in use until about 1600 B.C. Some authorities believe Stonehenge was an astronomical observatory, but this viewpoint is controversial.

Tehuacán Valley, Mexico   Valley in which evidence for a gradual shift from hunting and gathering to deliberate cultivation of squashes and other minor crops, then maize, has been documented. Tehuacán was occupied as early as 10,000 B.C., with maize agriculture appearing before 2700 B.C.

Telloh, Iraq   Sumerian city where the civilization of that name was first recognized in the 1870s.

Tenochtitlán, Mexico   Spectacular capital of the Aztec civilization in the Valley of Mexico, founded in A.D. 1325 and destroyed by Spanish conquistador Hernan Cortés in 1521.

Teotihuacán, Mexico   A vast pre-Columbian city in highland Mexico that flourished from as early as 200 B.C. until it declined in around A.D. 750. Teotihuacán maintained extensive political and trade contacts with lowland Mexico, and is famed for its enormous public buildings and pyramids.

Tepe Yahya, Iran   Important trading city on the Iranian Plateau, famous for its steatite markets in the third millennium B.C. Maintained trade connections with Mesopotamia and the Indus Valley.

Tikal, Guatemala   Classic Maya city in the Guatemalan lowlands, which reached its height in about A.D. 600.

Tollund, Denmark   Site of a bog corpse dating to the Danish Iron Age, c. 2,000 years ago.

Ubar, Saudi Arabia   Desert city of the first millennium A.D. Celebrated for its spice trading.

Uluburun, Turkey   Spectacular Bronze Age shipwreck dating to 1305 B.C. with cargo from all over the eastern Mediterranean.

Ur, Iraq   Biblical city in southern Iraq that grew from a tiny farming hamlet founded as early as 4700 B.C. Known for its Early Dynastic Sumerian burials, where a ruler's entire retinue committed institutionalized suicide.

Uxmal, Mexico   Late Classic Maya city and ceremonial center in the northern Yucatán.

Valley of Kings, Egypt   Narrow, dry valley where Egypt's New Kingdom pharaohs were buried, including Tutankhamun.

Wroxeter, England   Roman city in west-central England dating to the first few centuries after Christ.

Guide To Further Reading

The technical literature of archaeology is immense; we can guide you to no more than a few key references on each of the major topics covered in this book. For more detailed information, consult one of the major summaries listed here or ask your instructor.

General Summaries

Two major college texts provide a comprehensive background on the method and theory of prehistoric archaeology. This text is a much shortened version of my own *In the Beginning*, 9th ed. (New York: Addison Wesley Longman, 1997). R. J. Sharer and Wendy Ashmore, *Archaeology: Discovering the Past*, 3d ed. (Mountain View, CA: Mayfield, 1995), is an equivalent volume. The most comprehensive survey of archaeological methods available is Colin Renfrew and Paul Bahn, *Archaeology: Theories, Methods, and Practice* 2nd ed. (New York: Thames and Hudson, 1996). For a textbook on-line, try British archaeologist Kevin Green's *Archaeology: An Introduction*, 3rd ed. (London: Duckworth, 1996): http://www.ncl.ac.uk/~nktg/wintro/index.htm.

The major developments of world prehistory are described in my *People of the Earth*, 9th ed. (New York: Addison Wesley Longman, 1998), also in *World Prehistory: A Brief Introduction*, 4th ed. (New York: Addison Wesley Longman, 1996). Another excellent account is Robert Wenke, *Patterns in Prehistory*, 3d ed. (New York: Oxford University Press, 1990). *The Adventure of Archaeology* (Washington, DC: National Geographic Society, 1985) is a beautifully illustrated description of how archaeology began.

Special Fields of Archaeology

Historical archaeology: James Deetz, *In Small Things Forgotten*, 2d ed. (New York: Natural History Press, 1996), is a minor classic; Charles Orser and Brian Fagan, *Historical Archaeology* (New York: HarperCollins, 1995), is a basic text. Classical archaeology is summarized in Simon Hornblower and Antony Spawforth (eds.), *The Oxford Classical Dictionary*, 3d ed. (New York: Oxford University Press, 1996). For biblical archaeology, see T. E. Levy, ed., *The Archaeology of Society in the Holy Land* (New York: Facts on File, 1995). Underwater archaeology is covered by George Bass, *Archaeology Underwater* (New York: Praeger, 1966), and by the same author's magnificent *A History of Seafaring Based on Underwater Archaeology* (London: Thames and Hudson, 1972) and *Ships and Shipwrecks of the Americas* (London: Thames and Hudson, 1988). There is currently no good book that introduces cultural resource management to a general audience. Consult your instructor for references.

Atlases and Encyclopedias

The best atlas for the general reader is Chris Scarre, ed., *Past Worlds: The Times Atlas of Archaeology* (London: Times Books, 1988). *The Oxford Companion to Archaeology* (New York: Oxford University Press, 1996) is a comprehensive guide to the field on a global scale and tells you all you want to know about archaeology, and perhaps some things you do not.

Major Archaeological Journals

The dozens of international, national, and local archaeological journals are designed mainly for specialists. Among those carrying popular articles on archaeology are *Discover, National Geographic, Natural History, Smithsonian*, and *Scientific American*. *Archaeology* is a well-illustrated magazine for enthusiasts; *Antiquity*, the *Journal of World Prehistory*, and *World Archaeology* carry articles of wide interest to serious archaeologists. American archaeologists rely heavily on *American Antiquity* and *Latin American Antiquity*, the journals of the Society for American Archaeology. *American Anthropologist* and *Current Anthropology* sometimes carry archaeological pieces, and Old World archaeologists publish in *Nature* and the *Proceedings of the Prehistoric Society*. More specialized archaeological journals abound, among them the *Journal of Archaeological Science* and *Geoarchaeology*. The *Journal of Field Archaeology* is of high technical value and carries regular articles on looting issues.

Web Sites

The World Wide Web is becoming a preferred medium of communication for archaeologists, like everyone else. This is a confusing universe for those unfamiliar with the Web, especially because so much is changing all the time. However, the major Web sites are here to stay and offer links to other important locations. Everything operates on Uniform Resource Locators (URLs), some of which we list here.

The Virtual Library for archaeology worldwide is ArchNet: http://spirit.lib.uconn.edu/archaeology/html. This is both geographically and subject matter based, covering everything from the archaeology of Australia to method and theory and site tours. There are also listings of academic departments, museums, and other archaeological organizations, even of journals. ArchNet is an extraordinary resource, which does not claim to be comprehensive, but it covers a huge range of topics. The European equivalent is ARGE, the Archaeological Resource Guide for Europe: http://www.bham.ac.uk/ARGE. This also lists areas and subjects and is multilingual. Both ArchNet and ARGE have links to virtually any kind of archaeology you are looking for.

Chapter 1: *The Birth of a Science*

The history of archaeology is easily accessible. Paul Bahn, ed., *The Cambridge Illustrated History of Archaeology* (Cambridge: Cambridge University Press, 1997), is a lavishly illustrated global summary of the subject. *The Adventure of Archaeology*, already mentioned, is a more popular account. Gordon Willey and Jeremy Sabloff, *A History of American Archaeology*, 2d ed. (New York: W. H. Freeman, 1990), is widely quoted. Bruce Trigger's *A History of Archaeological Interpretation* (Cambridge: Cambridge University Press, 1989) is the definitive work on the subject.

Chapter 2: *The World of Scientific Archaeology*

James Deetz, *Invitation to Archaeology* (Garden City, NY: Natural History Press, 1967), is a gem of an essay on archaeology and covers many of the points in this chapter. So does Grahame Clark, *Archaeology and Society* (New York: Barnes & Noble, 1965)—an old account that has never been bettered. Gordon Willey and Philip Phillips, *Method and Theory in American Archaeology* (Chicago: University of Chicago Press, 1958), is a standard work. Rose Macaulay, *The Pleasure of Ruins* (London: Thames and Hudson, 1959), is a delight for tourists. Massimo Pallotino, *The Meaning of Archaeology* (New York: Abrams, 1968), is a thoughtful account of the issues raised in this chapter. Karl Meyer, *The Plundered Past* 2nd ed. (New York: Athenaeum, 1993), is a popular account of the international antiquities trade that makes for sobering reading. Things are bad, if not worse, a quarter century later. Regrettably there is little modern writing on the role of archaeology in today's world. We have become too specialized. World prehistory: Grahame Clark, *World Prehistory,* 3d ed. (Cambridge, England: Cambridge University Press, 1977), is somewhat outdated. My *People of the Earth,* 9th ed. (New York: Addison Wesley Longman, 1998) is updated regularly.

Chapter 3: *Culture*

Few archaeologists have dared to write a summary of the controversial issues covered in this chapter. Gordon Willey and Philip Phillips, *Method and Theory in American Archaeology* (Chicago: University of Chicago Press, 1958), is fundamental. So is V. Gordon Childe's insightful *Piecing Together the Past* (London: Routledge and Kegan Paul, 1956). R. L. Lyman and R. C. Dunnell, *The Rise and Fall of Culture History* (New York: Plenum, 1997), is a recent assessment of the history of this approach. Processual archaeology can be surveyed in Lewis Binford's somewhat biased *In Pursuit of the Past* (London: Thames and Hudson, 1983). A magnificent assessment of contemporary American archaeology appears in David Meltzer, Don Fowler, and Jeremy Sabloff, eds., *American Archaeology Past and Future* (Washington, DC: Smithsonian Institution Press, 1986). Guy Gibbon, *Anthropological Archaeology* (New York: Columbia University Press, 1984), is a good guide. For more recent theoretical literature, see Chapter 13.

Chapter 4: *The Present and the Past*

The study of site-formation processes is fundamental to this chapter. Michael Schiffer, *Site Formation Processes of the Archaeological Record* (New York: Academic Press, 1987), is a good starting point. Preservation: Nicholas Reeves, *The Complete Tutankhamun* (London: Thames and Hudson, 1990), tells you all you want to know about the boy pharaoh and more. Walter Alva and Christopher Donnan, *The Royal Tombs of Sipán* (Los Angeles: Fowler Museum of Cultural History, 1992), is a comprehensive account of one of the most spectacular archaeological discoveries of this century. P. V. Glob, *The Bog People* (London: Faber and Faber, 1969), describes a number of well-preserved prehistoric corpses from waterlogged Danish bogs; even the skin and intestines survive. The remarkable Ozette site is described by Ruth Kirk, with Richard Daugherty, in *Hunters of the Whale* (New York: Morrow, 1975). Payson D. Sheets, *The Cerén Site* (New York: Harcourt, Brace, Jovanovich, 1992), offers a clear and well-written account of this remarkable site.

Middle-range theory is best summarized by Lewis Binford, *In Pursuit of the Past* (London: Thames and Hudson, 1983). His *Nunamiut Eskimo Ethnoarchaeology* (New York: Academic Press, 1977) is a detailed account of his own attempts to grapple with issues of middle-range theory and ethnoarchaeology. For living archaeology, see Richard Gould, *Living Archaeology* (Cambridge: Cambridge University Press, 1980). The !Kung San: Richard B. Lee, *The !Kung San* (Cambridge: Cambridge University Press, 1979). John Yellen, *Archaeological Approaches to the Present* (Orlando, FL: Academic Press, 1977), covers ethnoarchaeological work in the Kalahari. This book provides background on all aspects of !Kung lifestyle referred to in these pages. John Coles, *Archaeology by Experiment* (London: Hutchinson University Press, 1973), is the best summary of this subject. For a project combining both approaches: Brian Hayden, ed., *Lithic Studies Among the Contemporary Highland Maya* (Tucson: University of Arizona Press, 1987).

Chapter 5: *Time and Space*

Thomas Hester, Harry J. Shafer, and Kenneth L. Feder, *Field Methods in Archaeology,* 7th ed. (Mountain View, CA: Mayfield, 1997), contains invaluable essays on stratigraphy and dating. No one has yet rivaled Sir Mortimer Wheeler's classic description of stratigraphy in his *Archaeology from the Earth* (Oxford: Clarendon Press, 1954). E. C. Harris and M. R. Brown, III, *Principles of Archaeological Stratigraphy,* 2d ed. (New York: Academic Press, 1989), offer a more technical analysis. Dating techniques are mainly described in journal articles, but M. J. Aitken, *Science-Based Dating in Archaeology* (New York: Longman's, 1990), is informative. R. E. Taylor, *Radiocarbon Dating: An Archaeological Perspective* (Orlando, FL: Academic Press, 1987), is an excellent account. A. G. Wintle's paper "Archaeologically Relevant Dating Techniques for the Next Century," *Journal of Archaeological Science* 23 (1996): 123–138, is up to date, technical, and invaluable. Space: Once again, V. Gordon Childe, *Piecing Together the Past* (London: Routledge and Kegan Paul, 1956), is one of the few accounts. Kent V. Flannery, ed., *The Early Mesoamerican Village* (New York: Academic Press, 1976), covers some key concepts, but is better read in the context of Chapter 10. For the law of association, read John Rowe's paper: "Worsaae's Law and the Use of Grave Lots for Archaeological Dating," *American Antiquity* 28:2 (1962): 129–137. Much of the literature for this chapter is scattered in periodicals: consult an expert.

Chapter 6: *Ancient Climate and Environment*

Karl Butzer, *Archaeology as Human Ecology* (Cambridge: Cambridge University Press, 1982), is fundamental; so is his *Environment and Archaeology*, 2d ed. (Chicago: Aldine, 1971). Jared Diamond's *Guns, Germs, and Steel* (New York: W.W. Norton, 1997) argues for the importance of environment and climate change in the past in a stimulating essay for the general reader. A growing literature deals with shorter term climatic change, best summarized for the general reader in two books: William Ryan and Walter Pitman, *Noah's Flood: The New Scientific Discoveries About the Event That Changed History* (New York: Simon & Schuster, 1998), describes the extraordinary detective work that went into the reconstruction of the Black Sea catastrophe of 5500 B.C. This book describes cutting-edge paleoclimatic research little known outside specialist circles. My own *Floods, Famines, and Emperors: El Niño and the Fate of Civilizations* (New York: Basic Books, 1999) analyzes the impacts of long- and short-term climatic change on history. Both these works have comprehensive references.

For the Moche, read Walter Alva and Christopher Donnan, *The Royal Tombs of Sipán* (Los Angeles: UCLA Fowler Museum of Cultural History, 1983). Andean ice core research is described by L. Thompson and others, "El Niño-Southern Oscillation and Events Recorded in the Stratigraphy of the Tropical Quelccaya Ice Cap," *Science* 225: 50–53, and in "A 1500-Year Tropical Ice Core Record of Climate: Potential Relations to Man in the Andes." *Science* 234 (1986): 361–364. Tree-ring research is well described by Jeffrey Dean: "Demography, Environment, and Subsistence Stress," in Joseph A. Tainter and Bonnie Bagley Tainter, eds., *Evolving Complexity and Environmental Risk in the Prehistoric Southwest* (Reading, MA: Addison Wesley, 1996), pp. 25–56. Also his "A Model of Anasazi Behavioral Adaptation," in George Gumerman, ed., *The Anasazi in a Changing Environment* (Cambridge: Cambridge University Press, 1988), pp. 25–44.

Chapter 7: *Finding and Assessing Archaeological Sites*

Archaeological survey is a hotly debated subject at the moment, but mainly in specialist journals. Thomas Hester, Harry J. Shafer, and Kenneth L. Feder, *Field Methods in Archaeology,* 7th ed. (Mountain View, CA: Mayfield, 1997), contains invaluable essays on aspects of survey and excavation, including stratigraphy and dating. Any serious student will likely encounter this book at some stage in his or her career. More specialized works include Irwin Scollar and others, *Archaeological Prospecting and Remote Sensing* (Cambridge: Cambridge University Press, 1990). Sampling in archaeology: James Mueller, ed., *Sampling in Archaeology* (Tucson: University of Arizona Press, 1975). H. D. G. Maschner, ed., *New Methods, Old Problems: Geographic Information Systems in Modern Archaeological Research* (Carbondale: Southern Illinois University Press, 1996), is a very useful volume on GIS. See also Vincent Gaffney and Zoran Stancic's *GIS Approaches to Regional Analysis: A Case Study of the Island of Hvar* (Ljubljana, Jugoslavia: Znanstveni Institut Filozofske Fakultete, 1990). Also A. Clark, *Seeing Below the Soil* (London: Batsford, 1996), and the more technical Lawrence B. Conyers and Dean Goodman, *Ground Penetrating Radar: An Introduction for Archaeologists* (Walnut Creek, CA: AltaMira Press, 1997). Cultural resource management is another difficult subject, remarkable for the complexity of its jargon. Charles McGimsey, *Public Archaeology* (New York: Seminar Press, 1972), is a pioneer work. George Gumerman's *A View from Black Mesa: The Changing Face of Archaeology* (Tucson: University of Arizona Press, 1984) gives the general reader a good impression of rapid changes in CRM approaches. See also T. F. King, P. P. Hickman, and G. Berg, *Anthropology in Historic Preservation: Caring for Culture's Clutter* (New York: Academic Press, 1977).

Chapter 8: *Excavation*

Thomas Hester, Harry J. Shafer, and Kenneth L. Feder, *Field Methods in Archaeology*, 7th ed. (Mountain View, CA: Mayfield, 1997), contains invaluable essays on excavation and is a standard work for American archaeologists. H. S. Dancey, *Archaeological Field Methods: An Introduction* (Minneapolis: Burgess, 1981), is also valuable. Mortimer Wheeler, *Archaeology from the Earth* (Oxford: Clarendon Press, 1954), is a timeless account of basic principles, based on larger sites. Quite apart from its other merits, it is readable! Phillip Barker, *Understanding Archaeological Excavation* (London: Batsford, 1986), has a strong European orientation, but is very perceptive. The same author's *The Techniques of Archaeological Excavation*, 2d ed. (London: Batsford, 1995), and Martha Joukowsky, *A Complete Manual of Field Archaeology* (Englewood Cliffs, NJ: Prentice-Hall, 1981), are basic sources for the serious student. For sampling: John A. Mueller, ed., *Sampling in Archaeology* (Tucson: University of Arizona Press, 1974). Two exemplary case studies of archaeological excavation in historical settings are Ivor Nöel Hume, *Martin's Hundred* (New York: Alfred Knopf, 1983), and Kathleen Deagan, *Spanish St. Augustine: The Archaeology of a Colonial Creole Community* (New York: Academic Press, 1983).

Chapter 9: *Analyzing the Past: Technology*

V. Gordon Childe, *Piecing Together the Past* (London: Routledge and Kegan Paul, 1956), is still one of the best accounts of the problems of ordering. So is Gordon Willey and Philip Phillips, *Method and Theory in American Archaeology* (Chicago: University of Chicago Press, 1958), which describes some of the archaeological units used in the New World. Robert Dunnell's *Systematics in Prehistory* (New York: Free

Press, 1970) is a technical but fascinating account of classification problems. Robert Whallon and James A. Brown, eds., *Essays on Archaeological Typology* (Kampsville, IL: Center for American Archaeology, 1982), updates the earlier literature and is a fundamental source. The latest major treatment: W. Y. Adams and Ernest W. Adams, *Archaeological Typology and Practical Reality* (Cambridge: Cambridge University Press, 1991). For quantitative methods in archaeology, try Stephen Shennan, *Quantifying Archaeology,* 2d ed. (Orlando, FL: Academic Press, 1996), which is intelligible to a beginner, as is Robert Drennan, *Statistics for Archaeologists: A Commonsense Approach* (New York: Plenum, 1996).

Chapter 10: *Subsistence*

Zooarchaeology is well served by S. J. M. Davis, *The Archaeology of Animals* (London: Batsford, 1987). Richard Klein and Kathryn Cruz-Uribe, *The Analysis of Animal Bones from Archaeological Sites* (Chicago: University of Chicago Press, 1984), and Donald Grayson, *Quantitative Zooarchaeology* (New York: Academic Press, 1984), are more advanced essays. Lewis Binford's widely read and controversial *Bones* (New York: Academic Press, 1981) is an essay about the basic problems of animal bones in archaeological sites. For plants: Deborah Pearsall, *Paleoethnobotany: A Handbook of Procedures* (New York: Academic Press, 1989), is an excellent starting point. For the origins of agriculture, see Bruce Smith, *The Emergence of Agriculture* (New York: Scientific American Library, 1994). Frank Hole, Kent V. Flannery, and A. J. Neely, *Prehistory and Human Ecology of the Deh Luran Plain* (Ann Arbor: Museum of Anthropology, University of Michigan, 1969), describe the Deh Luran finds. David Harris and Gordon Hillman, eds., *Foraging and Farming* (London: Unwin Hayman, 1989), is a fundamental source on plant remains of all kinds. Andrew Moore, Gordon Hillman, and Anthony Legge, *Abu Hureyra and the Advent of Agriculture* (New York: Oxford University Press, 1998), is not only a monograph on this important site, but a seminal foray into early farming. For shell middens, see Julie Stein, ed., *Deciphering a Shell Midden* (Orlando, FL: Academic Press, 1992).

Chapter 11: *Settlement and Trade*

K. C. Chang, *Settlement Archaeology* (Palo Alto: National Press, 1968), is a basic source, and Kent V. Flannery, ed., *The Early Mesoamerican Village* (New York: Academic Press, 1976), is essential reading for everyone interested in this subject, if only for the fascinating and hypothetical dialogues that communicate different viewpoints about contemporary archaeology. Teotihuacán: René Millon and others, *Urbanization at Teotihuacán, Mexico,* vol. 1 (Austin: University of Texas Press, 1973). A superb monograph on settlement archaeology: W. T. Sanders, Jeffrey R. Parsons, and Robert S. Santley, *The Basin of Mexico: Ecological Processes in the Evolution of a Civilization* (New York: Academic Press, 1979). More recent survey projects are usually summarized in periodical literature. Ask your instructor for details. Jeremy A. Sabloff and Karl Lamberg-Karlovsky, eds., *Ancient Civilizations and Trade* (Albuquerque: University of New Mexico Press, 1975), and E. Brumfiel and T. K. Earle, eds., *Specialization, Exchange, and Complex Societies* (Cambridge:

Cambridge University Press, 1987), discuss long-distance exchange; Robin Torrence, *Production and Exchange of Stone Tools* (Cambridge: Cambridge University Press, 1986), is an admirable study of the obsidian trade of the Aegean Sea.

Chapter 12: *The Archaeology of Society*

The Ice Man is well described by Konrad Spindler, *The Man in the Ice* (London: Weidenfeld and Nicholson, 1994), although new and obscurely published articles are updating the portrait in Spindler's summary. The literature on social evolution and complexity is enormous and very confusing. Elman Service, *Primitive Social Organization* (New York: Random House, 1973), is a classic that discusses socioeconomic classification of human societies. Social ranking is well covered by Robert Chapman et al., eds., *The Archaeology of Death* (Cambridge: Cambridge University Press, 1981). Christopher Peebles, "Moundville from 1000–1500 A.D.," in R. D. Drennan and C. A. Uribe, (eds.), *Chiefdoms in the Americas* (Lanham, NJ: University Press of the Americas, 1987), pp. 21–41, is a fine example of research into this topic. Ethnic diversity is a relatively new concern in archaeology. There are some excellent essays in Randall McGuire and Robert Paynter, eds., *The Archaeology of Inequality* (Oxford: Blackwell, 1991), pp. 64–78. These include articles on the examples cited here. Leland Ferguson, *Uncommon Ground* (Washington, DC: Smithsonian Institution Press, 1991), is a fascinating essay on African American archaeology that reveals some of the potential of this approach to historical archaeology. See also Sian Jones, *The Archaeology of Ethnicity: Constructing Identities in the Past and Present* (London: Routledge, 1997). The literature on the archaeology of gender is proliferating rapidly, although good case studies are still rare. Joan Gero and Margaret Conkey, eds., *Engendering Archaeology* (Oxford: Blackwell, 1991), is currently the definitive starting point. Sarah Nelson, *Gender in Archaeology* (Walnut Creek, CA: AltaMira Press, 1997), is a masterly critique of gender in archaeology with a comprehensive bibliography. Prehistoric religion: I have attempted a summary in my *From Black Land to Fifth Sun* (Reading, MA: Helix, 1998). Two of the best studies come from Maya civilization: Linda Schele and Mary Miller, *The Blood of Kings* (New York: Thames and Hudson, 1992), is based on art and hieroglyphs and is excellent on attitudes and beliefs of the Maya. Linda Schele and David Friedel, *A Forest of Kings* (New York: William Morrow, 1991), is a popular account of Maya civilization that is a mine of information on religion, iconography, and social ranking. The same authors' *Maya Cosmos* (New York: William Morrow, 1993) is an informative sequel. The best set of essays on the whole area of the intangible appears under the title "What Is Cognitive Archaeology" in the *Cambridge Archaeological Journal* 3(2) (1993): 247–270.

Chapter 13: *Explaining the Past*

The literature is enormous and sometimes acrimonious. Two good starting points are Bruce D. Trigger, *A History of Archaeological Thought* (Cambridge: Cambridge University Press, 1989), and Lewis Binford's *In Pursuit of the Past* (London: Thames and Hudson, 1983). Also, P. J. Watson, Steven A. LeBlanc, and C. L. Redman, *Archaeological Explanation* (New York: Columbia University Press, 1984), and Guy

Gibbon's *Anthropological Archaeology* (New York: Columbia University Press, 1984). Postprocessual archaeology has generated a profuse literature, summarized in two books by M. Shanks and C. Tilley: *Reconstructing Archaeology; Theory and Practice*, 2d ed. (London: Routledge, 1993), and *Social Theory and Archaeology* (Albuquerque: University of New Mexico Press, 1987). For a devastating commentary on the contemporary theoretical scene, see John Bintcliff, "Post-Modernism, Rhetoric, and Scholasticism at TAG: The Current State of British Archaeological Theory," *Antiquity* 65 (247) (1991): 274–278. A series of essays on the emerging approach called cognitive-processual archaeology appears in Colin Renfrew and others, "What Is Cognitive Archaeology?" *Cambridge Archaeological Journal* 3(2) (1993): 247–270. A useful introduction to general anthropological theory: Robert Layton, *An Introduction to Theory in Anthropology* (Cambridge, England: Cambridge University Press, 1997). An excellent anthology of writings about archaeological theory over the past 20 years is Robert Preucel and Ian Hodder, eds., *Contemporary Archaeology in Theory: A Reader* (Oxford, England: Blackwell, 1996). For a dispassionate analysis of current theoretical approaches, see Bruce Trigger, "Distinguished Lecture in Archaeology: Constraint and Freedom," *American Anthropologist* 93(3) (1992): 551–569.

Chapter 14: *Archaeology Tomorrow*

There is surprisingly little literature on archaeology in the modern world. More's the pity, for it is a major issue in contemporary archaeological scholarship. Karl Meyer, *The Plundered Past*, 2d ed. (New York: Athenaeum Press, 1993), is required reading for everyone. Charles McGimsey, *Public Archaeology* (New York: Seminar Press, 1972), highlights the crisis in archaeology. Archaeological ethics in general are explored by Mark J. Lynott and Alison Wylie, eds., *Ethics in American Archaeology: Challenges for the 1990s* (Washington, DC: Society for American Archaeology, 1995), and in Lynott's admirable "Ethical Principles and Archaeological Practice," *American Antiquity* 61 (1997): 589–599.

Glossary

This glossary gives informal definitions of key words and ideas in the text. It is not a comprehensive dictionary of archaeology. Jargon is kept to a minimum, but a few technical expressions are inevitable. Terms such as adaptation and mutation, which are common in contexts other than archaeology, are not listed. A good dictionary will clarify these and other such terms.

absolute chronology Dating in calendar years before the present; chronometric dating.

accelerator mass spectrometry (AMS) Method of radiocarbon dating that counts actual 14C atoms. Requires much smaller samples for precise dates.

activity area Patterning of artifacts in a site indicating that a specific activity, such as stone toolmaking, took place.

activity set Set of artifacts that reveals the activities of an individual.

analogy Process of reasoning whereby two entities that share some similarities are assumed to share many others.

analysis Stage of archaeological research that involves describing and classifying artifactual and nonartifactual data.

anthropology Study of humanity in the widest possible sense. Anthropology studies humanity from the earliest times up to the present, and it includes cultural and physical anthropology and archaeology.

antiquarian Someone interested in the past who collects and digs up antiquities unscientifically, in contrast to the scientific archaeologist.

archaeological context See *context.*

archaeological data Material recognized as significant evidence by the archaeologist and collected and recorded as part of the research. The four main classes of archaeological data are artifacts, features, structures, and food remains.

archaeological record Material remains of the past, archaeological sites, artifacts, food remains, and so on, which form the surviving database for the study of the human past.

archaeological survey   Systematic attempts to locate, identify, and record the distribution of archaeological sites on the ground and against the natural geographic and environmental background.

archaeological theory   Body of theoretical concepts providing both a framework and a means for archaeologists to look beyond the facts and material objects for explanations of events that took place in prehistory.

archaeological unit   Arbitrary unit of classification set up by archaeologists to conveniently separate in time and space one grouping of artifacts from another.

archaeologist   Someone who studies the past using scientific methods, with the motive of recording and interpreting ancient cultures rather than collecting artifacts for profit or display.

archaeology   Special form of anthropology that uses material remains to study extinct human societies. The objectives of archaeology are to construct culture history, reconstruct past lifeways, and study cultural process.

area excavation   Excavation of a large, horizontal area, usually used to uncover houses and prehistoric settlement patterns.

artifact   Any object manufactured or modified by human beings.

assemblage   All of the artifacts found at a site, including the sum of all subassemblages at the site.

association   Relationship between an artifact and other archaeological finds and a site level or other artifact, structure, or feature in the site.

attribute   Well-defined feature of an artifact that cannot be further subdivided. Archaeologists identify types of attributes, including form, style, and technology, in order to classify and interpret artifacts.

attritional age profile   Distribution of ages in an animal population that results from selective hunting or predation.

band   Simple form of human social organization that flourished for most of prehistory. Bands consist of a family or a series of families, usually ranging from 20 to 50 people.

battleship curve   Shape on a seriation graph formed by plotted points representing, for instance, the rise in popularity of an artifact, its period of maximum popularity, and its eventual decline.

biosphere   All of the earth's living organisms interacting with the physical environment.

blade   In stone technology, a term applied to punch-struck flakes, usually removed from a cylindrical core. Often characteristic of prehistoric societies after 35,000 years ago.

cambium   Viscid substance under the bark of trees, in which the annual growth of wood and bark takes place.

catastrophic age profile   Distribution of ages in an animal population as a result of death by natural causes.

characterization   Methods of identifying the sources of prehistoric artifacts, especially those in clay, metal, and stone.

chiefdom   Form of social organization more complex than a tribal society that has evolved some form of leadership structure and some mechanisms for distributing goods and services throughout the society. The chief who heads such a society and the specialists who work for the chief are supported by the voluntary contributions of the people.

chronological types   Types defined by form that are time markers.

chronometric chronology   Dating in years before the present; absolute dating.

Classical archaeologist   Student of the Classical civilizations of Greece and Rome.

classification   Ordering of archaeological data into groups and classes, using various ordering systems.

cluster sampling   Sampling using clusters of elements.

cognitive archaeology   See *cognitive-processual archaeology.*

cognitive-processual archaeology   Theoretical approach to archaeology that combines processual approaches with other data to study religious beliefs and other intangibles.

community   In archaeology, the tangible remains of the activities of the maximum number of people who together occupy a settlement at any one period.

component   Association of all the artifacts from one occupation level at a site.

conchoidal fracture   Type of fracture characteristic of crystalline rocks used for ancient stone tool manufacture.

conservation archaeology   See cultural resource management.

context   Position of an archaeological find in time and space, established by measuring and assessing its associations, matrix, and provenance. The assessment includes study of what has happened to the find since it was buried in the ground.

coprolite   Excrement preserved by desiccation or fossilization.

core   In archaeology, a lump of stone from which human-struck flakes have been removed.

crop mark   Differential growth in crops and vegetational cover that reveals from the air the outlines of archaeological sites.

cross-dating   Dating of sites by objects of known age, or artifact association of known age.

cultural anthropology   Aspect of anthropology focusing on cultural facets of human societies (a term widely used in the United States).

cultural ecology   Study of the dynamic interactions between human societies and their environments. Under this approach, culture is the primary adaptive mechanism used by human societies.

cultural evolution   Theory similar to that of biological evolution, which argues that human cultures change gradually throughout time as a result of a number of cultural processes.

cultural process   Deductive approach to archaeological research that is designed to study the changes and interactions in cultural systems and the processes by which human cultures change throughout time. Processual archaeologists use both descriptive and explanatory models.

cultural resource management   Conservation and management of archaeological sites and artifacts as a means of protecting the past.

cultural system   Perspective on culture that thinks of culture and its environment as a number of linked systems in which change occurs through a series of minor linked variations in one or more of these systems.

culture   Theoretical concept used by archaeologists and anthropologists to describe humankind's external means of adapting to the natural environment. Human culture is a set of designs for living that help mold our responses to different situations. It is our primary means of adapting to our environment. A "culture" in archaeology is an arbitrary unit meaning similar assemblages of artifacts found at several sites, defined in a precise context of time and space.

culture history   Approach to archaeology assuming that artifacts can be used to build up a generalized picture of human culture and descriptive models in time and space, and that these can be interpreted.

dendrochronology   Tree-ring chronology.

descriptive types   Types based on the physical or external properties of an artifact.

diffusion (diffusionism)   Spread of a culture trait from one area to another by means of contact between people.

direct historical approach   Archaeological technique of working backward in time from historic sites of known age into earlier times.

ecofact   Object not modified by human manufacture brought into a site (e.g., an unworked pebble brought into an early human occupation site).

ecosystem   Environmental system maintained by the regulation of vertical food chains and patterns of energy flow.

element sampling   Sampling that uses an arbitrary grid system.

epiphysis   Articular end of a long bone, which fuses at adulthood.

ethnoarchaeology   Living archaeology, a form of ethnography that deals mainly with material remains. Archaeologists carry out living archaeology to document the relationships between human behavior and the patterns of artifacts and food remains in the archaeological record.

ethnographer   Anthropologists who study the culture, technology, and economy of human societies.

ethnographic analogy   Use of analogies from living societies and cultures to interpret those from the past.

ethnologist   Anthropologists engaged in the comparative study of human cultures.

excavation   Digging of archaeological sites, removal of the matrix, and observance of the provenance and context of the finds therein, and the recording of them in a three-dimensional way.

exchange system   System for exchanging goods and services between individuals and communities.

experimental archaeology   Use of carefully controlled modern experiments to provide data to aid in interpretation of the archaeological record.

feature   Artifact such as a house or storage pit, which cannot be removed from a site; normally, it is only recorded.

feces   Excrement.

feedback   Concept in archaeological applications of systems theory reflecting the continually changing relationship between cultural variables and their environment.

flotation   In archaeology, recovering plant remains by using water to separate seeds from their surrounding deposit.

foot survey   Archaeological reconnaissance on foot, often with a set interval between members of the survey team.

formation processes   Humanly caused or natural processes by which an archaeological site is modified during or after occupation and abandonment.

functional type   Type based on cultural use or function rather than on outward form or chronological position.

general systems theory   Notion that any organism or organization can be studied as a system broken down into many interacting subsystems, or parts; sometimes called cybernetics.

geoarchaeology   Study of archaeology using the methods and concepts of the earth sciences.

Geographic Information Systems (GIS)   Computer-generated mapping systems that allow archaeologists to plot and analyze site distributions against environmental and other background data derived from remote sensing, digitized maps, and other sources.

Ground penetrating radar   Radar sets used to detect subsurface features on archaeological sites without excavation.

half-life   Time required for one half of a radioactive isotope to decay into a stable element. Used as a basis for radiocarbon and other dating methods.

historical archaeology   Study of archaeological sites in conjunction with historical records. It is sometimes called historic sites archaeology.

history   Study of the past through written records.

Holocene   From the Greek word "holos," meaning "recent," and covering geological time since the end of the Ice Age 15,000 years ago.

horizon   Widely distributed set of culture traits and artifact assemblages whose distribution and chronology allow one to assume that they spread rapidly. Horizons are often formed of artifacts that were associated with widespread, distinctive religious beliefs.

horizontal (area) excavation   Archaeological excavation designed to uncover large areas of a site, especially settlement layouts.

household group Arbitrary archaeological unit defining artifact patterns reflecting the activities that take place around a house and assumed to belong to one household.

human culture See *culture.*

inevitable variation Notion that cultures change and vary with time, cumulatively. The reasons for these changes are little understood.

inorganic materials Material objects that are not part of the animal or vegetable kingdom.

interpretation Stage in research at which the results of archaeological analyses are synthesized and we attempt to explain their meaning.

invention Creation or evolution of a new idea.

Linguistic anthropology The study of human languages and culture.

lithic analysis Analysis of stone tools and stone tool technology.

market Place where people congregrate to buy, sell, and exchange goods and commodities, usually with relative stable prices.

material culture Normally refers to technology and artifacts.

matriarchal Family authority resting with the woman's family.

Matuyama-Brunhes event Moment 730,000 years ago when the earth's magnetic polarity reversed; named after the two geologists who identified it.

Mesolithic ("Middle Stone Age" from Greek *mesos,* middle) Rather dated name sometimes applied by Old World archaeologists to the period of transition between the Palaeolithic and Neolithic eras. No precise economic or technological definition has ever been formulated.

mica Mineral that occurs in a glittering, scaly form; widely prized for ornament.

midden In archaeology, an accumulation of food remains and other occupation debris. Often used to describe accumulations of shells and mollusks, hence "shell midden."

middle-range theory Way of seeking accurate means for identifying and measuring specified properties of past cultural systems.

migration Movements of entire societies who decide to change their own sphere of influence.

multilinear cultural evolution Theory of cultural evolution that sees each human culture evolving in its own way by adaptation to diverse environments. Sometimes divided into four broad stages of evolving of social organization (band, tribe, chiefdom, and state-organized society).

natural type Archaeological type coinciding with an actual category recognized by the original toolmaker.

Natural type An archaeological type constructed from the archaeologists' own cultural experience.

Neolithic ("New Stone Age" from Greek *neos,* new) Somewhat outmoded Old World term referring to that period of the Stone Age when people were cultivating without metals.

noncultural processes   Events and processes of the natural environment that impact on the archaeological record.

normative view   View of human culture arguing that one can identify the abstract rules regulating a particular culture; a commonly used basis for studying archaeological cultures throughout time.

obsidian   Volcanic glass.

organic materials   Materials such as bone, wood, horn, or hide that were once living organisms.

paleobotanist   One who studies prehistoric botany.

palynology   Pollen analysis.

patterns of discard   Remains left for investigation after natural destructive forces have affected artifacts and food remains abandoned by their original users.

permafrost   Permanently frozen subsoil.

phase   Archaeological unit defined by characteristic groupings of culture traits that can be identified precisely in time and space. It lasts for a relatively short time and is found at one or more sites in a locality or region. Its culture traits are clear enough to distinguish it from other phases.

physical anthropology   Basically, biological anthropology, which includes the study of fossil human beings, genetics, primates, and blood groups.

Pleistocene   The last major geological epoch, extending from about 2.5 million years ago until about 13,000 B.C. It is sometimes called the Quaternary, or the Great Ice Age.

population   In sampling methods, the sum of sampling units selected within a data universe.

postprocessual archaeology   Theoretical approaches to archaeology that are critical of processual archaeology and emphasize social factors in human societies.

potassium-argon dating   Absolute dating technique based on the decay rate of potassium 40K, which becomes 40Ar.

potsherd   Fragment of a clay vessel.

prehistory   Millennia of human history preceding written records. Prehistorians study prehistoric archaeology.

prestate society   Small-scale society based on the community, band, or village.

probabilistic sampling   Means of relating small data samples in mathematical ways to much larger populations.

process   In archaeology, the process of cultural change that takes place as a result of interactions between a cultural system's elements and the system and its environment.

processual archaeology   Approach to archaeology that uses research design, and the scientific method to analyze conditions of cultural change.

public archaeology   Basically archaeological education, informing the general public about archaeology and the past.

Quaternary.   See *Pleistocene.*

radiocarbon dating   Absolute dating method based on measuring the decay rate of the carbon isotope, carbon 14, to stable nitrogen. The resulting dates are calibrated with tree-ring chronologies, from radiocarbon ages into dates in calendar years.

random sampling   Sampling method using random choice of samples to obtain unbiased samples.

reciprocity   In archaeology, the exchange of goods between two parties.

redistribution   Dispersal of trade goods from a central place throughout a society, a complex process that was a critical part of the evolution of civilization.

reductive technology   Technology where an artisan acquires material, then shapes it by removing flakes or other fragments until it is shaped to the finished product. Normally applied to stone technology.

refitting (retrofitting)   Reassembling of stone debitage and cores to reconstruct ancient lithic technologies.

relative chronology   Time scale developed by the law of superposition or artifact ordering.

remote sensing   Reconnaissance and site survey methods using such devices as aerial photography to detect subsurface features and sites.

research design   Carefully formulated and systematic plan for executing archaeological research.

resistivity survey   Measurement of differences in electrical conductivity in soils, used to detect buried features such as walls and ditches.

sampling   Science of assessing the reliability of data through the use of probability theory.

satellite sensor imagery   Method of recording sites from the air using infrared radiation that is beyond the practical spectral response of photographic film. Useful for tracing prehistoric agricultural systems that have disturbed the topsoil over wide areas.

seriation techniques   Methods used to place artifacts in chronological order; artifacts closely similar in form or style are placed close to one another.

settlement archaeology   Study of ancient settlements and settlement distributions in the context of their landscape.

settlement pattern   Distribution of human settlement on the landscape and within archaeological communities.

Shovel Pits   Test pits, typically laid out in lines, excavated with a few shovel strokes. Used to define the limits of shallow sites.

site   Any place where objects, features, or ecofacts manufactured or modified by human beings are found. A site can range from a living site to a quarry site, and it can be defined in functional and other ways.

site catchment analysis   Inventorying natural resources within a given distance of a site.

site-formation processes   The processes, natural and humanly caused, that modify the material remains of the past in the ground after their abandonment.

social anthropologist   Anthropologists who organize social organization.

sourcing   See *characterization.*

spatial analysis   Analysis of spatial relationships in the archaeological record.

spectrographic analysis   Chemical analysis that involves passing the light from a number of trace elements through a prism or diffraction grating that spreads out the wavelengths in a spectrum. This enables researchers to separate the emissions and identify different trace elements. A useful approach for studying metal objects and obsidian artifacts.

state-organized society   Preindustrial civilization marked by cities, centralized government, and social stratification and large-scale social complexity.

stratified sampling   Probabilistic sampling technique used to cluster and isolate sample units when regular spacing is inappropriate for cultural reasons.

stratigraphy   Observation of the superimposed layers in an archaeological site.

stratum   Single-deposited or cultural level.

stylistic type   Type based on stylistic distinctions.

subassemblage   Association of artifacts denoting a particular form of prehistoric activity practiced by a group of people.

subtractive technology   See Reductive technology.

superposition   Principle, borrowed from geology, that states a stratigraphic layer overlying another is younger than the one below it.

surface survey   Collection of archaeological finds from sites, with the objective of gathering representative samples of artifacts from the surface. Surface survey also establishes the types of activity on the site, locates major structures, and gathers information on the most densely occupied areas of the site that could be most productive for total or sample excavation.

systematics   In archaeology, procedures for creating sets of archaeological units derived from a logical system for a particular purpose.

systems-ecological approach   Approach to archaeology that involves three models of cultural change: systems models, cultural ecology, and multilinear evolution.

taphonomy   Study of the processes by which animal bones and other fossil remains are transformed after deposition.

taxonomy   Ordered set of operations that results in the subdividing of objects into ordered classifications.

tell   Arabic word for an occupation mound; a term referring to archaeological sites of this type in the Near East.

test pit   Excavation unit used to sample or probe a site before large-scale excavation or to check surface surveys.

thermoluminescence (TL)   Chronometric dating method that measures the amount of light energy released by a baked clay object when heated rapidly. Gives an indication of the time elapsed since the object was last heated.

three age system   Technological subdivision of the prehistoric past developed for Old World prehistory in 1806.

tool kit Basic set of tools used by a culture.

total data station An electronic surveying device used for surveying sites and excavations.

trace element analysis Means of identifying the sources of artifacts and raw materials using X-ray spectrometry and other techniques that identify distinctive trace elements in stones and minerals. Trace element analysis is used to study the sources of obsidian and other materials traded over long distances.

tradition Persistent technological or cultural patterns identified by characteristic artifact forms. These persistent forms outlast a single phase and can occur over a wide area.

tribe Larger group of bands unified by sodalities and governed by a council of representatives from the bands, kin groups, or sodalities within it.

type In archaeology, a grouping of artifacts created for comparison with other groups. This grouping may or may not coincide with the actual tool types designed by the original manufacturers.

typology Classification of types.

underwater archaeology Study of archaeological sites and shipwrecks beneath the surface of the water.

uniformitarianism Doctrine that states the earth was formed by the same natural geological processes operating today.

unilinear cultural evolution Late nineteenth-century evolutionary theory envisaging all human societies as evolving along one track of cultural evolution, from simple hunting and gathering to literate civilization.

unit In archaeology, an artificial grouping used for describing artifacts.

vertical excavation Excavation undertaken to establish a chronological sequence, normally covering a limited area.

zooarchaeology Study of animal remains in archaeology.

References

Belzoni, Giovanni Battista. 1820. *Narrative of the Operations and Recent Discoveries in Egypt and Nubia.* London: John Murray.

Bintcliff, John. 1991. "Post-Modernism, Rhetoric, and Scholasticism at TAG: The Current State of British Archaeological Theory." *Antiquity* 65(247): 274–278.

Flannery, Kent. (ed.) 1976. *The Early Mesoamerican Village.* Orlando, FL: Academic Press.

— and Joyce Marcus. 1993 "Cognitive Archaeology." *Cambridge Archaeological Journal* 3(2): 260–267.

Huxley, Thomas. 1863. *Man's Place in Nature.* London: Macmillan.

Layard, Austen Henry. 1849. *Nineveh and Its Remains.* London: John Murray.

Schiffer, Michael. 1987. *Site Formation Processes of the Archaeological Record.* Albuquerque: University of New Mexico Press.

Specter, Janet. 1983. *What This Awl Means.* St. Paul, MN: Minnesota History Society.

Stephens, John L. 1841. *Incidents of Travel in Chiapas and Yucatan.* New York: Harpers.

Tedlock, Dennis. 1996. *Popol Vuh.* New York: Simon and Schuster.

Trigger, Bruce. 1991. "Distinguished Lecture in Archaeology: Constraint and Freedom." *American Anthropologist* 93(3): 551–569.

Tylor, Sir Edward. 1871. *Anthropology.* London: Longman.

Wheeler, Mortimer. 1943. *Maiden Castle.* London: Society of Antiquaries.

Woolley, Sir Leonard. 1982. *Excavations at Ur.* New York: Barnes and Noble.

Illustration Credits

Chapter 1-_Opening illustration,_ from M.C. Bishop, Antiquity 63, 241, 1989, p. 698. Reprinted by permission; **Page 4:** _Gentleman's Magazine,_ 1840; **7:** Bettmann Archive; **9:** Mansell Collection; **11:** Corbis-Bettmann; **15:** Copyright © George Gardner/ The Image Works; **18:** Courtesy of Anthony Pitt-Rivers, from the Salisbury and South Wiltshire Museum. **Chapter 2-Page 23:** Copyright © 1999 Robert Frerck/Odyssey/Chicago; **29:** Colonial Williamsburg Foundation. **Chapter 3-Page 42:** Werner Forman Archive/Field Museum of Natural History, Chicago/Art Resource; **44:** Adapted from Stuart Piggot, _Ancient Europe._ Copyright © 1965 by Stuart Piggot. Used by permission of Aldine de Gruyter (a division of Walter de Gruyter, Inc.) and Edinburgh University Press; **50:** Copyright © President & Fellows of Harvard College. All rights reserved. Peabody Museum, Harvard University. Photo: Hillel Burger; **52:** Steven A. LeBlanc. **Chapter 4-**_Opening illustration:_ Joanna Richards, from Francis Pryor, Flag Fen, B.T. Batsford Limited, 1991; **Page 58:** Griffith Institute, Ashmolean Museum, Oxford; **62:** Redrawn from "The Swanacombe Skull: A Survey of Research on a Pleistocene Site" (Occasional Paper no. 20, fig. 26.3) with permission of the Royal Anthropological Institute of Great Britain and Ireland; **64:** Fowler Museum of Cultural History, UCLA/ Photo by Susan Einstein; **65:** Utah Museum of Natural History, University of Utah; **66:** National Museum, Copenhagen; **67 top:** Ruth Kirk, and Richard Daugherty, Hunters of the Whale, William Morrow, and Company, New York, 1974. Photography by Harvey Rice; **67 bottom:** From Payson Sheets, _The Cerén Site,_ Harcourt Brace Jovanovich; **69:** Col. Charles Worthington Furnell; 71: Dr. F. L. Van Noten, Musee Royale d, Afrique Centrale; **73:** Brian Hayden. **Chapter 5-Page 82:** From James Deetz, _Invitation to Archaeology,_ illustrated by Eric G. Engstrom. Copyright © 1967 by James Deetz. Reproduced by permission of Doubleday and Co., Inc.; **83:** Adapted from R.S. MacNeish, _The Prehistory of the Tehuacan Valley,_ Vol. 3. Copyright © 1970 by the University of Texas Press, Austin; **86:** Adapted from D.R. Brotherwell and Eric Higgs, _Science in Archaeology._ London: Thames and Hudson, Ltd.; **96:** The Society of Antiquaries of London. **Chapter 6-**_Opening illustration:_ P.O. Schousbo, 1983; **102:** From N.J. Shackleton and N.D. Opdyke, "Oxygen Isotope and Paleomagnetic Stratigraphy of Equatorial Pacific Ocen Core V28-238" in _Quaternary_

Research 3:38-55. Reprinted by permission; **106 top:** From *Foundations of Archaeology* by Jason W. Smith. Reprinted with permission of Macmillan Publishing Company; **106 bottom:** From Payson Sheets, The Cerén Site, Harcourt Brace Jovanovich, 1992; **107:** From Colin Renfrew and Paul Bahn, *Archaeology,* Thames & Hudson Ltd. **Chapter 7-**Opening illustration: From Michael E. Mosley, *The Incas and Their Ancestors,* Thames & Hudson, Ltd., 1992. Drawing by Guaman Poma; **123:** Joe Ben Wheat, University of Colorado Museum; **128:** QUERY AU; **132:** Vincent Gaffney and Zoran Stancic Punc; **135 top and bottom:** Payson Sheets, *The Cerén Site,* Harcourt Brace Jovanovich. **Chapter 8-Page 140:** Redrawn from Stuart Struever and James A. Brown, "The Organization of Archaeological Research: An Illinois example" Fig. 1, p. 278 in Charles L. Redman, *Research and Theory in Current Archaeology.* New York: John Wiley & Sons, Inc., 1973; **143:** The Society of Antiquaries of London; **144:** James Tuck; **151:** Henry T. Bunn; **152:** Peabody Museum, Harvard University; **153:** The Society of Antiquaries of London; **154:** Wilfred Shawcross; **156:** Photographed by Ledyard Smith. Courtesy of the Peabody Museum, Harvard University. **Chapter 9-Page166:** Phoebe A. Hearst Museum of Anthropology, University of California at Berkeley; **167:** From James Deetz, *Invitation to Archaeology,* illustrated by Eric G. Engstrom. Copyright © 1967 by James Deetz. Reproduced by permission of Doubleday and Co., Inc.; **170:** From "Nine-thousand-year-old Mesolithic Artifacts," Fig. 35 in *Excavations at Star Carr* by J.C.D. Clark. London: Cambridge University Press, 1954. Copyright © 1954. Reprinted by Permission; **173:** The Bodleian Library, Oxford. MS. Arch. Selden A.1, fol. 67r; **177:** Copyright © Loren McIntyre; **180:** Wyatt Davis, The Museum of New Mexico (neg. no. 44191); **182:** G.H. Bushnell, *The First Americans: The Pre-Columbian Civilization,* p. 132. London: Thames & Hudson, Ltd. and New York: McGraw-Hill. Copyright © 1968 by Thames & Hudson, Ltd. and McGraw-Hill. **Chapter 10-Page 185:** After Sonia Cole, *The Neolithic Revolution,* 1959. Reproduced by permission of the Trustees of the British Museum (Natural History); **188:** Fig. 1.1. from *The Archaeology of Amimals* by S.J.M. Davies. London: Battsford, 1987. Reprinted by permission; **190 bottom:** Redrawn from *Animals Bones in Archaeology* by M.L. Ryder. Oxford: Blackwell Scientific Publications, Ltd., 1969; **194:** From *The Analysis of Animal Bones from Archaeological Sites* by Richard G. Klein. Chicago: University of Chicago Press, 1984; **196 top:** Cambridge Museum of Archaeology and Anthropology, Cambridge, England; **196 bottom:** From Colin Renfrew and Paul Bahn, *Archaeology,* Thames & Hudson Ltd.; **199:** Patricia Vincombe, "A Fishing Scene from the Tsoelike River, South-Eastern Basutoland," *South African Archaeological Bulletin,* 15:57, March 1960, fig. 1, p. 15. **Chapter 11-**Opening illustration: Geoffrey H.S. Bushnell, Peru, Thames & Hudson, Ltd., 1965. Drawn by Mrs. G.E. Daniel; **204:** Redrawn from James Mellaart, *Catal Huyuk.* Thames & Hudson. Reprinted by permission; **208:** Lee Boltin; **211 left:** Redrawn from *The Early Mesoamerican Village,* edited by Kent V. Flannery. New York: Academic Press, 1976; **217:** Institute of Nautical Archaeology; **219:** Superstock. **Chapter 12-***Opening illustration:* Geoffrey H.S. Bushnell, *Peru,* Thames & Hudson, Ltd., 1965. Drawn by Mrs. G.E. Daniel; **223:** Copyright © Wieslav Smetek/ Stern/ Black Star; **225:** Ancient Art & Architecture Collection, London; **226:** The British Museum; **229:** South Carolina Insitutue of Archaeology and Anthropology;

232: Adapted from *The Aztecs* by Brain Fagan. New York: W.H. Freeman and Co., 1984, p. 142; **235:** Musee de L,Homme; **236:** National Museum of the American Indian, Smithsonian Institution, #21598; **238:** Thomas Dowson, Rock Art Research Unit, University of the Witwatersrand; **239:** Kent V. Flannery; **Chapter 13-***Opening illustration:* From *Ancient Egypt* by Barry Kemp. London: Routledge, 1989, Fig. 6, p. 28; **244:** From James Deetz, *Invitation to Archaeology,* illustrated by Eric G. Engstrom. Copyright © 1967 by James Deetz. Reproduced by permission of Doubleday and Co., Inc.; **255:** Fowler Museum of Cultural History, UCLA, Photograph by Susan Einstein.

Index